FAERIES' LANDING

Volume 5

By

You Hyun

HAMBURG // LONDON // LOS ANGELES // TOKYO

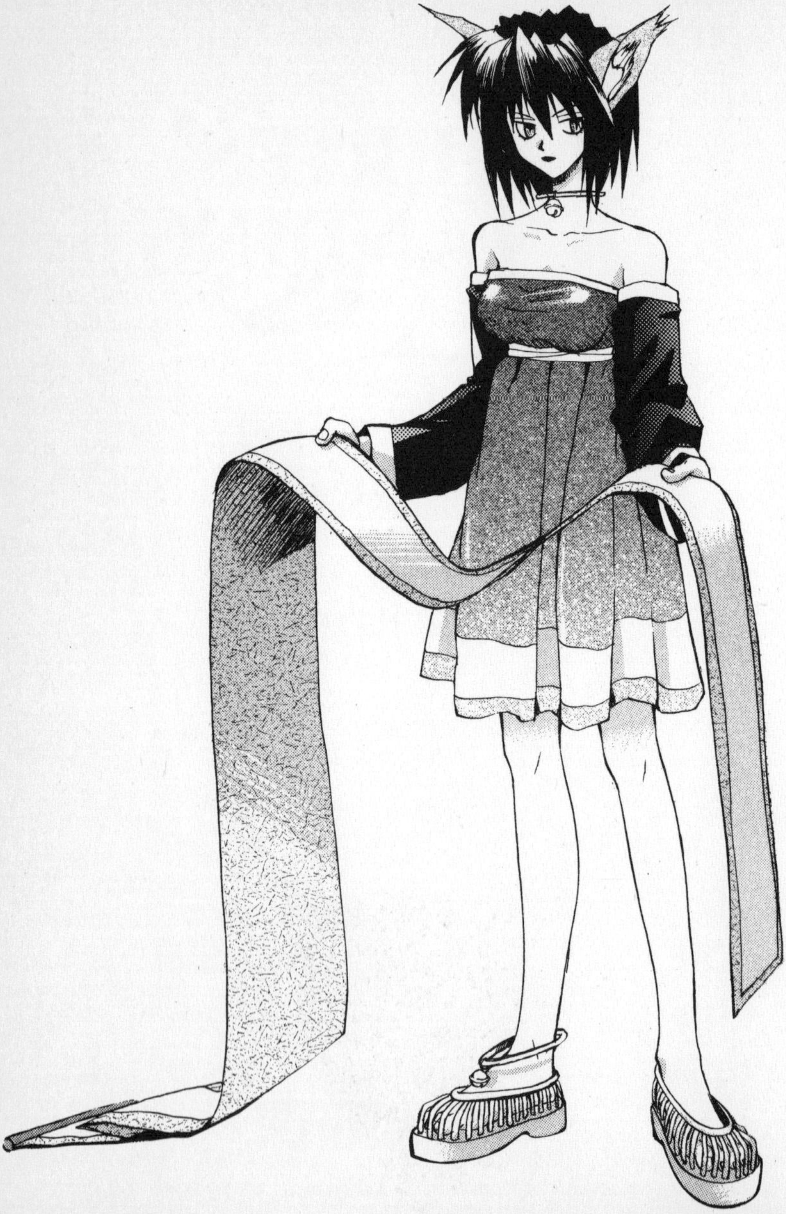

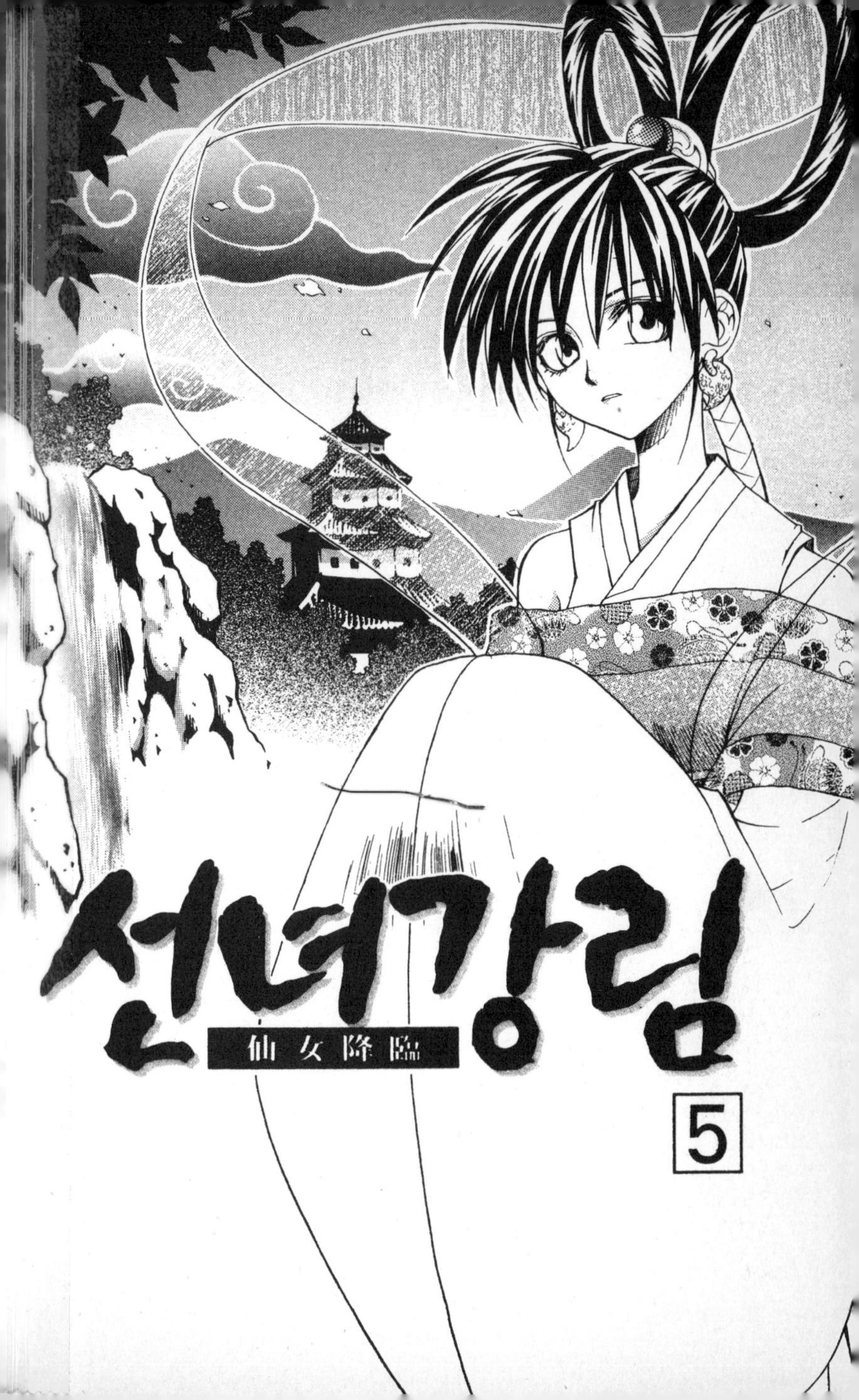
선녀강림
仙女降臨
5

Faeries' Landing Vol. 5
Created by You Hyun

Translation - Woo Sok Park
English Adaptation - Tim Beedle
Associate Editor - Tim Beedle
Retouch and Lettering - Norine Lukaczyk
Production Artist - Yoohae Yang
Cover Design - Raymond Makowski

Editor - Paul Morrissey
Digital Imaging Manager - Chris Buford
Pre-Press Manager - Antonio DePietro
Production Managers - Jennifer Miller and Mutsumi Miyazaki
Art Director - Matt Alford
Managing Editor - Jill Freshney
VP of Production - Ron Klamert
President and C.O.O. - John Parker
Publisher and C.E.O. - Stuart Levy

A  Manga

TOKYOPOP Inc.
5900 Wilshire Blvd. Suite 2000
Los Angeles, CA 90036

E-mail: info@TOKYOPOP.com
Come visit us online at www.TOKYOPOP.com

ISBN: 1-59182-613-6

First TOKYOPOP printing: September 2004
10 9 8 7 6 5 4 3 2 1
Printed in the USA

Ryang Jegal

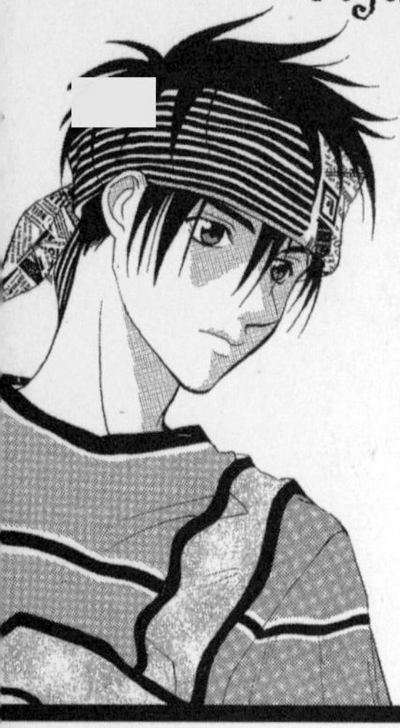

Our hapless bandanna-wearing protagonist. He's harboring Fanta, a fetching faerie grounded on Earth. Due to a magical curse, Ryang must suffer through 108 doomed relationships. This guy's gonna have major girl troubles!

Mungyeong Seong

Ryang's buddy. Boy, is he a sucker for pretty girls.

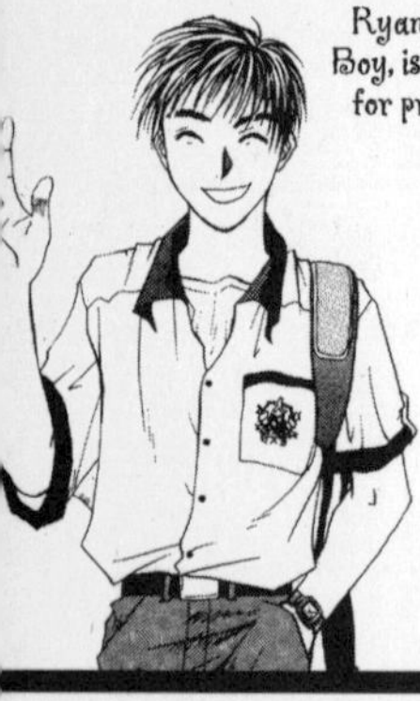

Hun Jegal and Taeyeong

Hun is Ryang's older brother, and Taeyeong is Hun's lovely wife. Ryang currently lives with them.

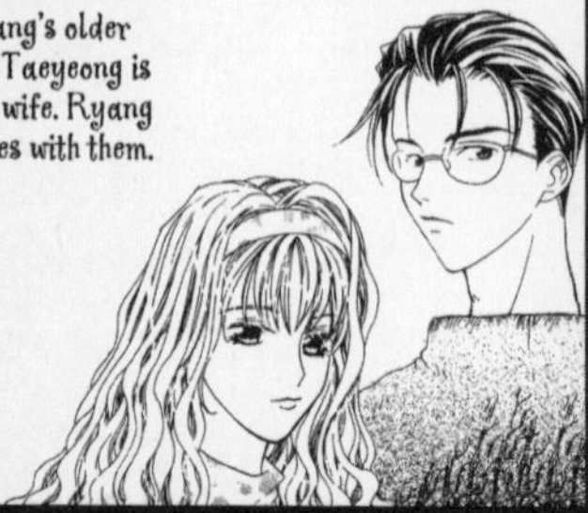

FROM THE REALM OF MAN

Fanta

A gorgeous faerie from the mystical realm of Avalon. She must stay in the human world after her winged gown is torn. Much to Ryang's delight—and frequent dismay—she now lives with him.

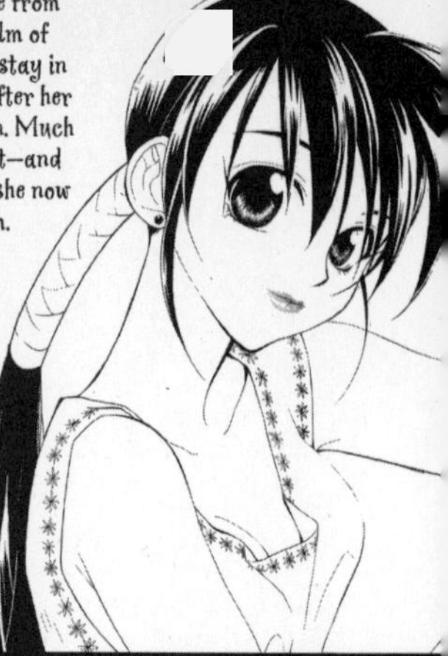

Goodfellow

An impish, Pan-like creature from Avalon who introduced Ryang to Fanta.

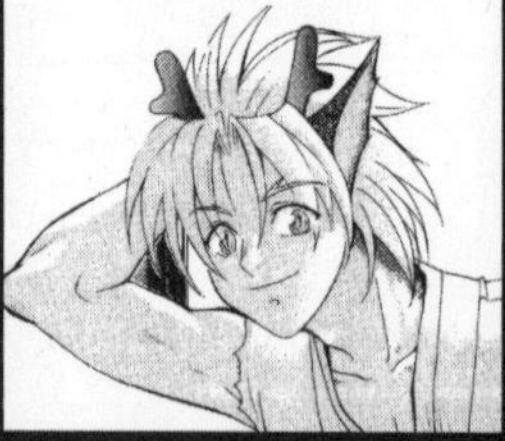

Pain

A flamboyant faerie in every sense of the word, Pain is Avalon's royal inspector and Fanta's brother.

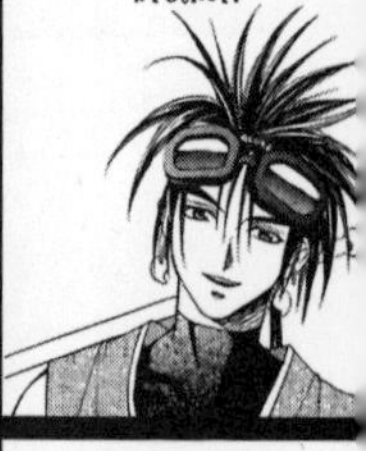

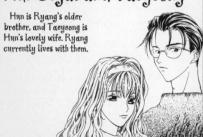

Charon

As the right-hand man of the faerie God, he overlooks all of the important administrative duties in Avalon. He's also Medea's older brother.

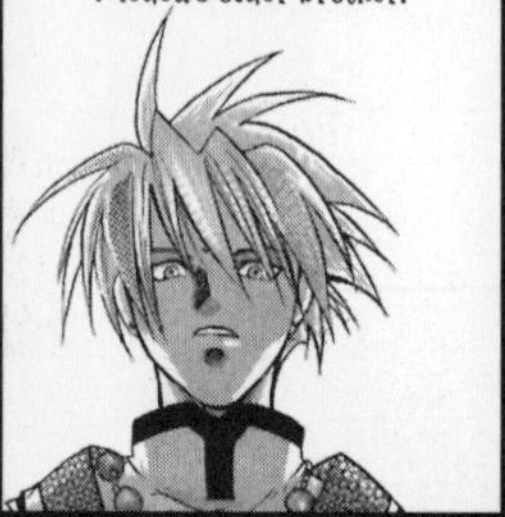

Medea

Fanta's devious and ambitious rival. She aspires to be the queen of Avalon.

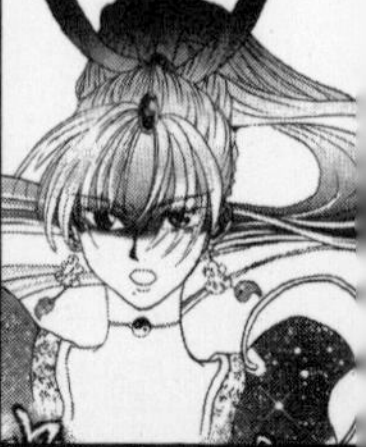

FROM THE REALM OF AVALON

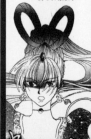

STORY SO FAR...

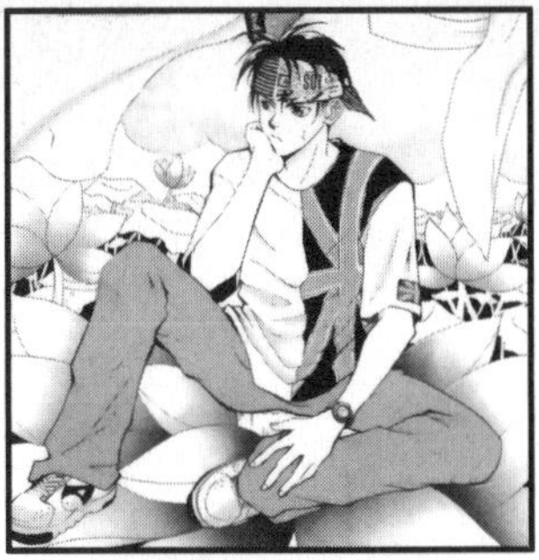

Meet Ryang, an average,
everyday high school student.
Ryang lives in Faeries' Landing,
a small suburban town in Korea.

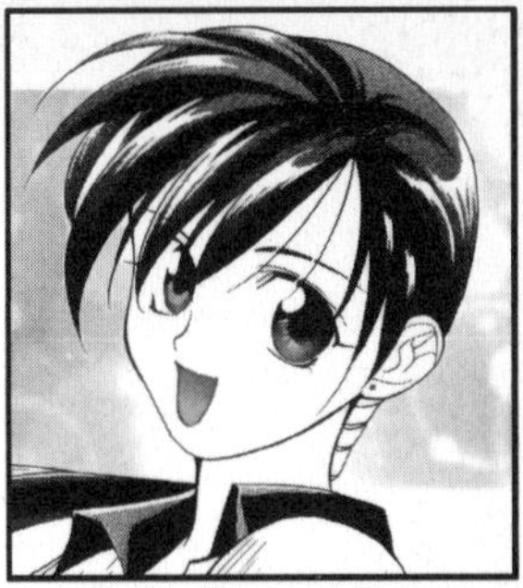

One day Ryang met Fanta,
a powerful (and pretty cute) faerie.
Fanta wants nothing more than to
experience human life, and since meeting
Ryang she has—as his roommate.

Ryang has
a problem. After
he accidentally
confused a faerie
serum with eye
drops, he found
himself cursed.
Any girl he
looks in the eye
becomes a host for
an "evil affinity."
This is destined
to happen 108
times in his life.

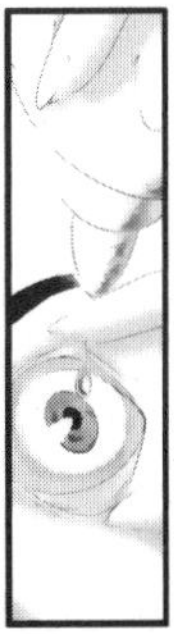

This is Medea,
the faerie who
put the curse
on Ryang.
After word of
her evildoing
got out, she was
banished from
Avalon and now
lives with Ryang,
helping Fanta
purify the evil
affinities.

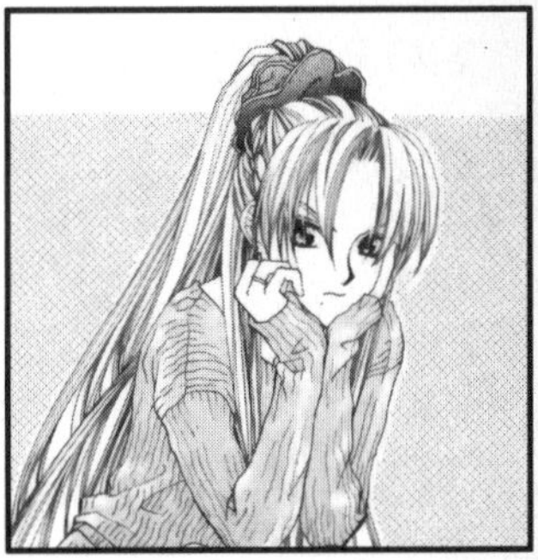

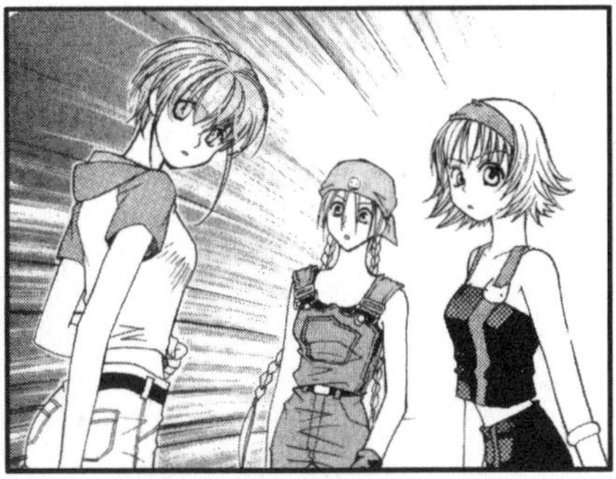

Recently, at a skateboarding competition,
Ryang accidentally created three evil affinities at once.
Two of the hosts were purified by Fanta...

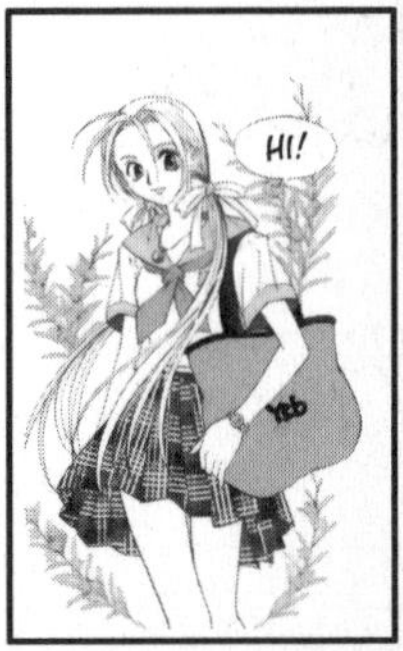
HI!

...while one of them—a girl named
Jinhui—managed to escape. Fanta
and Medea have kept a close eye
on her, aware that the evil affinity
could emerge at any time...

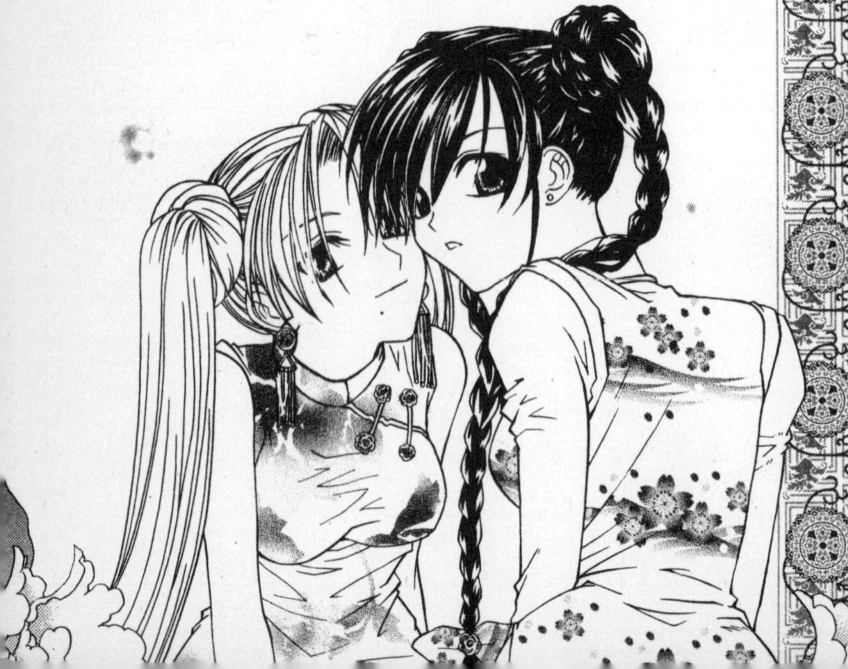

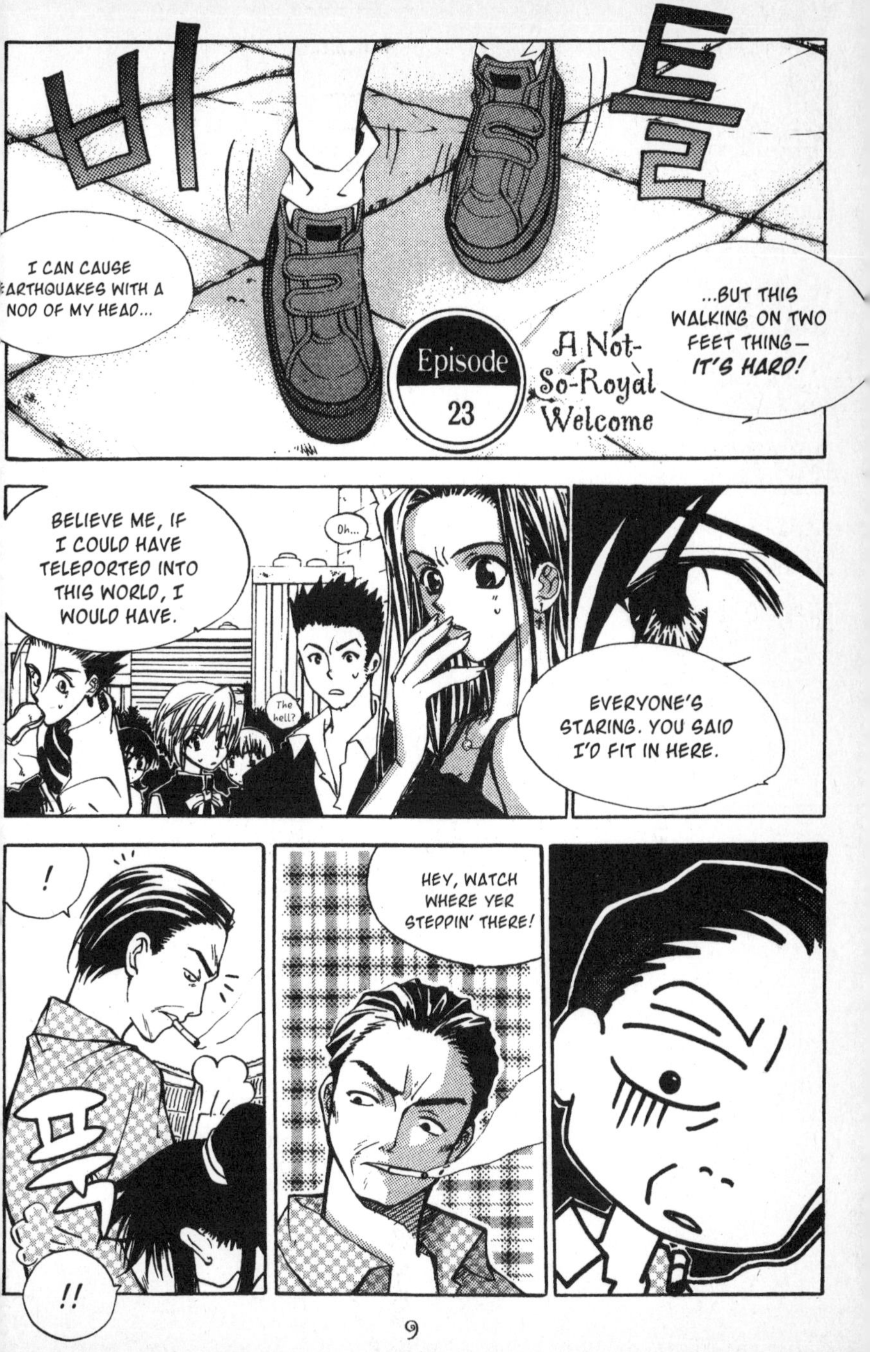
비틀
I CAN CAUSE EARTHQUAKES WITH A NOD OF MY HEAD...
Episode 23
A Not-So-Royal Welcome
...BUT THIS WALKING ON TWO FEET THING— IT'S HARD!
BELIEVE ME, IF I COULD HAVE TELEPORTED INTO THIS WORLD, I WOULD HAVE.
Oh...
The hell?
EVERYONE'S STARING. YOU SAID I'D FIT IN HERE.
!
!!
HEY, WATCH WHERE YER STEPPIN' THERE!

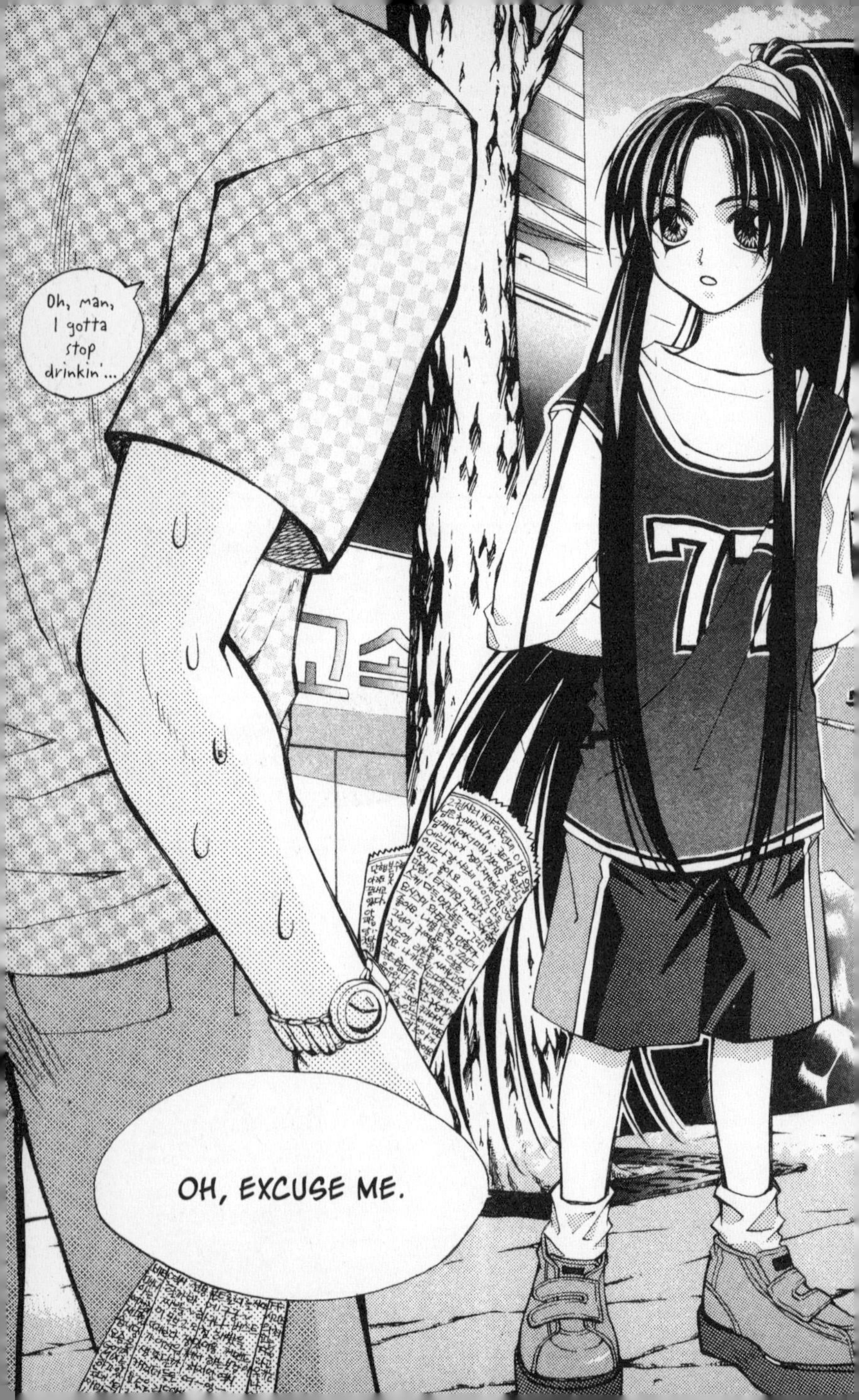
Oh, man, I gotta stop drinkin'...
OH, EXCUSE ME.

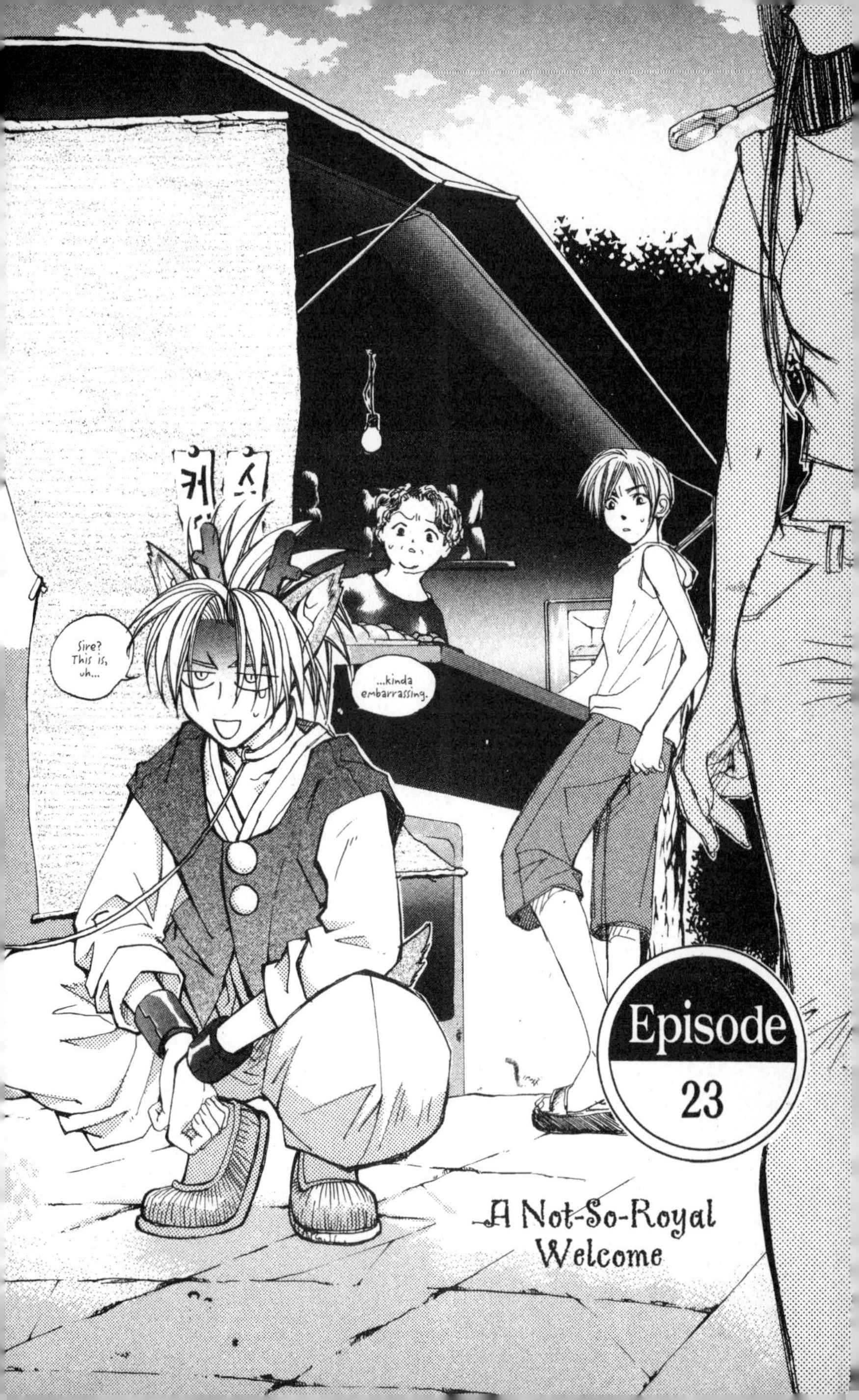
Sire? This is, uh...
...kinda embarrassing.
Episode 23
A Not-So-Royal Welcome

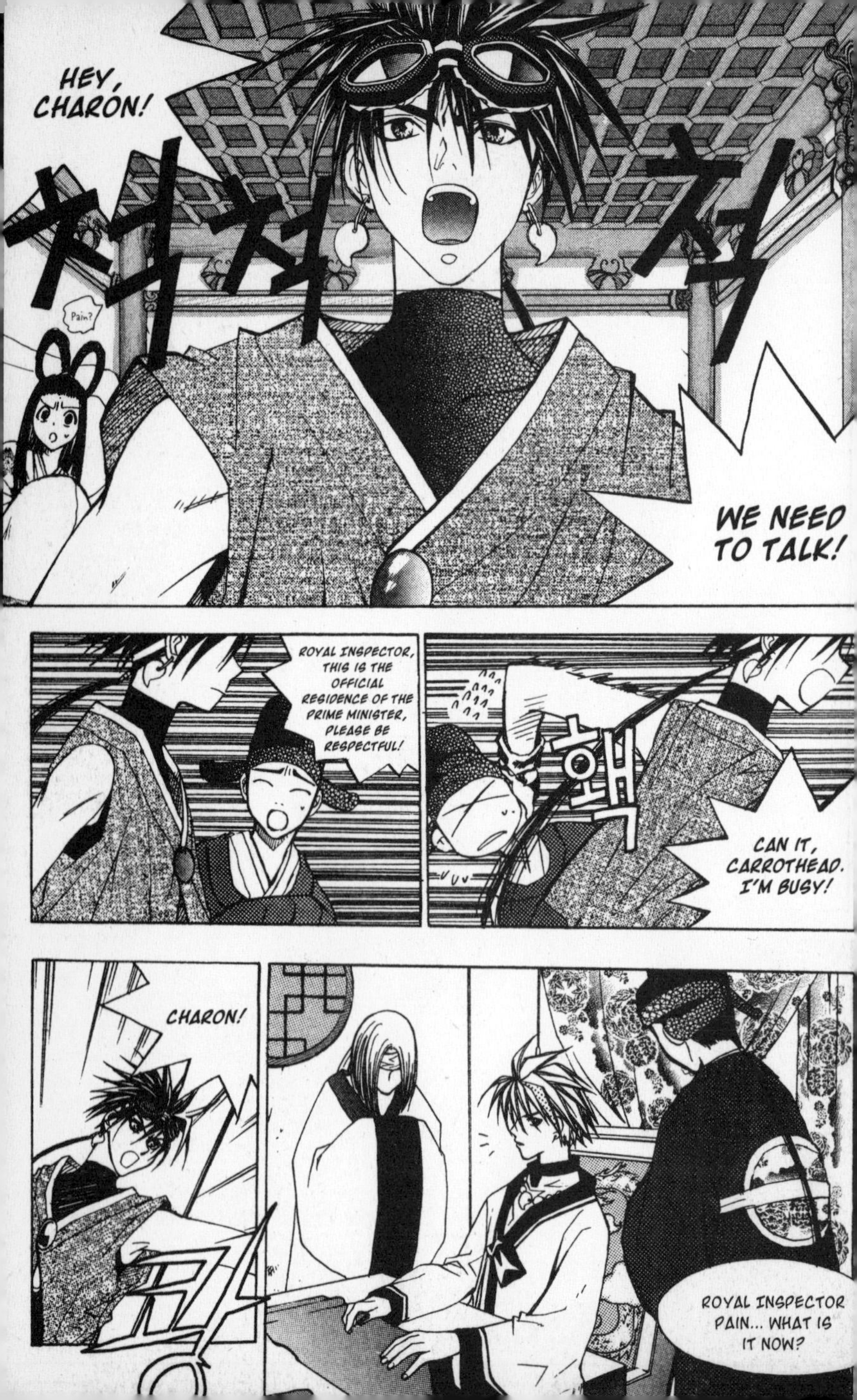
HEY, CHARON!
Pain?
WE NEED TO TALK!
ROYAL INSPECTOR, THIS IS THE OFFICIAL RESIDENCE OF THE PRIME MINISTER, PLEASE BE RESPECTFUL!
CAN IT, CARROTHEAD. I'M BUSY!
CHARON!
ROYAL INSPECTOR PAIN... WHAT IS IT NOW?

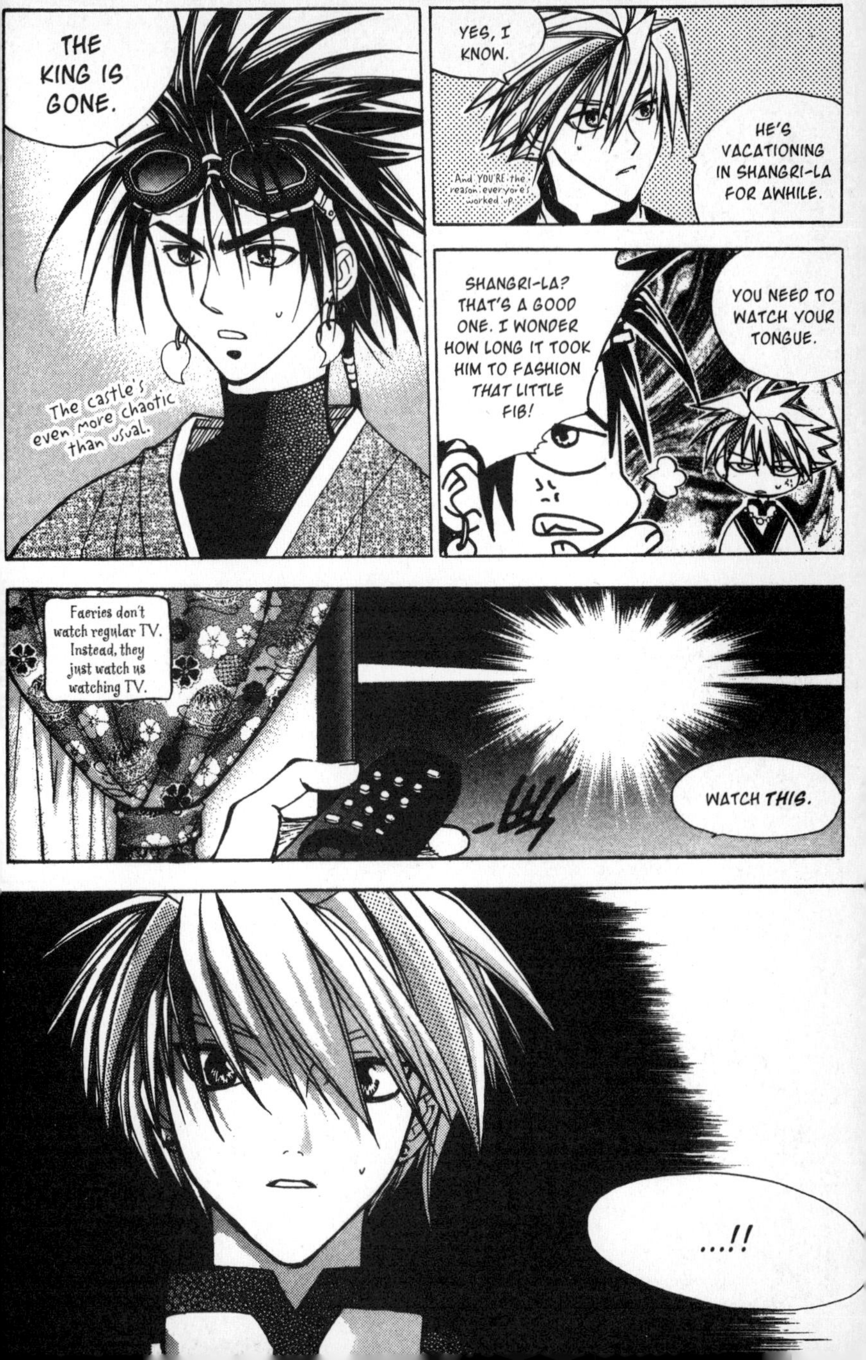
THE KING IS GONE.
The castle's even more chaotic than usual.
YES, I KNOW.
And YOU'RE the reason everyone's worked up.
HE'S VACATIONING IN SHANGRI-LA FOR AWHILE.
SHANGRI-LA? THAT'S A GOOD ONE. I WONDER HOW LONG IT TOOK HIM TO FASHION THAT LITTLE FIB!
YOU NEED TO WATCH YOUR TONGUE.
Faeries don't watch regular TV. Instead, they just watch us watching TV.
WATCH THIS.
...!!

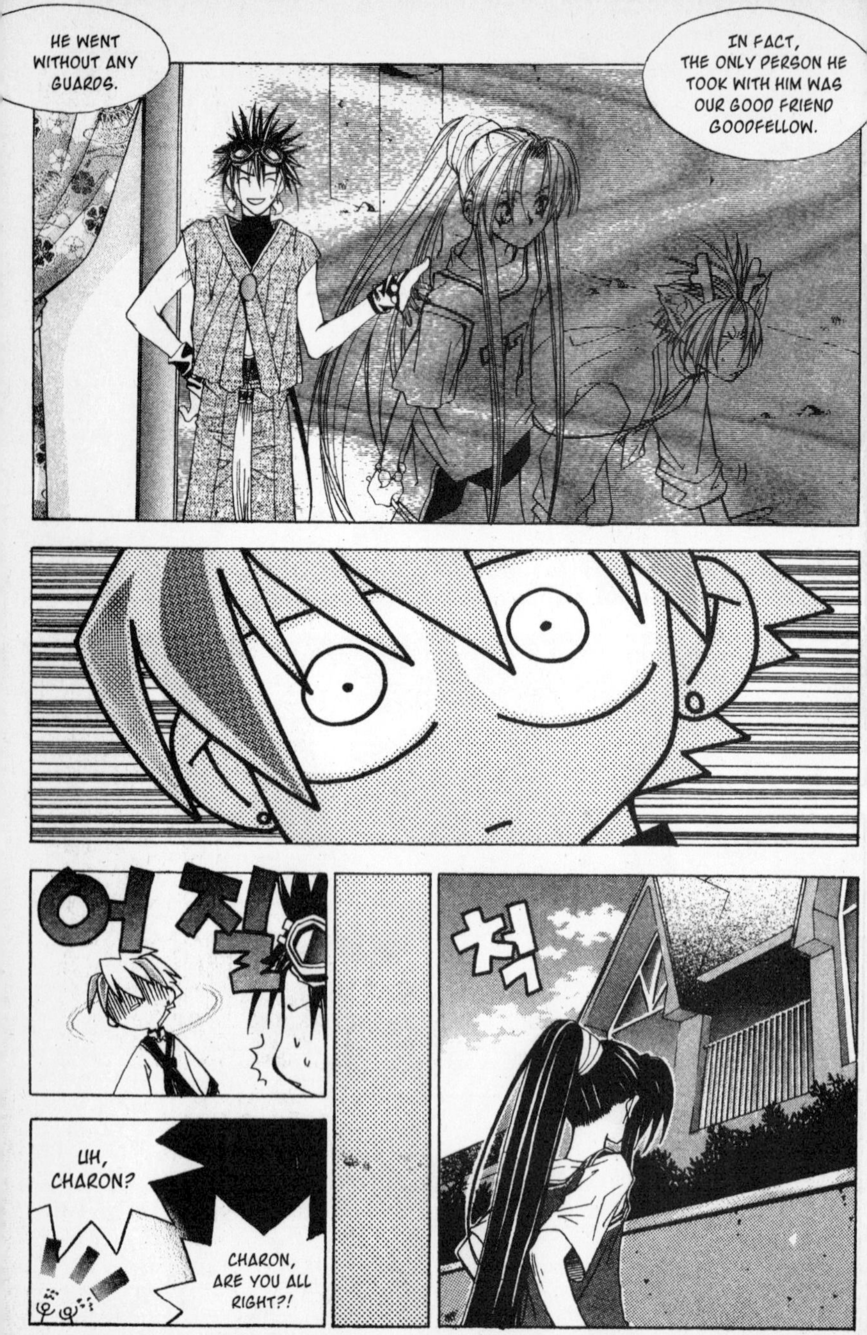
HE WENT WITHOUT ANY GUARDS.
IN FACT, THE ONLY PERSON HE TOOK WITH HIM WAS OUR GOOD FRIEND GOODFELLOW.
어질
UH, CHARON?
CHARON, ARE YOU ALL RIGHT?!
척

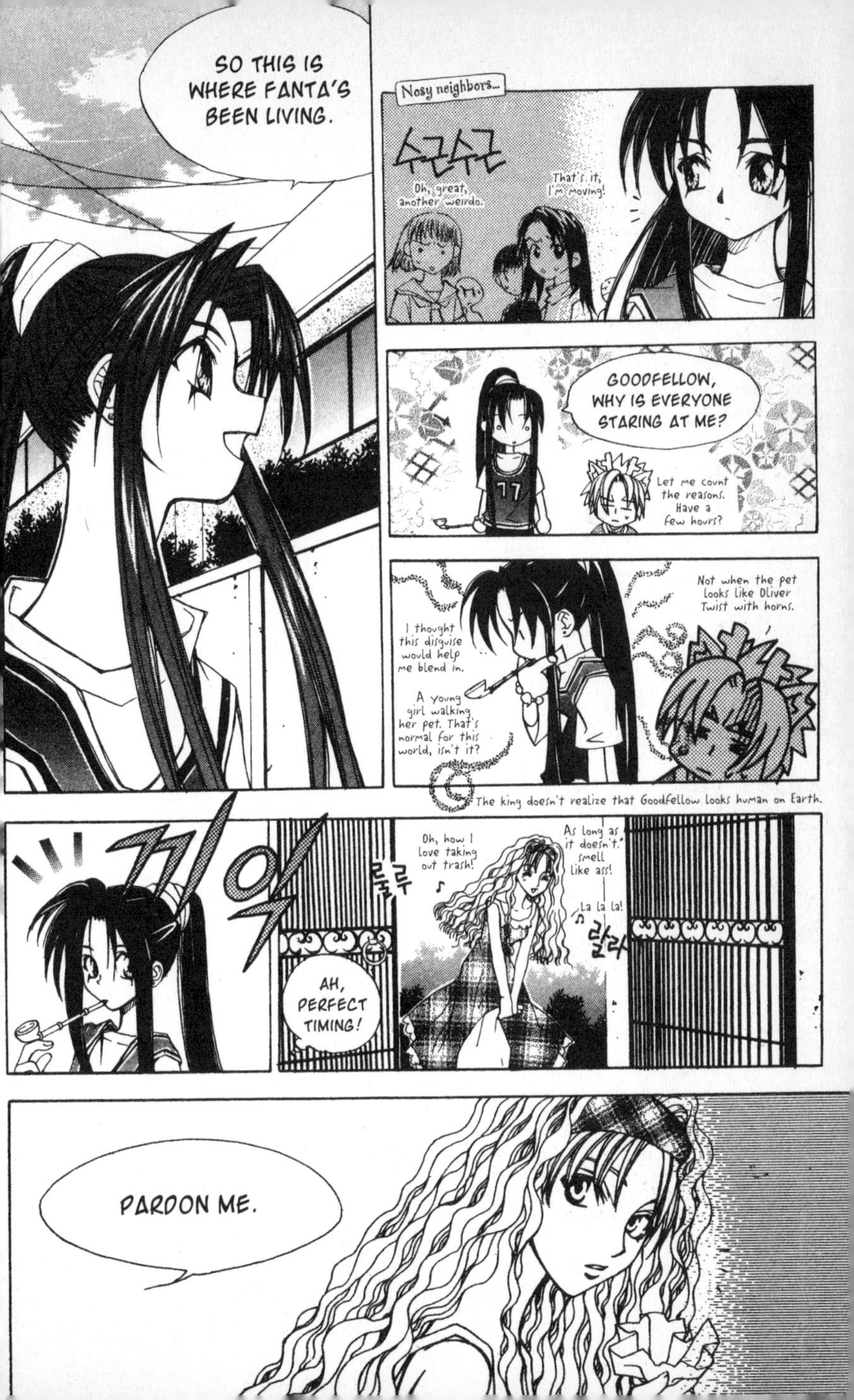
SO THIS IS WHERE FANTA'S BEEN LIVING.
Nosy neighbors...
수군수군
Oh, great, another weirdo.
That's it, I'm moving!
GOODFELLOW, WHY IS EVERYONE STARING AT ME?
Let me count the reasons. Have a few hours?
I thought this disguise would help me blend in.
A young girl walking her pet. That's normal for this world, isn't it?
Not when the pet looks like Oliver Twist with horns.
The king doesn't realize that Goodfellow looks human on Earth.
끼익
AH, PERFECT TIMING!
룰루
Oh, how I love taking out trash!
As long as it doesn't smell like ass!
La la la!
랄라
PARDON ME.

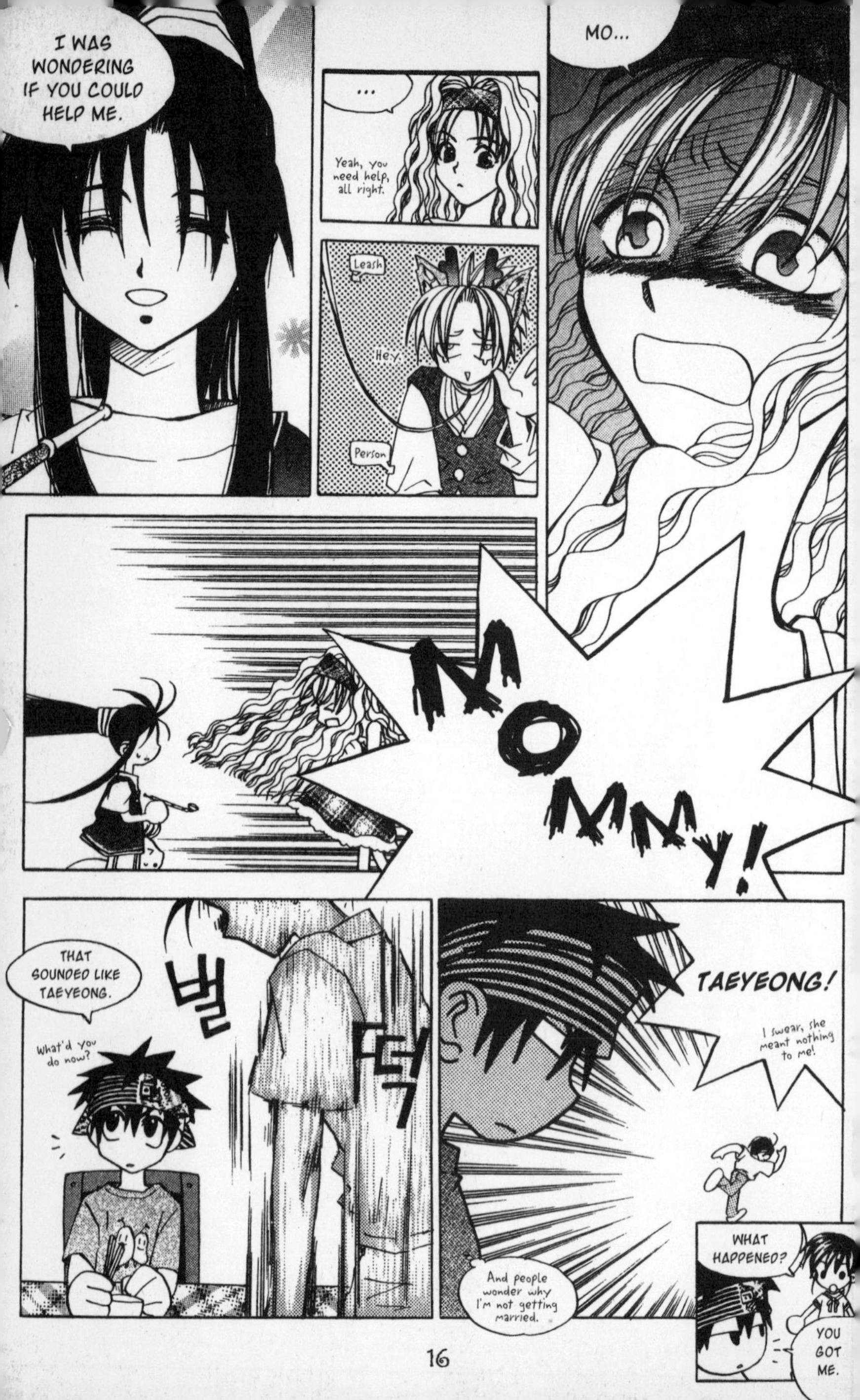
I WAS WONDERING IF YOU COULD HELP ME.
...
Yeah, you need help, all right.
Leash
Hey.
Person
MO...
MOMMY!
THAT SOUNDED LIKE TAEYEONG.
What'd you do now?
벌떡
TAEYEONG!
I swear, she meant nothing to me!
And people wonder why I'm not getting married.
WHAT HAPPENED?
YOU GOT ME.

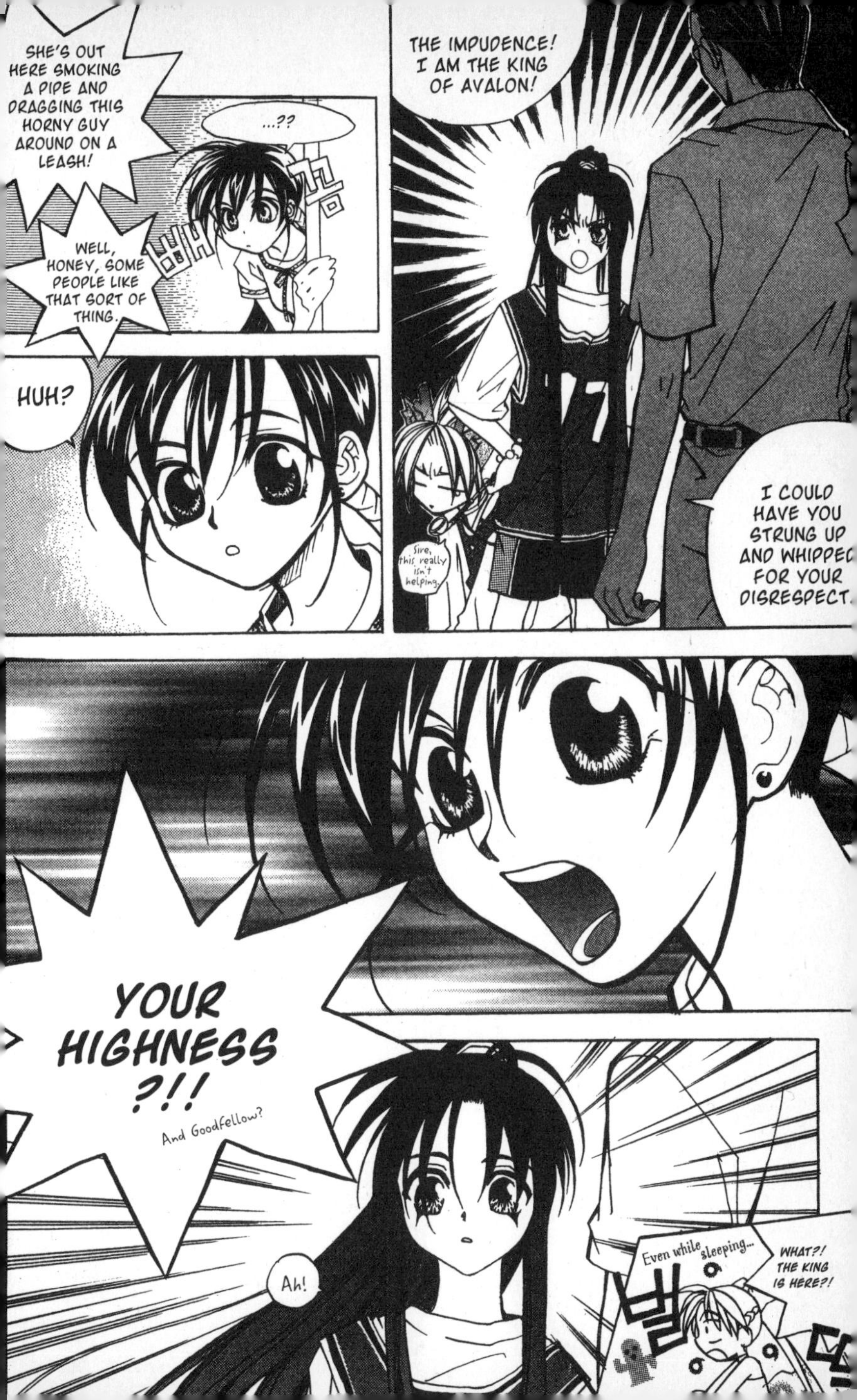
SHE'S OUT HERE SMOKING A PIPE AND DRAGGING THIS HORNY GUY AROUND ON A LEASH!
...??
WELL, HONEY, SOME PEOPLE LIKE THAT SORT OF THING.
HUH?
THE IMPUDENCE! I AM THE KING OF AVALON!
Sire, this really isn't helping.
I COULD HAVE YOU STRUNG UP AND WHIPPED FOR YOUR DISRESPECT.
YOUR HIGHNESS ?!!
And Goodfellow?
Ah!
Even while sleeping...
WHAT?! THE KING IS HERE?!

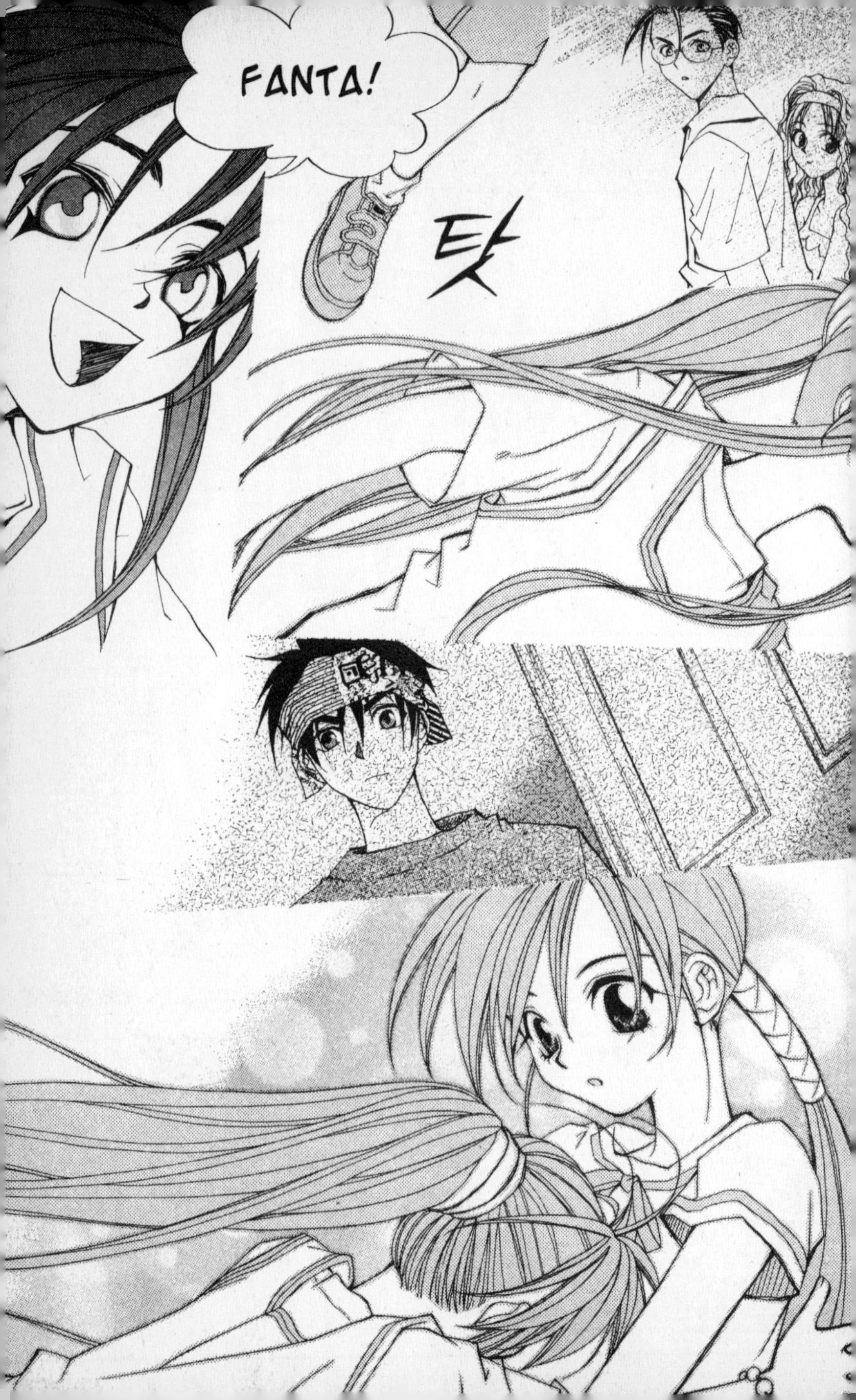
FANTA!
탓

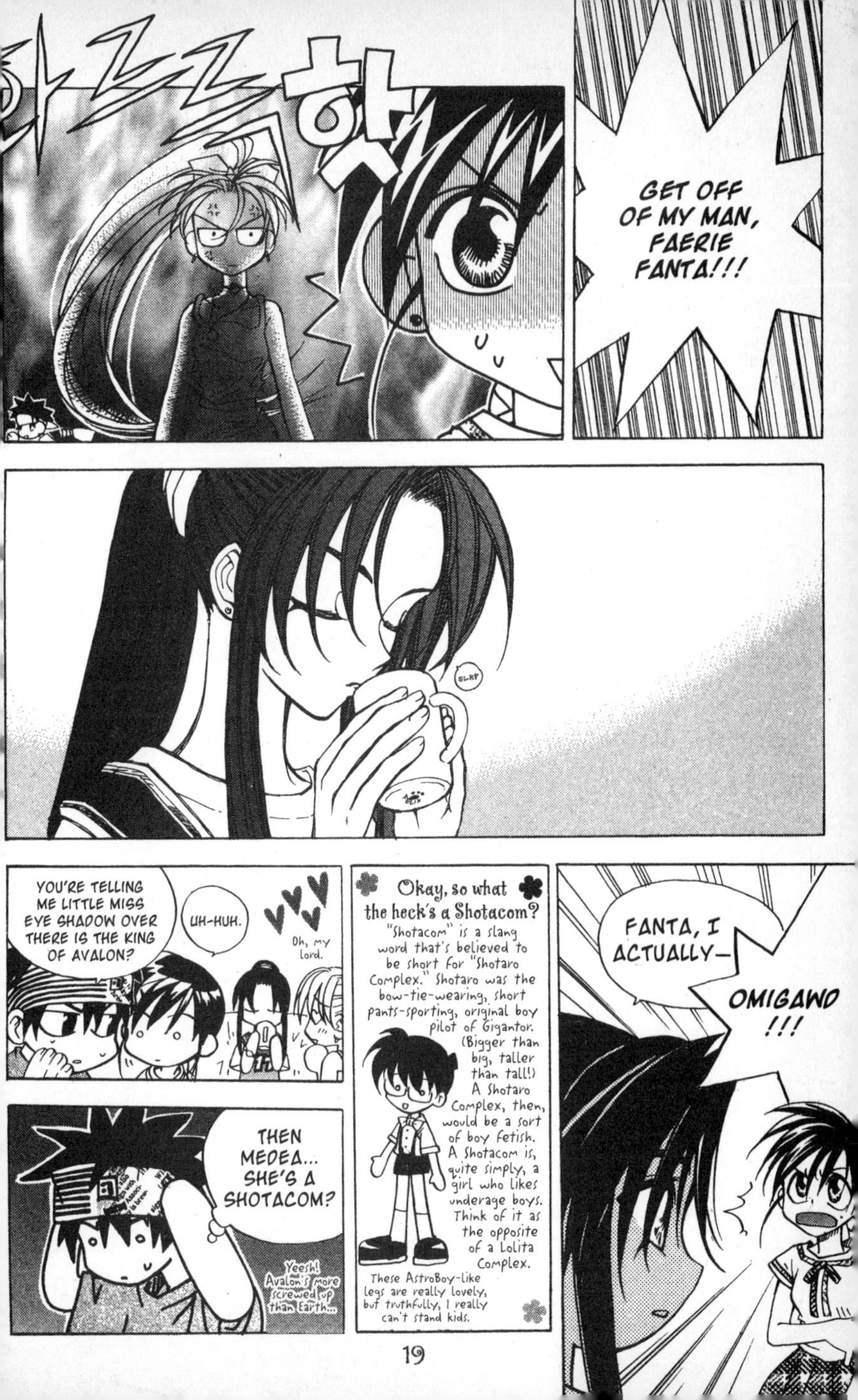
ZZZ
하
GET OFF OF MY MAN, FAERIE FANTA!!!
SLRF
YOU'RE TELLING ME LITTLE MISS EYE SHADOW OVER THERE IS THE KING OF AVALON?
UH-HUH.
Oh, my lord.
THEN MEDEA... SHE'S A SHOTACOM?
Yeesh! Avalon's more screwed up than Earth...
Okay, so what the heck's a Shotacom?
"Shotacom" is a slang word that's believed to be short for "Shotaro Complex." Shotaro was the bow-tie-wearing, short pants-sporting, original boy pilot of Gigantor. (Bigger than big, taller than tall!) A Shotaro Complex, then, would be a sort of boy fetish. A Shotacom is, quite simply, a girl who likes underage boys. Think of it as the opposite of a Lolita Complex.
These AstroBoy-like legs are really lovely, but truthfully, I really can't stand kids.
FANTA, I ACTUALLY—
OMIGAWD!!!

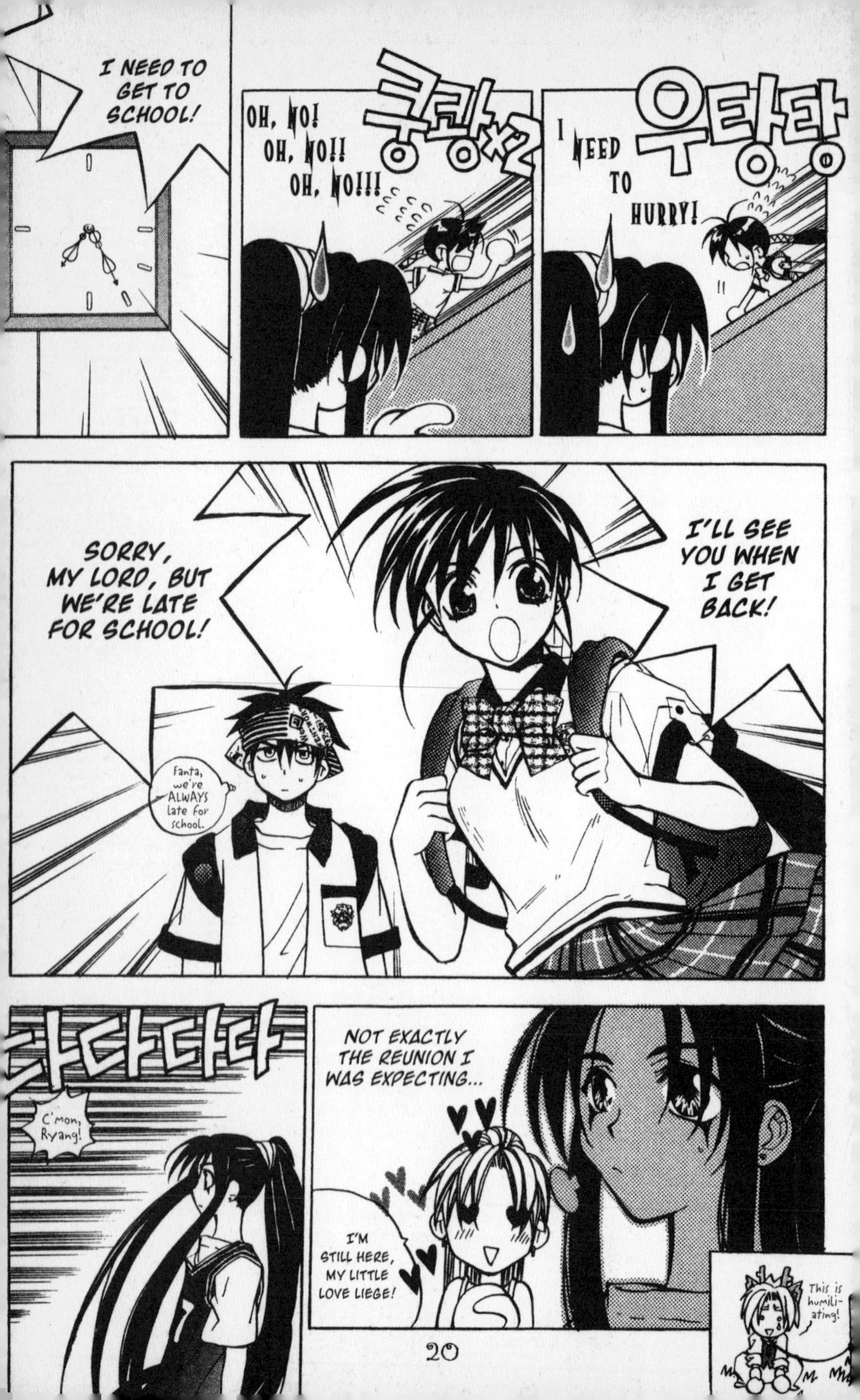
I NEED TO GET TO SCHOOL!
OH, NO! OH, NO!! OH, NO!!!
쿵쾅×2
I NEED TO HURRY!
우탕탕
SORRY, MY LORD, BUT WE'RE LATE FOR SCHOOL!
Fanta, we're ALWAYS late for school.
I'LL SEE YOU WHEN I GET BACK!
다다다다다
C'mon, Ryang!
NOT EXACTLY THE REUNION I WAS EXPECTING...
I'M STILL HERE, MY LITTLE LOVE LIEGE!
This is humili-ating!

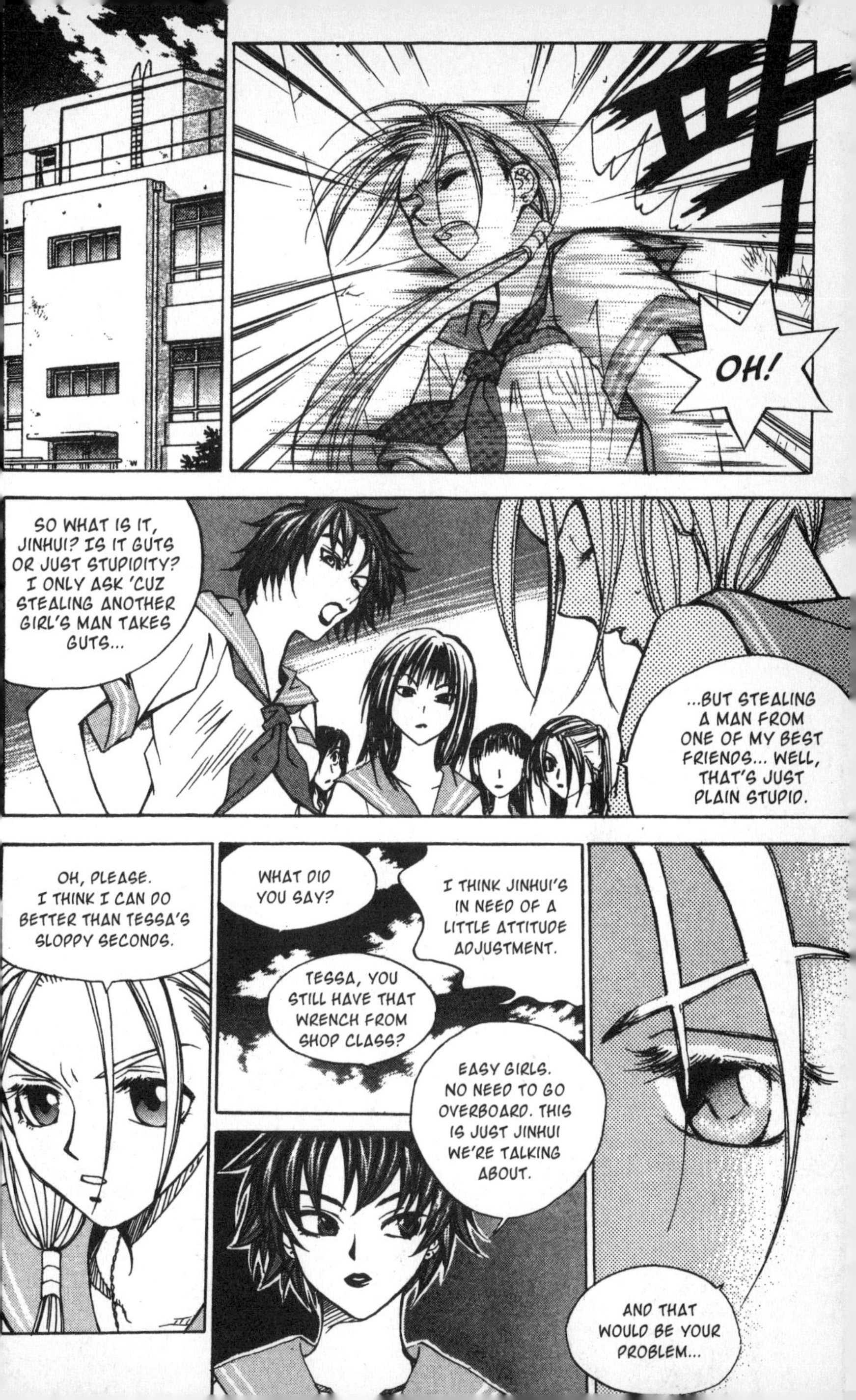
OH!
SO WHAT IS IT, JINHUI? IS IT GUTS OR JUST STUPIDITY? I ONLY ASK 'CUZ STEALING ANOTHER GIRL'S MAN TAKES GUTS...
...BUT STEALING A MAN FROM ONE OF MY BEST FRIENDS... WELL, THAT'S JUST PLAIN STUPID.
OH, PLEASE. I THINK I CAN DO BETTER THAN TESSA'S SLOPPY SECONDS.
WHAT DID YOU SAY?
I THINK JINHUI'S IN NEED OF A LITTLE ATTITUDE ADJUSTMENT.
TESSA, YOU STILL HAVE THAT WRENCH FROM SHOP CLASS?
EASY GIRLS. NO NEED TO GO OVERBOARD. THIS IS JUST JINHUI WE'RE TALKING ABOUT.
AND THAT WOULD BE YOUR PROBLEM...

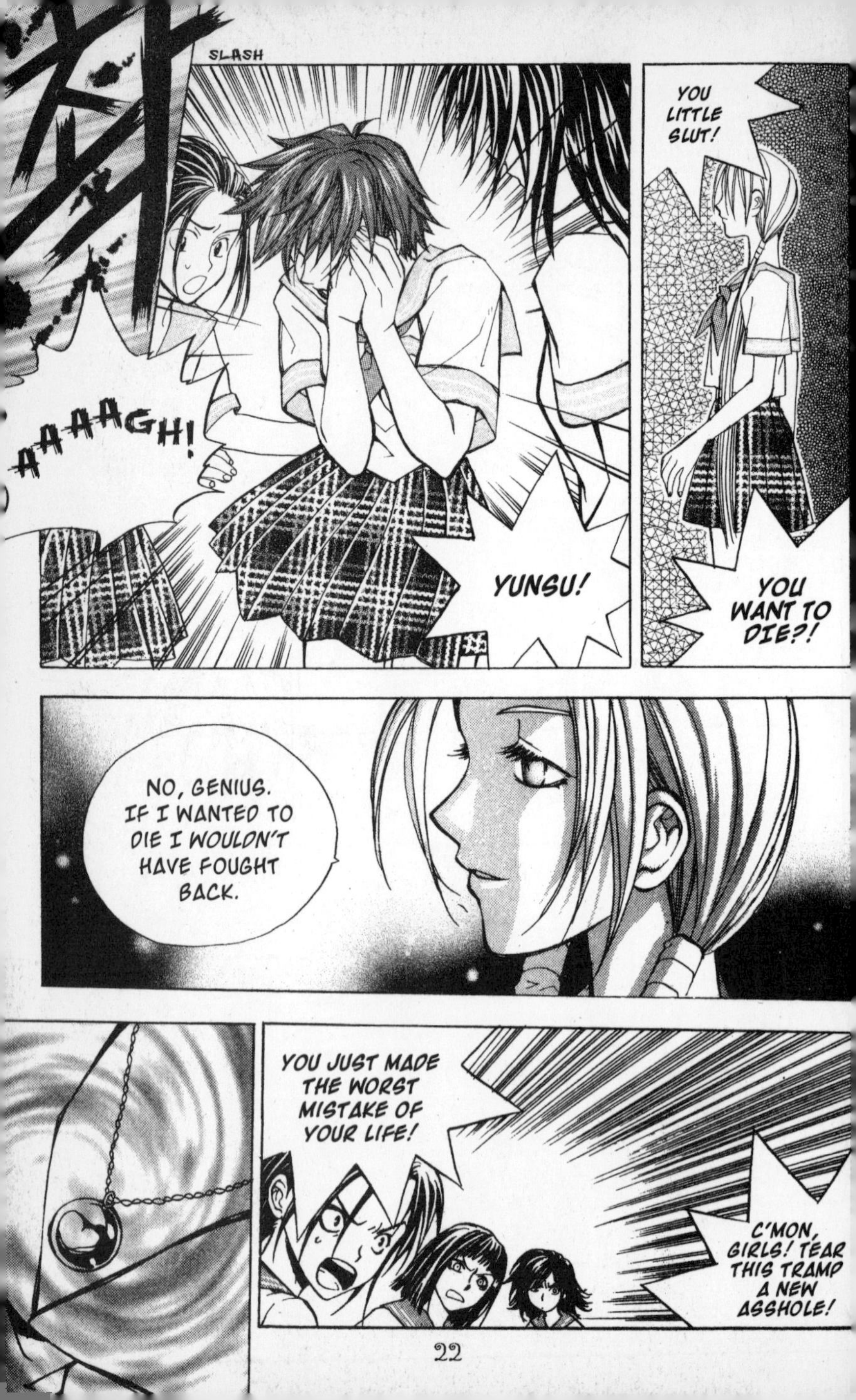
SLASH
AAAAGH!
YUNSU!
YOU LITTLE SLUT!
YOU WANT TO DIE?!
NO, GENIUS. IF I WANTED TO DIE I WOULDN'T HAVE FOUGHT BACK.
YOU JUST MADE THE WORST MISTAKE OF YOUR LIFE!
C'MON, GIRLS! TEAR THIS TRAMP A NEW ASSHOLE!

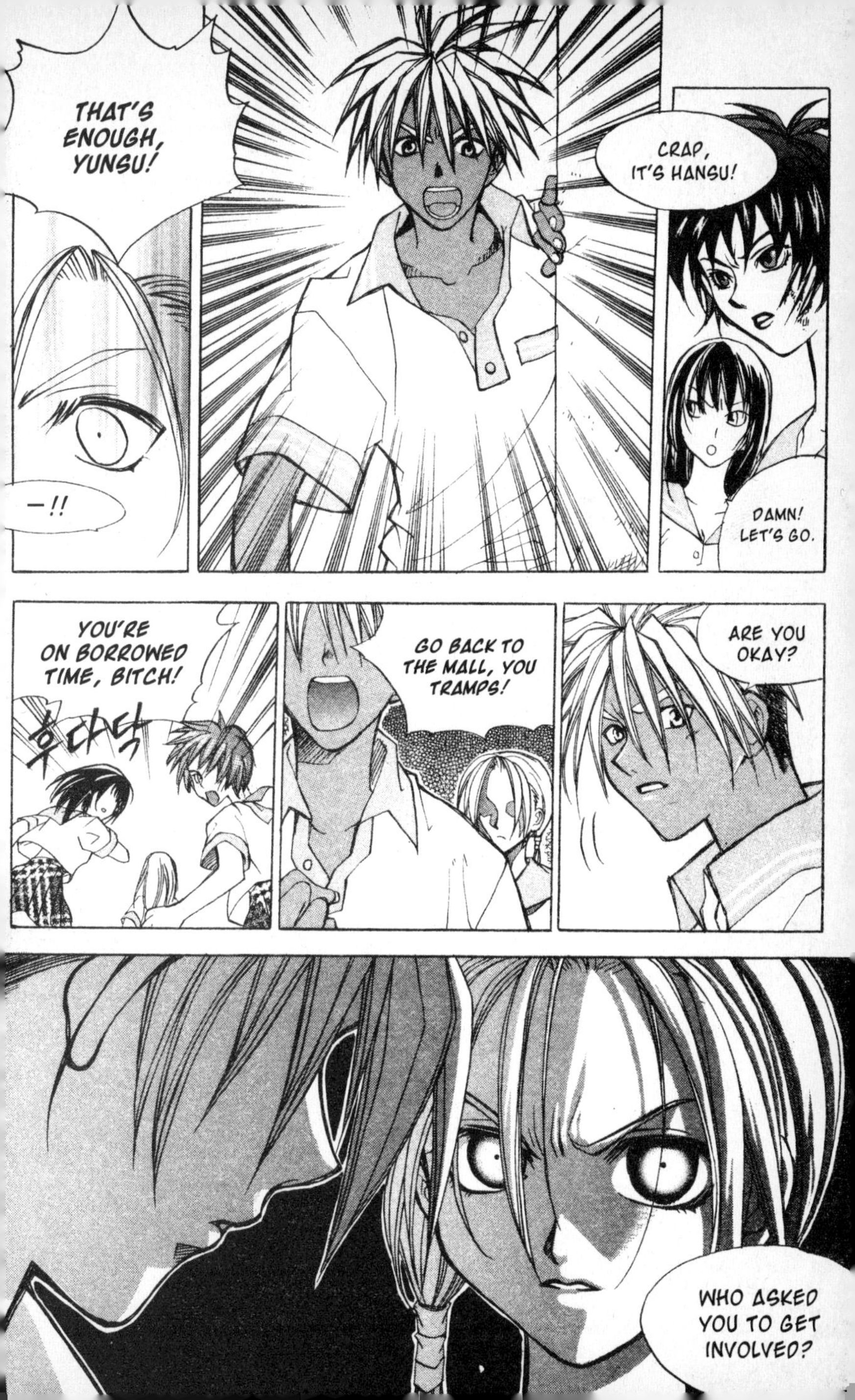
THAT'S ENOUGH, YUNSU!
—!!
CRAP, IT'S HANSU!
DAMN! LET'S GO.
YOU'RE ON BORROWED TIME, BITCH!
후다닥
GO BACK TO THE MALL, YOU TRAMPS!
ARE YOU OKAY?
WHO ASKED YOU TO GET INVOLVED?

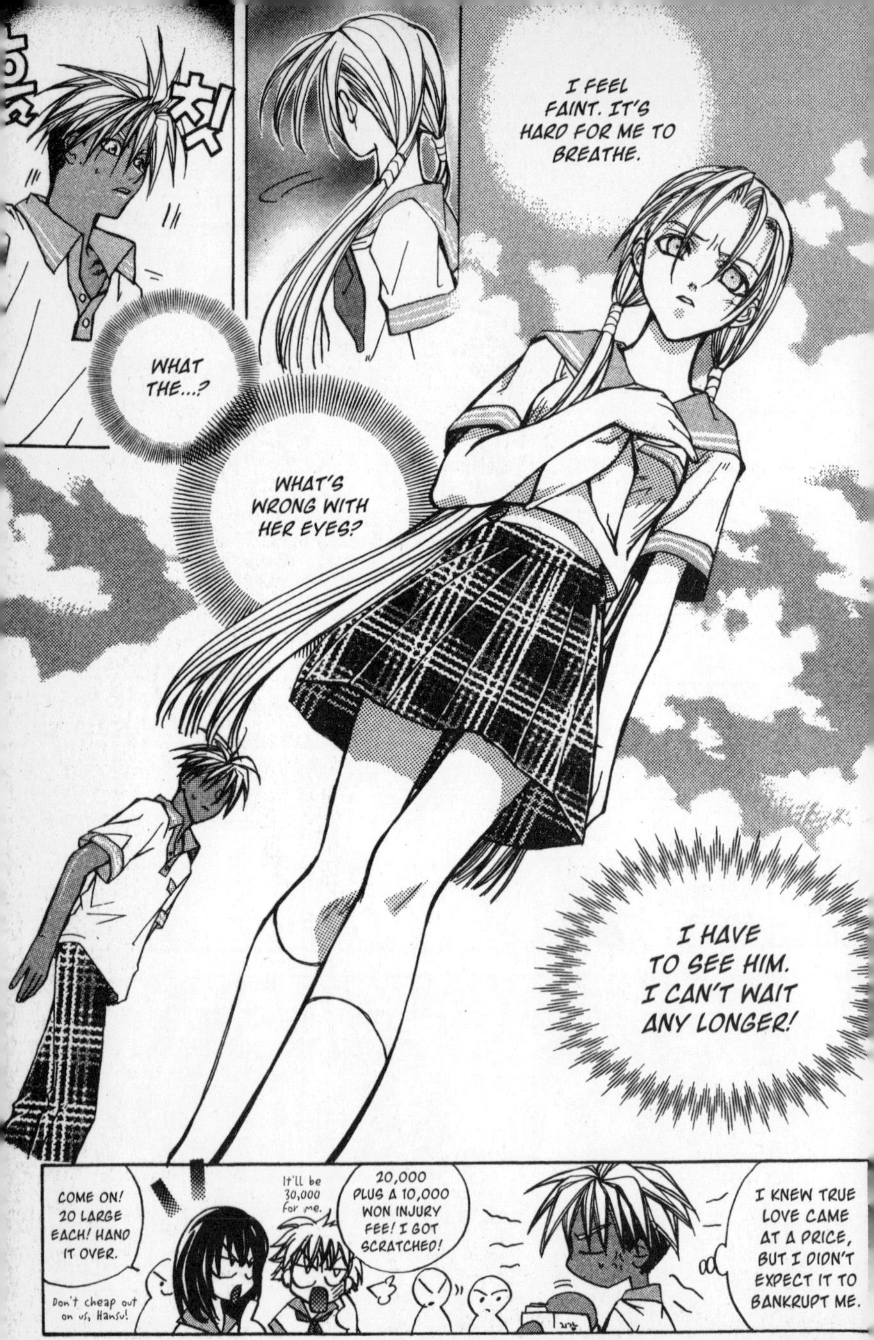
WHAT THE...?
I FEEL FAINT. IT'S HARD FOR ME TO BREATHE.
WHAT'S WRONG WITH HER EYES?
I HAVE TO SEE HIM. I CAN'T WAIT ANY LONGER!
COME ON! 20 LARGE EACH! HAND IT OVER.
Don't cheap out on us, Hansu!
It'll be 30,000 for me.
20,000 PLUS A 10,000 WON INJURY FEE! I GOT SCRATCHED!
I KNEW TRUE LOVE CAME AT A PRICE, BUT I DIDN'T EXPECT IT TO BANKRUPT ME.

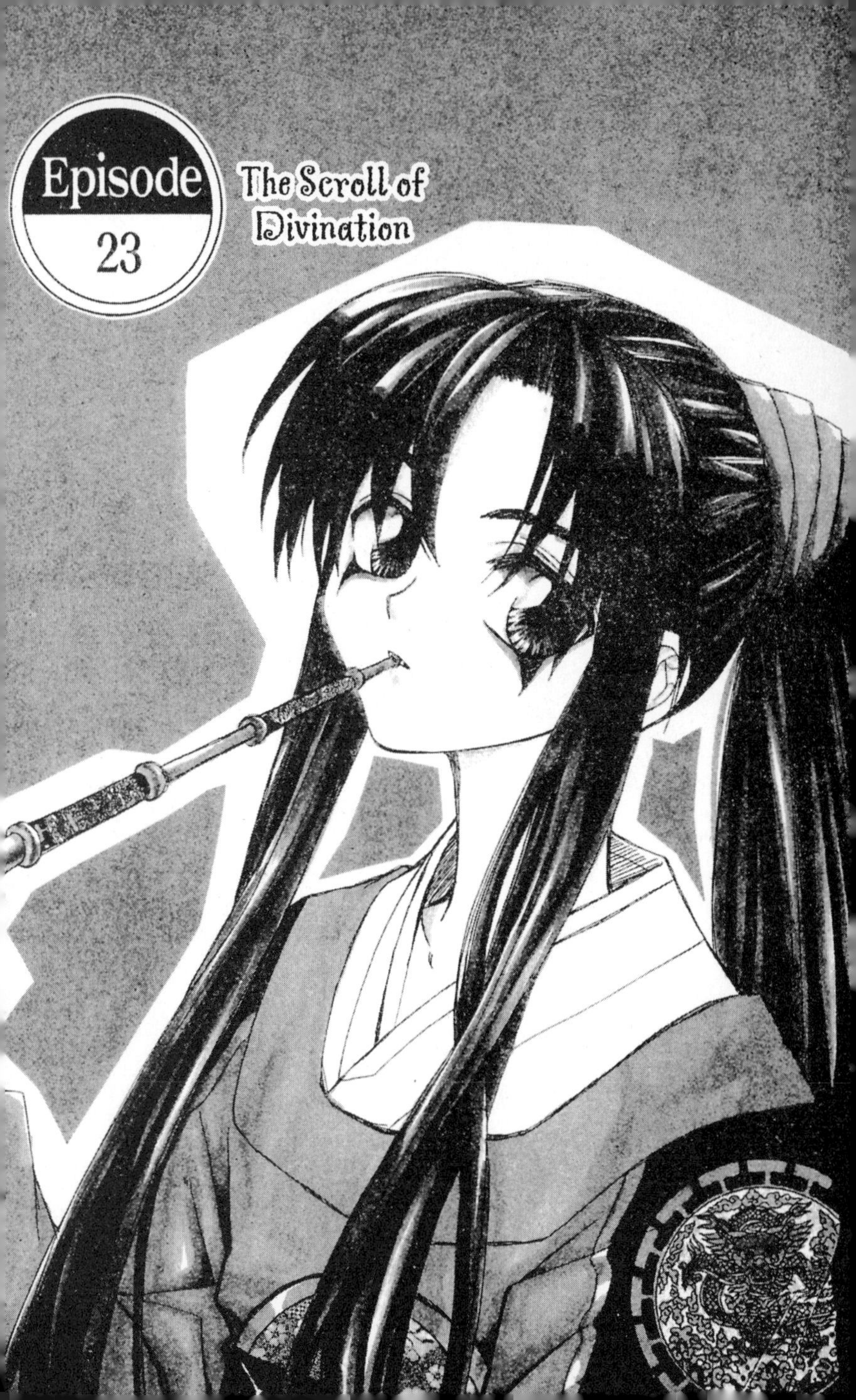
Episode
23
The Scroll of Divination

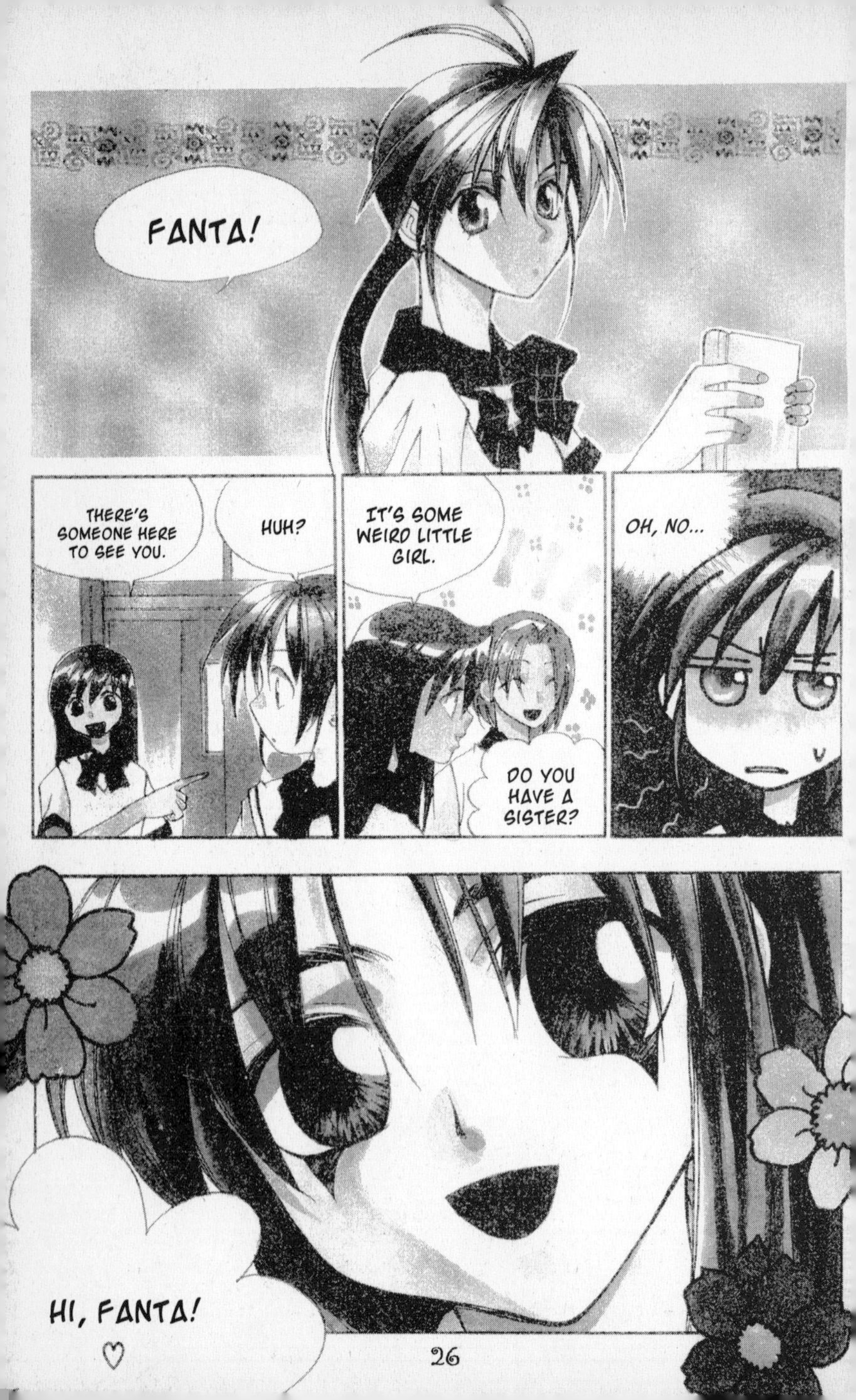
FANTA!
THERE'S SOMEONE HERE TO SEE YOU.
HUH?
IT'S SOME WEIRD LITTLE GIRL.
DO YOU HAVE A SISTER?
OH, NO...
HI, FANTA! ♡

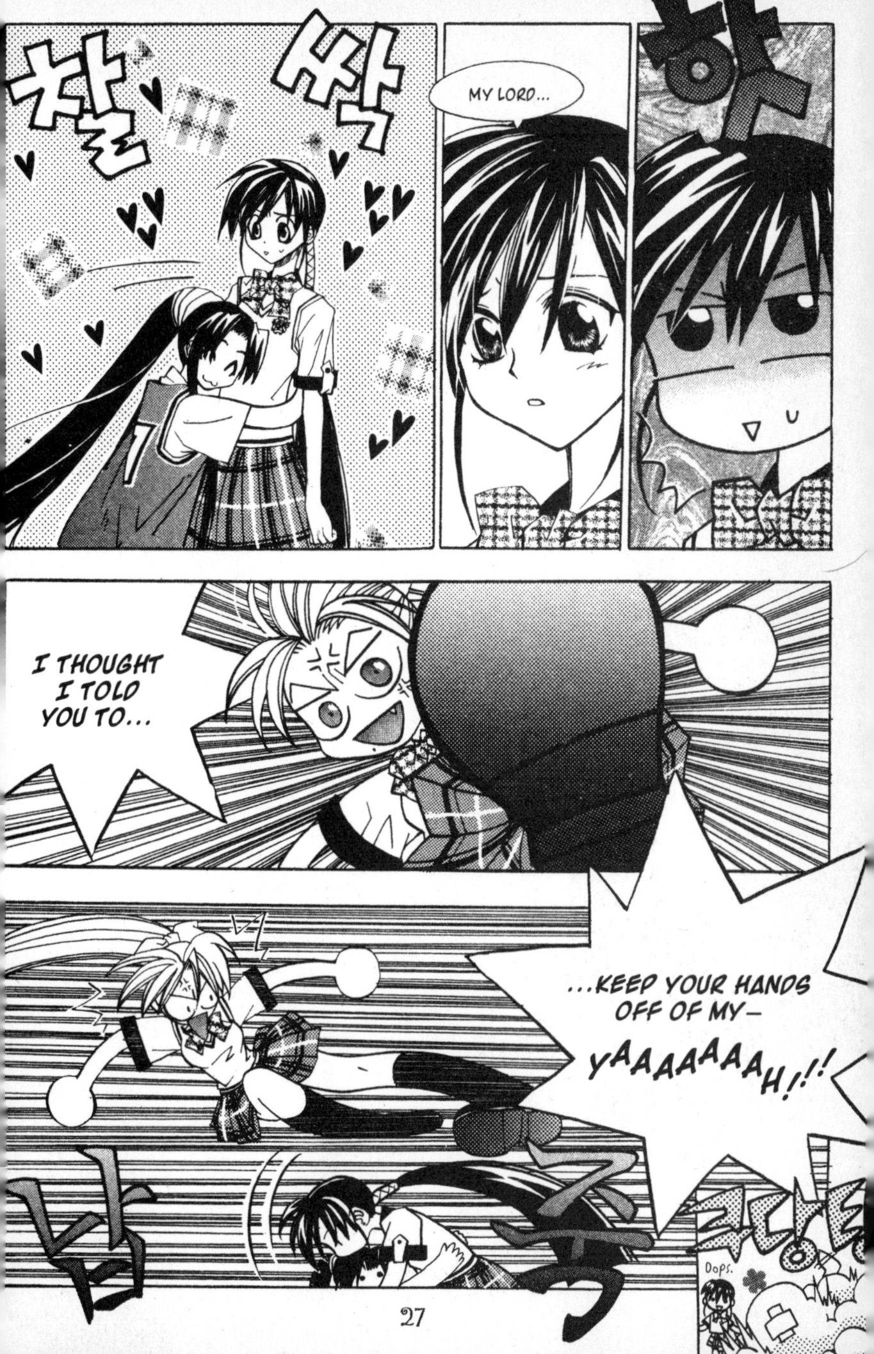
찰싹
MY LORD...
I THOUGHT I TOLD YOU TO...
...KEEP YOUR HANDS OFF OF MY—
YAAAAAAAH!!!
Oops.

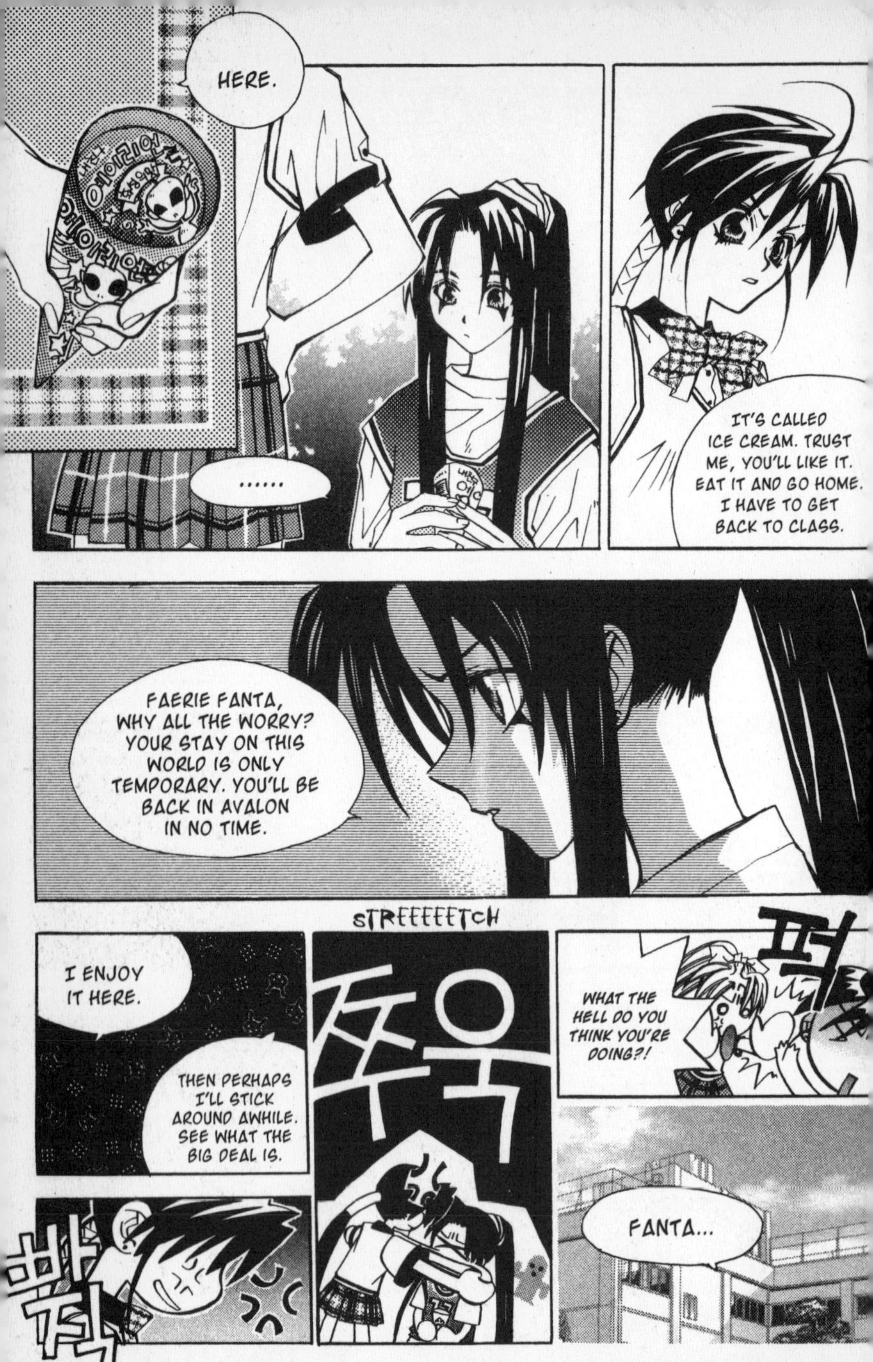
HERE.
......
IT'S CALLED ICE CREAM. TRUST ME, YOU'LL LIKE IT. EAT IT AND GO HOME. I HAVE TO GET BACK TO CLASS.
FAERIE FANTA, WHY ALL THE WORRY? YOUR STAY ON THIS WORLD IS ONLY TEMPORARY. YOU'LL BE BACK IN AVALON IN NO TIME.
I ENJOY IT HERE.
THEN PERHAPS I'LL STICK AROUND AWHILE. SEE WHAT THE BIG DEAL IS.
STREEEEETCH
WHAT THE HELL DO YOU THINK YOU'RE DOING?!
FANTA...

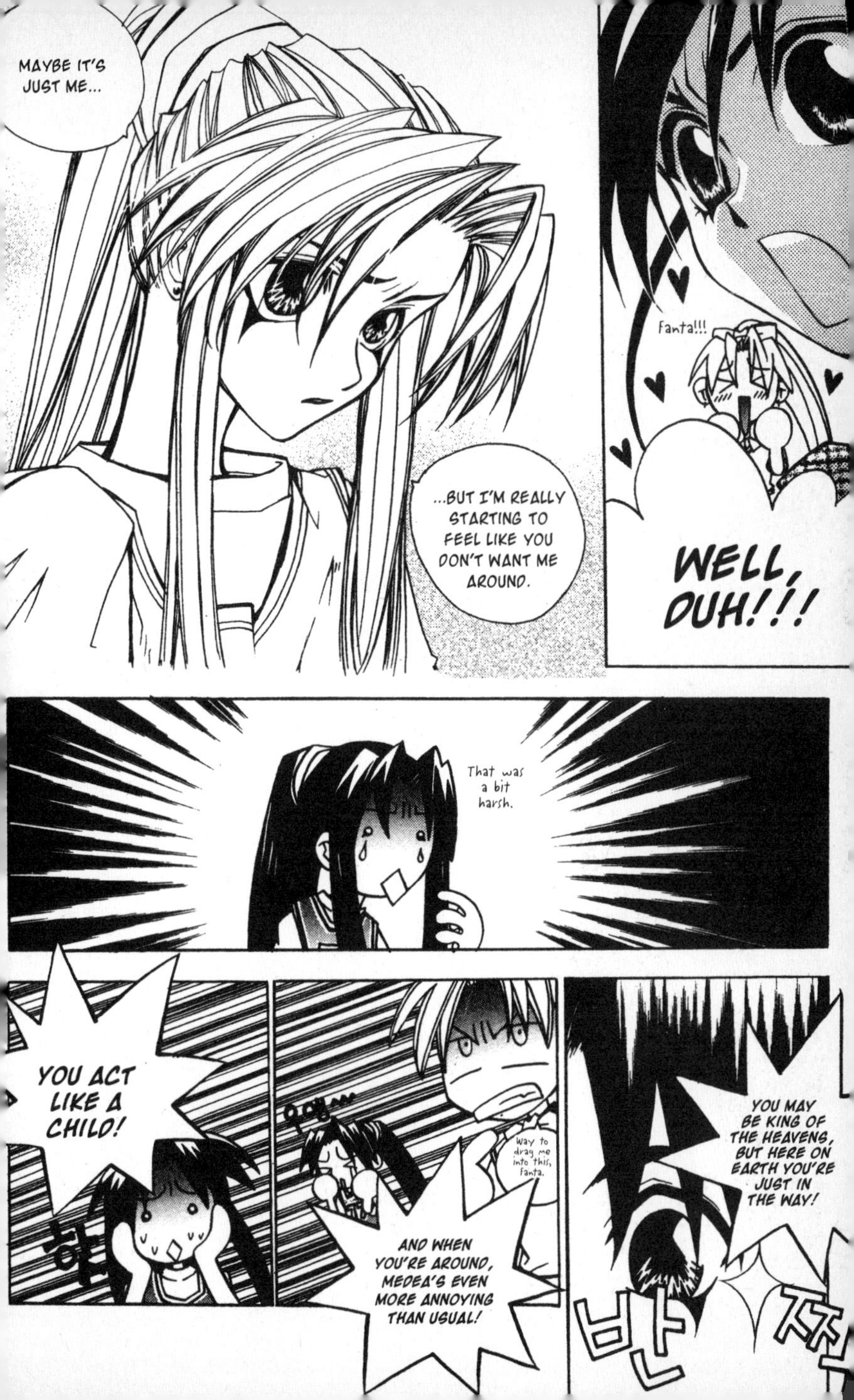

MAYBE IT'S JUST ME...
...BUT I'M REALLY STARTING TO FEEL LIKE YOU DON'T WANT ME AROUND.
Fanta!!!
WELL, DUH!!!
That was a bit harsh.
YOU ACT LIKE A CHILD!
Way to drag me into this, Fanta.
AND WHEN YOU'RE AROUND, MEDEA'S EVEN MORE ANNOYING THAN USUAL!
YOU MAY BE KING OF THE HEAVENS, BUT HERE ON EARTH YOU'RE JUST IN THE WAY!

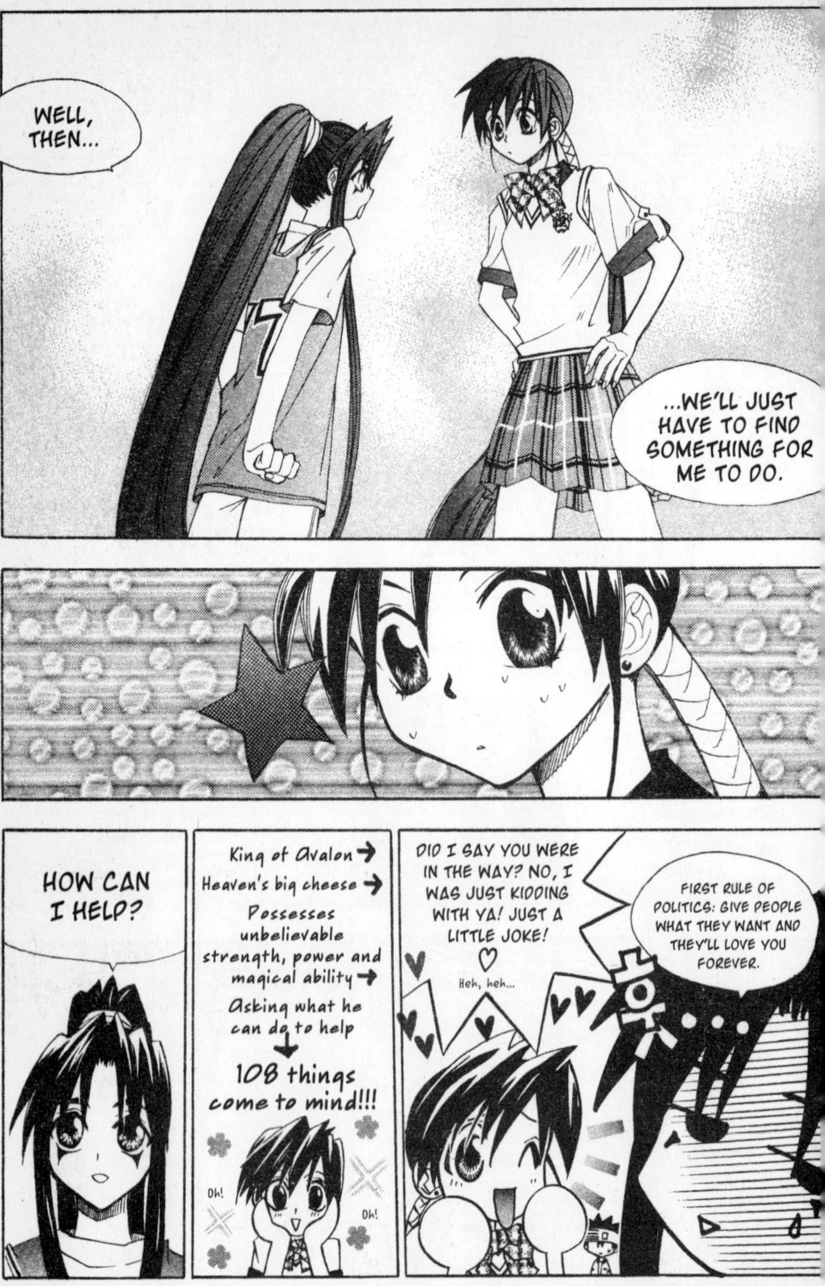
WELL, THEN...
...WE'LL JUST HAVE TO FIND SOMETHING FOR ME TO DO.
HOW CAN I HELP?
King of Avalon →
Heaven's big cheese →
Possesses unbelievable strength, power and magical ability →
Asking what he can do to help
108 things come to mind!!!
Oh!
Oh!
DID I SAY YOU WERE IN THE WAY? NO, I WAS JUST KIDDING WITH YA! JUST A LITTLE JOKE! ♡
Heh, heh...
FIRST RULE OF POLITICS: GIVE PEOPLE WHAT THEY WANT AND THEY'LL LOVE YOU FOREVER.

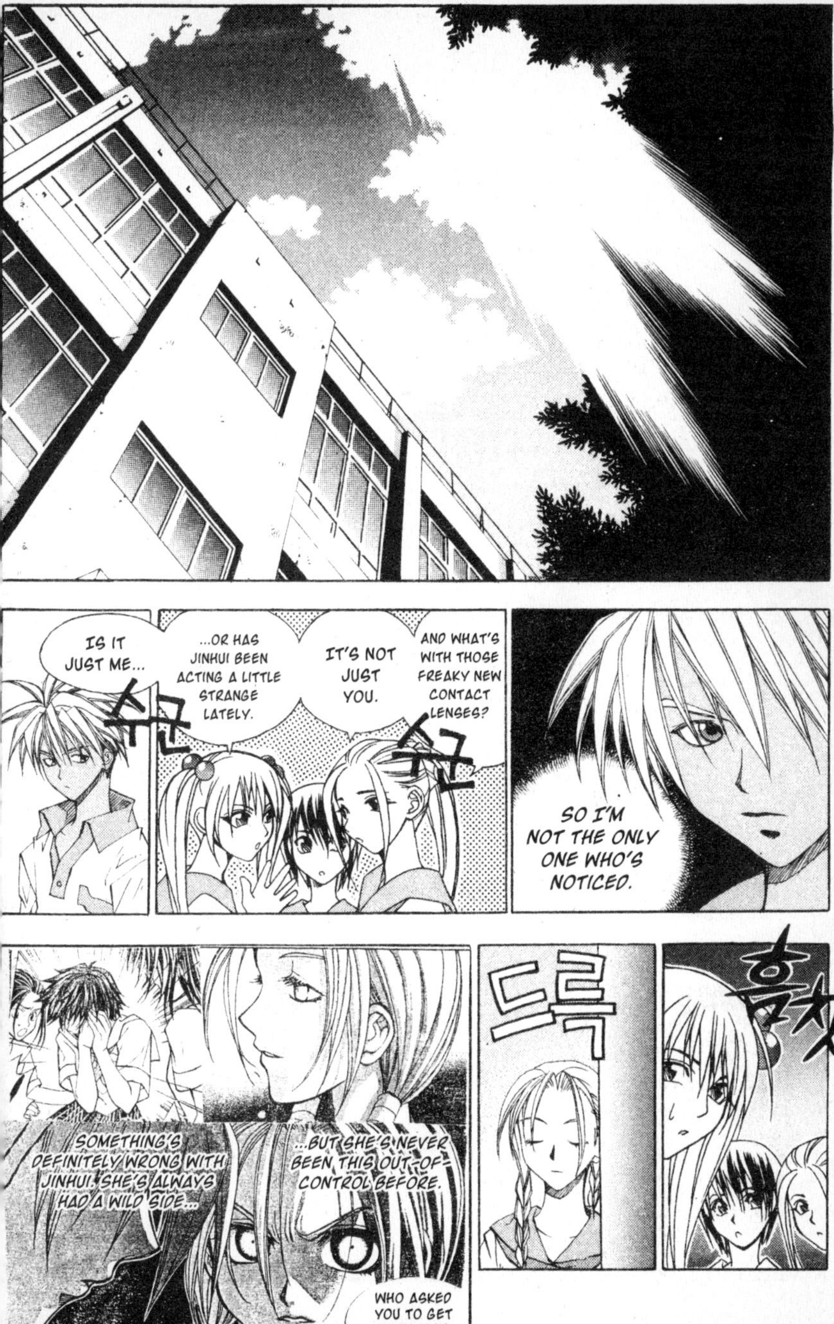
IS IT JUST ME...
수군
...OR HAS JINHUI BEEN ACTING A LITTLE STRANGE LATELY.
IT'S NOT JUST YOU.
AND WHAT'S WITH THOSE FREAKY NEW CONTACT LENSES?
수군
SO I'M NOT THE ONLY ONE WHO'S NOTICED.
SOMETHING'S DEFINITELY WRONG WITH JINHUI. SHE'S ALWAYS HAD A WILD SIDE...
...BUT SHE'S NEVER BEEN THIS OUT-OF-CONTROL BEFORE.
WHO ASKED YOU TO GET INVOLVED?
드르륵
흠칫

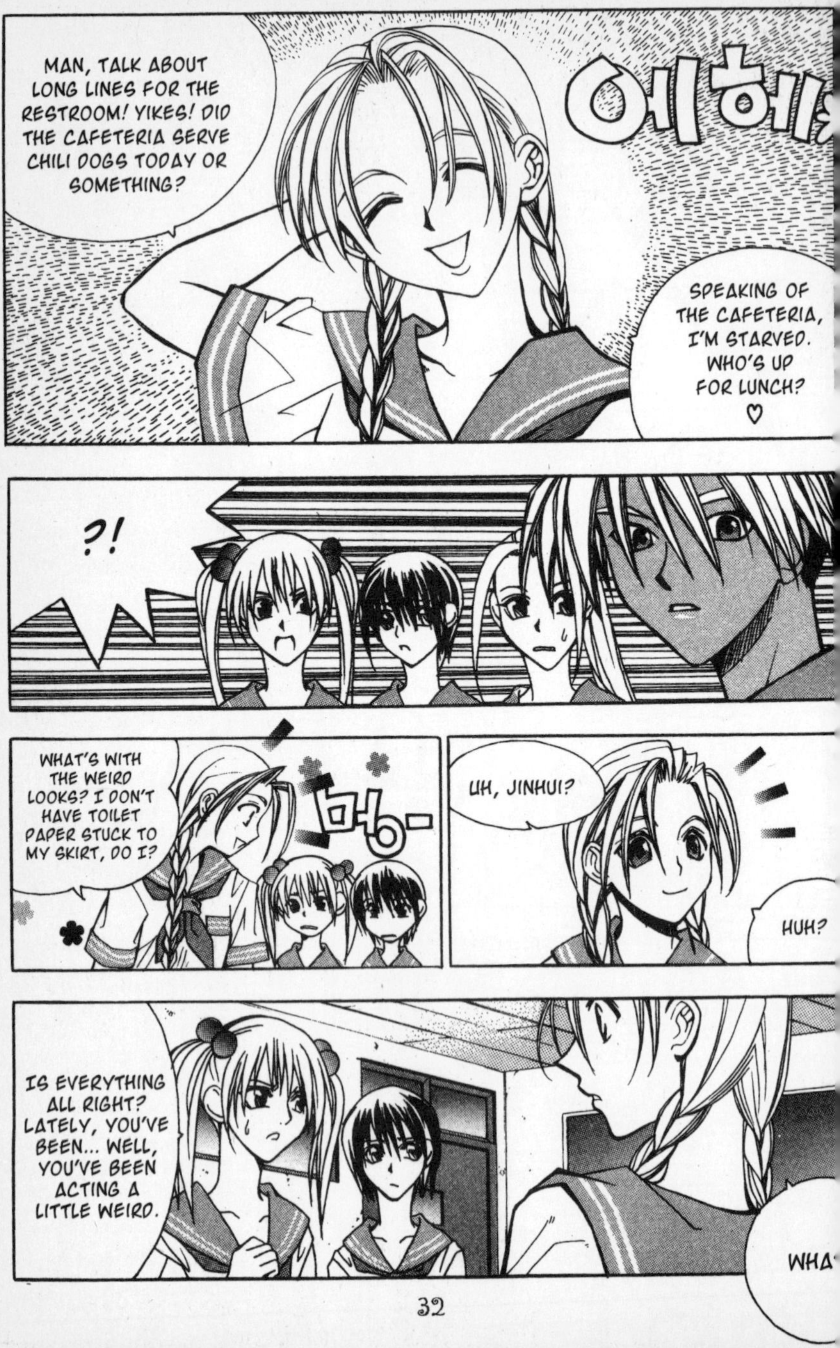
MAN, TALK ABOUT LONG LINES FOR THE RESTROOM! YIKES! DID THE CAFETERIA SERVE CHILI DOGS TODAY OR SOMETHING?
에헤
SPEAKING OF THE CAFETERIA, I'M STARVED. WHO'S UP FOR LUNCH? ♡
?!
WHAT'S WITH THE WEIRD LOOKS? I DON'T HAVE TOILET PAPER STUCK TO MY SKIRT, DO I?
UH, JINHUI?
HUH?
IS EVERYTHING ALL RIGHT? LATELY, YOU'VE BEEN... WELL, YOU'VE BEEN ACTING A LITTLE WEIRD.
WHA

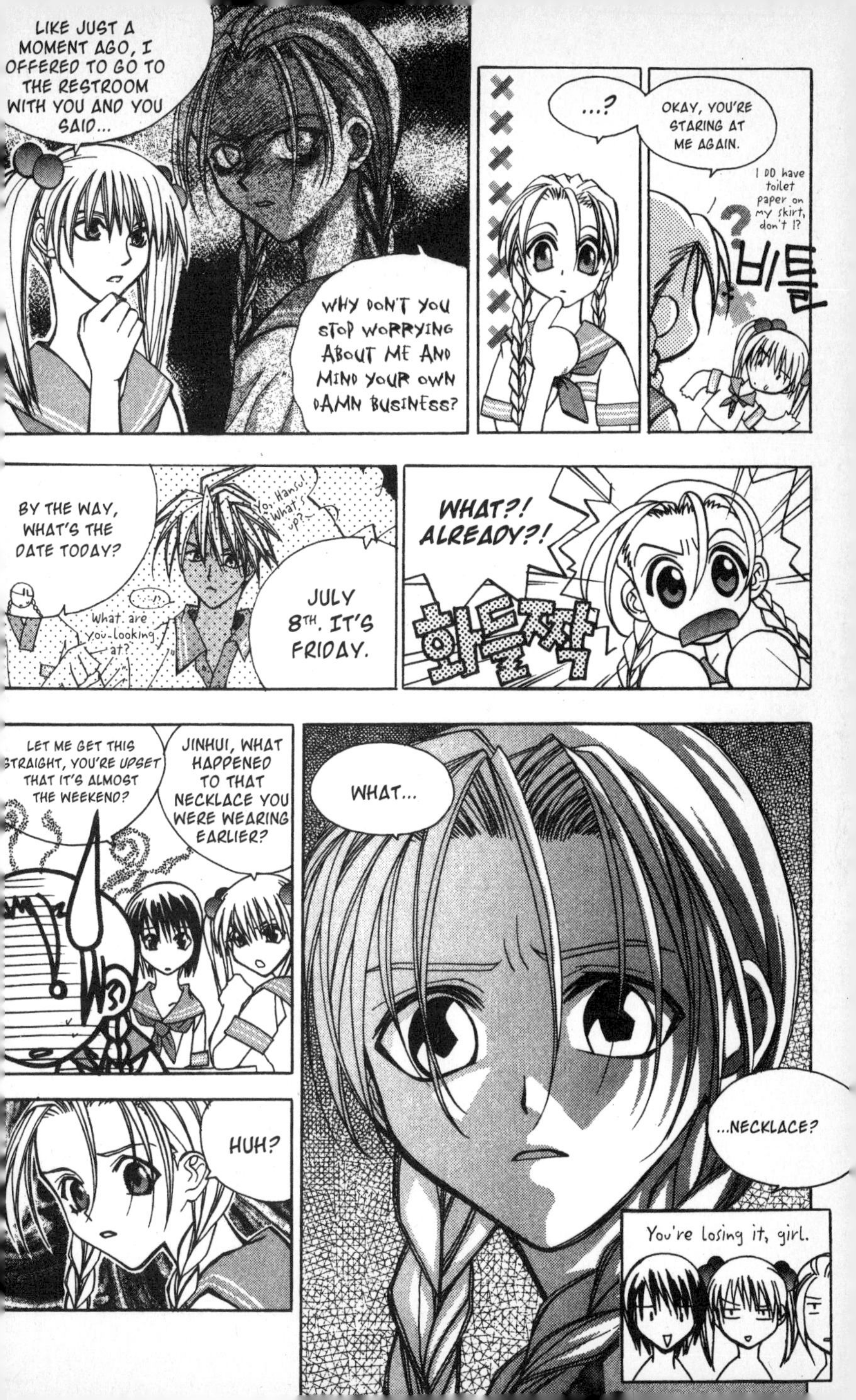
LIKE JUST A MOMENT AGO, I OFFERED TO GO TO THE RESTROOM WITH YOU AND YOU SAID...
WHY DON'T YOU STOP WORRYING ABOUT ME AND MIND YOUR OWN DAMN BUSINESS?
...?
OKAY, YOU'RE STARING AT ME AGAIN.
I DO have toilet paper on my skirt, don't I?
비틀
BY THE WAY, WHAT'S THE DATE TODAY?
Yo, Hansu! What's up?
...!
What are you looking at?
JULY 8TH. IT'S FRIDAY.
WHAT?! ALREADY?!
화들짝
LET ME GET THIS STRAIGHT, YOU'RE UPSET THAT IT'S ALMOST THE WEEKEND?
JINHUI, WHAT HAPPENED TO THAT NECKLACE YOU WERE WEARING EARLIER?
HUH?
WHAT...
...NECKLACE?
You're losing it, girl.

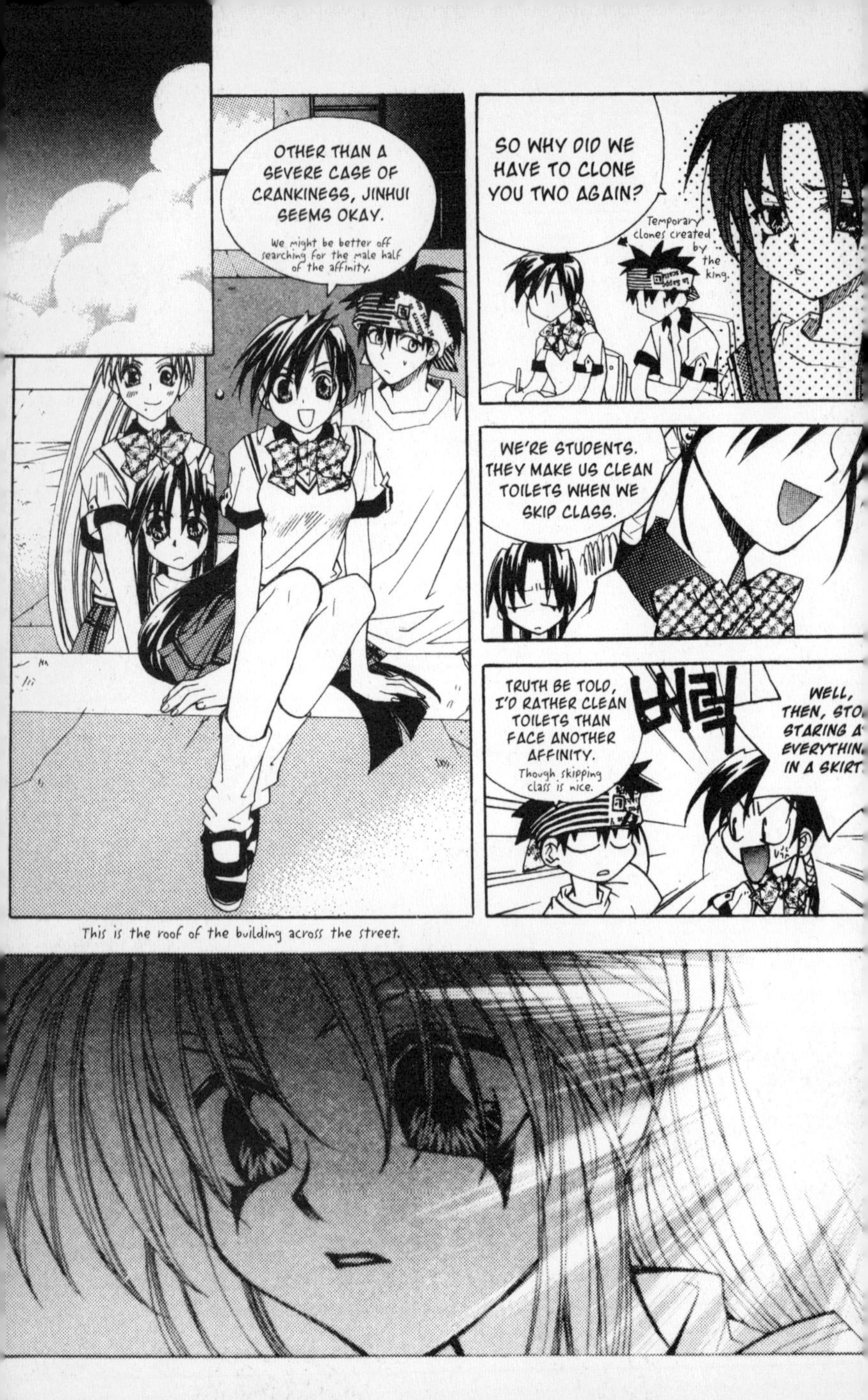
OTHER THAN A SEVERE CASE OF CRANKINESS, JINHUI SEEMS OKAY.
We might be better off searching for the male half of the affinity.
This is the roof of the building across the street.
SO WHY DID WE HAVE TO CLONE YOU TWO AGAIN?
Temporary clones created by the king.
WE'RE STUDENTS. THEY MAKE US CLEAN TOILETS WHEN WE SKIP CLASS.
TRUTH BE TOLD, I'D RATHER CLEAN TOILETS THAN FACE ANOTHER AFFINITY.
Though skipping class is nice.
버럭
WELL, THEN, STO STARING A EVERYTHIN IN A SKIRT

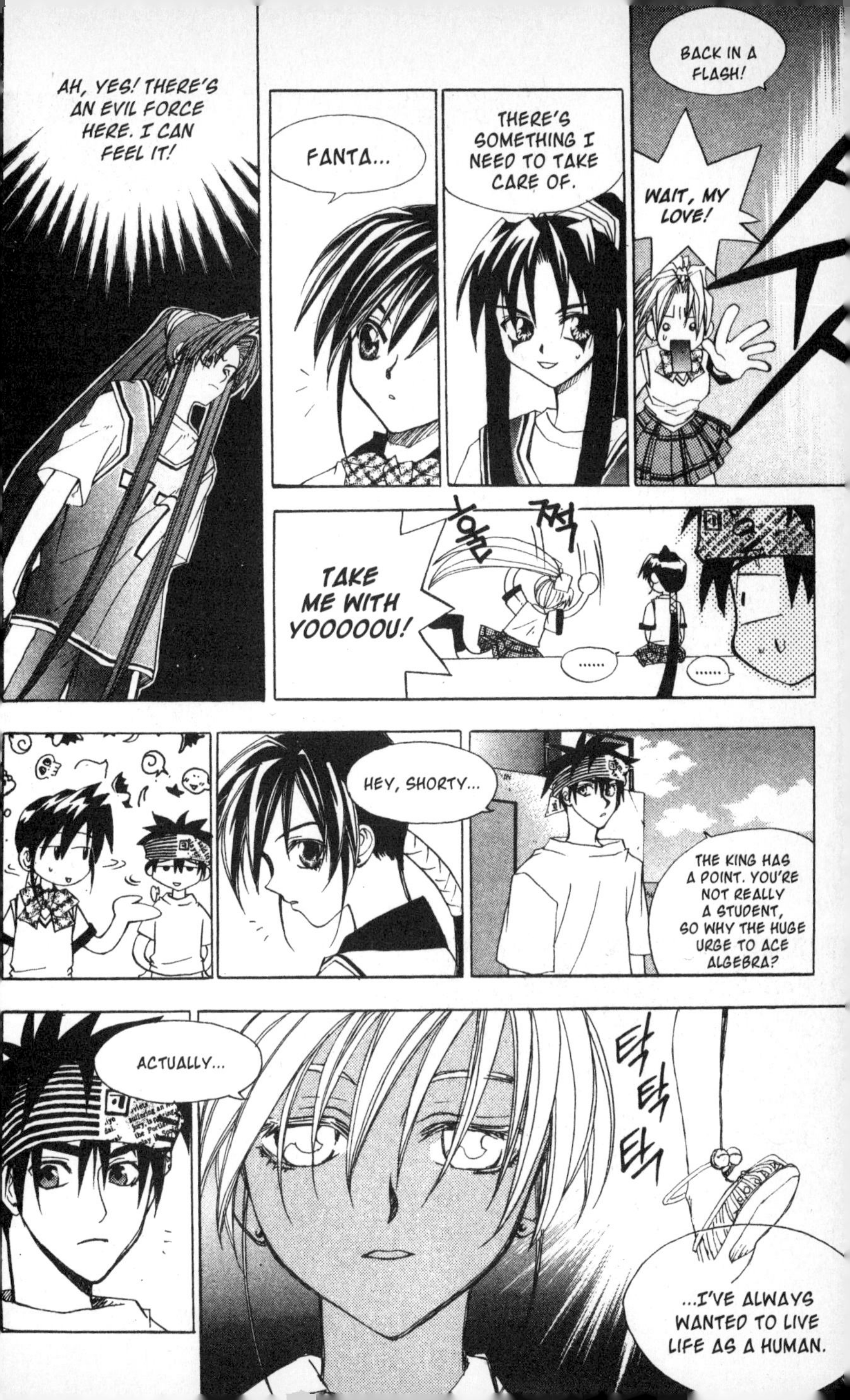
AH, YES! THERE'S AN EVIL FORCE HERE. I CAN FEEL IT!
FANTA...
THERE'S SOMETHING I NEED TO TAKE CARE OF.
BACK IN A FLASH!
WAIT, MY LOVE!
TAKE ME WITH YOOOOOU!
훌쩍
......
......
HEY, SHORTY...
THE KING HAS A POINT. YOU'RE NOT REALLY A STUDENT, SO WHY THE HUGE URGE TO ACE ALGEBRA?
ACTUALLY...
탁
탁
탁
...I'VE ALWAYS WANTED TO LIVE LIFE AS A HUMAN.

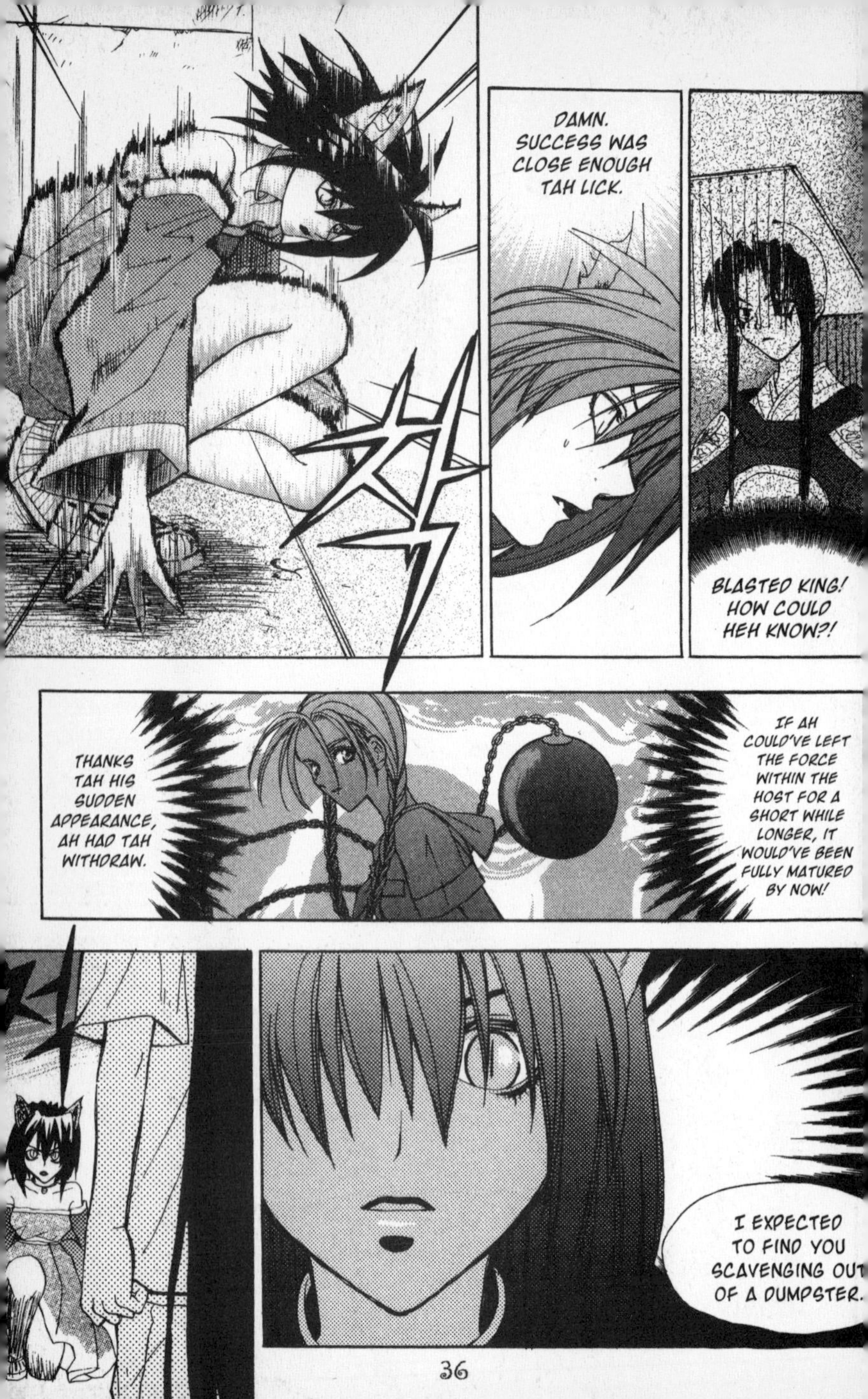
DAMN. SUCCESS WAS CLOSE ENOUGH TAH LICK.
BLASTED KING! HOW COULD HEH KNOW?!
THANKS TAH HIS SUDDEN APPEARANCE, AH HAD TAH WITHDRAW.
IF AH COULD'VE LEFT THE FORCE WITHIN THE HOST FOR A SHORT WHILE LONGER, IT WOULD'VE BEEN FULLY MATURED BY NOW!
I EXPECTED TO FIND YOU SCAVENGING OUT OF A DUMPSTER.

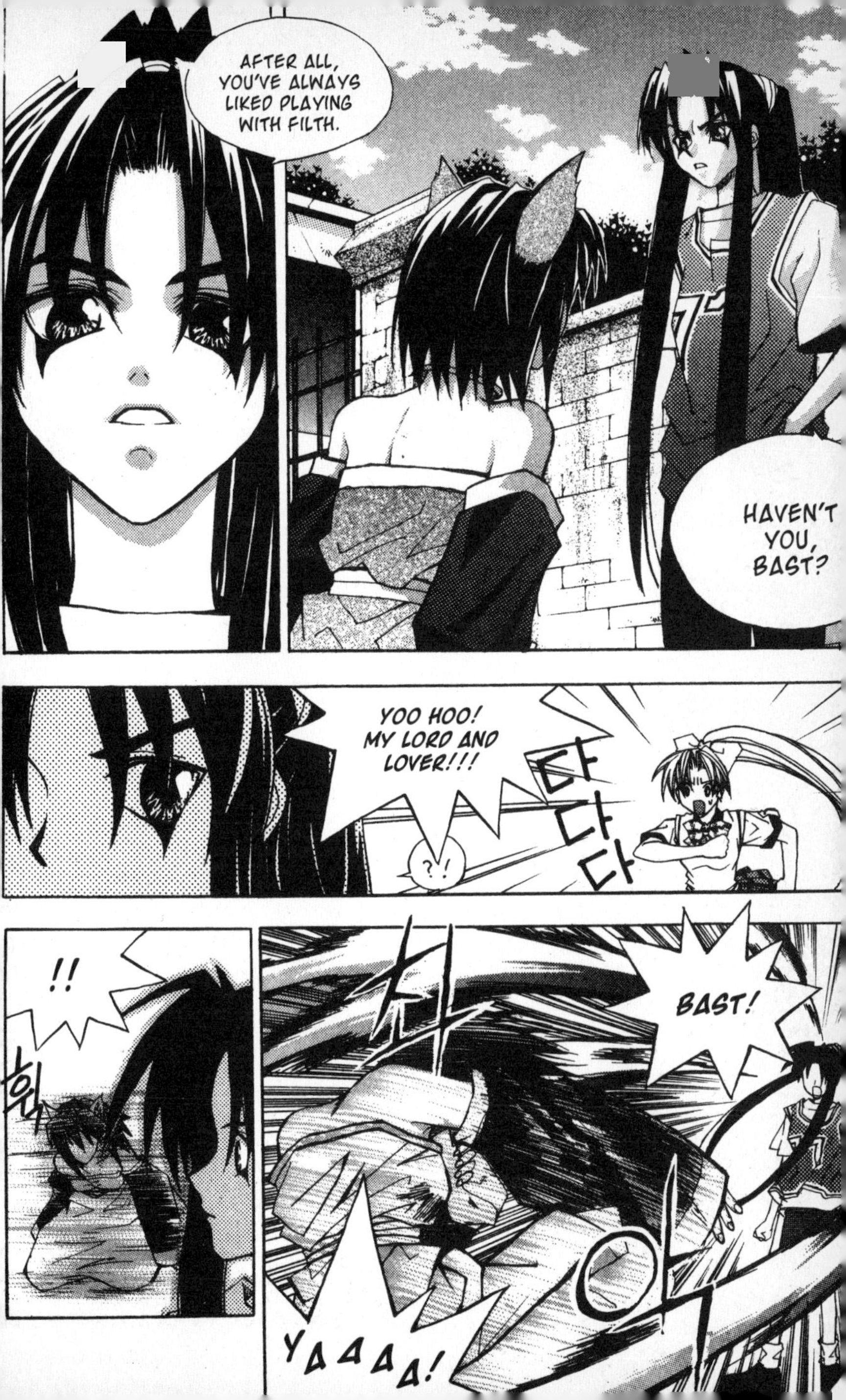
AFTER ALL, YOU'VE ALWAYS LIKED PLAYING WITH FILTH.
HAVEN'T YOU, BAST?
YOO HOO! MY LORD AND LOVER!!!
다 다 다
?!
!!
BAST!
YAAAAA!

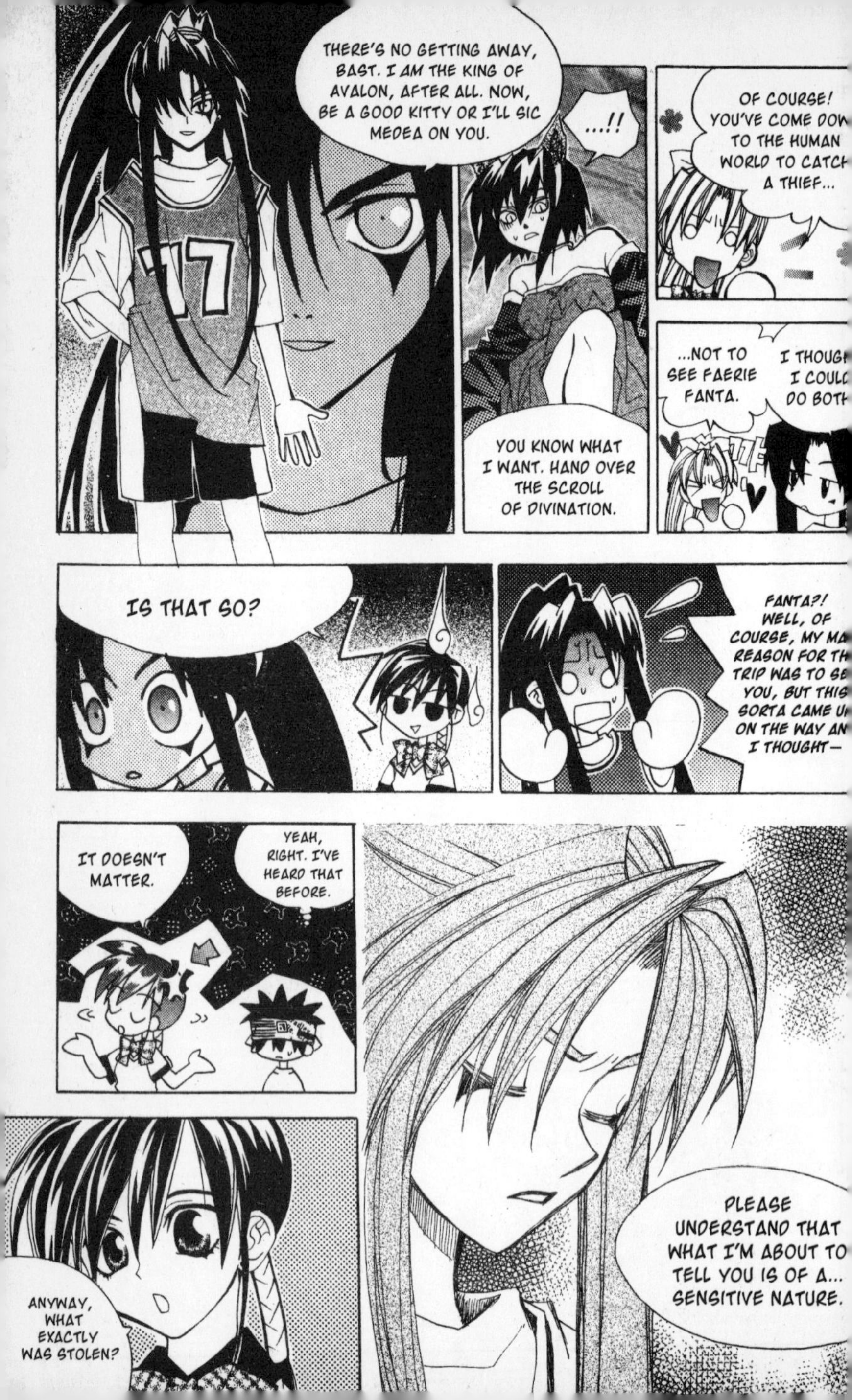

THERE'S NO GETTING AWAY, BAST. I AM THE KING OF AVALON, AFTER ALL. NOW, BE A GOOD KITTY OR I'LL SIC MEDEA ON YOU.
...!!
YOU KNOW WHAT I WANT. HAND OVER THE SCROLL OF DIVINATION.
OF COURSE! YOU'VE COME DOW TO THE HUMAN WORLD TO CATCH A THIEF...
...NOT TO SEE FAERIE FANTA.
I THOUGH I COULD DO BOTH
IS THAT SO?
FANTA?! WELL, OF COURSE, MY MA REASON FOR TH TRIP WAS TO SE YOU, BUT THIS SORTA CAME U ON THE WAY AN I THOUGHT—
IT DOESN'T MATTER.
YEAH, RIGHT. I'VE HEARD THAT BEFORE.
ANYWAY, WHAT EXACTLY WAS STOLEN?
PLEASE UNDERSTAND THAT WHAT I'M ABOUT TO TELL YOU IS OF A... SENSITIVE NATURE.

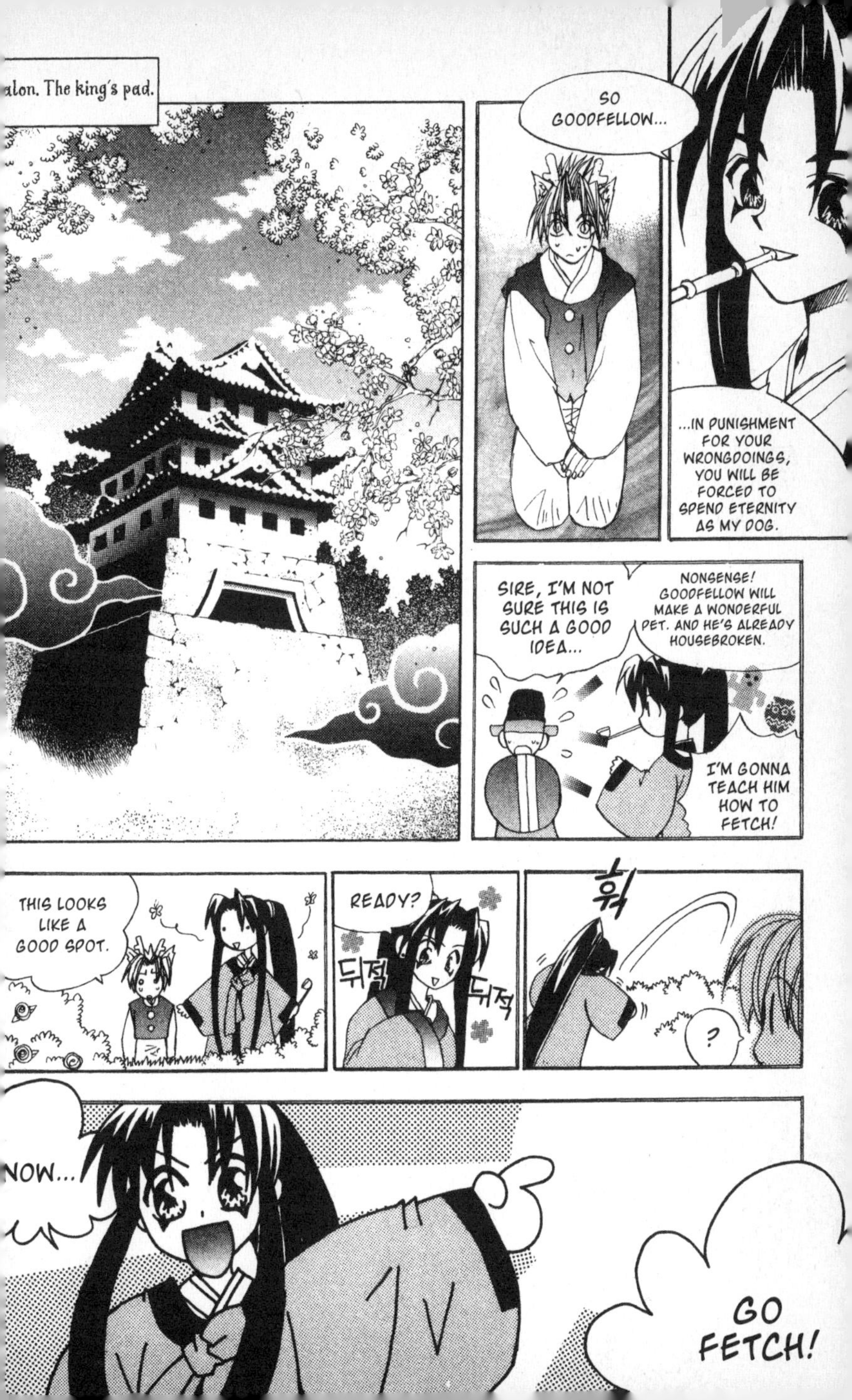
alon. The king's pad.
SO GOODFELLOW...
...IN PUNISHMENT FOR YOUR WRONGDOINGS, YOU WILL BE FORCED TO SPEND ETERNITY AS MY DOG.
SIRE, I'M NOT SURE THIS IS SUCH A GOOD IDEA...
NONSENSE! GOODFELLOW WILL MAKE A WONDERFUL PET. AND HE'S ALREADY HOUSEBROKEN.
I'M GONNA TEACH HIM HOW TO FETCH!
THIS LOOKS LIKE A GOOD SPOT.
READY?
뒤적
뒤적
휙
?
NOW...
GO FETCH!

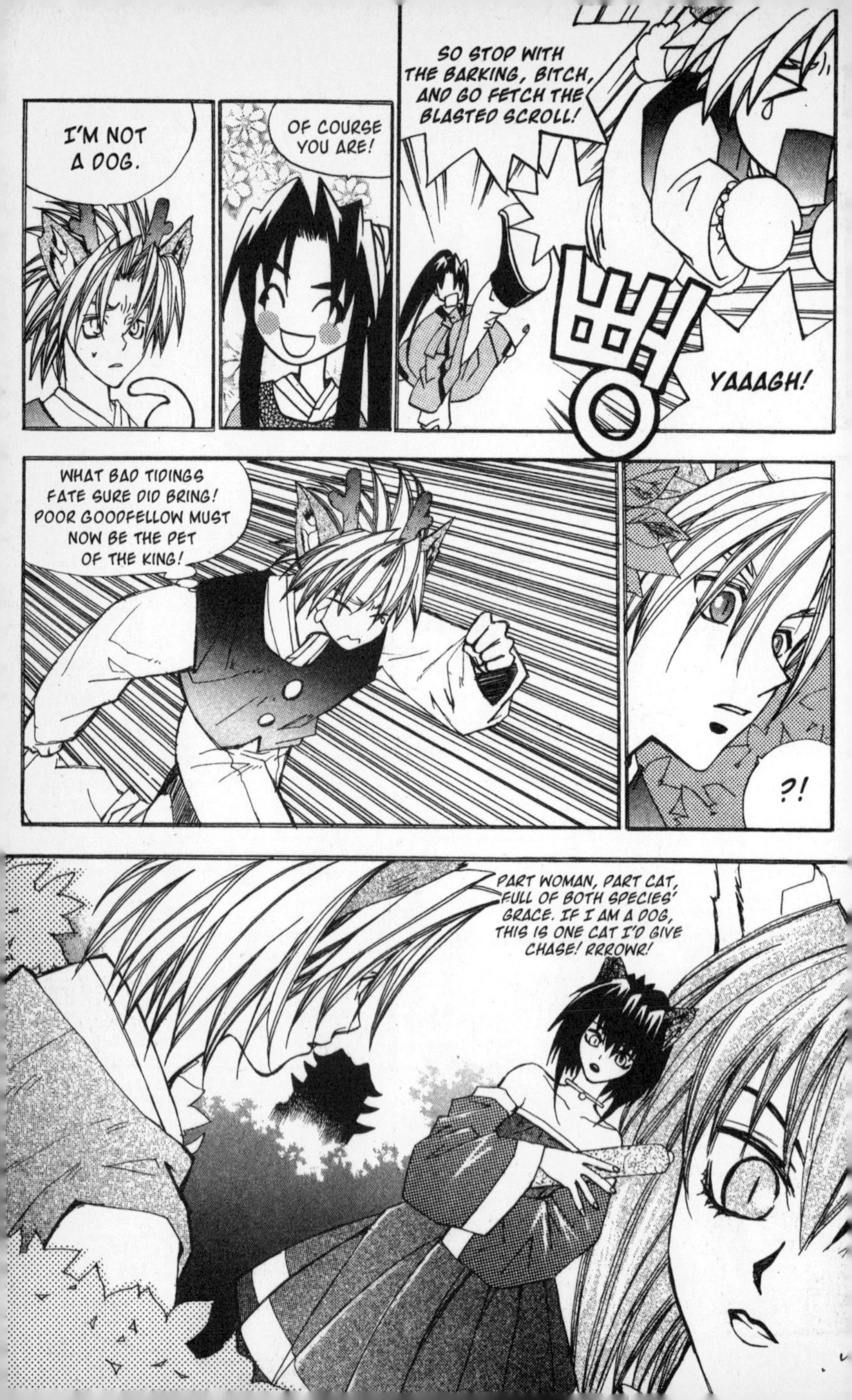
I'M NOT A DOG.
OF COURSE YOU ARE!
SO STOP WITH THE BARKING, BITCH, AND GO FETCH THE BLASTED SCROLL!
YAAAGH!
WHAT BAD TIDINGS FATE SURE DID BRING! POOR GOODFELLOW MUST NOW BE THE PET OF THE KING!
?!
PART WOMAN, PART CAT, FULL OF BOTH SPECIES' GRACE. IF I AM A DOG, THIS IS ONE CAT I'D GIVE CHASE! RRROWR!

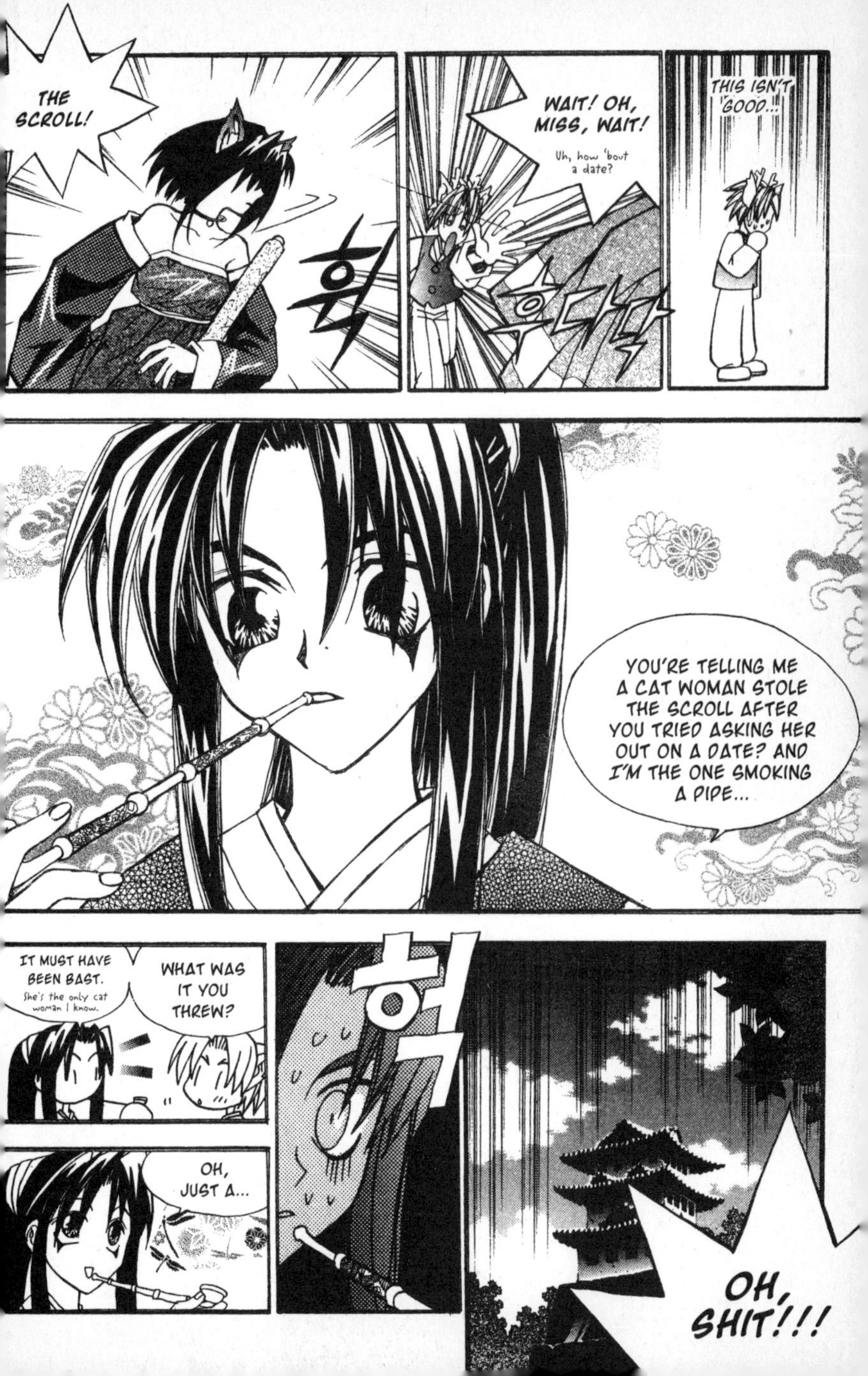
THE SCROLL!
WAIT! OH, MISS, WAIT!
Uh, how 'bout a date?
THIS ISN'T GOOD...
YOU'RE TELLING ME A CAT WOMAN STOLE THE SCROLL AFTER YOU TRIED ASKING HER OUT ON A DATE? AND I'M THE ONE SMOKING A PIPE...
IT MUST HAVE BEEN BAST.
She's the only cat woman I know.
WHAT WAS IT YOU THREW?
OH, JUST A...
헉
OH, SHIT!!!

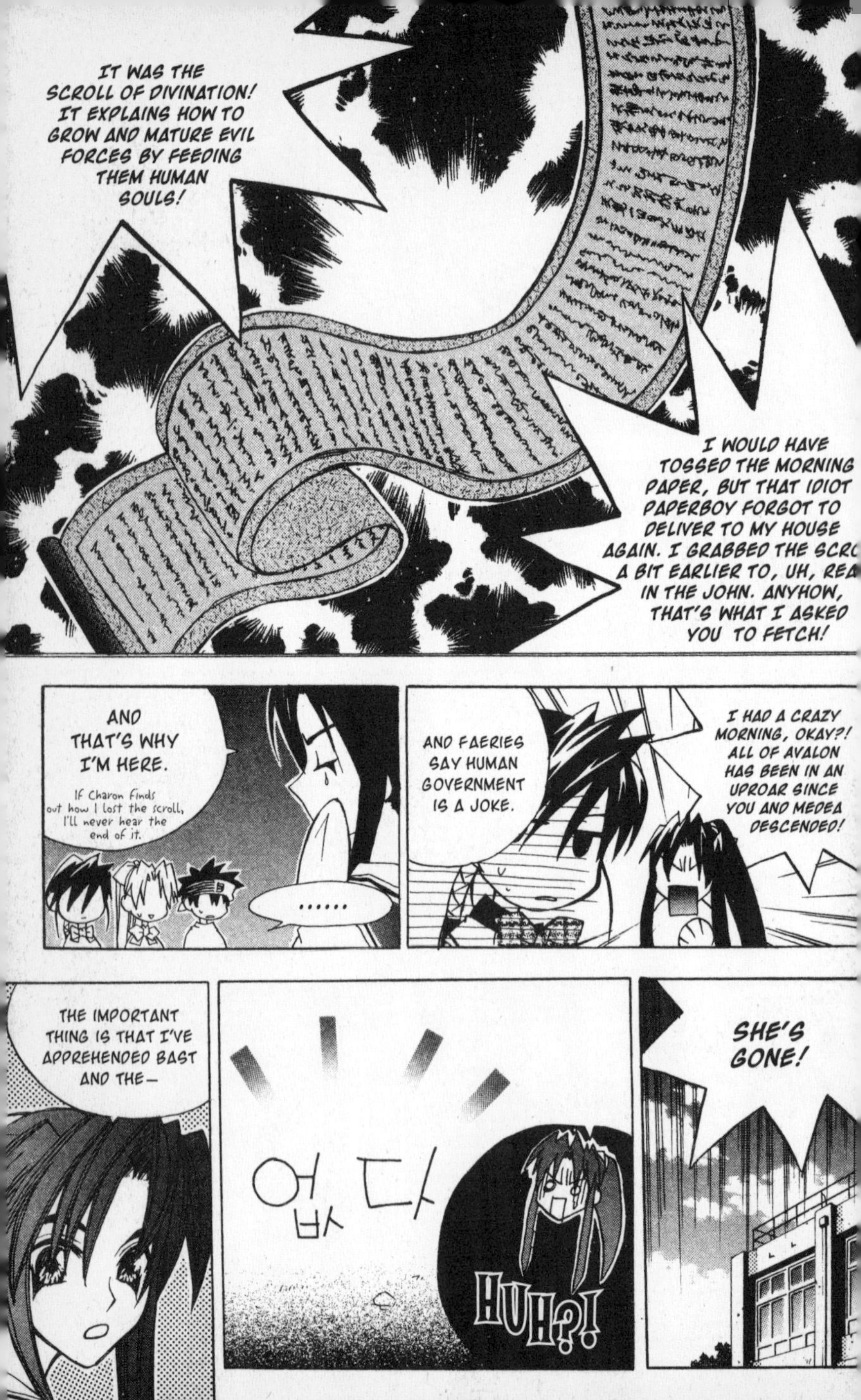

IT WAS THE SCROLL OF DIVINATION! IT EXPLAINS HOW TO GROW AND MATURE EVIL FORCES BY FEEDING THEM HUMAN SOULS!
I WOULD HAVE TOSSED THE MORNING PAPER, BUT THAT IDIOT PAPERBOY FORGOT TO DELIVER TO MY HOUSE AGAIN. I GRABBED THE SCRO A BIT EARLIER TO, UH, REA IN THE JOHN. ANYHOW, THAT'S WHAT I ASKED YOU TO FETCH!
AND THAT'S WHY I'M HERE.
If Charon finds out how I lost the scroll, I'll never hear the end of it.
......
AND FAERIES SAY HUMAN GOVERNMENT IS A JOKE.
I HAD A CRAZY MORNING, OKAY?! ALL OF AVALON HAS BEEN IN AN UPROAR SINCE YOU AND MEDEA DESCENDED!
THE IMPORTANT THING IS THAT I'VE APPREHENDED BAST AND THE—
없다
HUH?!
SHE'S GONE!

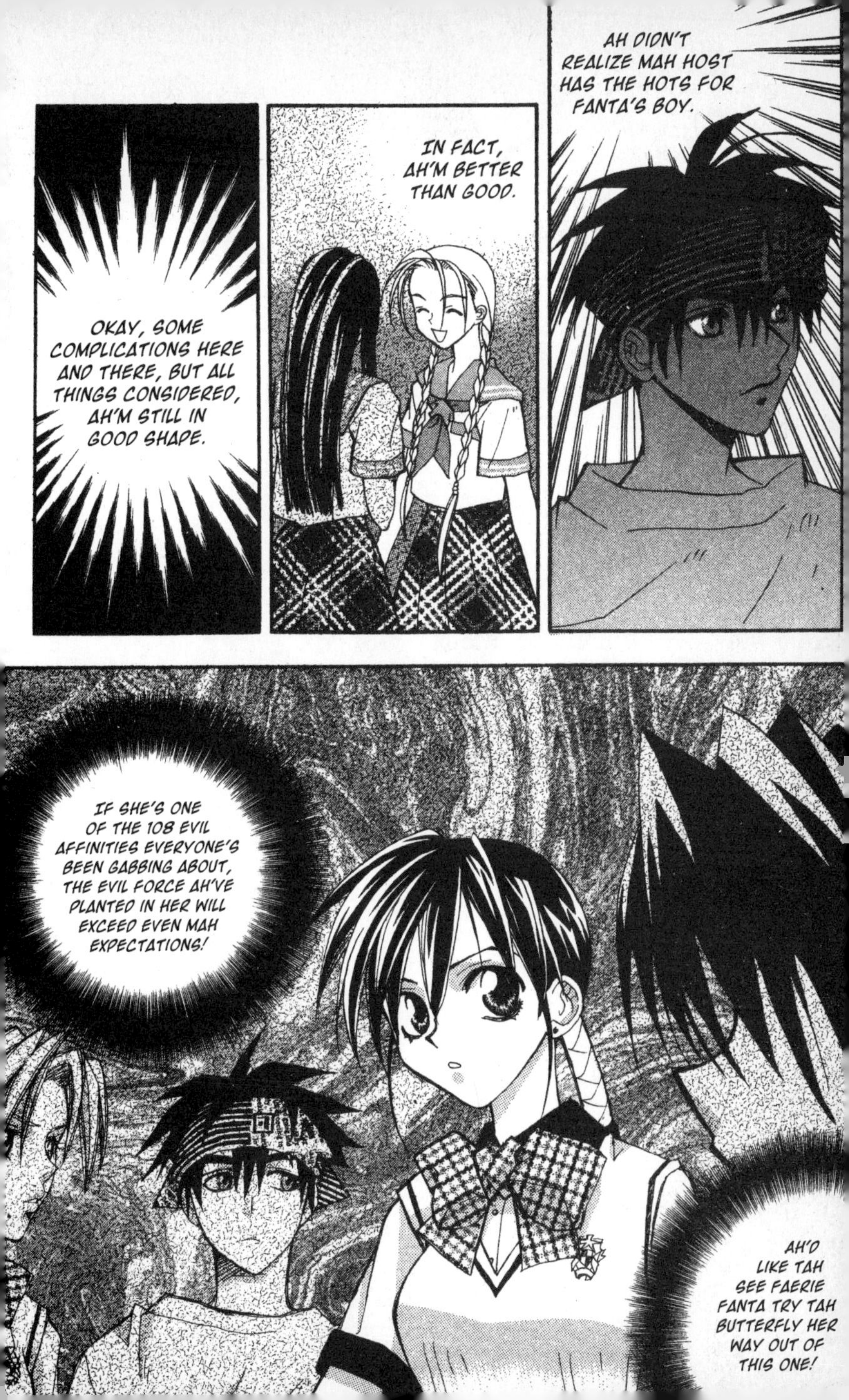
OKAY, SOME COMPLICATIONS HERE AND THERE, BUT ALL THINGS CONSIDERED, AH'M STILL IN GOOD SHAPE.
IN FACT, AH'M BETTER THAN GOOD.
AH DIDN'T REALIZE MAH HOST HAS THE HOTS FOR FANTA'S BOY.
IF SHE'S ONE OF THE 108 EVIL AFFINITIES EVERYONE'S BEEN GABBING ABOUT, THE EVIL FORCE AH'VE PLANTED IN HER WILL EXCEED EVEN MAH EXPECTATIONS!
AH'D LIKE TAH SEE FAERIE FANTA TRY TAH BUTTERFLY HER WAY OUT OF THIS ONE!

Daily Journal

EDITOR'S NOTE: Around the time You Hyun was working on Volume 5 of Faeries' Landing (1998–1999), there was a large, well-known cult making doomsday predictions in Korea. The story on this page satirizes that cult.

THE CLOCK IS TICKING, AND YOU TWO ARE SPENDING WHAT LITTLE TIME WE HAVE LEFT WORKING ON MANUSCRIPTS?!

IN 1999, THE GREAT KING OF TERROR WILL DESCEND TO EARTH, TRAILED BY HIS ARMY OF UNDEAD GLOWWORMS. HE'LL EAT THE SUN FOR BREAKFAST, BRINGING FORTH ARMAGEDDON.

Huijin

Jeong

The one and only Ms. You Hyun!

THE ECONOMY WILL COLLAPSE, NATIONS WILL GO TO WAR AND WHOOPI GOLDBERG WILL BE GIVEN ANOTHER SITCOM. IT WILL BE THE END OF THE WORLD AS WE KNOW IT! A NEW ERA OF MADNESS, SUFFERING AND DEATH!

I HAVE NO CHOICE BUT TO PUT THE SERIES ASIDE AND BLOW EVERY LAST CENT I HAVE ON CLOTHES, VIDEO GAMES AND CHEAP WINE!

THEN WHAT IF ARMAGEDDON DOESN'T HAPPEN?

FOOLS! THERE WILL BE GOOD FORTUNE FOR BELIEVERS!

HOW CAN THERE BE GOOD FORTUNE IF THE WORLD ENDS?

NICE TRY, YOU. NOW GET BACK TO WORK!

UNDEAD GLOW-WORMS... YEESH.

Man, reality really stinks.

Acupuncture works great for stress!

These are my thoughts after finishing the manuscript. The days have been increasingly warm. The hot weather makes me even more annoyed when I get hot-blooded. On top of that, it's humid, so the paper has been eating up water. And why do I always seem to catch a cold in the summer? Is it because I'm not even as good as a dog? Or is it because I'm not a dog? Once again, I have lots of help, which was not in the original plan. Rose drew a lot of the extras. I was also supposed to draw this journal, but in the interest of time, Hyeonjeong did it. Sniff. Huijin also works hard on the backgrounds. I even got help from Eunyeong. Thanks for diligently helping me even though my cats get in your way. (I love you, Eungyeong.) I wonder if the end will really come? Heh, heh... There are so many things I still want to do. Isn't the term "Great King of Terror" a Japanese term? (Who's going to complain about something like that? Damn, complain, complain.) If you're going to hit me, hit me. It's not like I committed a deadly sin, but there's always people who create a ruckus. Sorry if this is incoherent, I'm a bit broken.

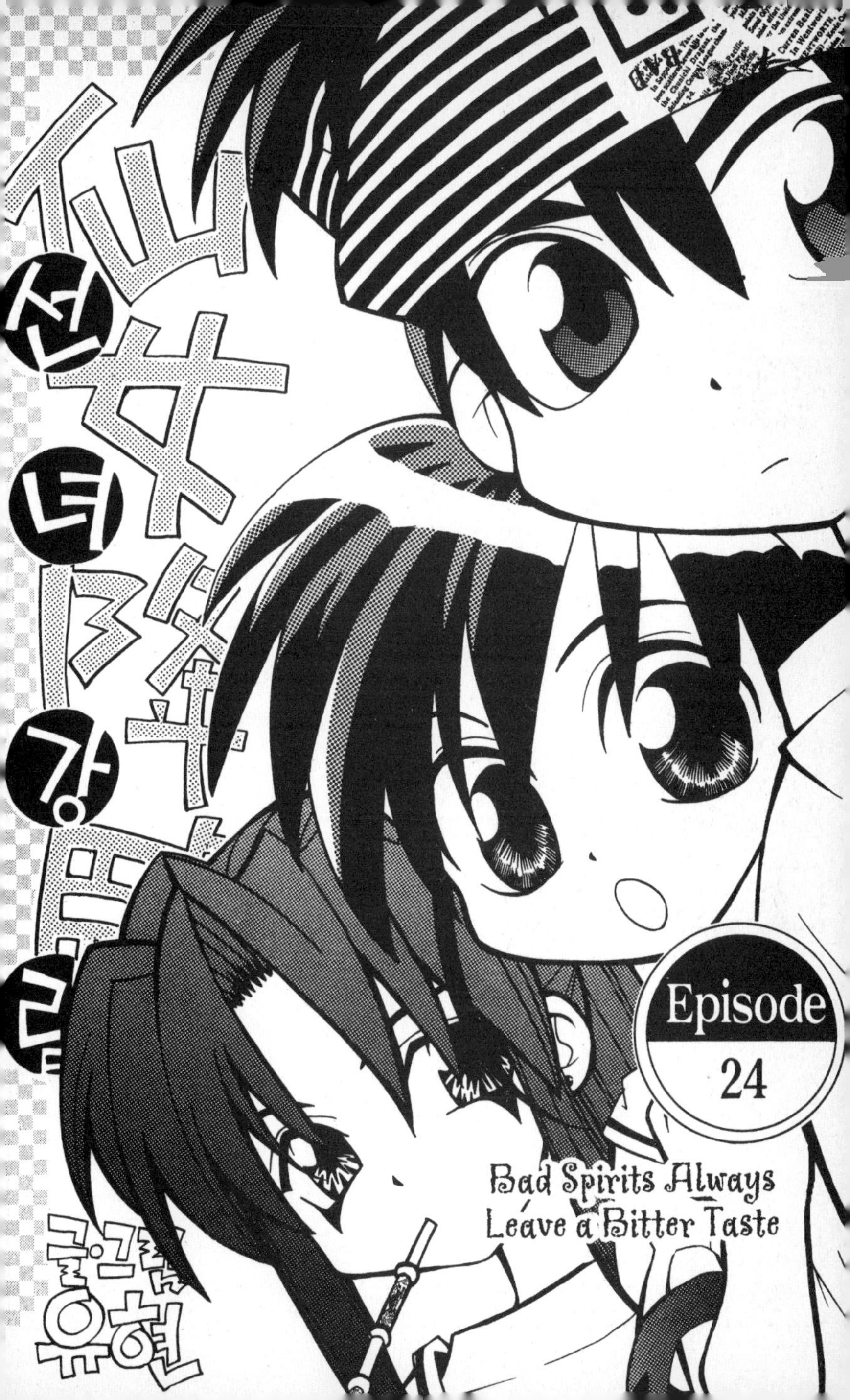
Episode
24
Bad Spirits Always Leave a Bitter Taste

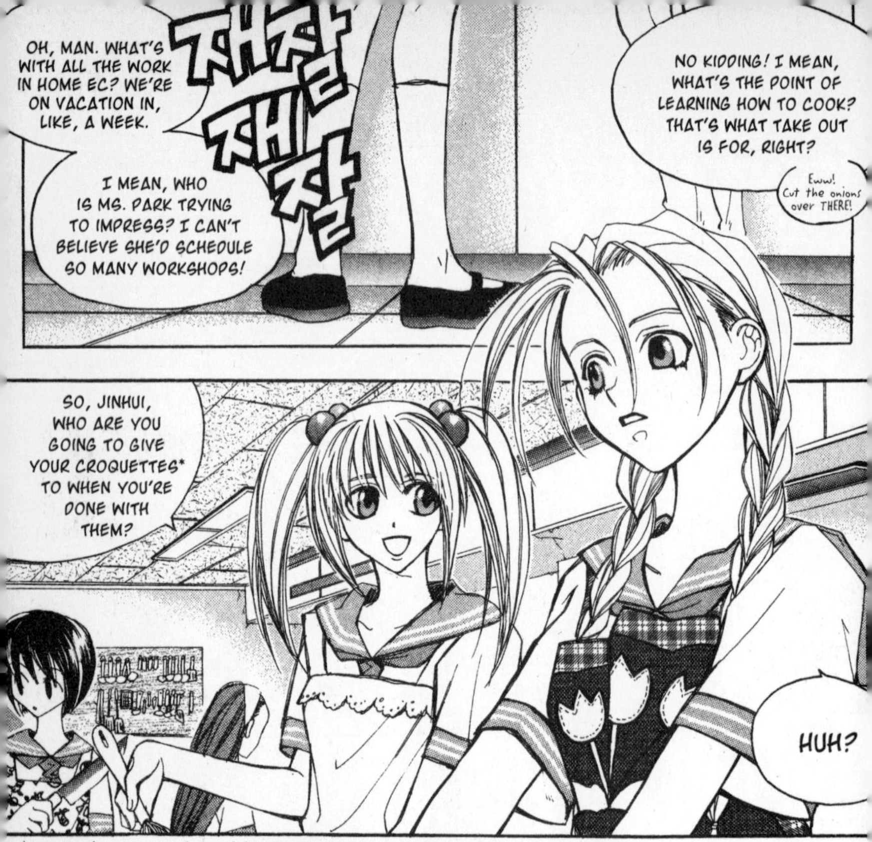
OH, MAN. WHAT'S WITH ALL THE WORK IN HOME EC? WE'RE ON VACATION IN, LIKE, A WEEK.
I MEAN, WHO IS MS. PARK TRYING TO IMPRESS? I CAN'T BELIEVE SHE'D SCHEDULE SO MANY WORKSHOPS!
재잘 재잘 재잘
NO KIDDING! I MEAN, WHAT'S THE POINT OF LEARNING HOW TO COOK? THAT'S WHAT TAKE OUT IS FOR, RIGHT?
Eww! Cut the onions over THERE!
SO, JINHUI, WHO ARE YOU GOING TO GIVE YOUR CROQUETTES* TO WHEN YOU'RE DONE WITH THEM?
HUH?

*Croquette: A popular snack food consisting of a glob of meat or vegetables deep-fried in fat. Yummmm!

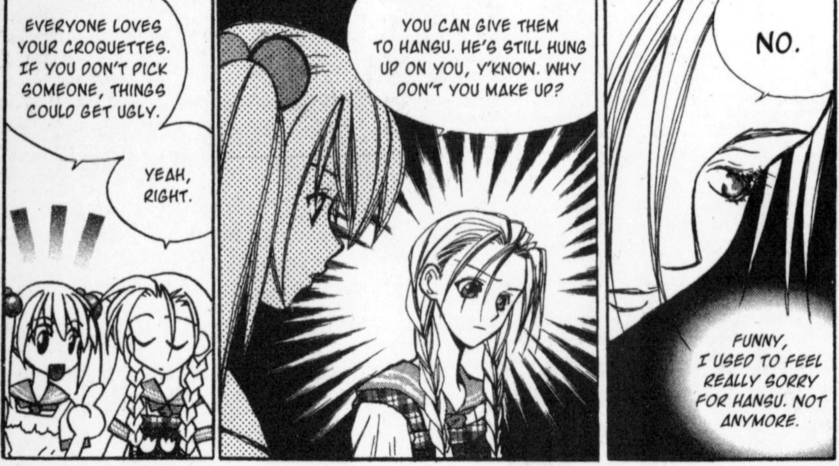
EVERYONE LOVES YOUR CROQUETTES. IF YOU DON'T PICK SOMEONE, THINGS COULD GET UGLY.
YEAH, RIGHT.
YOU CAN GIVE THEM TO HANSU. HE'S STILL HUNG UP ON YOU, Y'KNOW. WHY DON'T YOU MAKE UP?
NO.
FUNNY, I USED TO FEEL REALLY SORRY FOR HANSU. NOT ANYMORE.

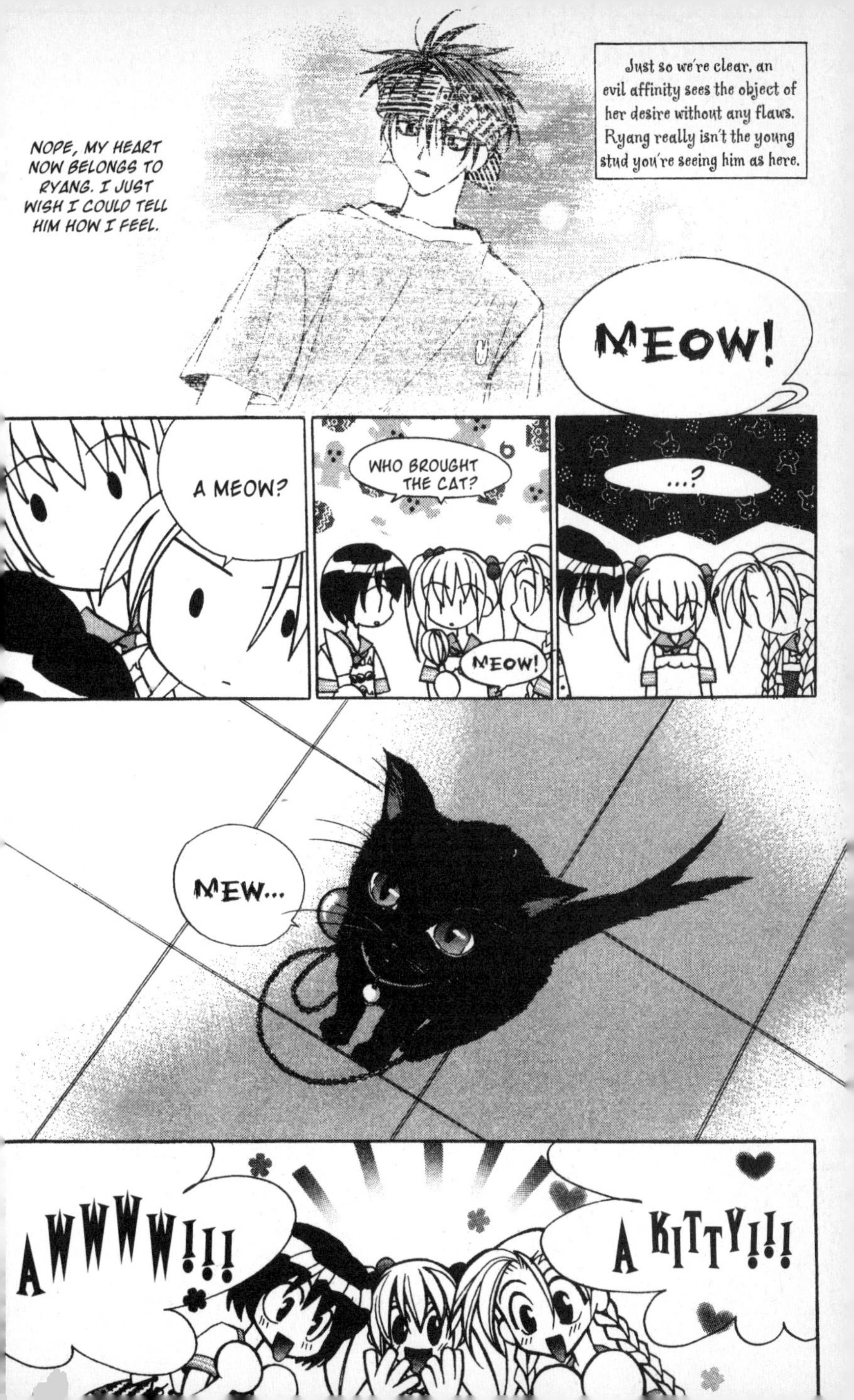
NOPE, MY HEART NOW BELONGS TO RYANG. I JUST WISH I COULD TELL HIM HOW I FEEL.
Just so we're clear, an evil affinity sees the object of her desire without any flaws. Ryang really isn't the young stud you're seeing him as here.
MEOW!
A MEOW?
WHO BROUGHT THE CAT?
MEOW!
...?
MEW...
AWWWW!!!
A KITTY!!!

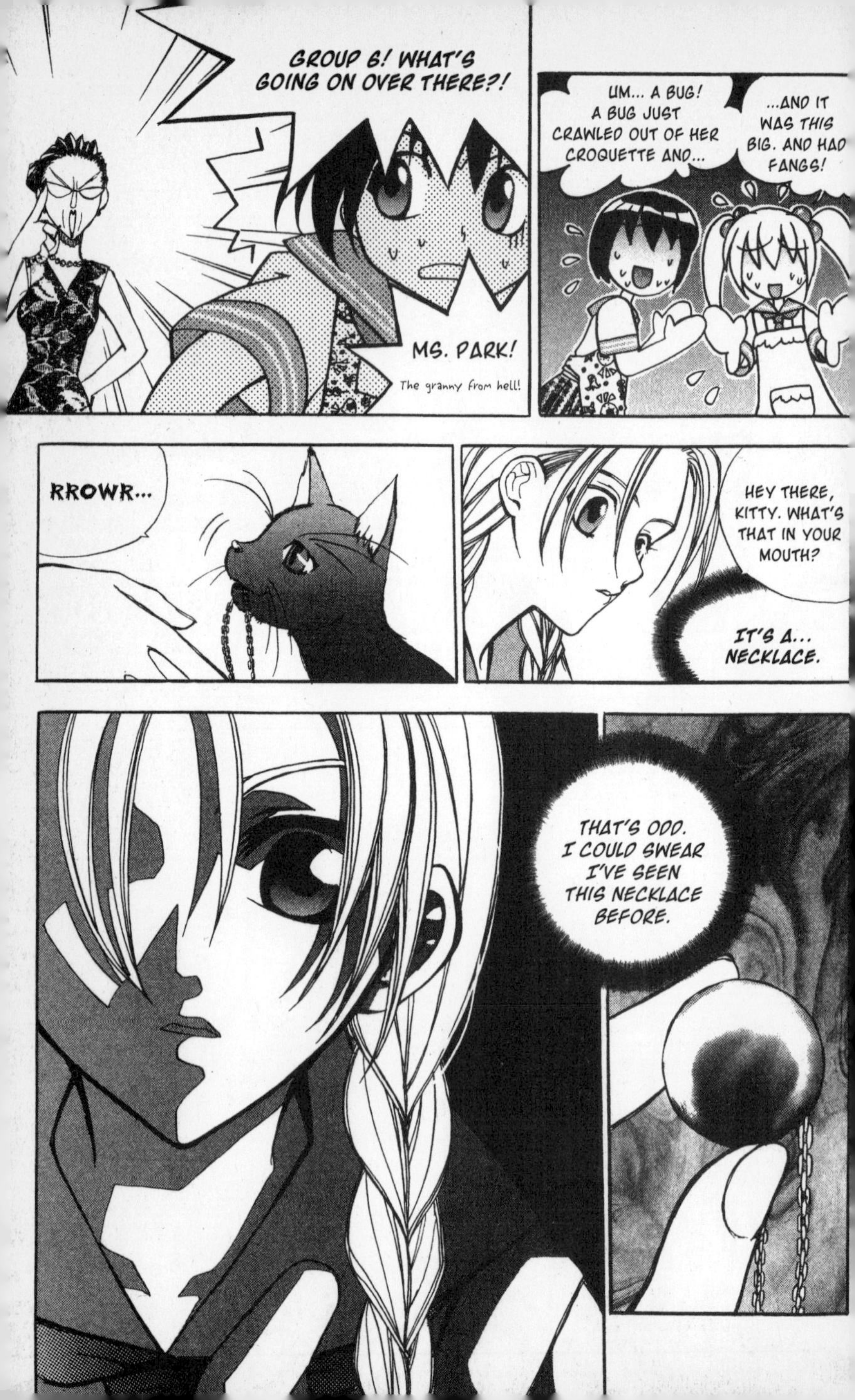
GROUP 6! WHAT'S GOING ON OVER THERE?!
MS. PARK!
The granny from hell!
UM... A BUG! A BUG JUST CRAWLED OUT OF HER CROQUETTE AND...
...AND IT WAS THIS BIG. AND HAD FANGS!
RROWR...
HEY THERE, KITTY. WHAT'S THAT IN YOUR MOUTH?
IT'S A... NECKLACE.
THAT'S ODD. I COULD SWEAR I'VE SEEN THIS NECKLACE BEFORE.

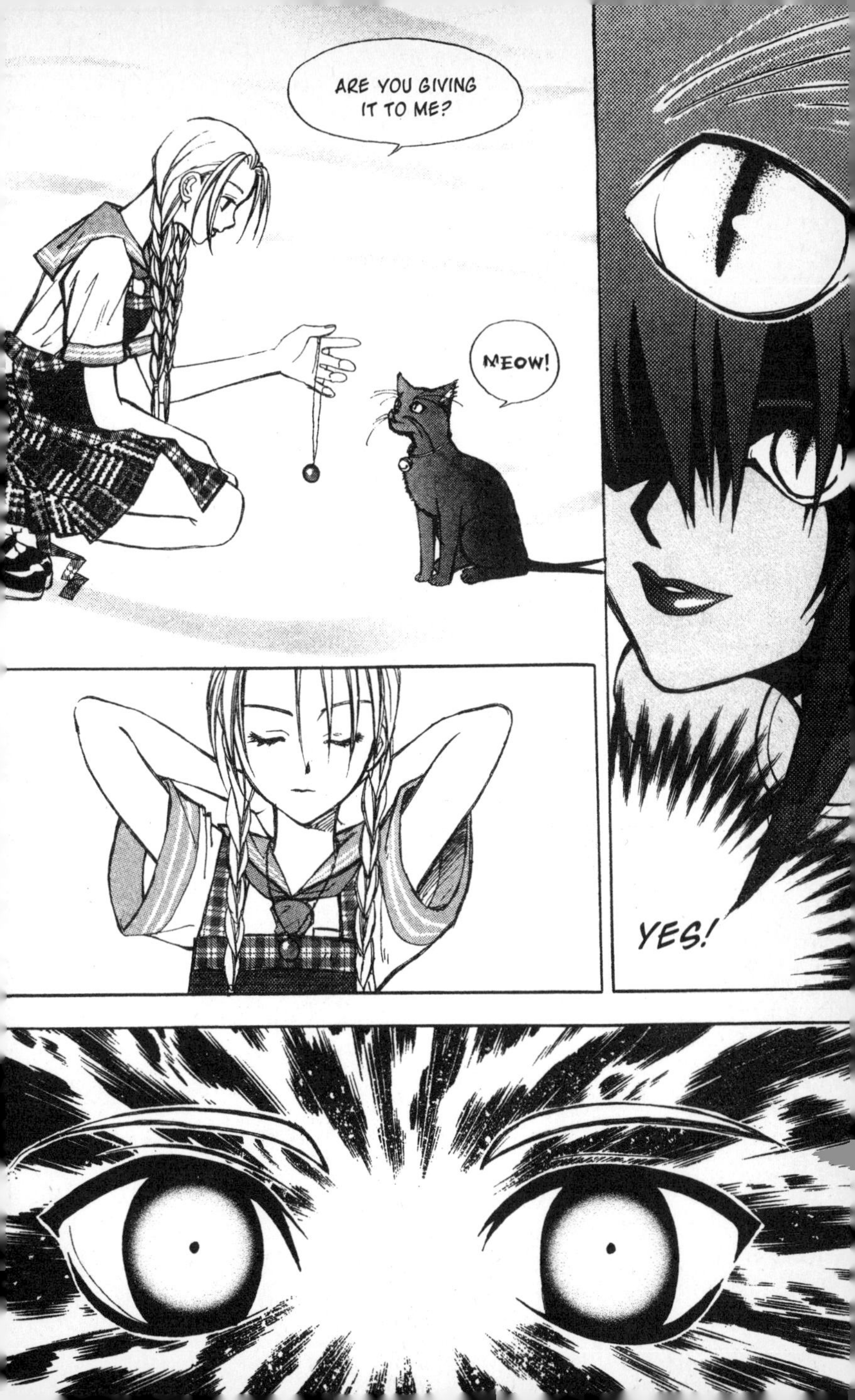
ARE YOU GIVING IT TO ME?
MEOW!
YES!

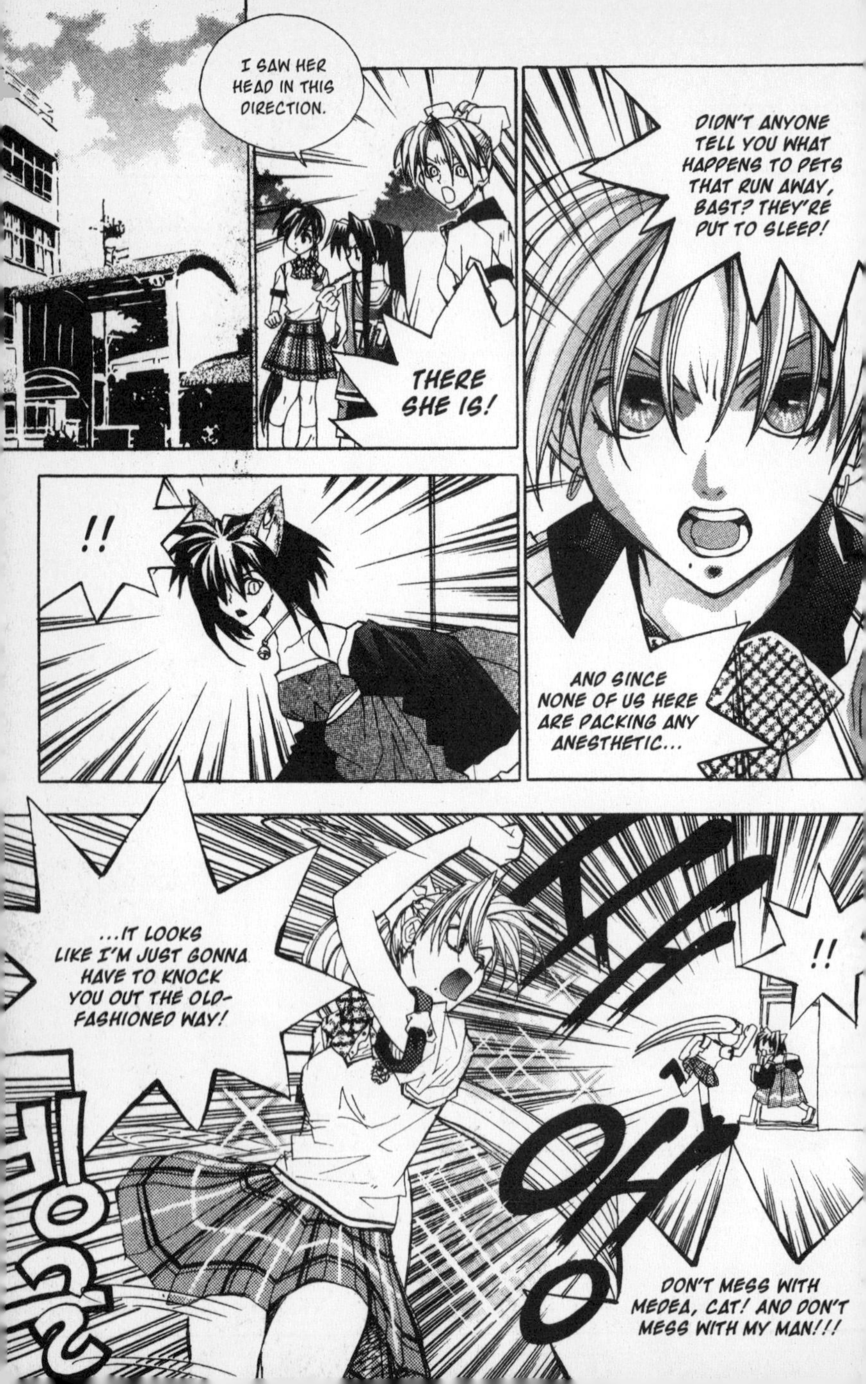
I SAW HER HEAD IN THIS DIRECTION.
THERE SHE IS!
!!
DIDN'T ANYONE TELL YOU WHAT HAPPENS TO PETS THAT RUN AWAY, BAST? THEY'RE PUT TO SLEEP!
AND SINCE NONE OF US HERE ARE PACKING ANY ANESTHETIC...
...IT LOOKS LIKE I'M JUST GONNA HAVE TO KNOCK YOU OUT THE OLD-FASHIONED WAY!
!!
DON'T MESS WITH MEDEA, CAT! AND DON'T MESS WITH MY MAN!!!

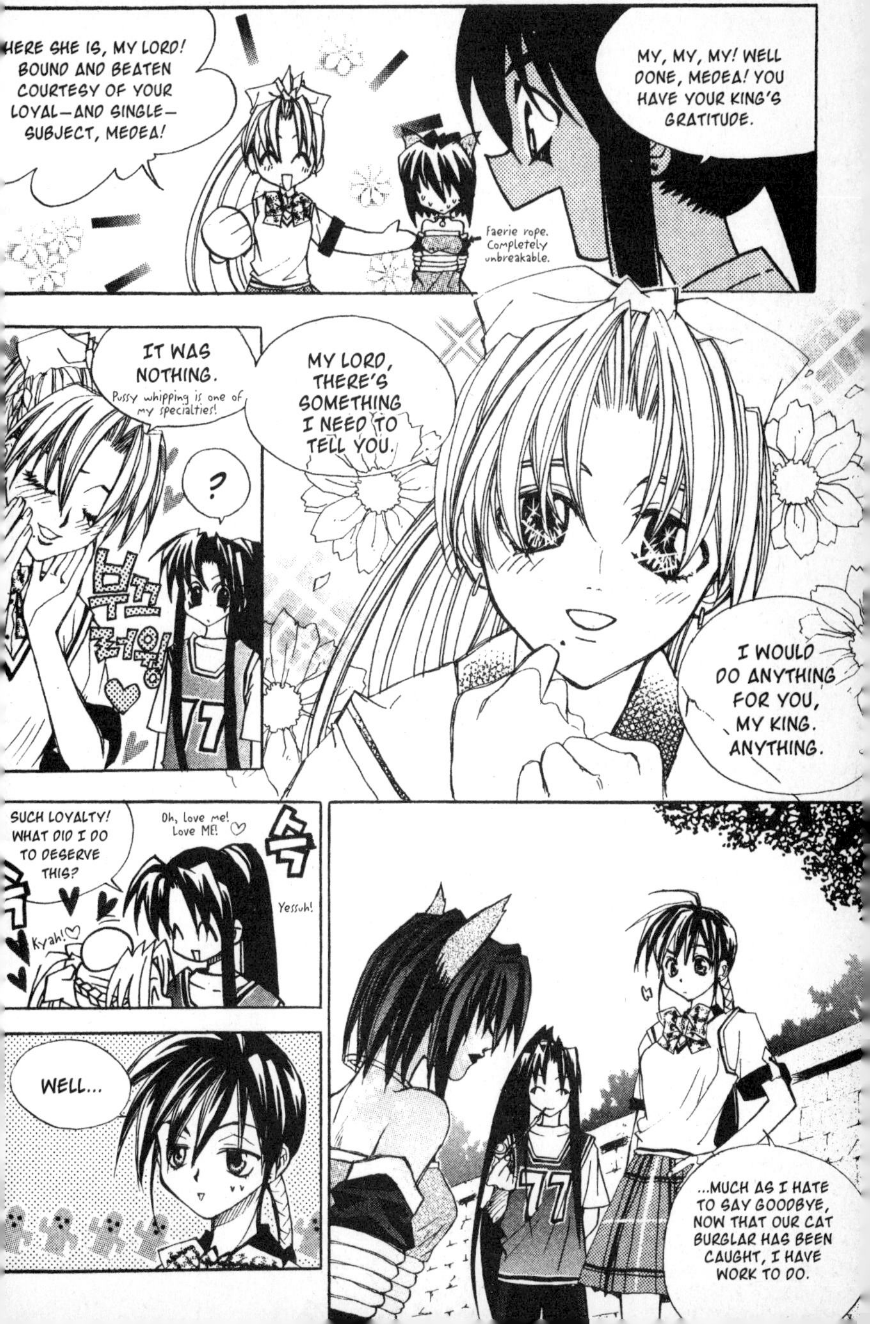
HERE SHE IS, MY LORD! BOUND AND BEATEN COURTESY OF YOUR LOYAL—AND SINGLE—SUBJECT, MEDEA!
Faerie rope. Completely unbreakable.
MY, MY, MY! WELL DONE, MEDEA! YOU HAVE YOUR KING'S GRATITUDE.
IT WAS NOTHING.
Pussy whipping is one of my specialties!
?
MY LORD, THERE'S SOMETHING I NEED TO TELL YOU.
I WOULD DO ANYTHING FOR YOU, MY KING. ANYTHING.
SUCH LOYALTY! WHAT DID I DO TO DESERVE THIS?
Oh, love me! Love ME!
Kyah!
Yessuh!
WELL...
...MUCH AS I HATE TO SAY GOODBYE, NOW THAT OUR CAT BURGLAR HAS BEEN CAUGHT, I HAVE WORK TO DO.

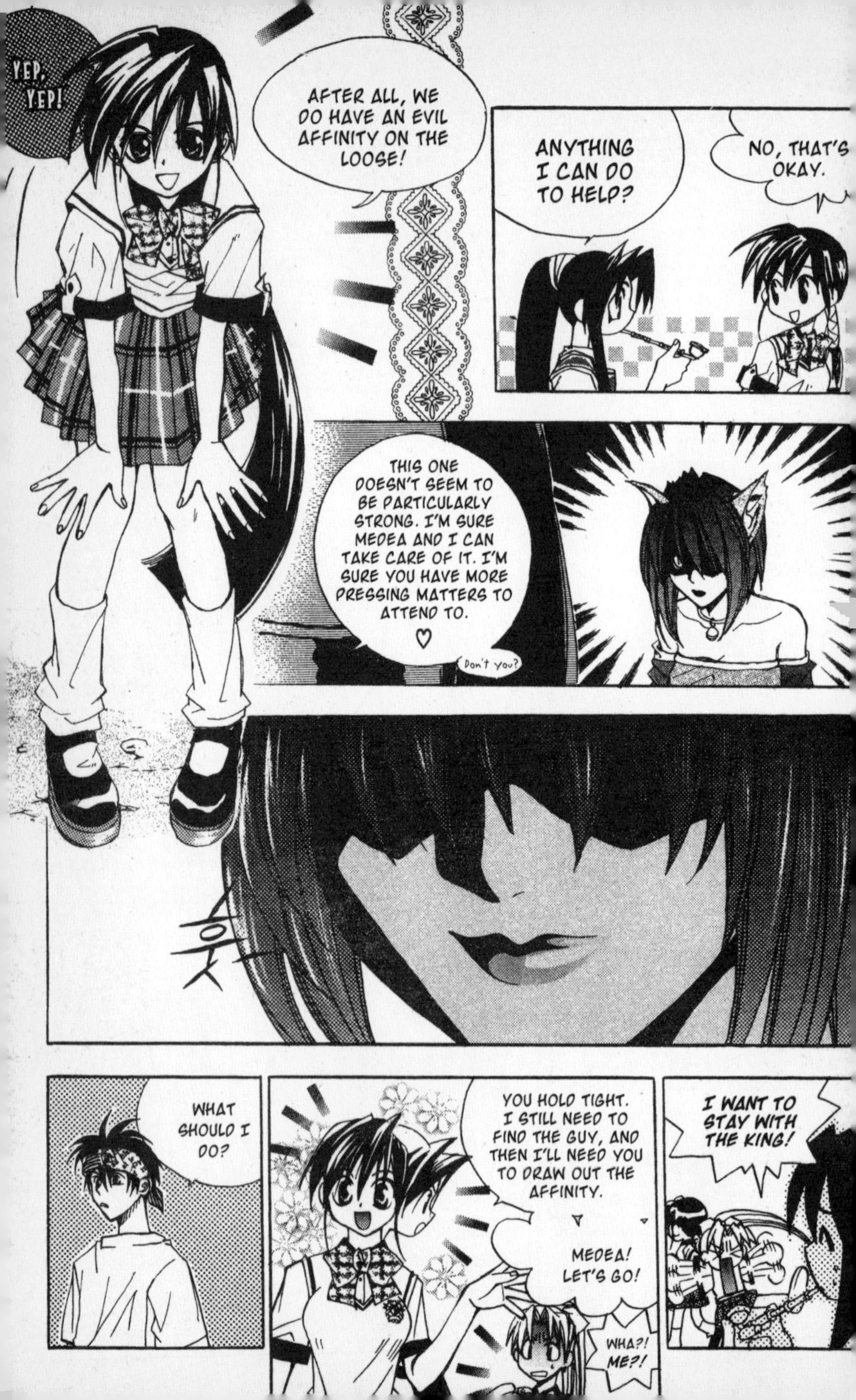
YEP, YEP!
AFTER ALL, WE DO HAVE AN EVIL AFFINITY ON THE LOOSE!
ANYTHING I CAN DO TO HELP?
NO, THAT'S OKAY.
THIS ONE DOESN'T SEEM TO BE PARTICULARLY STRONG. I'M SURE MEDEA AND I CAN TAKE CARE OF IT. I'M SURE YOU HAVE MORE PRESSING MATTERS TO ATTEND TO. ♡
Don't you?
WHAT SHOULD I DO?
YOU HOLD TIGHT. I STILL NEED TO FIND THE GUY, AND THEN I'LL NEED YOU TO DRAW OUT THE AFFINITY.
MEDEA! LET'S GO!
WHA?! ME?!
I WANT TO STAY WITH THE KING!

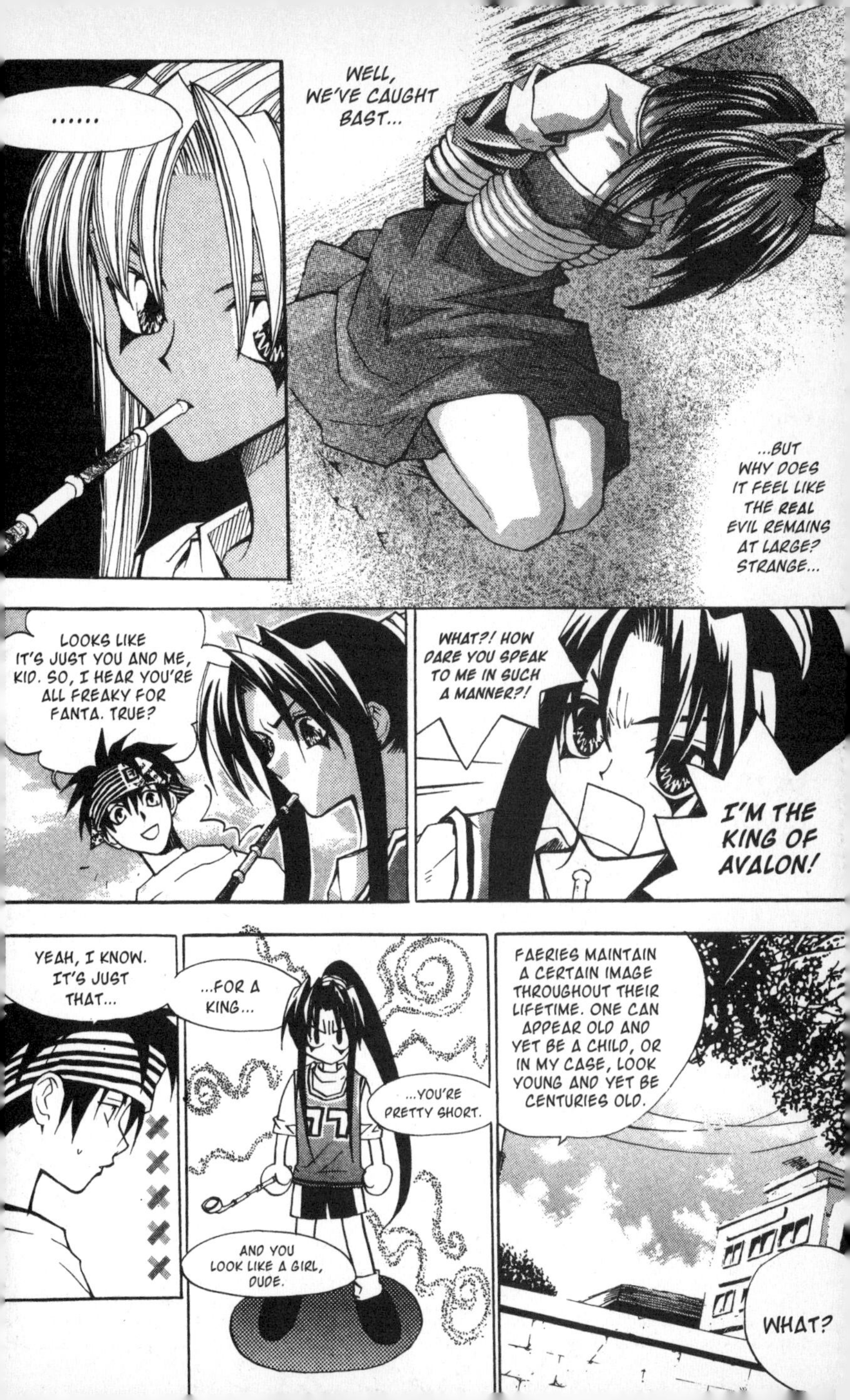
......
WELL, WE'VE CAUGHT BAST...
...BUT WHY DOES IT FEEL LIKE THE REAL EVIL REMAINS AT LARGE? STRANGE...
LOOKS LIKE IT'S JUST YOU AND ME, KID. SO, I HEAR YOU'RE ALL FREAKY FOR FANTA. TRUE?
WHAT?! HOW DARE YOU SPEAK TO ME IN SUCH A MANNER?!
I'M THE KING OF AVALON!
YEAH, I KNOW. IT'S JUST THAT...
...FOR A KING...
...YOU'RE PRETTY SHORT.
AND YOU LOOK LIKE A GIRL, DUDE.
FAERIES MAINTAIN A CERTAIN IMAGE THROUGHOUT THEIR LIFETIME. ONE CAN APPEAR OLD AND YET BE A CHILD, OR IN MY CASE, LOOK YOUNG AND YET BE CENTURIES OLD.
WHAT?

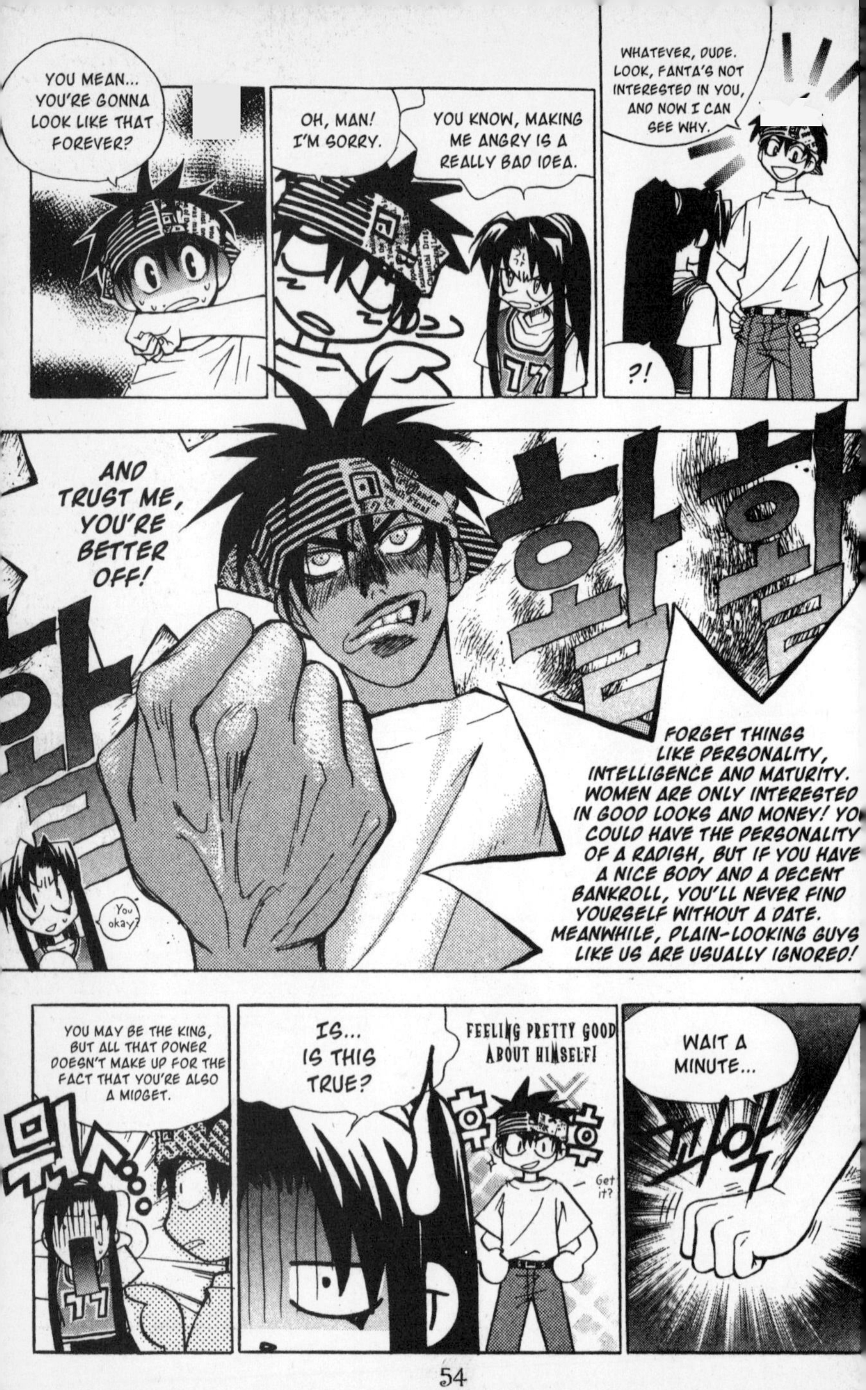
YOU MEAN... YOU'RE GONNA LOOK LIKE THAT FOREVER?
OH, MAN! I'M SORRY.
YOU KNOW, MAKING ME ANGRY IS A REALLY BAD IDEA.
WHATEVER, DUDE. LOOK, FANTA'S NOT INTERESTED IN YOU, AND NOW I CAN SEE WHY.
?!
AND TRUST ME, YOU'RE BETTER OFF!
You okay?
FORGET THINGS LIKE PERSONALITY, INTELLIGENCE AND MATURITY. WOMEN ARE ONLY INTERESTED IN GOOD LOOKS AND MONEY! YOU COULD HAVE THE PERSONALITY OF A RADISH, BUT IF YOU HAVE A NICE BODY AND A DECENT BANKROLL, YOU'LL NEVER FIND YOURSELF WITHOUT A DATE. MEANWHILE, PLAIN-LOOKING GUYS LIKE US ARE USUALLY IGNORED!
YOU MAY BE THE KING, BUT ALL THAT POWER DOESN'T MAKE UP FOR THE FACT THAT YOU'RE ALSO A MIDGET.
IS... IS THIS TRUE?
FEELING PRETTY GOOD ABOUT HIMSELF!
Get it?
WAIT A MINUTE...

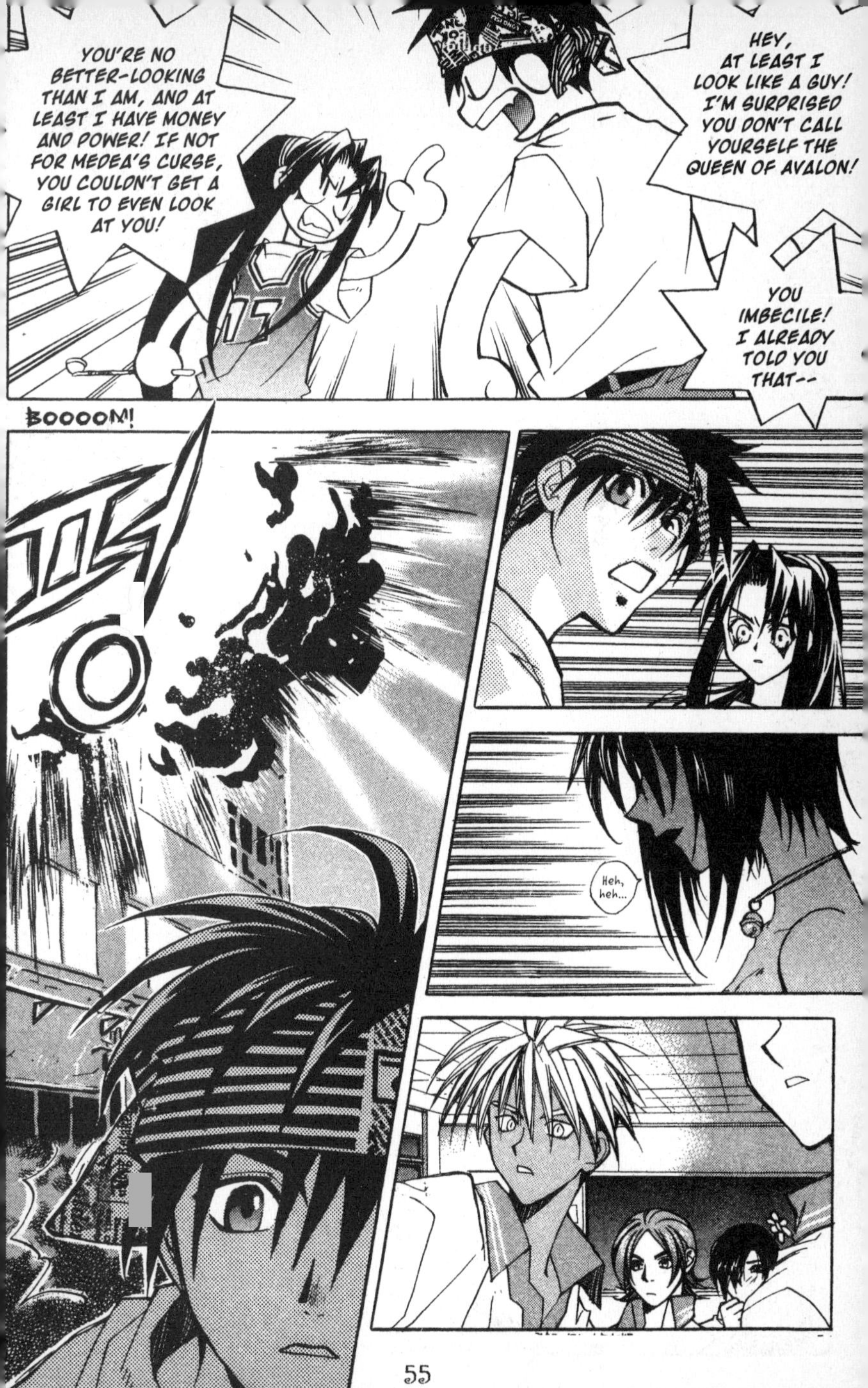
YOU'RE NO BETTER-LOOKING THAN I AM, AND AT LEAST I HAVE MONEY AND POWER! IF NOT FOR MEDEA'S CURSE, YOU COULDN'T GET A GIRL TO EVEN LOOK AT YOU!
HEY, AT LEAST I LOOK LIKE A GUY! I'M SURPRISED YOU DON'T CALL YOURSELF THE QUEEN OF AVALON!
YOU IMBECILE! I ALREADY TOLD YOU THAT--
BOOOOM!
Heh, heh...

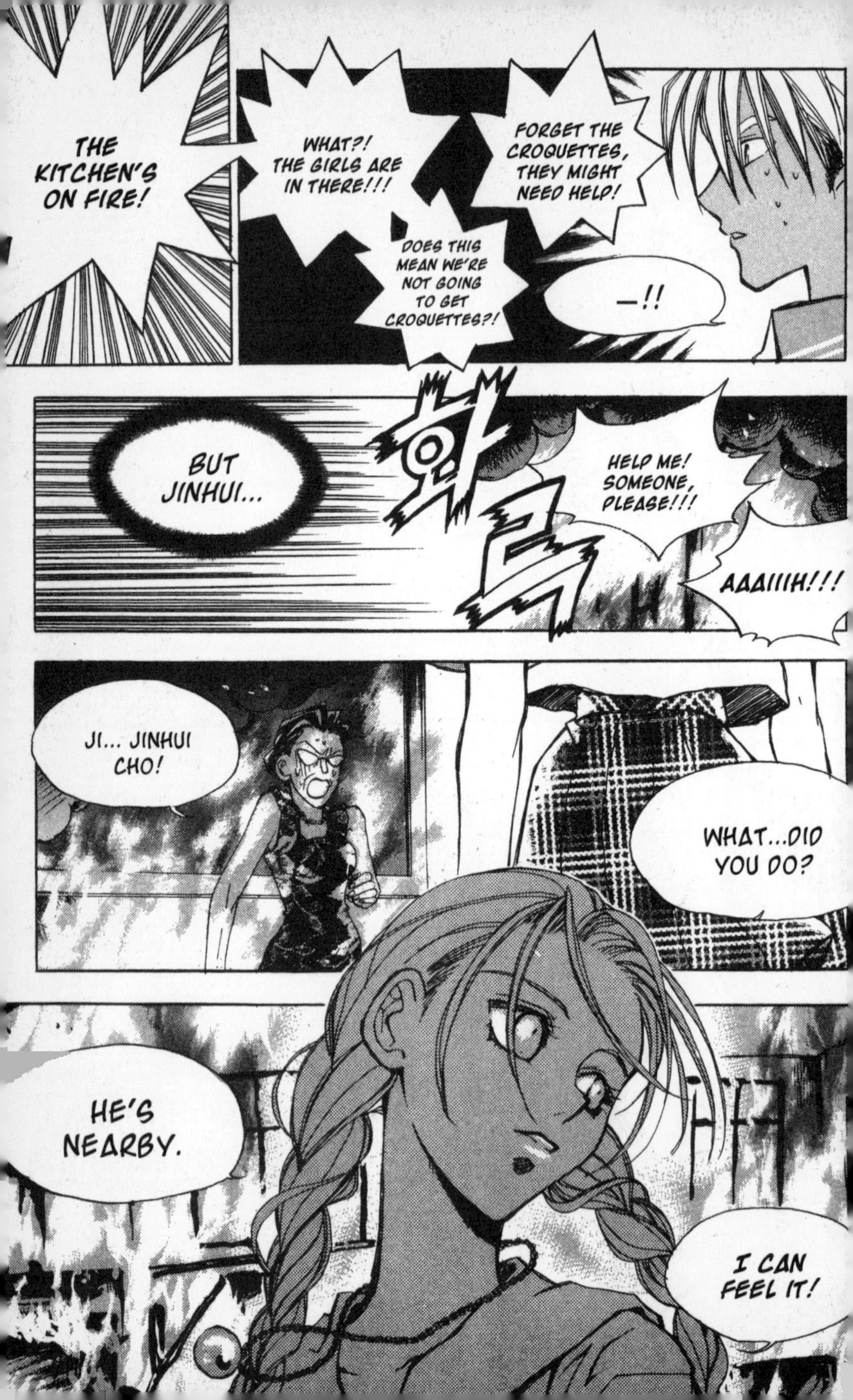
THE KITCHEN'S ON FIRE!
WHAT?! THE GIRLS ARE IN THERE!!!
DOES THIS MEAN WE'RE NOT GOING TO GET CROQUETTES?!
FORGET THE CROQUETTES, THEY MIGHT NEED HELP!
—!!
BUT JINHUI...
HELP ME! SOMEONE, PLEASE!!!
AAAIIIH!!!
JI... JINHUI CHO!
WHAT...DID YOU DO?
HE'S NEARBY.
I CAN FEEL IT!

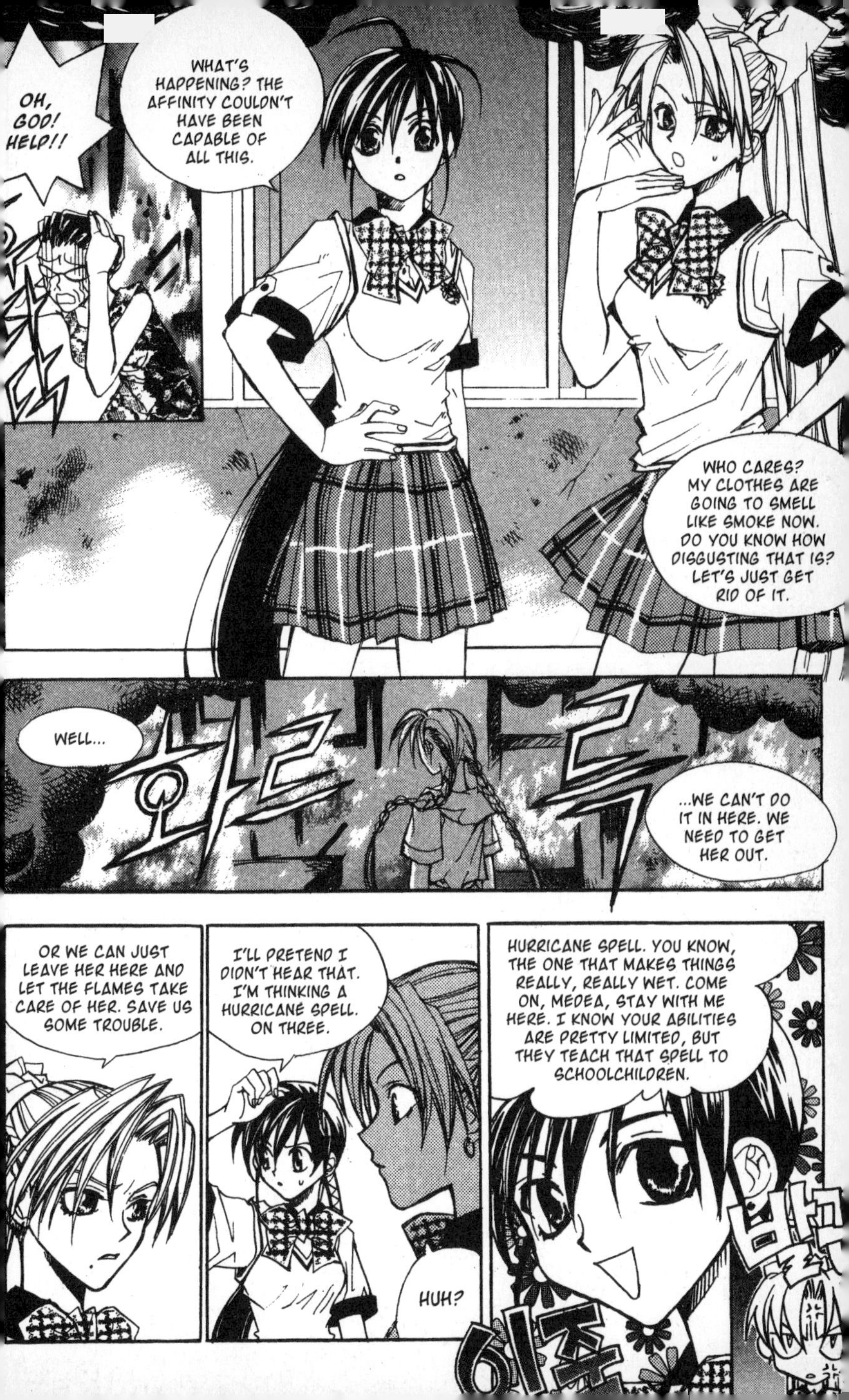
OH, GOD! HELP!!
WHAT'S HAPPENING? THE AFFINITY COULDN'T HAVE BEEN CAPABLE OF ALL THIS.
WHO CARES? MY CLOTHES ARE GOING TO SMELL LIKE SMOKE NOW. DO YOU KNOW HOW DISGUSTING THAT IS? LET'S JUST GET RID OF IT.
WELL...
...WE CAN'T DO IT IN HERE. WE NEED TO GET HER OUT.
OR WE CAN JUST LEAVE HER HERE AND LET THE FLAMES TAKE CARE OF HER. SAVE US SOME TROUBLE.
I'LL PRETEND I DIDN'T HEAR THAT. I'M THINKING A HURRICANE SPELL. ON THREE.
HUH?
HURRICANE SPELL. YOU KNOW, THE ONE THAT MAKES THINGS REALLY, REALLY WET. COME ON, MEDEA, STAY WITH ME HERE. I KNOW YOUR ABILITIES ARE PRETTY LIMITED, BUT THEY TEACH THAT SPELL TO SCHOOLCHILDREN.

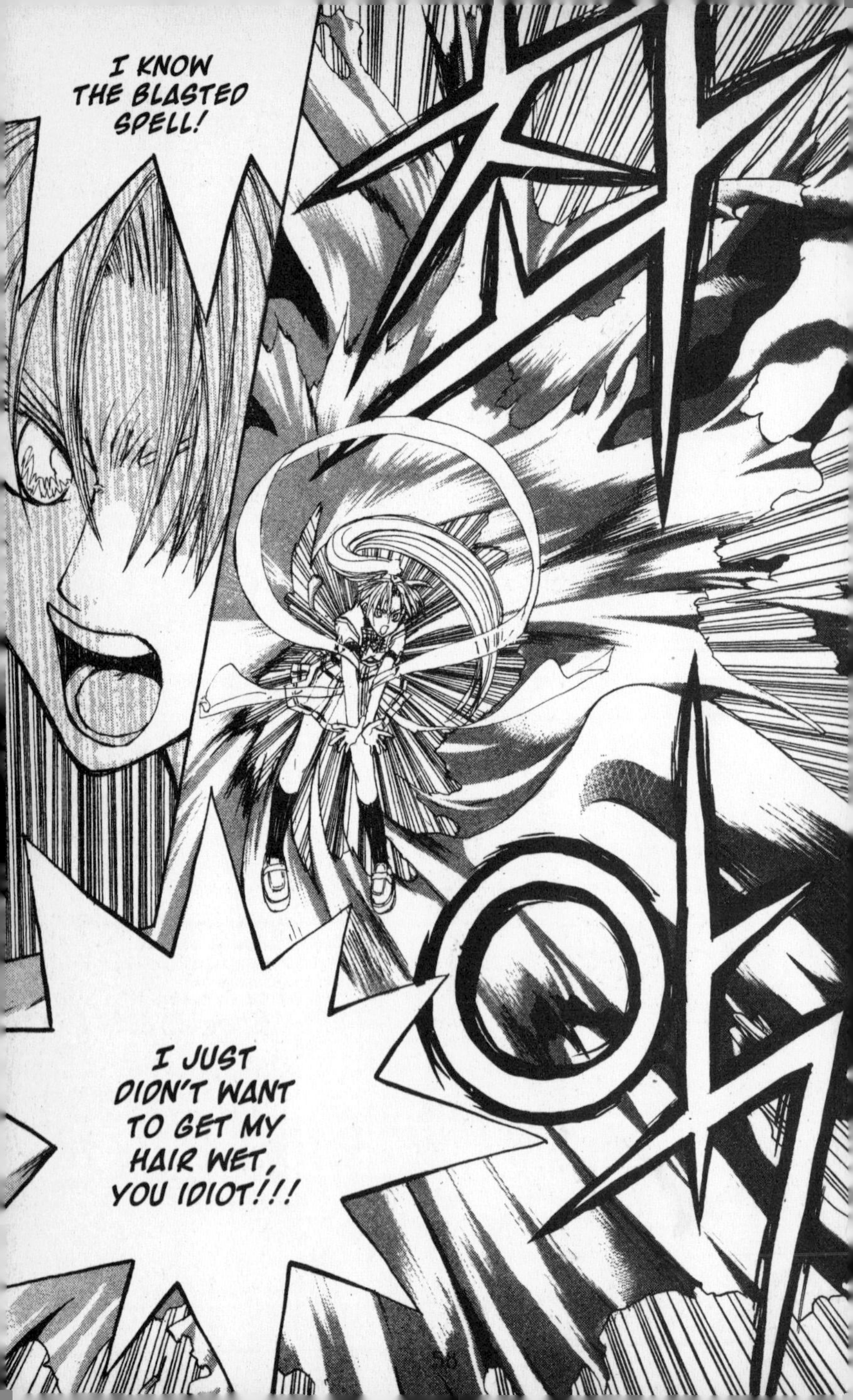
I KNOW THE BLASTED SPELL!
I JUST DIDN'T WANT TO GET MY HAIR WET, YOU IDIOT!!!

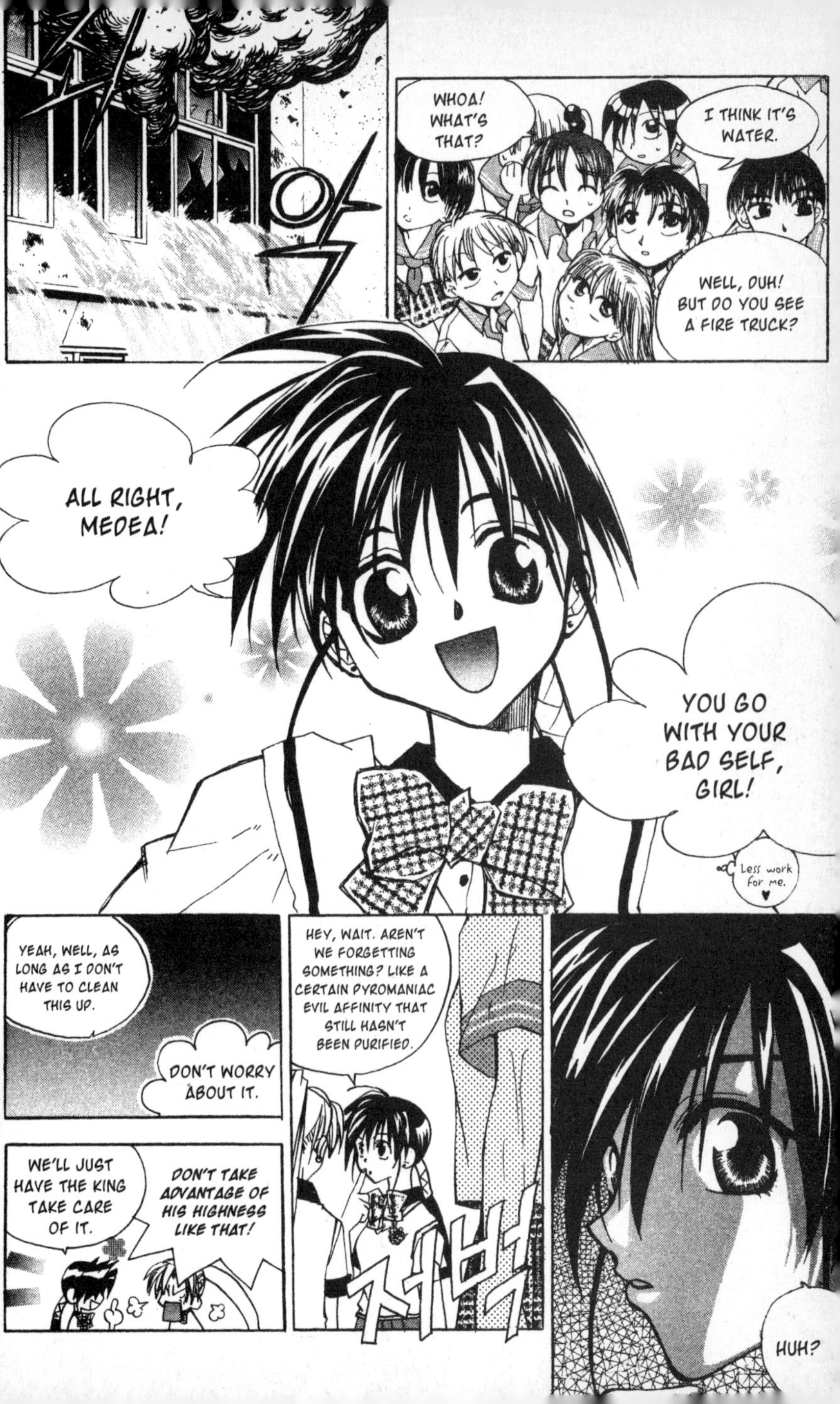
WHOA! WHAT'S THAT?
I THINK IT'S WATER.
WELL, DUH! BUT DO YOU SEE A FIRE TRUCK?
ALL RIGHT, MEDEA!
YOU GO WITH YOUR BAD SELF, GIRL!
Less work for me. ♥
YEAH, WELL, AS LONG AS I DON'T HAVE TO CLEAN THIS UP.
DON'T WORRY ABOUT IT.
WE'LL JUST HAVE THE KING TAKE CARE OF IT.
DON'T TAKE ADVANTAGE OF HIS HIGHNESS LIKE THAT!
HEY, WAIT. AREN'T WE FORGETTING SOMETHING? LIKE A CERTAIN PYROMANIAC EVIL AFFINITY THAT STILL HASN'T BEEN PURIFIED.
HUH?

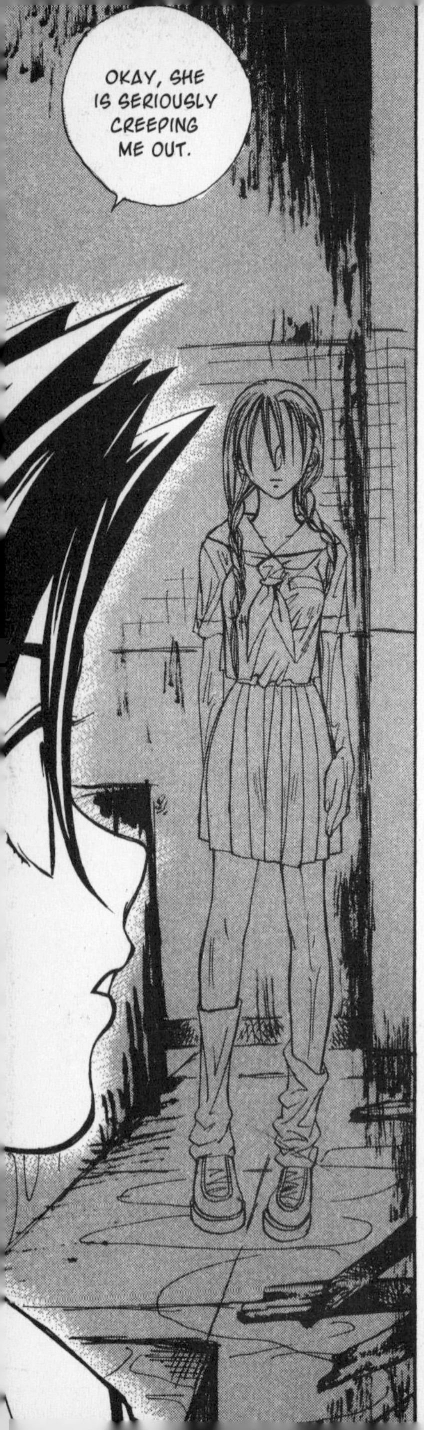
OKAY, SHE IS SERIOUSLY CREEPING ME OUT.

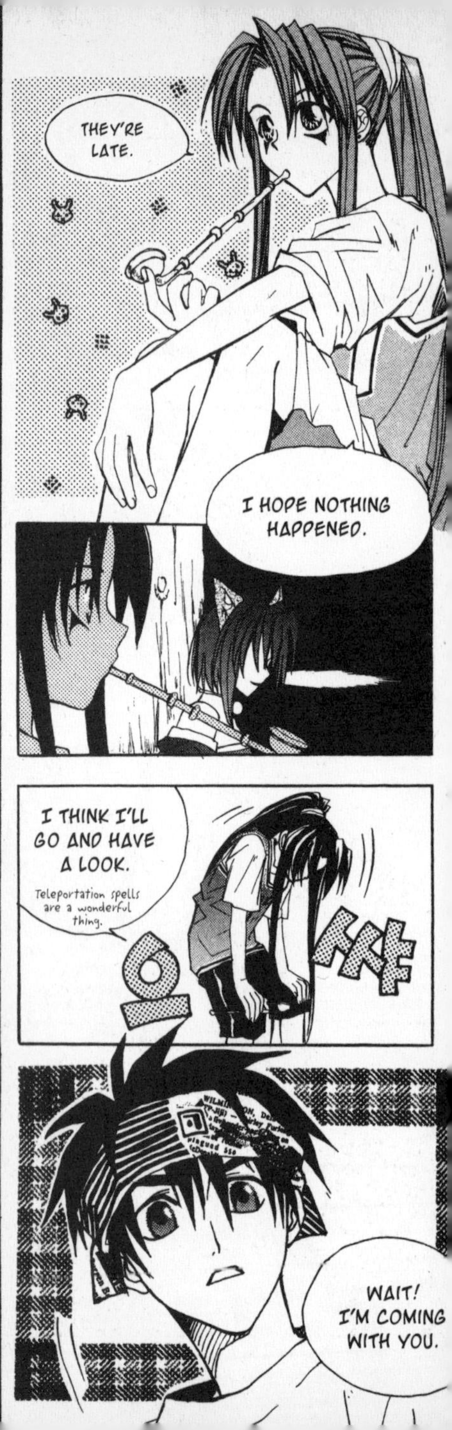
THEY'RE LATE.
I HOPE NOTHING HAPPENED.
I THINK I'LL GO AND HAVE A LOOK.
Teleportation spells are a wonderful thing.
WAIT! I'M COMING WITH YOU.

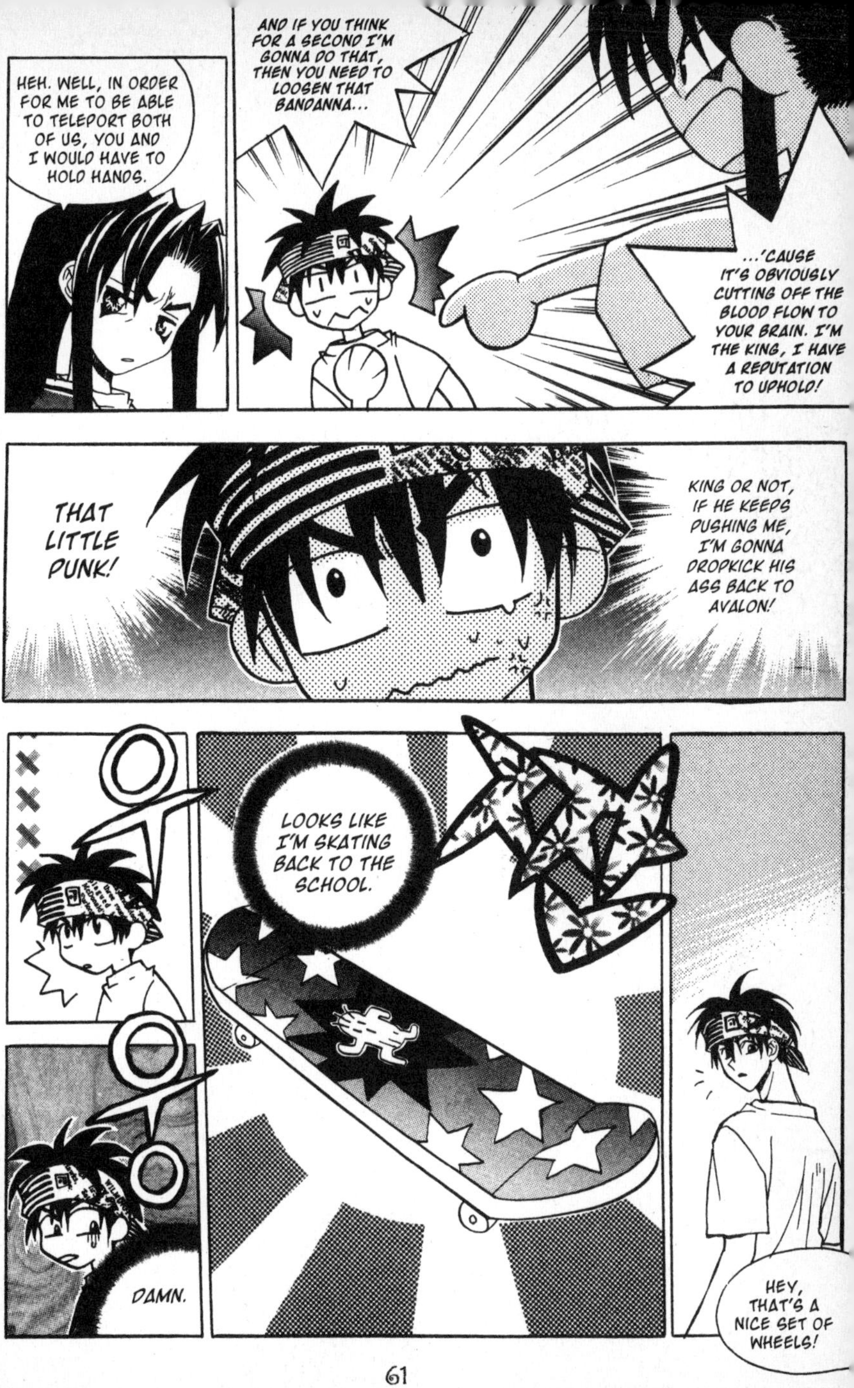
HEH. WELL, IN ORDER FOR ME TO BE ABLE TO TELEPORT BOTH OF US, YOU AND I WOULD HAVE TO HOLD HANDS.
AND IF YOU THINK FOR A SECOND I'M GONNA DO THAT, THEN YOU NEED TO LOOSEN THAT BANDANNA...
...'CAUSE IT'S OBVIOUSLY CUTTING OFF THE BLOOD FLOW TO YOUR BRAIN. I'M THE KING, I HAVE A REPUTATION TO UPHOLD!
THAT LITTLE PUNK!
KING OR NOT, IF HE KEEPS PUSHING ME, I'M GONNA DROPKICK HIS ASS BACK TO AVALON!
DAMN.
LOOKS LIKE I'M SKATING BACK TO THE SCHOOL.
HEY, THAT'S A NICE SET OF WHEELS!

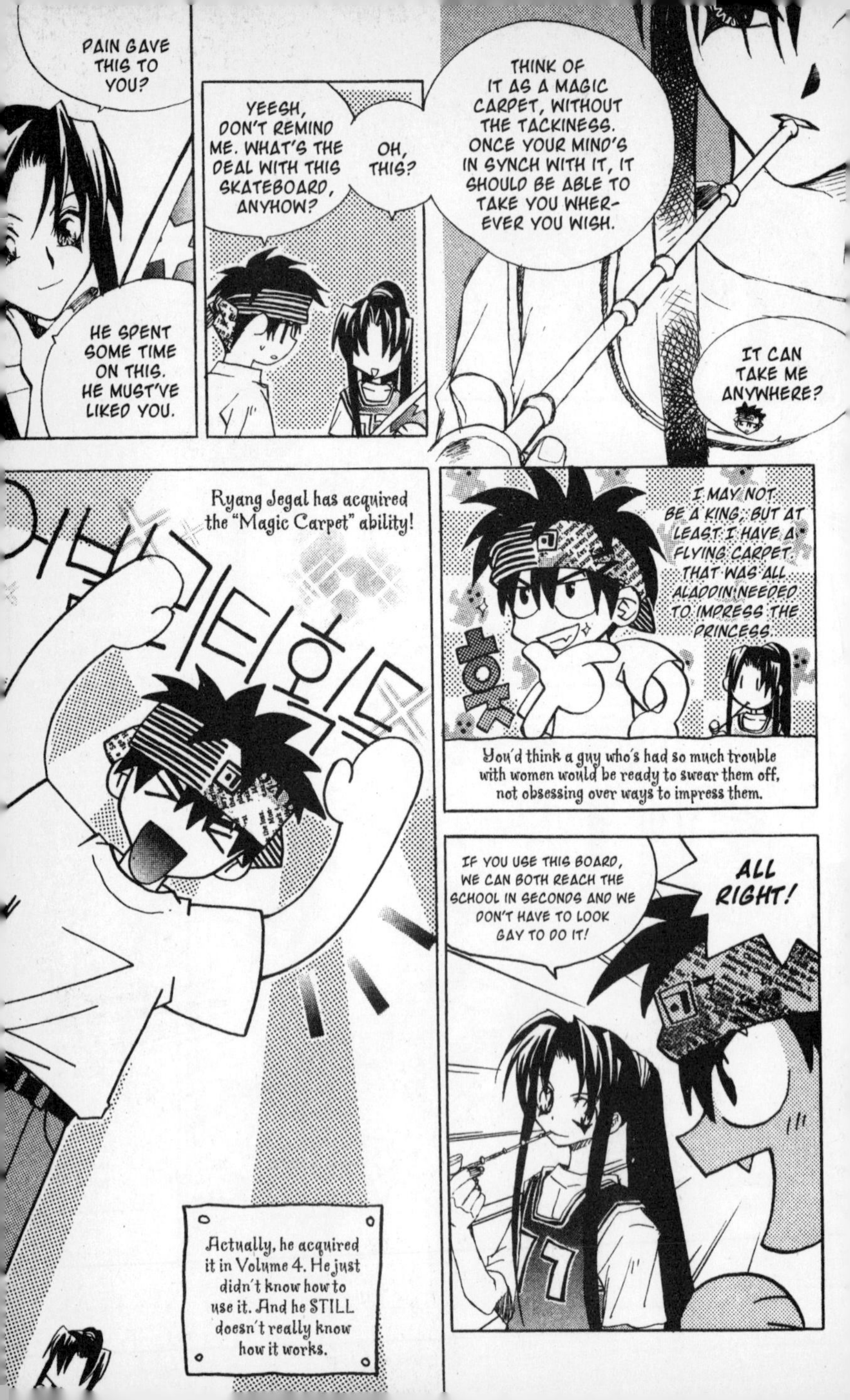
PAIN GAVE THIS TO YOU?
HE SPENT SOME TIME ON THIS. HE MUST'VE LIKED YOU.
YEESH, DON'T REMIND ME. WHAT'S THE DEAL WITH THIS SKATEBOARD, ANYHOW?
OH, THIS?
THINK OF IT AS A MAGIC CARPET, WITHOUT THE TACKINESS. ONCE YOUR MIND'S IN SYNCH WITH IT, IT SHOULD BE ABLE TO TAKE YOU WHEREVER YOU WISH.
IT CAN TAKE ME ANYWHERE?
Ryang Jegal has acquired the "Magic Carpet" ability!
Actually, he acquired it in Volume 4. He just didn't know how to use it. And he STILL doesn't really know how it works.
I MAY NOT BE A KING, BUT AT LEAST I HAVE A FLYING CARPET. THAT WAS ALL ALADDIN NEEDED TO IMPRESS THE PRINCESS.
You'd think a guy who's had so much trouble with women would be ready to swear them off, not obsessing over ways to impress them.
IF YOU USE THIS BOARD, WE CAN BOTH REACH THE SCHOOL IN SECONDS AND WE DON'T HAVE TO LOOK GAY TO DO IT!
ALL RIGHT!

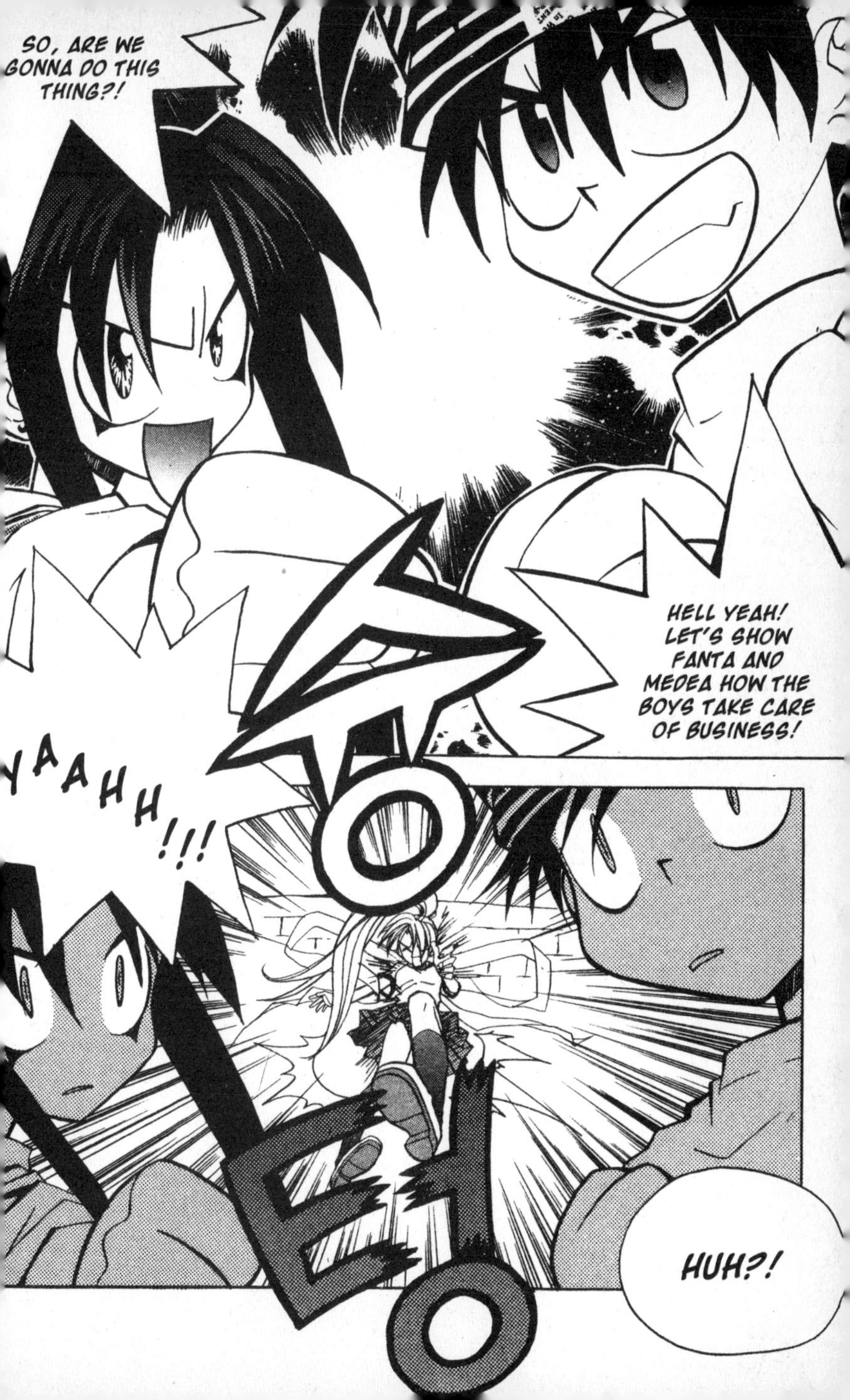
SO, ARE WE GONNA DO THIS THING?!
HELL YEAH! LET'S SHOW FANTA AND MEDEA HOW THE BOYS TAKE CARE OF BUSINESS!
YAAHH!!!
HUH?!

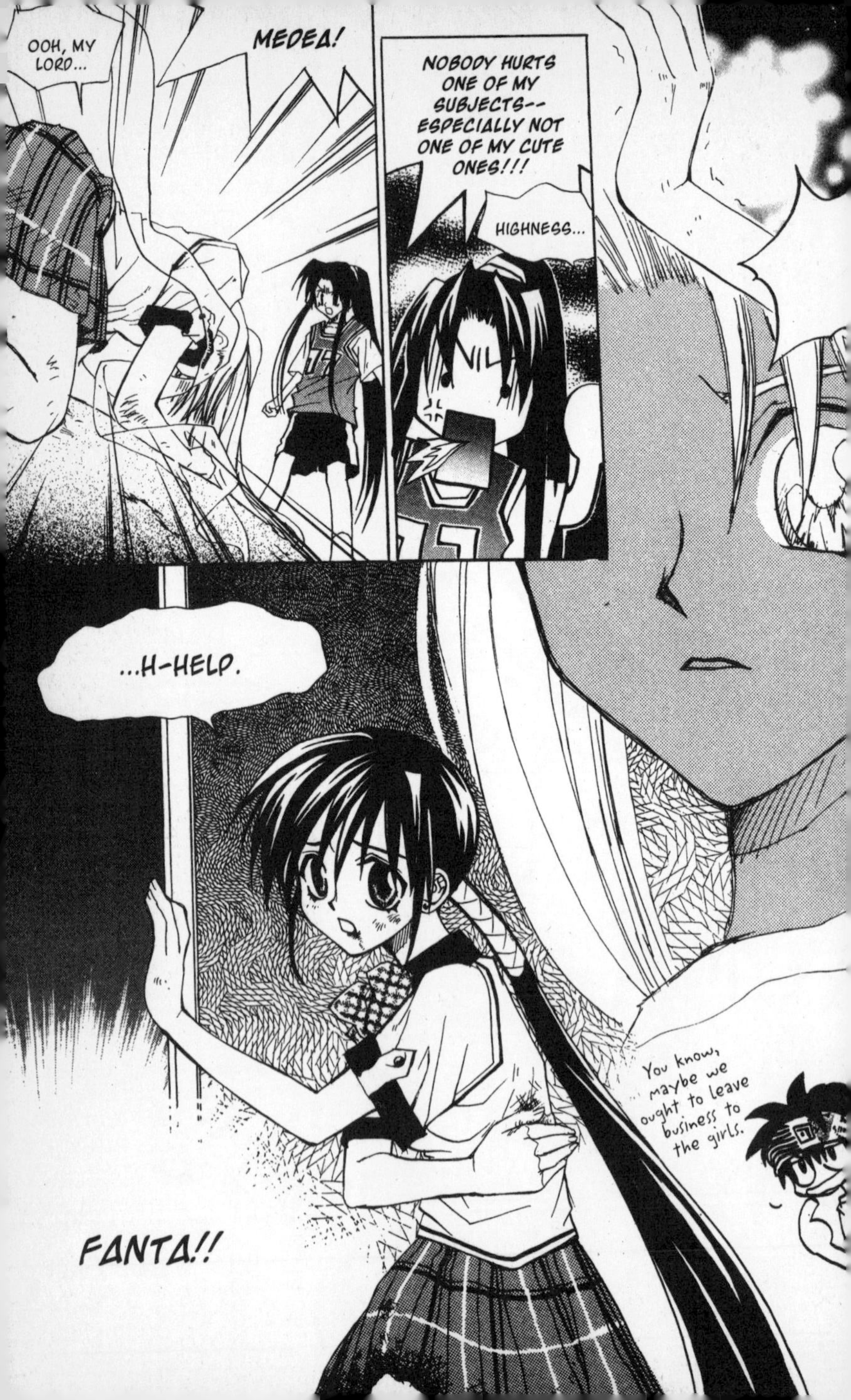
NOBODY HURTS ONE OF MY SUBJECTS-- ESPECIALLY NOT ONE OF MY CUTE ONES!!!
HIGHNESS...
MEDEA!
OOH, MY LORD...
...H-HELP.
You know, maybe we ought to leave business to the girls.
FANTA!!

Episode 25 Fanta's Scheme

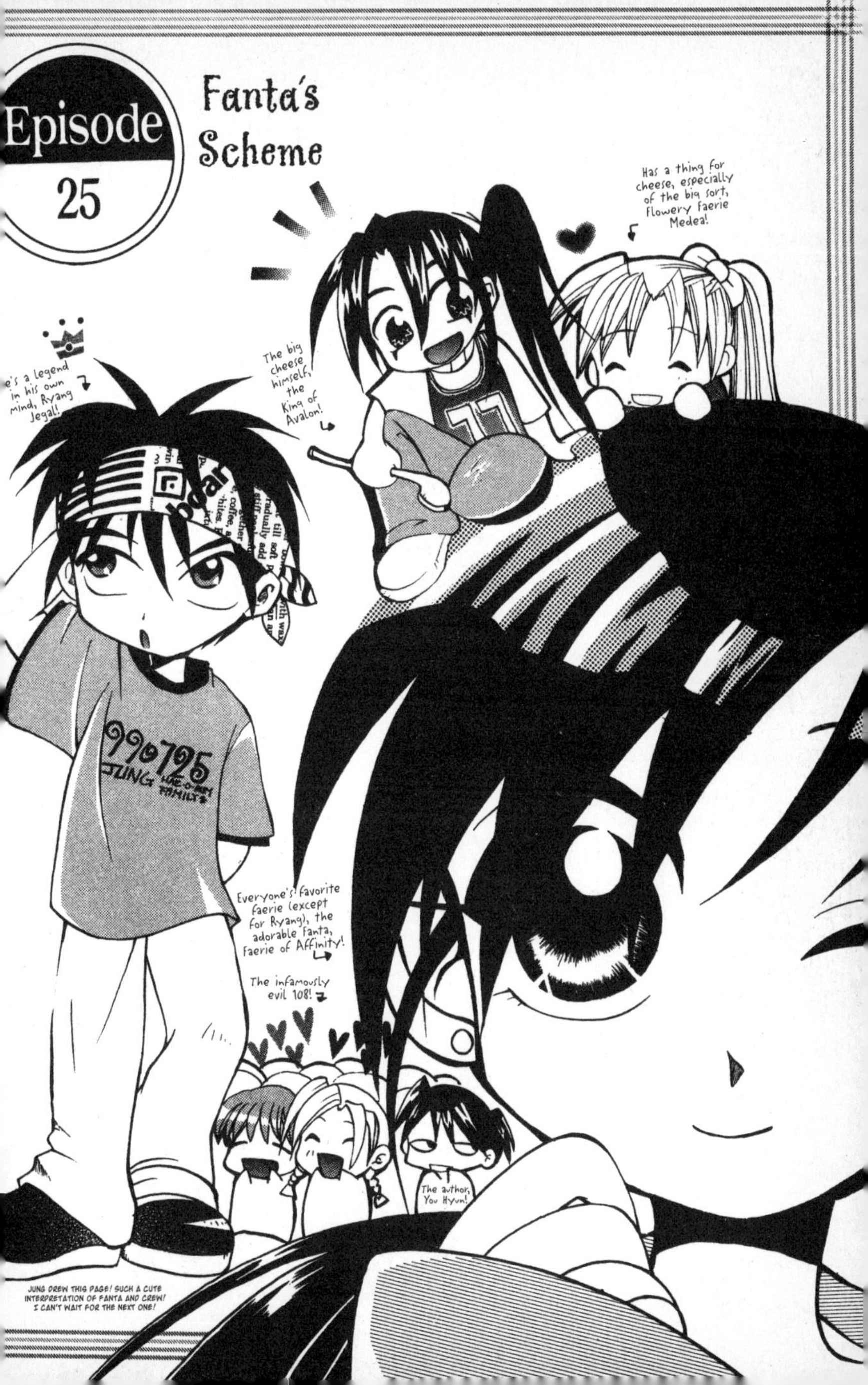
e's a legend in his own mind, Ryang Jegal!
The big cheese himself, the King of Avalon!
Has a thing for cheese, especially of the big sort, Flowery Faerie Medea!
Everyone's favorite faerie (except for Ryang), the adorable Fanta, Faerie of Affinity!
The infamously evil 108!
The author, You Hyun!
JUNG DREW THIS PAGE! SUCH A CUTE INTERPRETATION OF FANTA AND CREW! I CAN'T WAIT FOR THE NEXT ONE!

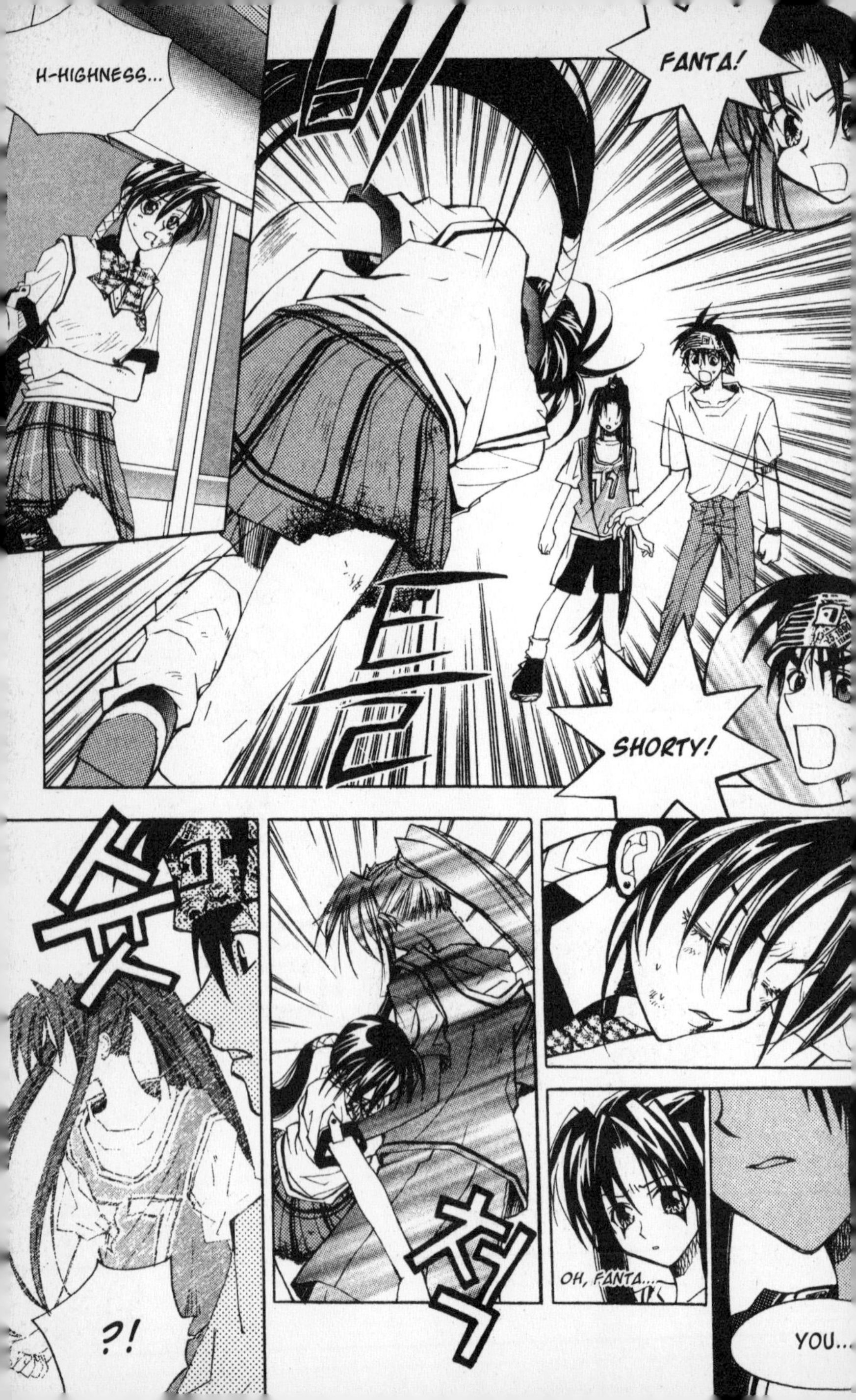
H-HIGHNESS...
FANTA!
SHORTY!
?!
OH, FANTA...
YOU...

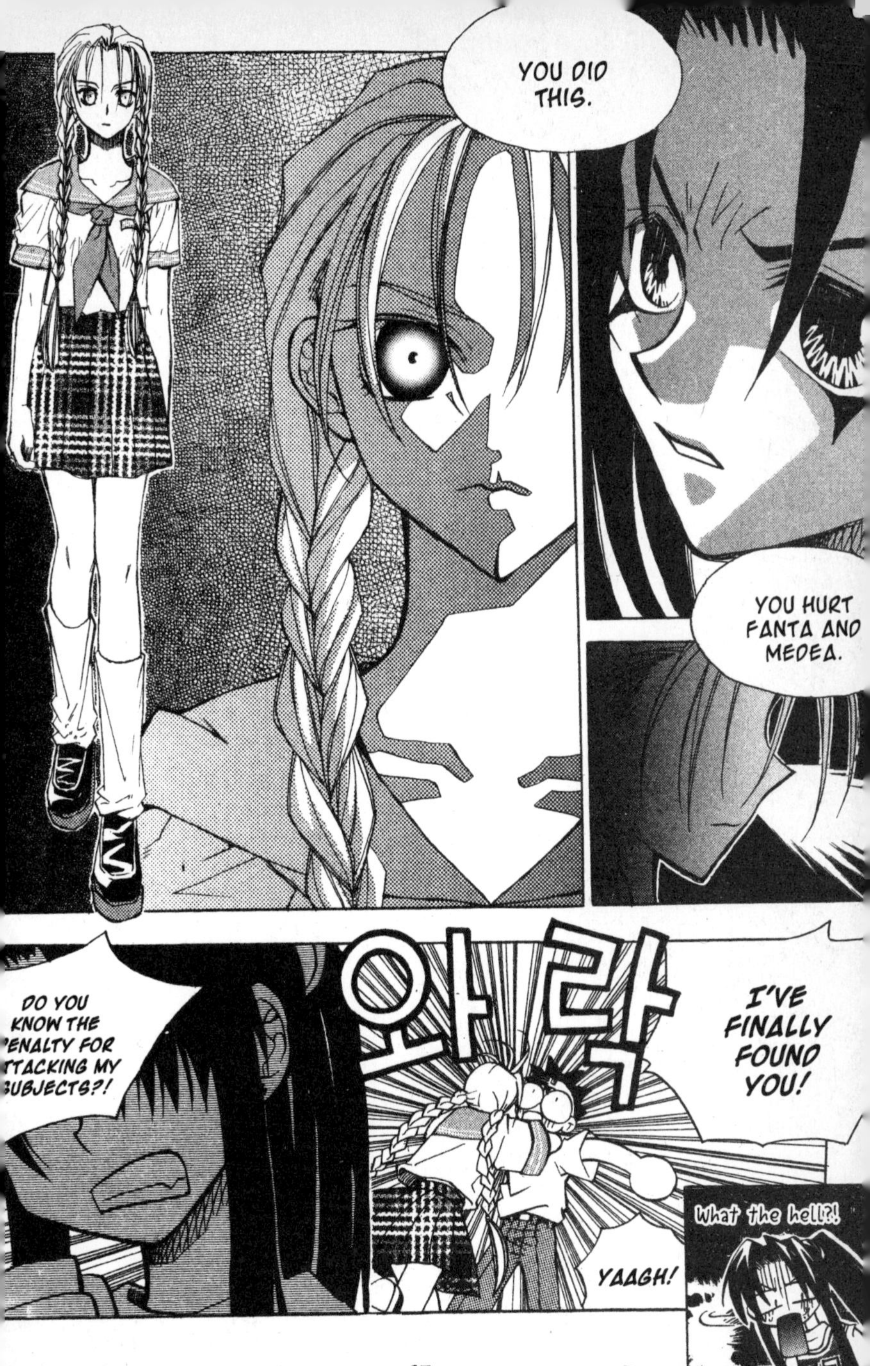
YOU DID THIS.
YOU HURT FANTA AND MEDEA.
DO YOU KNOW THE ENALTY FOR TTACKING MY UBJECTS?!
와락
I'VE FINALLY FOUND YOU!
YAAGH!
What the hell?!

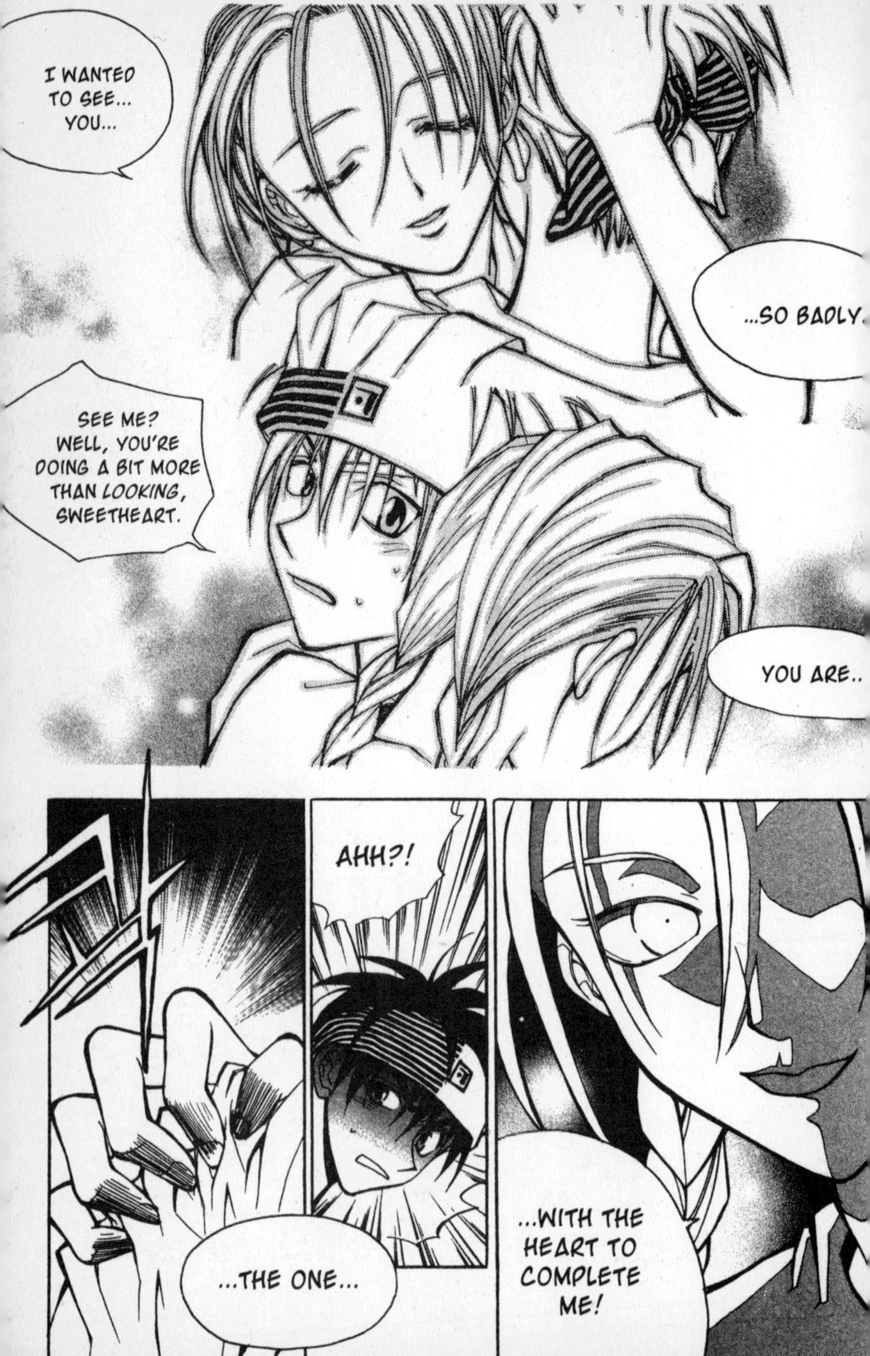
I WANTED TO SEE... YOU...
...SO BADLY.
SEE ME? WELL, YOU'RE DOING A BIT MORE THAN *LOOKING*, SWEETHEART.
YOU ARE..
...THE ONE...
AHH?!
...WITH THE HEART TO COMPLETE ME!

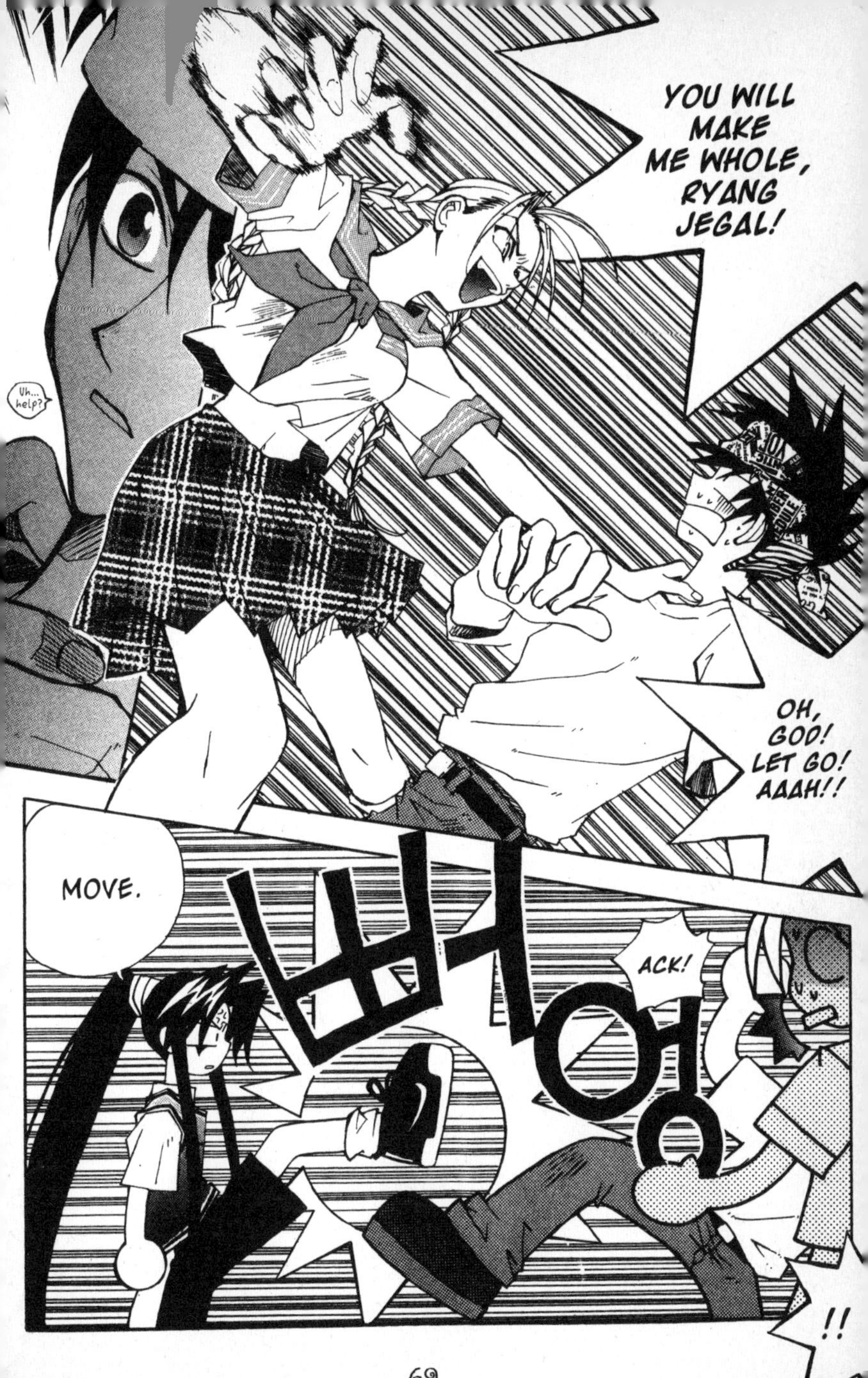

Uh... help?
YOU WILL MAKE ME WHOLE, RYANG JEGAL!
OH, GOD! LET GO! AAAH!!
MOVE.
ACK!
!!

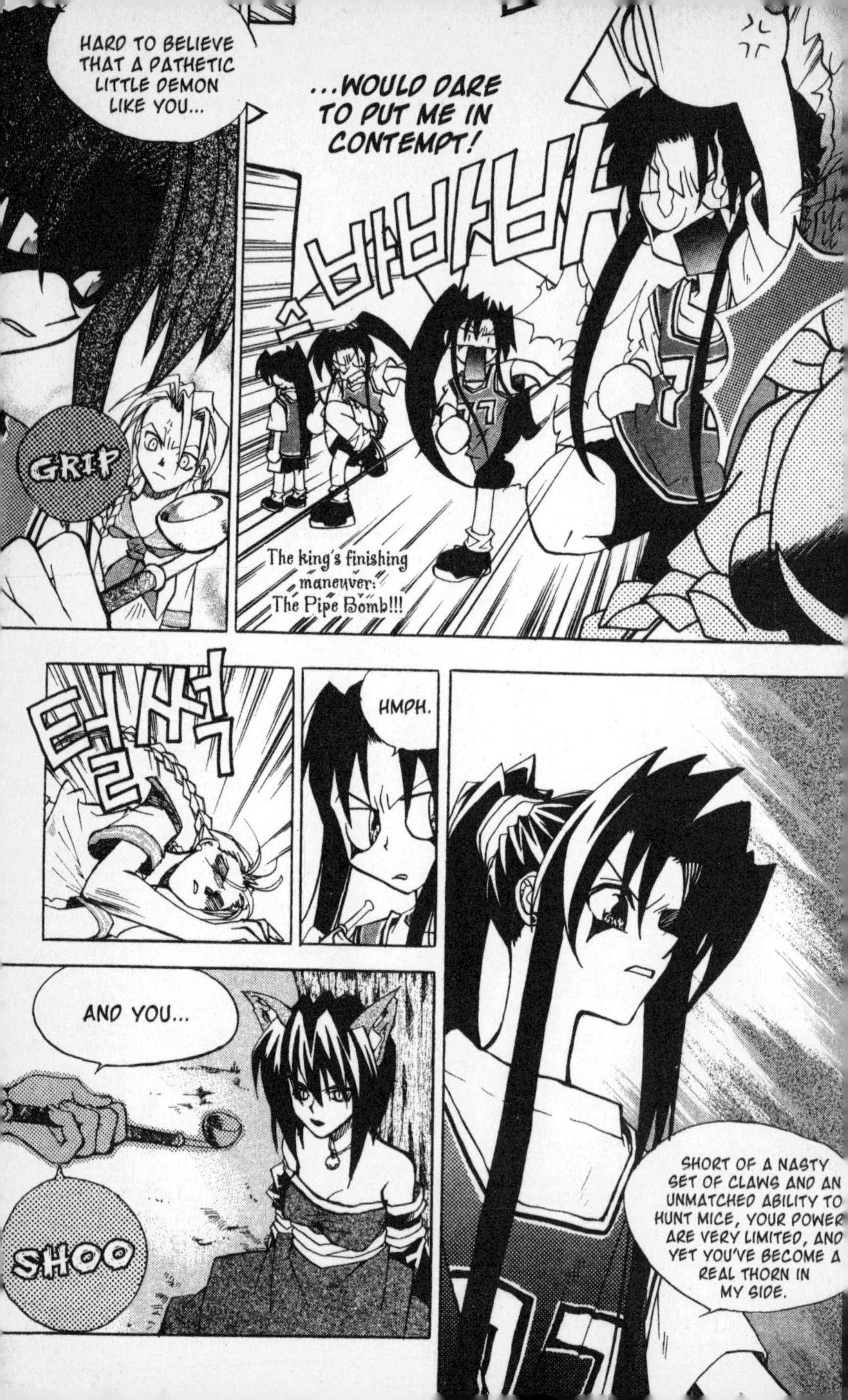
HARD TO BELIEVE THAT A PATHETIC LITTLE DEMON LIKE YOU...
GRIP
...WOULD DARE TO PUT ME IN CONTEMPT!
The king's finishing maneuver: The Pipe Bomb!!!
HMPH.
AND YOU...
SHOO
SHORT OF A NASTY SET OF CLAWS AND AN UNMATCHED ABILITY TO HUNT MICE, YOUR POWER ARE VERY LIMITED, AND YET YOU'VE BECOME A REAL THORN IN MY SIDE.

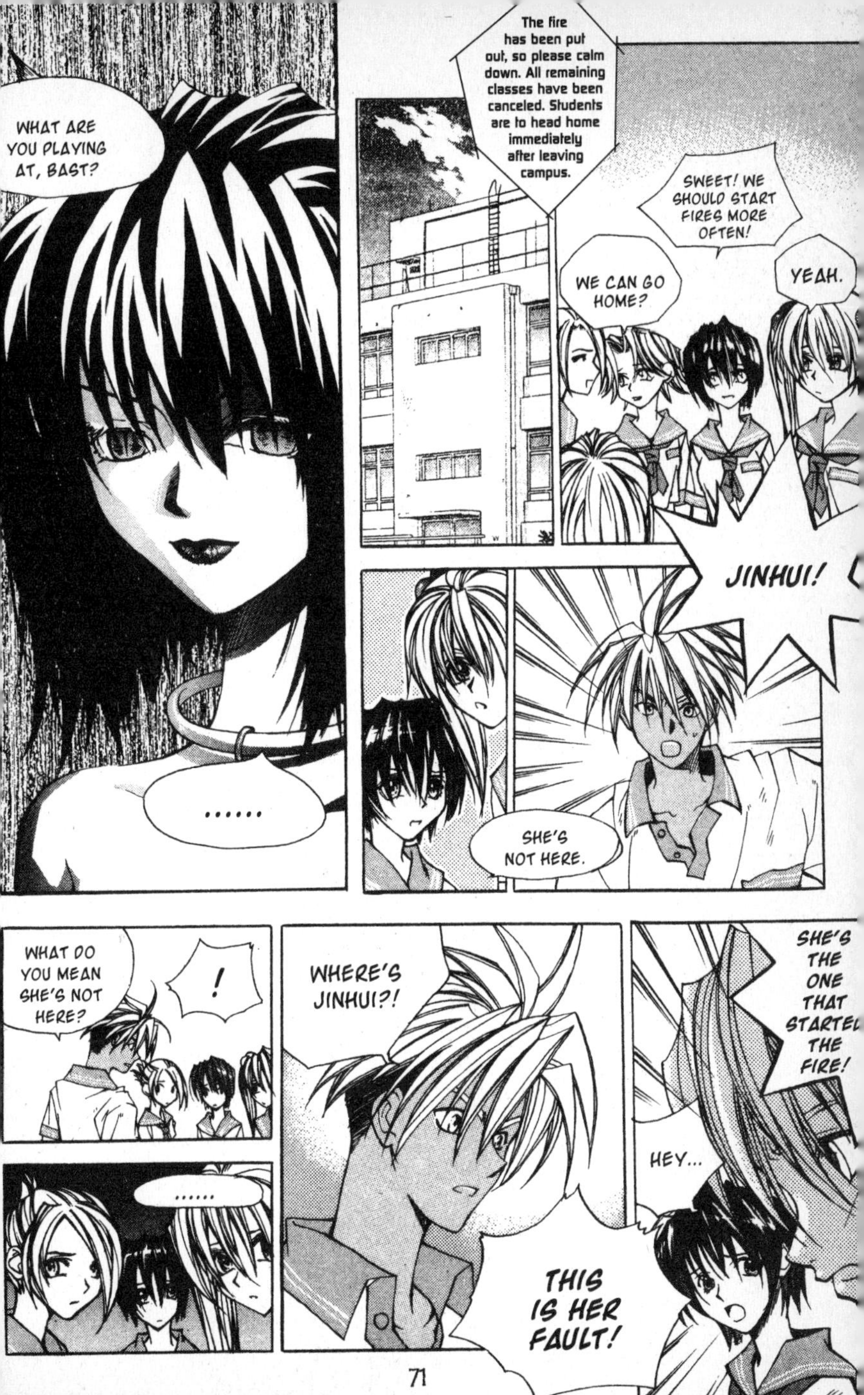
WHAT ARE YOU PLAYING AT, BAST?
......
The fire has been put out, so please calm down. All remaining classes have been canceled. Students are to head home immediately after leaving campus.
WE CAN GO HOME?
SWEET! WE SHOULD START FIRES MORE OFTEN!
YEAH.
JINHUI!
SHE'S NOT HERE.
WHAT DO YOU MEAN SHE'S NOT HERE?
!
......
WHERE'S JINHUI?!
THIS IS HER FAULT!
SHE'S THE ONE THAT STARTED THE FIRE!
HEY...

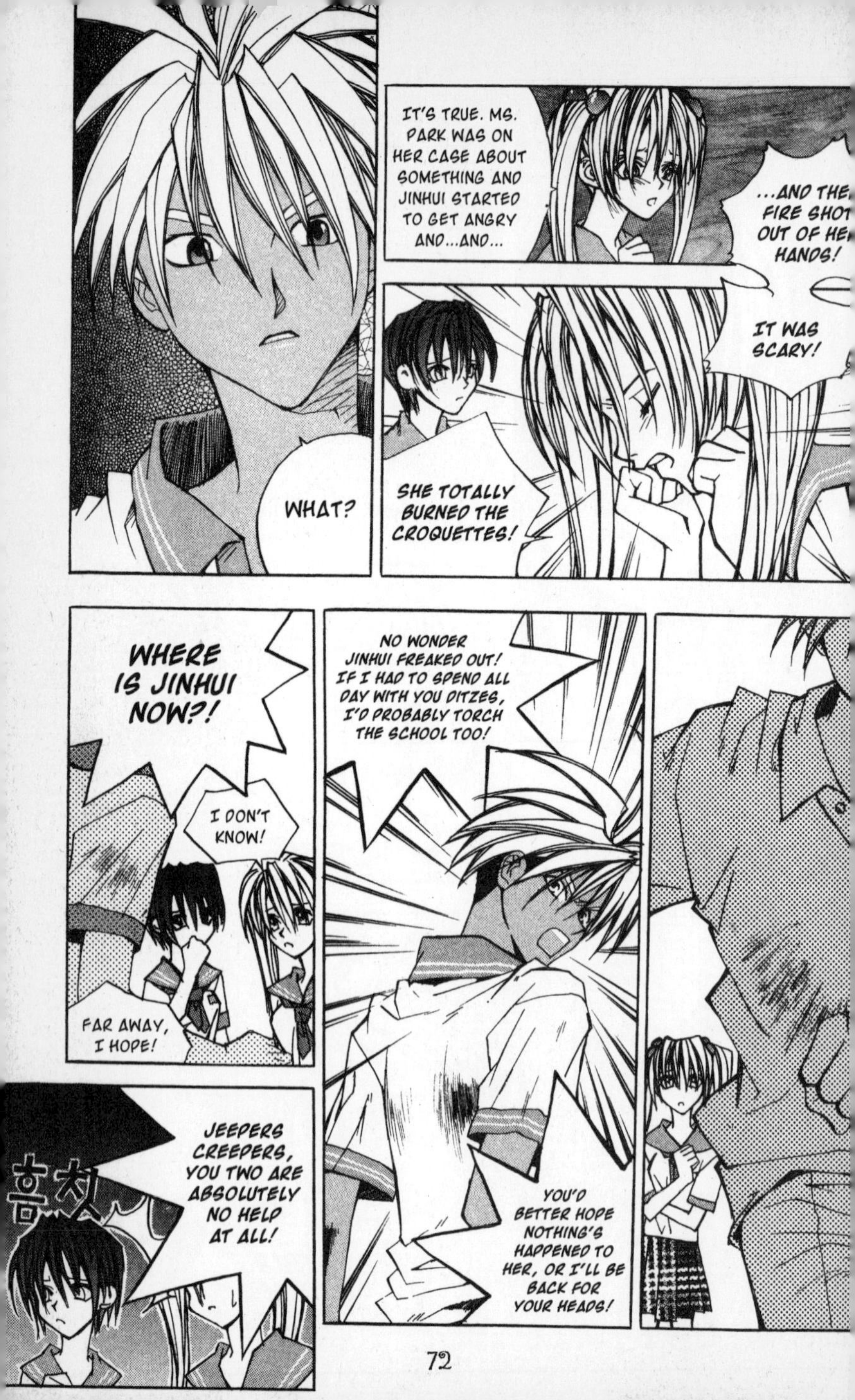
WHAT?
IT'S TRUE. MS. PARK WAS ON HER CASE ABOUT SOMETHING AND JINHUI STARTED TO GET ANGRY AND...AND...
...AND THE FIRE SHOT OUT OF HE HANDS!
IT WAS SCARY!
SHE TOTALLY BURNED THE CROQUETTES!
WHERE IS JINHUI NOW?!
I DON'T KNOW!
FAR AWAY, I HOPE!
흠칫
JEEPERS CREEPERS, YOU TWO ARE ABSOLUTELY NO HELP AT ALL!
NO WONDER JINHUI FREAKED OUT! IF I HAD TO SPEND ALL DAY WITH YOU DITZES, I'D PROBABLY TORCH THE SCHOOL TOO!
YOU'D BETTER HOPE NOTHING'S HAPPENED TO HER, OR I'LL BE BACK FOR YOUR HEADS!

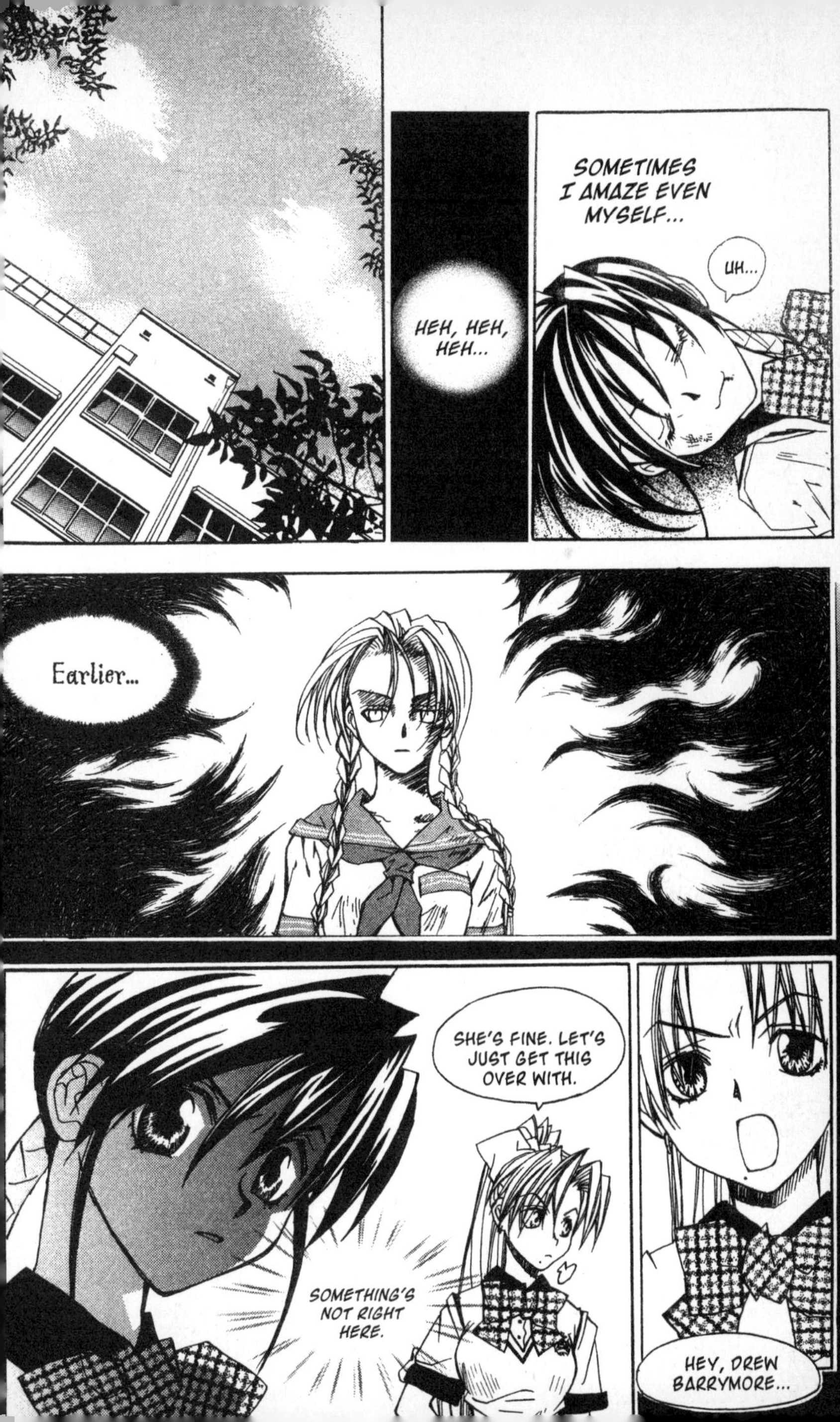
HEH, HEH, HEH...
SOMETIMES I AMAZE EVEN MYSELF...
UH...
Earlier...
SHE'S FINE. LET'S JUST GET THIS OVER WITH.
SOMETHING'S NOT RIGHT HERE.
HEY, DREW BARRYMORE...

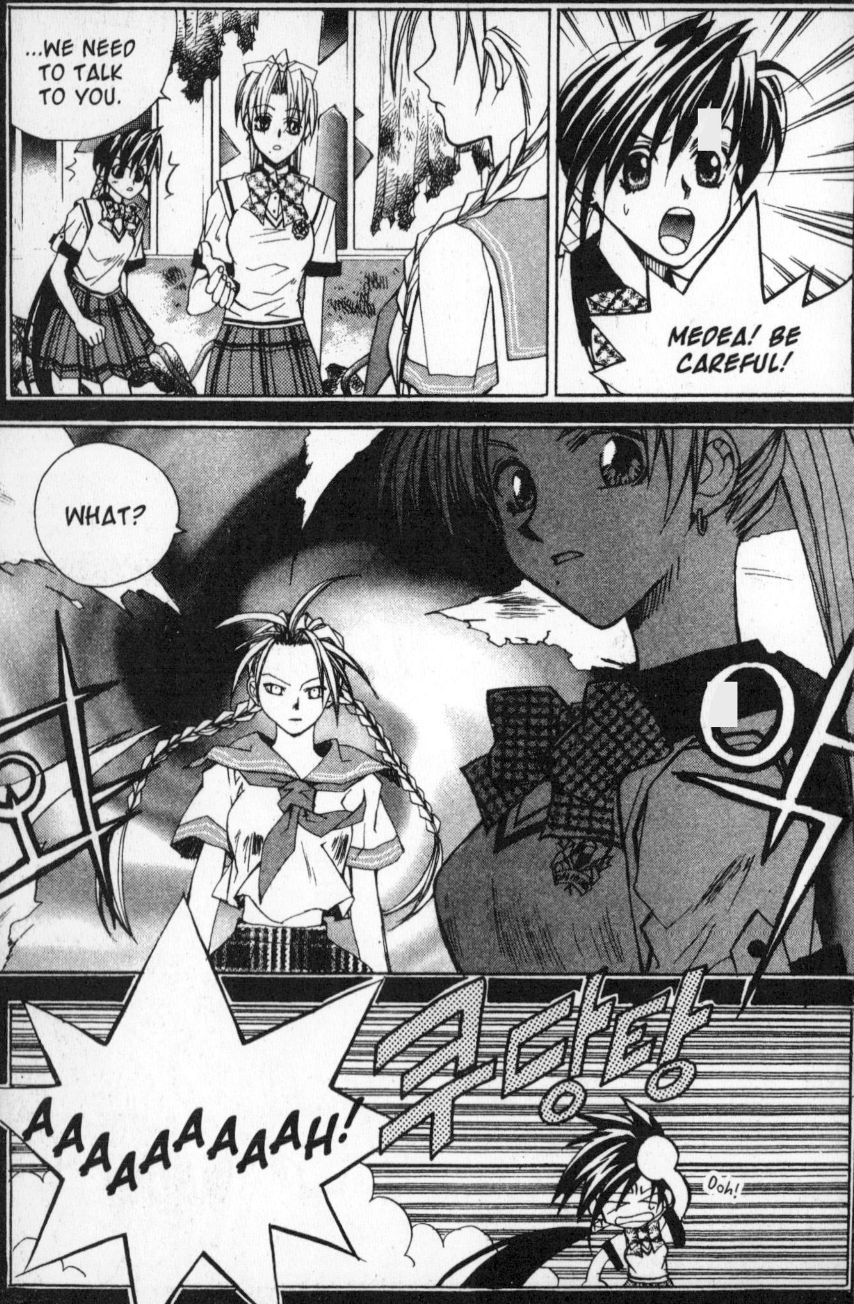
...WE NEED TO TALK TO YOU.
MEDEA! BE CAREFUL!
WHAT?
AAAAAAAAAAH!
주당탕!
Ooh!

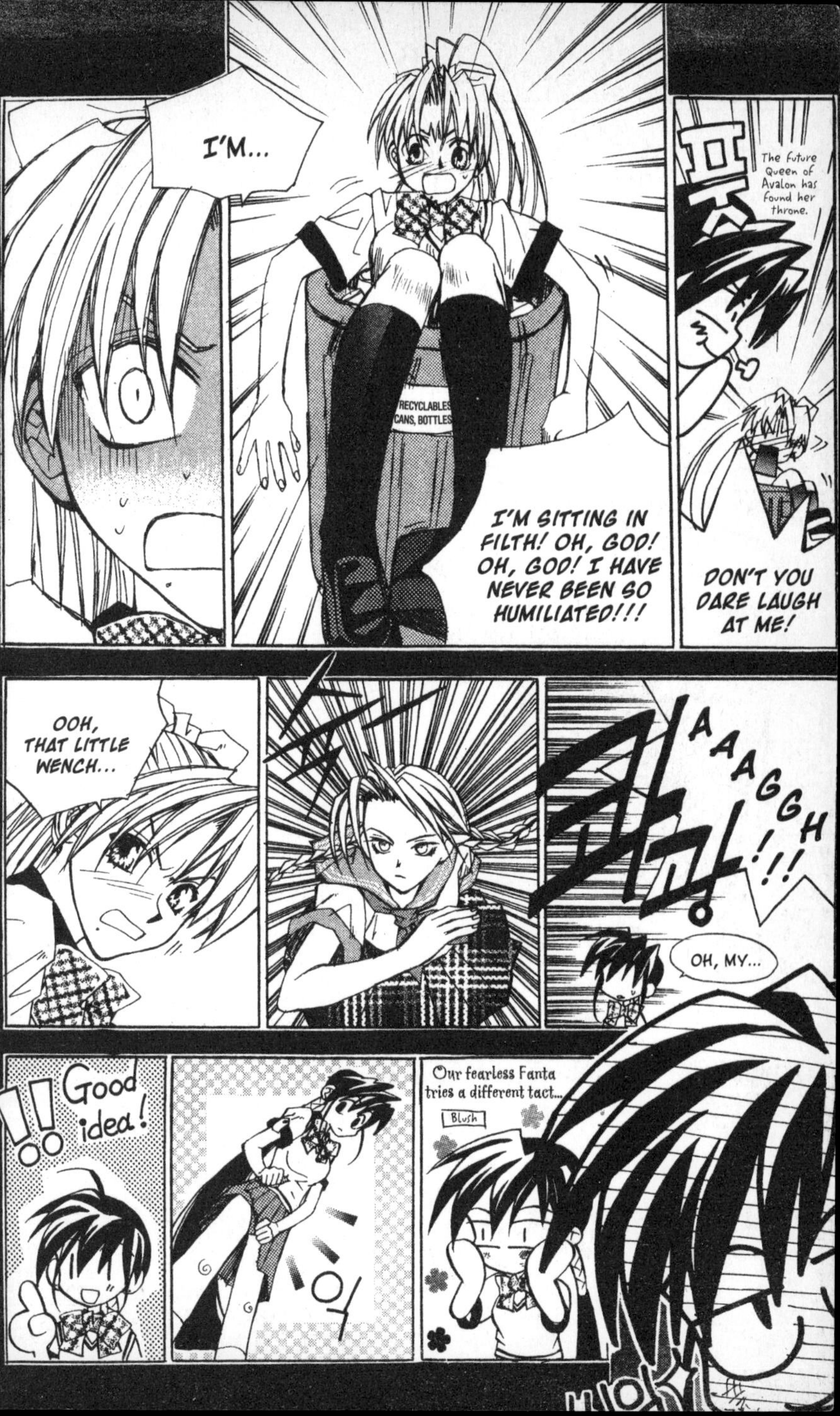

I'M...
RECYCLABLES
CANS, BOTTLES
I'M SITTING IN FILTH! OH, GOD! OH, GOD! I HAVE NEVER BEEN SO HUMILIATED!!!
The future Queen of Avalon has found her throne.
DON'T YOU DARE LAUGH AT ME!
OOH, THAT LITTLE WENCH...
AAAAGGH!!!!
OH, MY...
!! Good idea!
Our fearless Fanta tries a different tact...
Blush

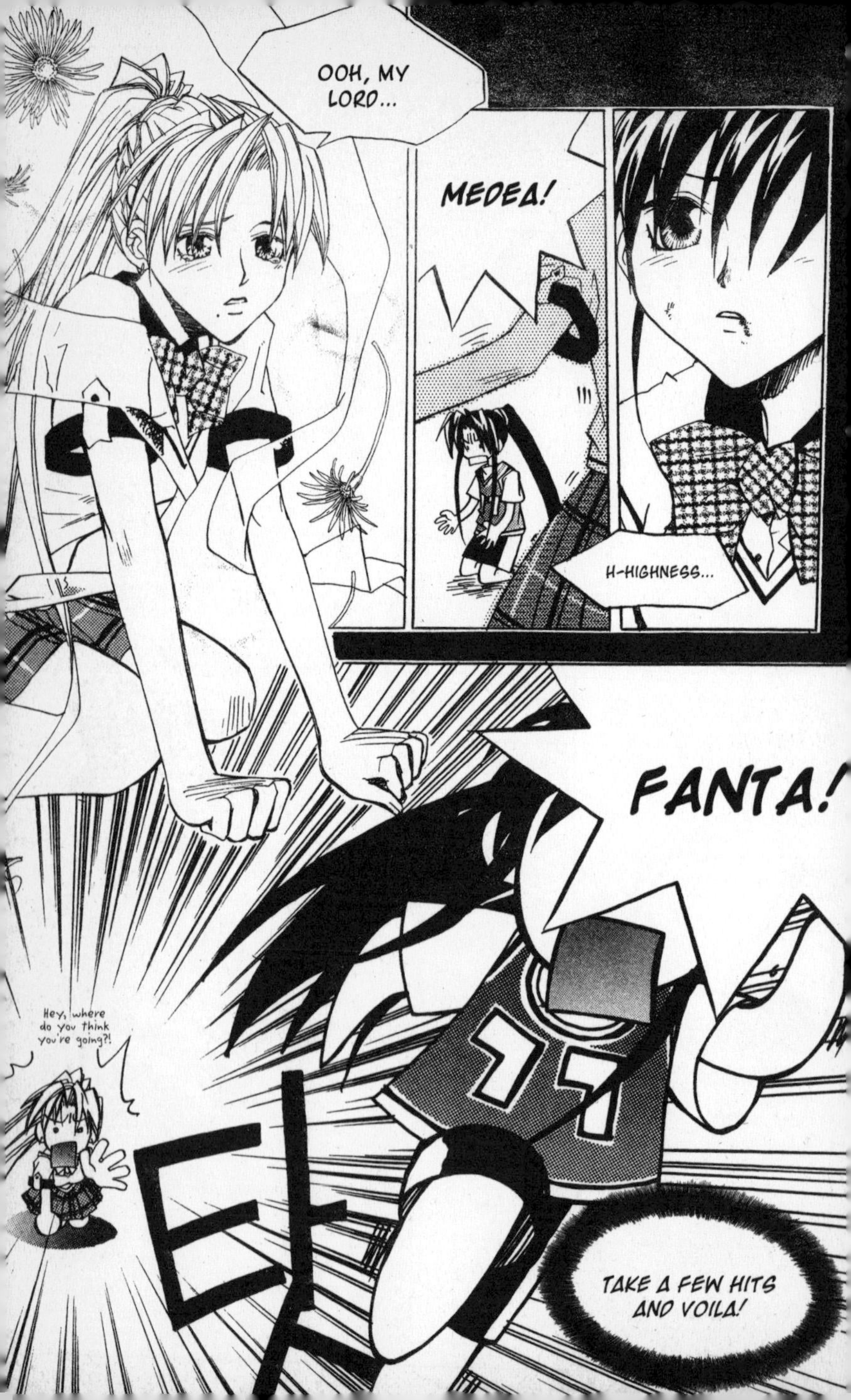
OOH, MY LORD...
MEDEA!
H-HIGHNESS...
FANTA!
Hey, where do you think you're going?!
TAKE A FEW HITS AND VOILA!

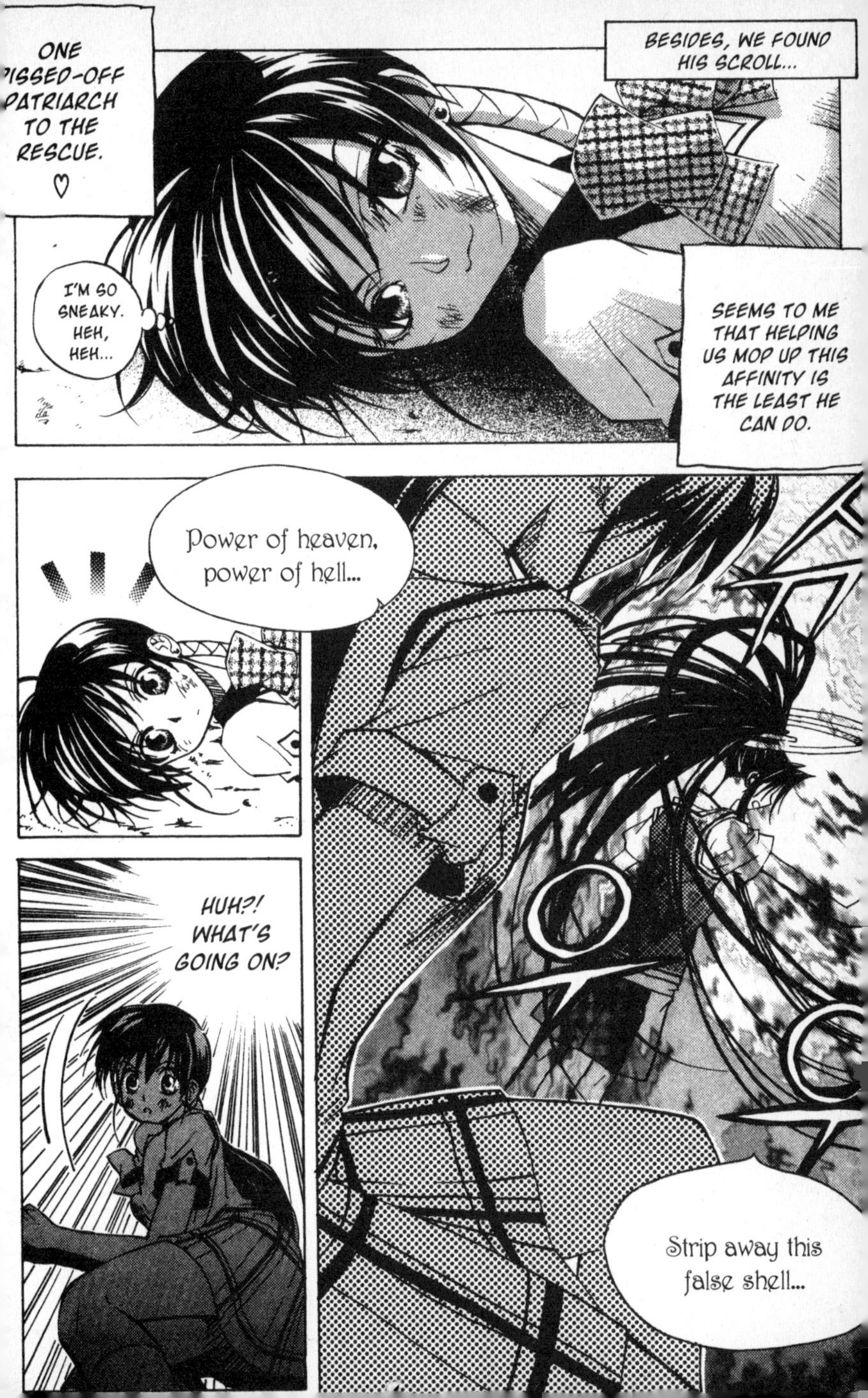
ONE PISSED-OFF PATRIARCH TO THE RESCUE. ♡
BESIDES, WE FOUND HIS SCROLL...
I'M SO SNEAKY. HEH, HEH...
SEEMS TO ME THAT HELPING US MOP UP THIS AFFINITY IS THE LEAST HE CAN DO.
Power of heaven, power of hell...
HUH?! WHAT'S GOING ON?
Strip away this false shell...

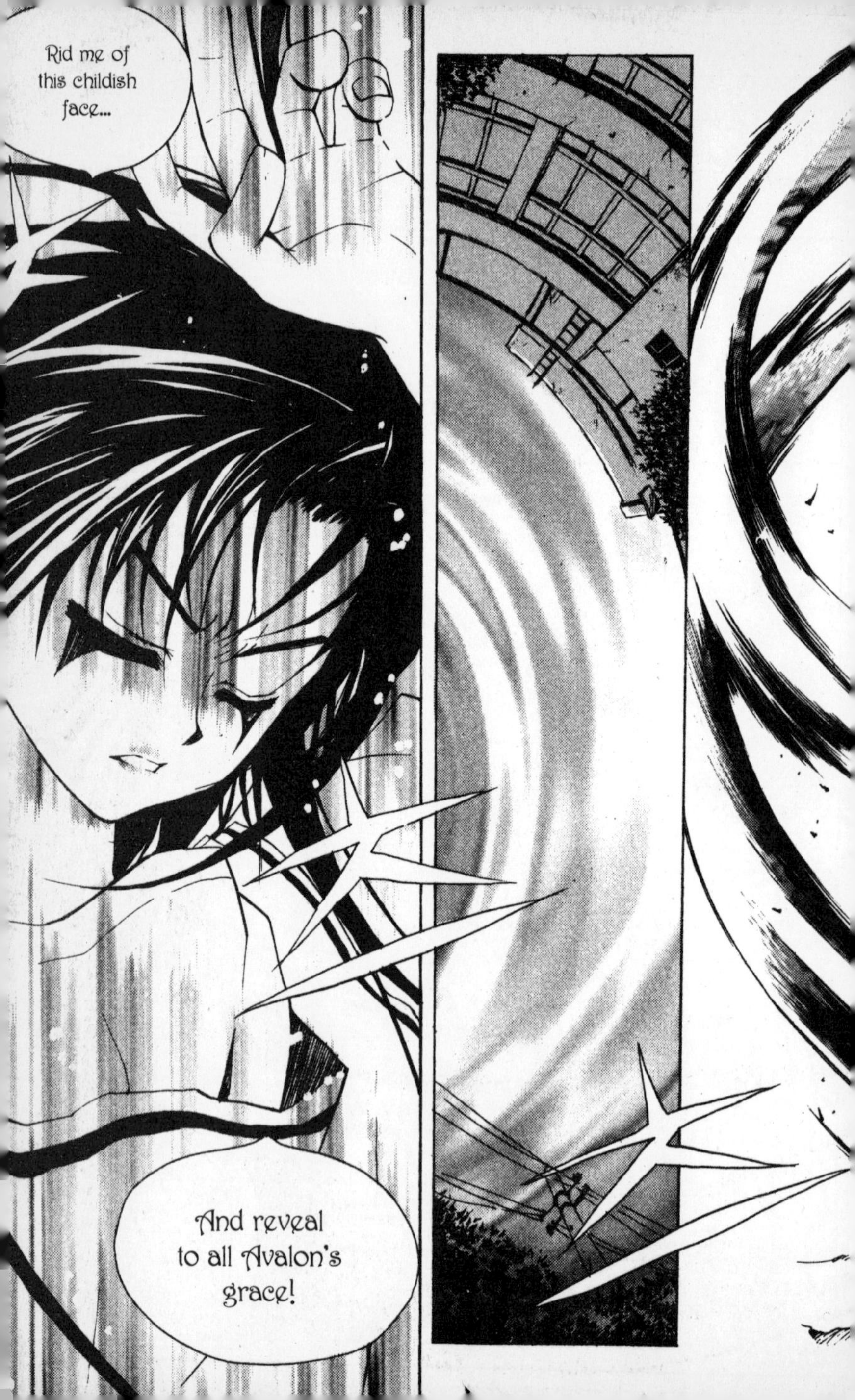
Rid me of this childish face...
And reveal to all Avalon's grace!

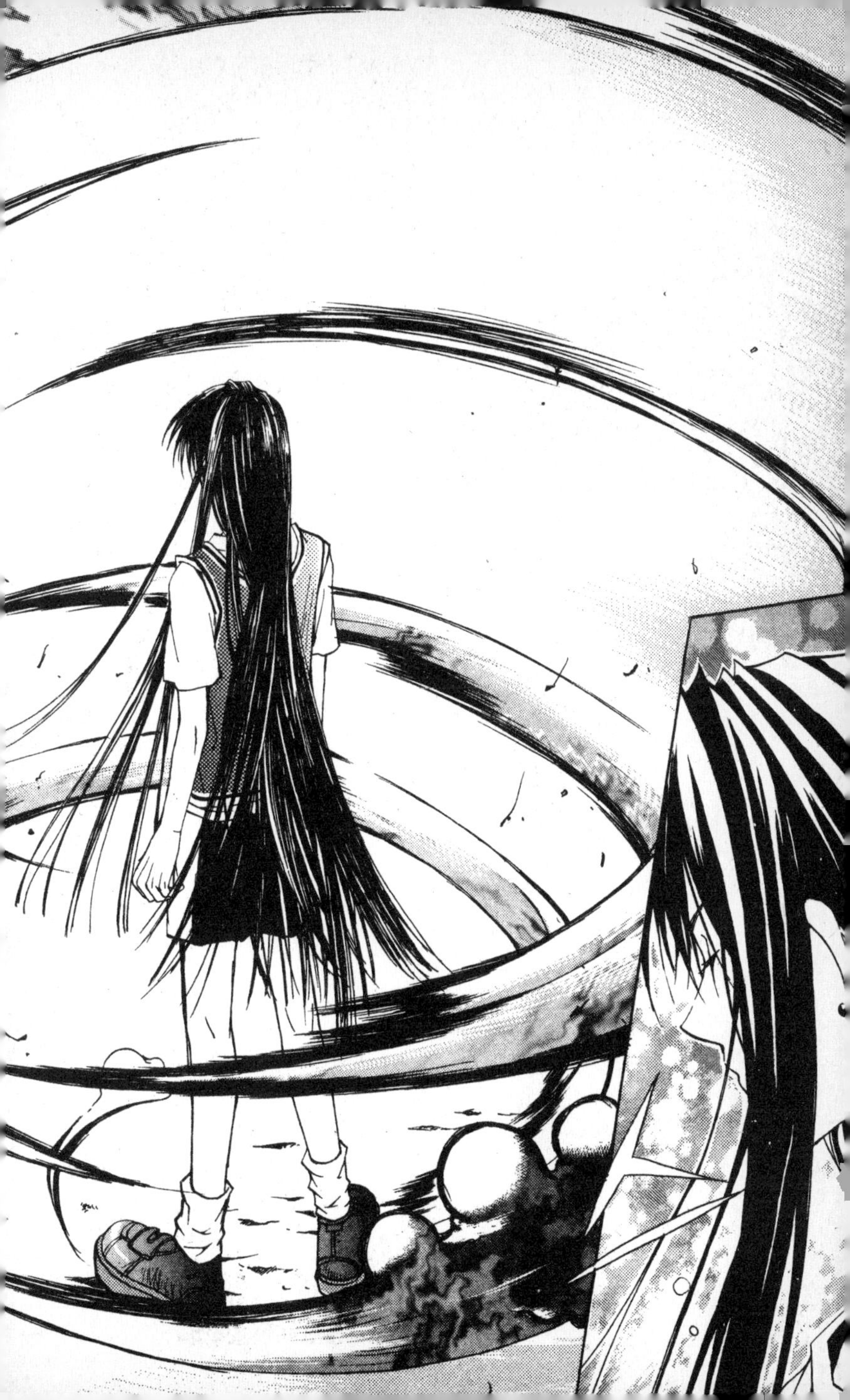

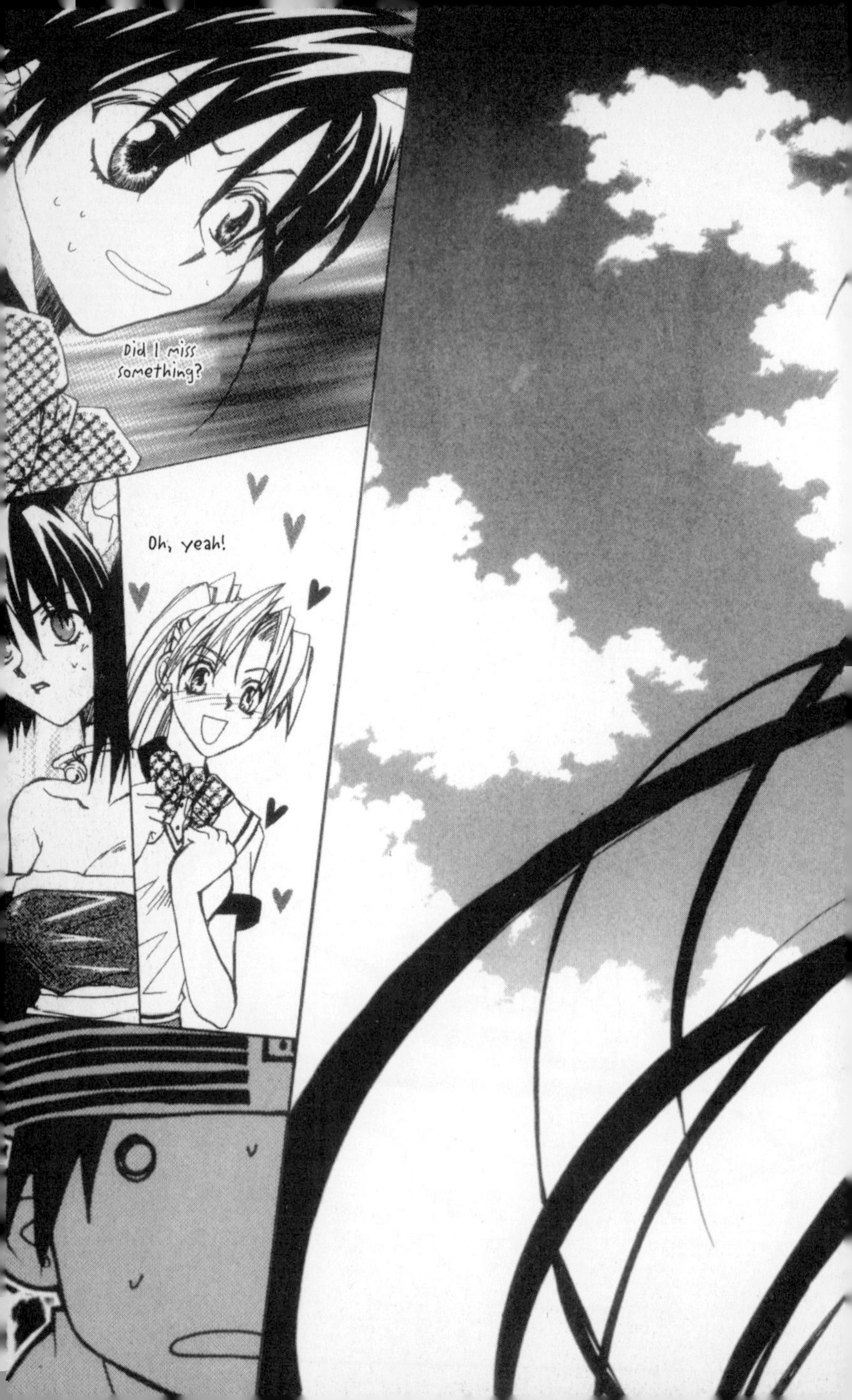
Did I miss something?
Oh, yeah!

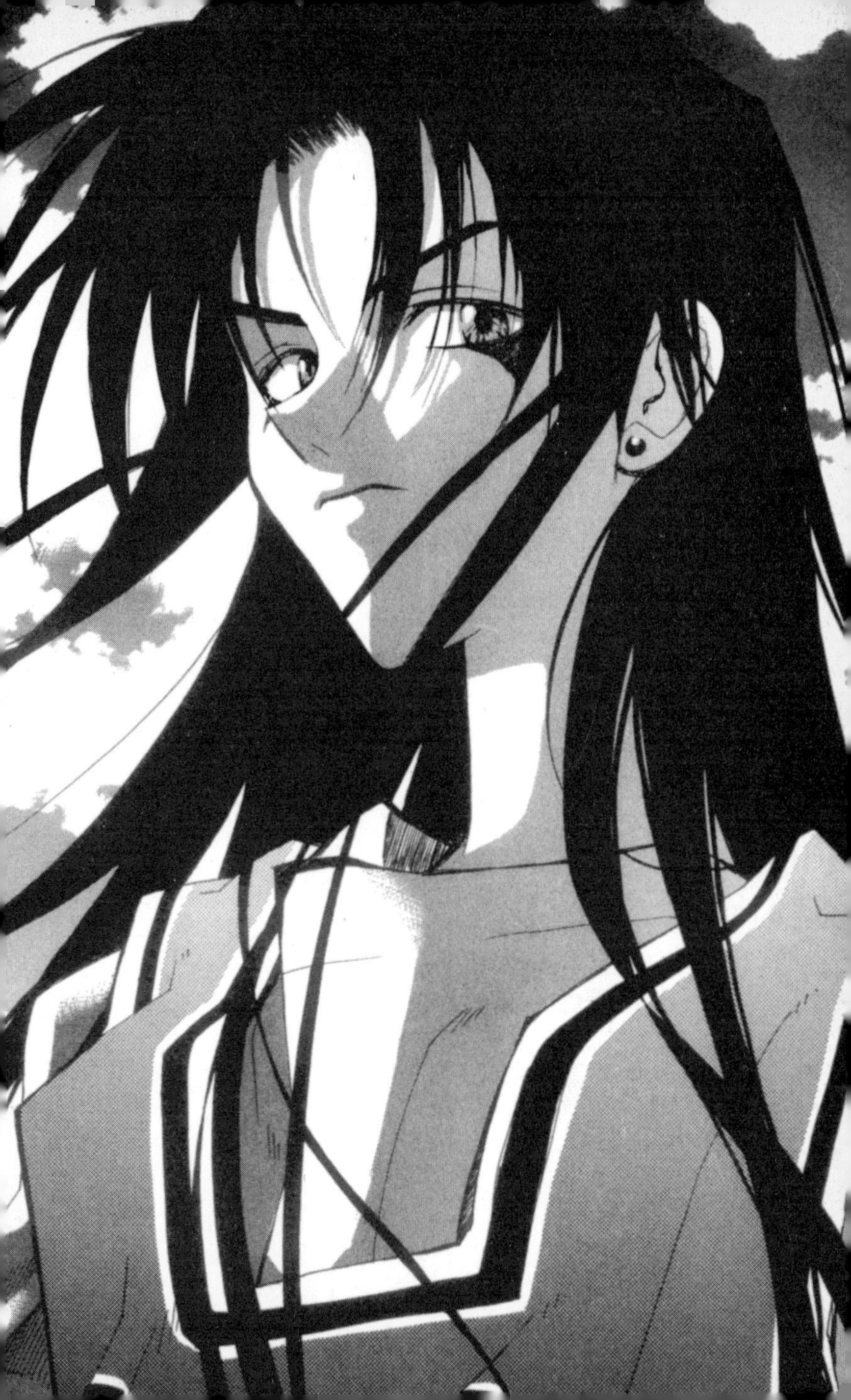

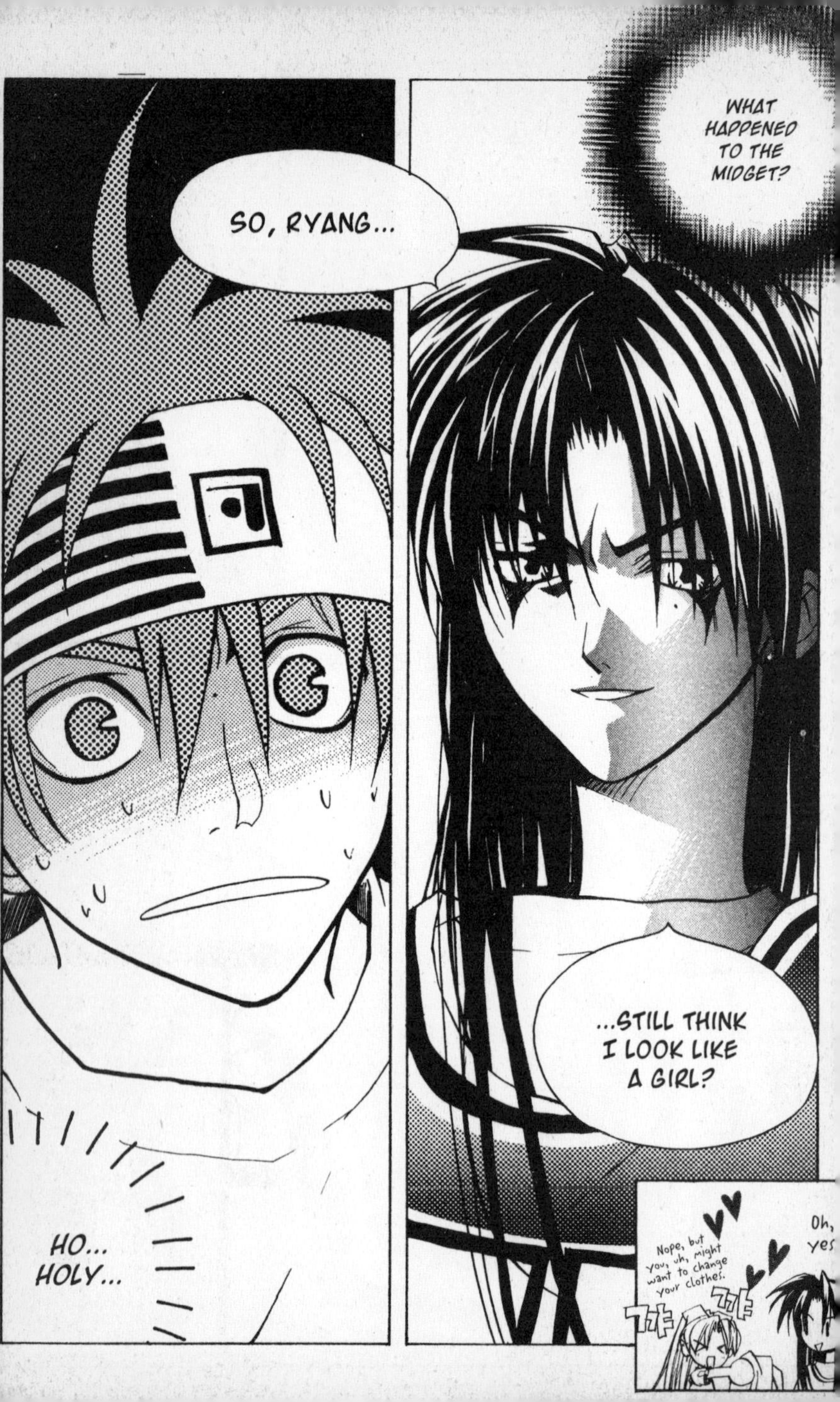
SO, RYANG...
HO... HOLY...
WHAT HAPPENED TO THE MIDGET?
...STILL THINK I LOOK LIKE A GIRL?
Nope, but you, uh, might want to change your clothes.
Oh, yes

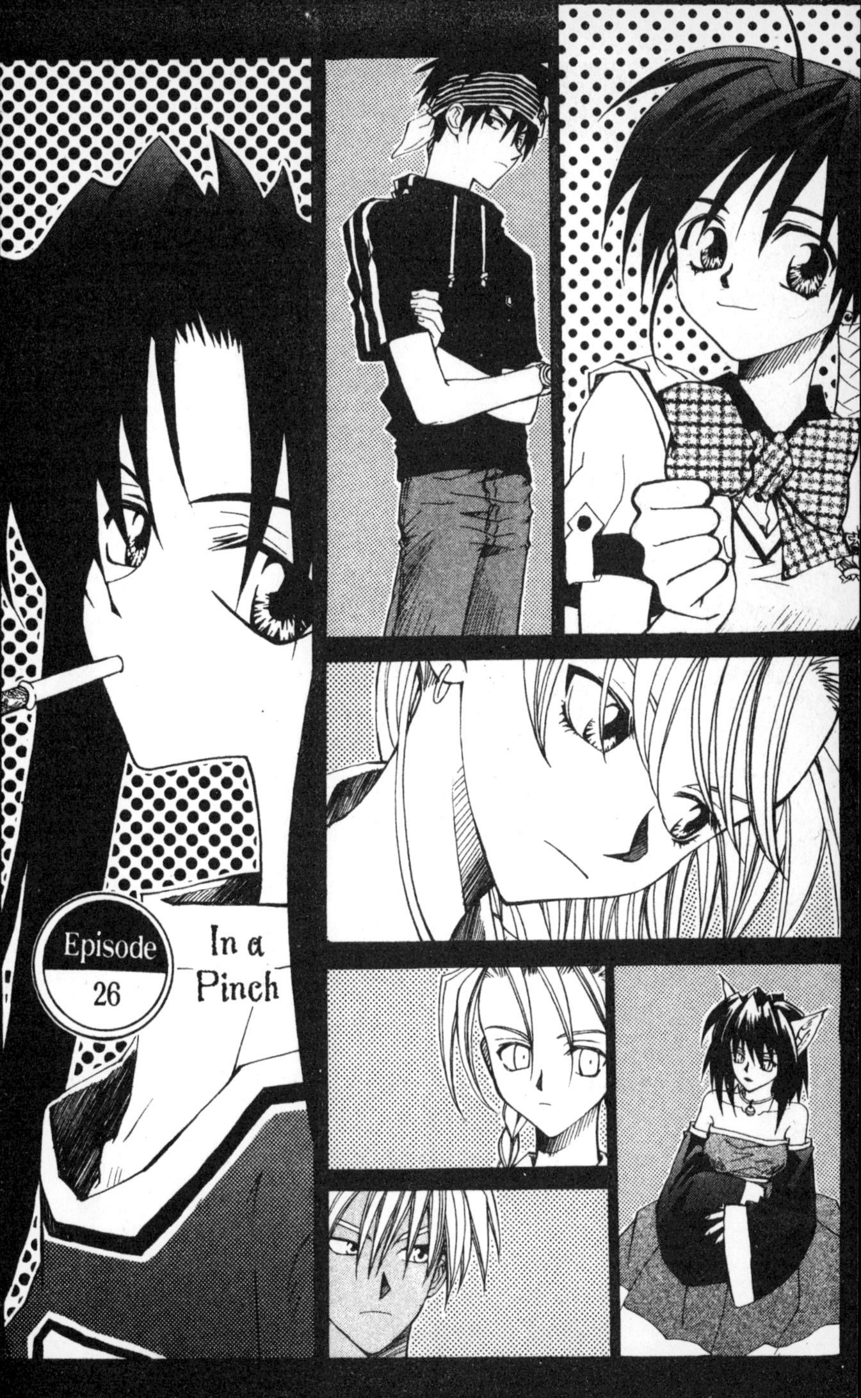
Episode 26
In a Pinch

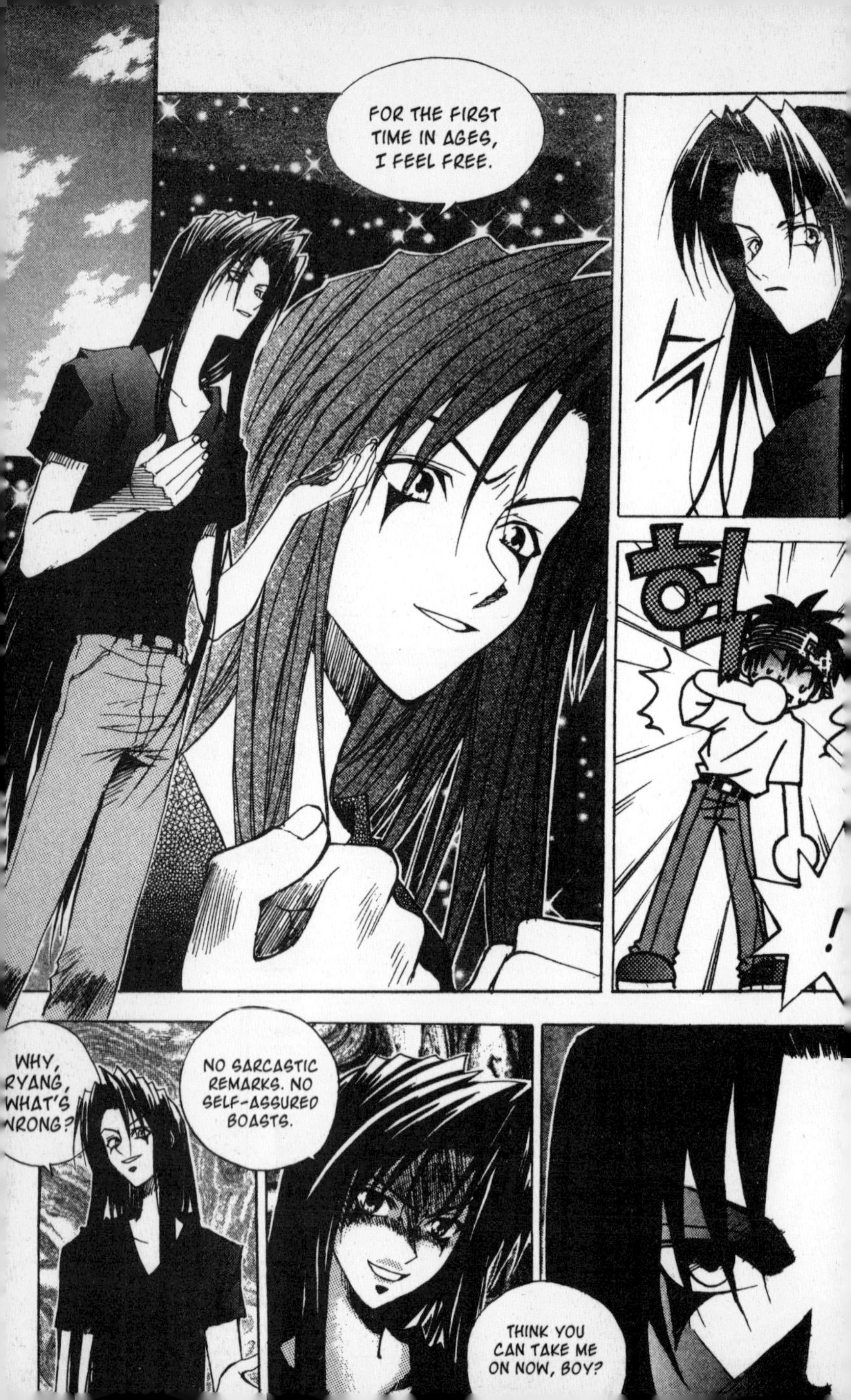
FOR THE FIRST TIME IN AGES, I FEEL FREE.
혀
!
WHY, RYANG, WHAT'S WRONG?
NO SARCASTIC REMARKS. NO SELF-ASSURED BOASTS.
THINK YOU CAN TAKE ME ON NOW, BOY?

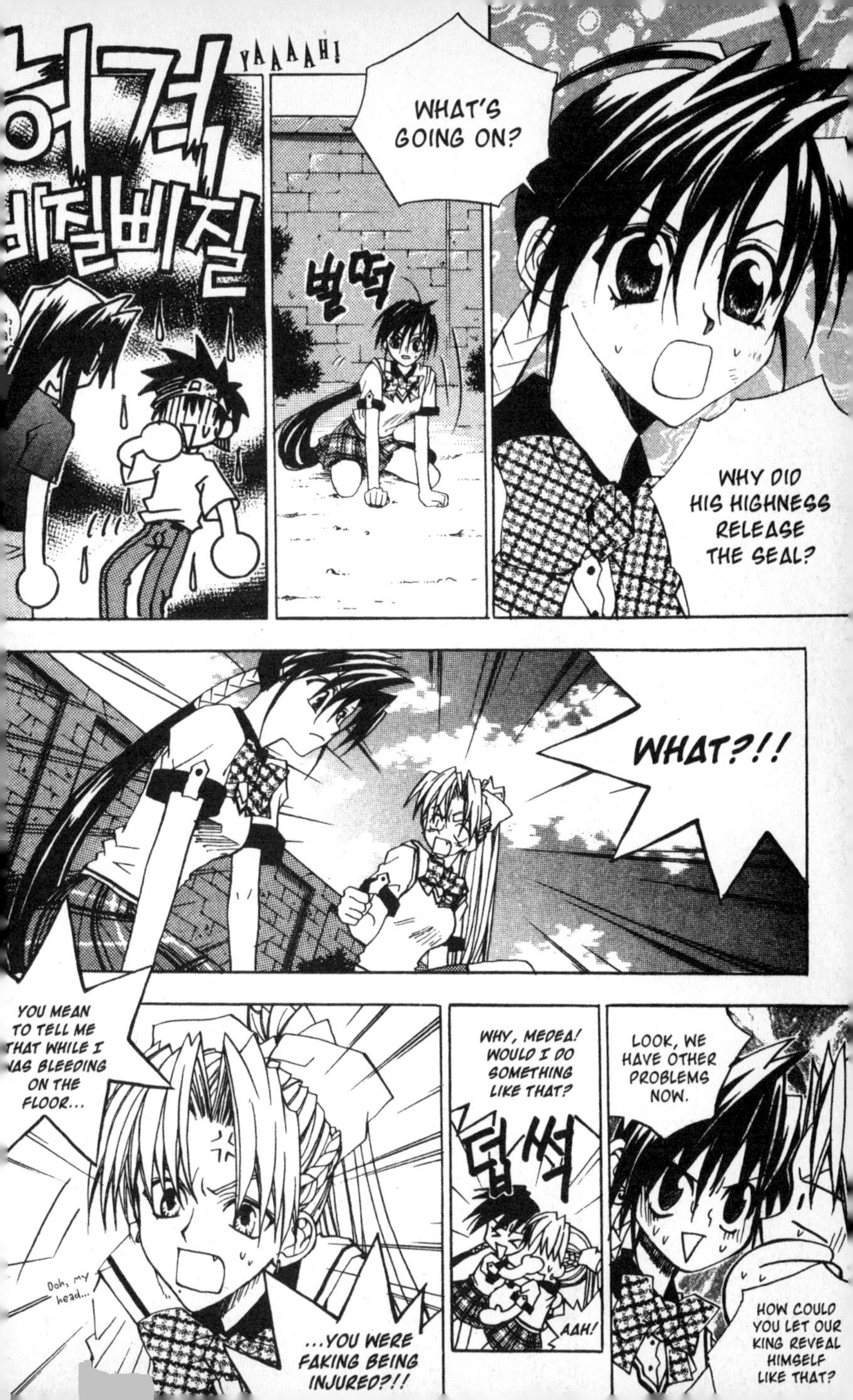
허걱
YAAAAH!
비질삐질
WHAT'S GOING ON?
벌떡
WHY DID HIS HIGHNESS RELEASE THE SEAL?
WHAT?!!
YOU MEAN TO TELL ME THAT WHILE I WAS BLEEDING ON THE FLOOR...
Ooh, my head...
...YOU WERE FAKING BEING INJURED?!!
WHY, MEDEA! WOULD I DO SOMETHING LIKE THAT?
덥석
AAH!
LOOK, WE HAVE OTHER PROBLEMS NOW.
HOW COULD YOU LET OUR KING REVEAL HIMSELF LIKE THAT?

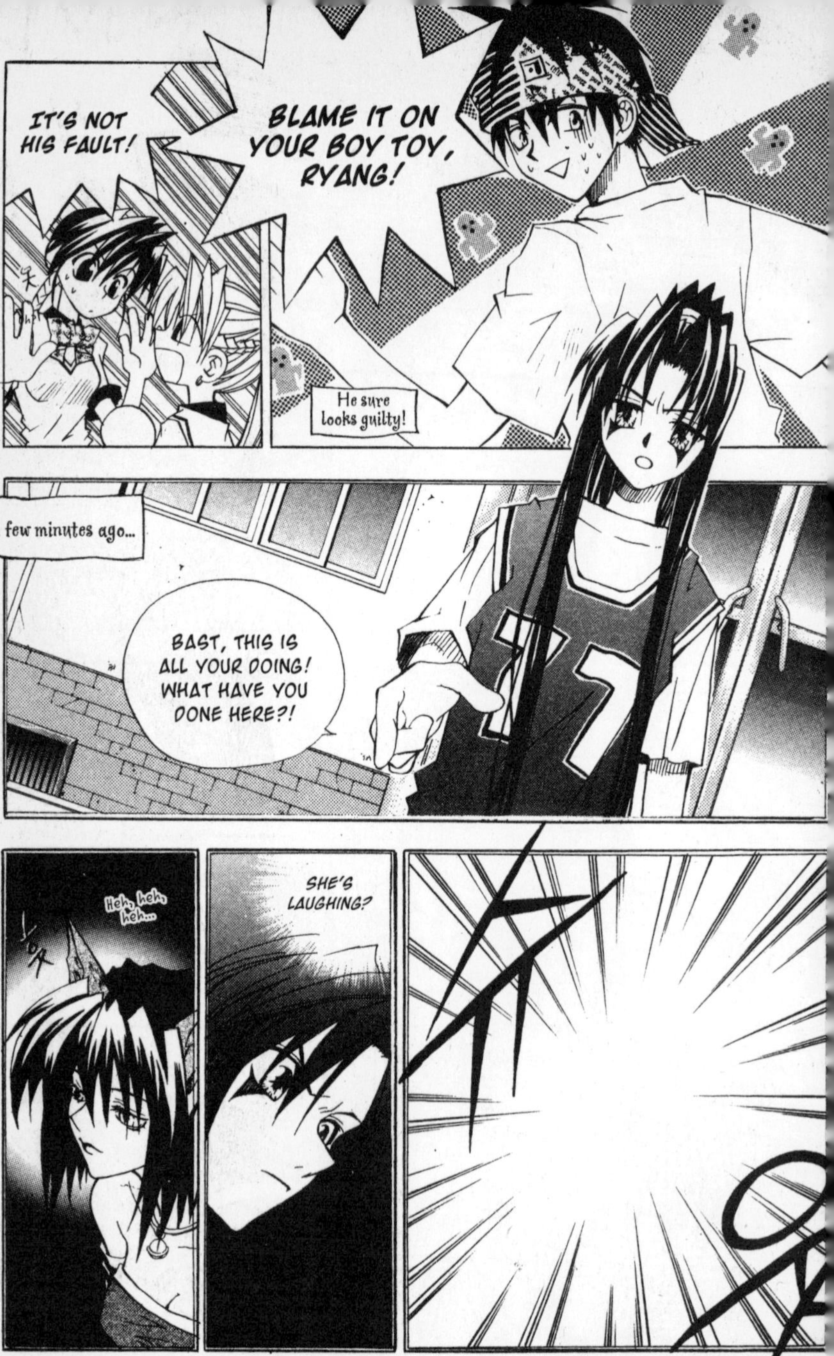
IT'S NOT HIS FAULT!
BLAME IT ON YOUR BOY TOY, RYANG!
He sure looks guilty!
A few minutes ago...
BAST, THIS IS ALL YOUR DOING! WHAT HAVE YOU DONE HERE?!
Heh, heh, heh...
SHE'S LAUGHING?

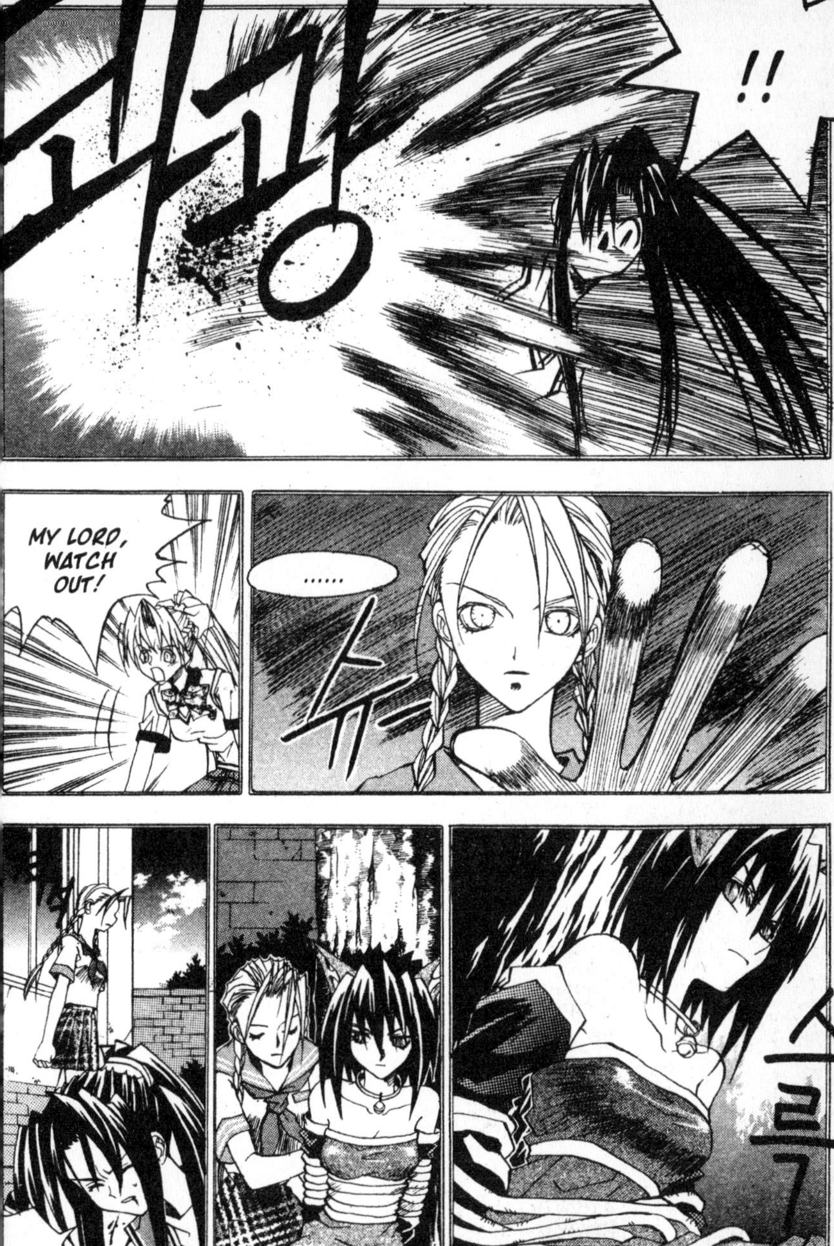
!!
MY LORD, WATCH OUT!
......
OOH!

Faerie rope. Completely unbreakable, but NOT untieable.

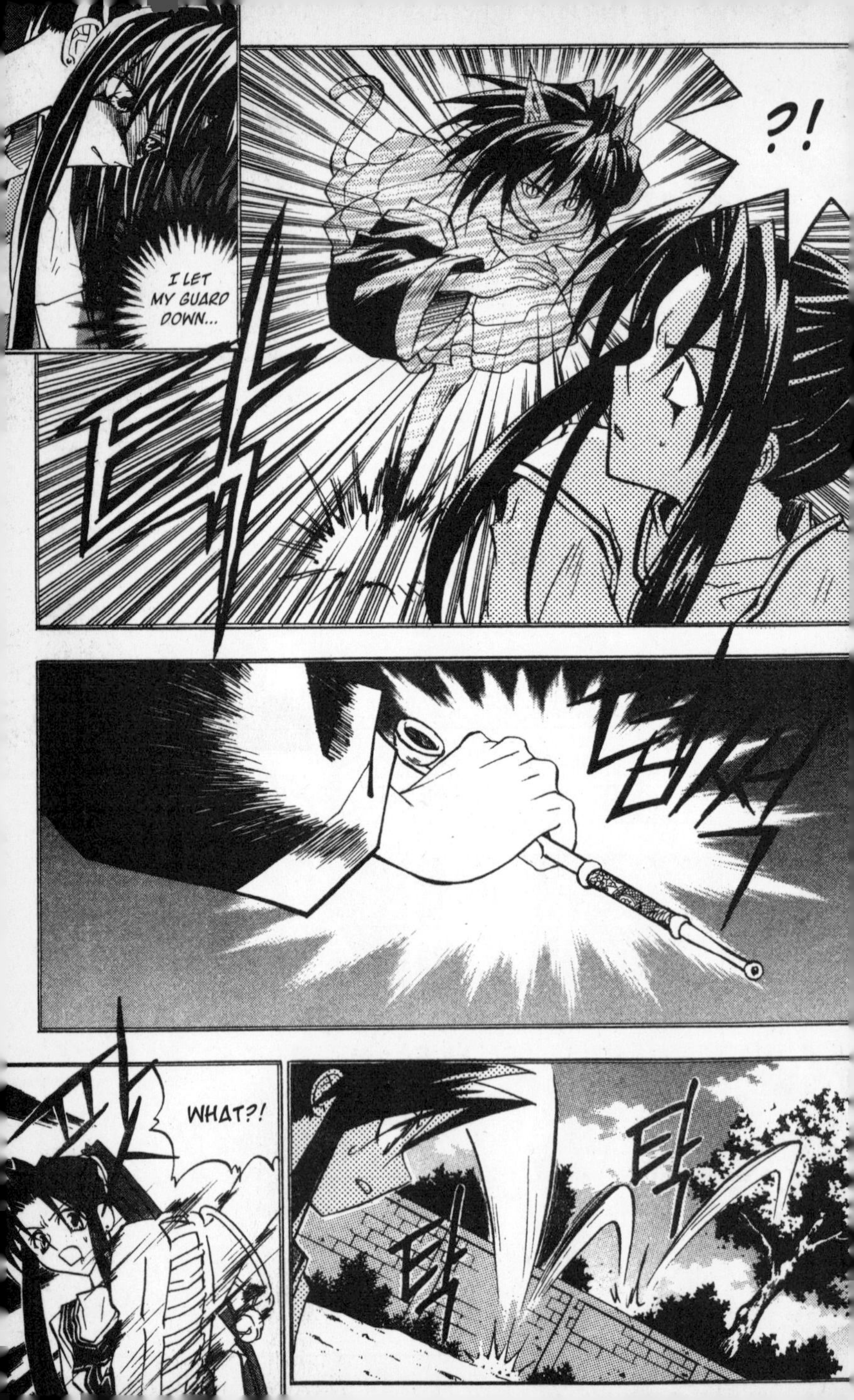
I LET MY GUARD DOWN...
?!
WHAT?!

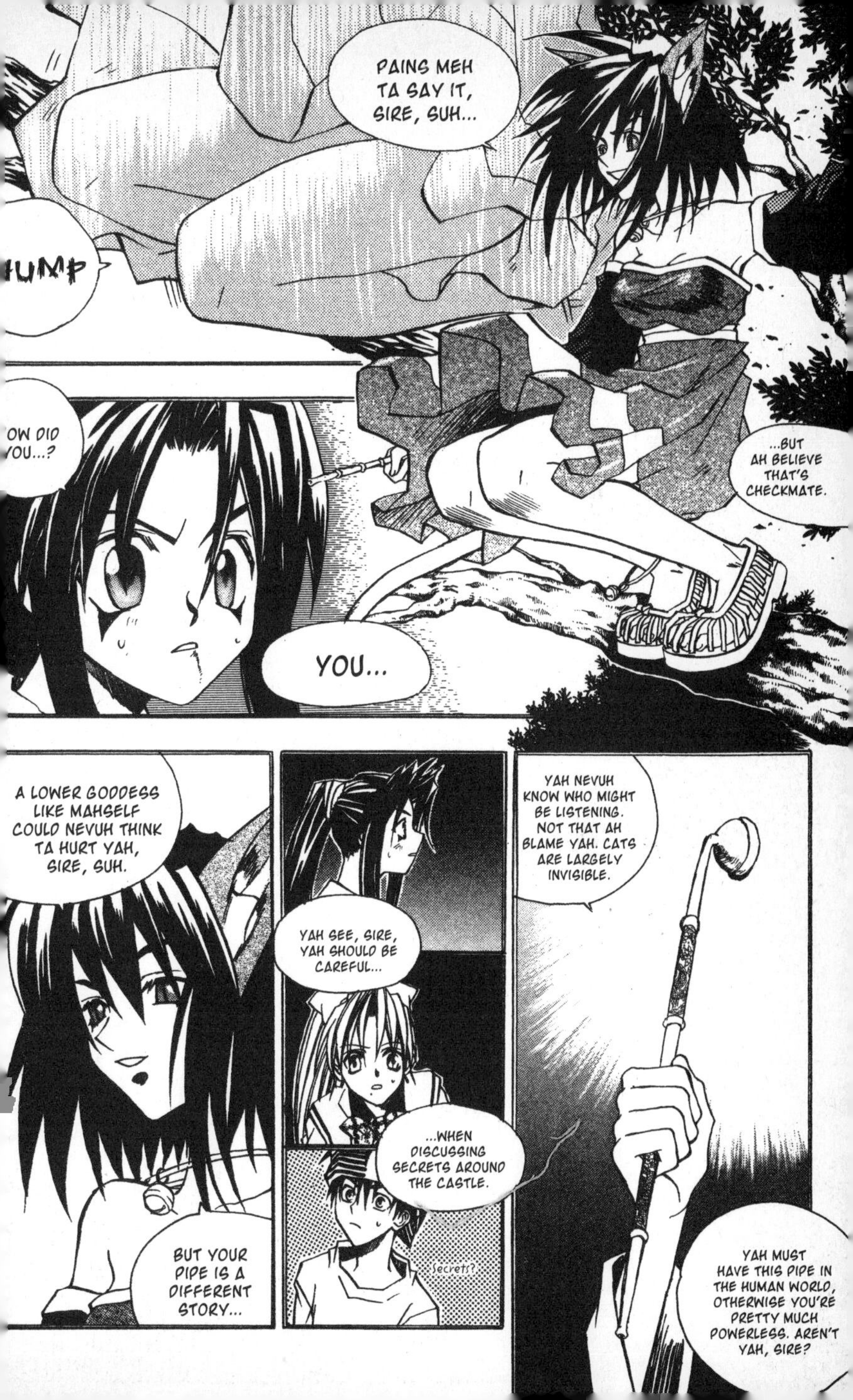
PAINS MEH TA SAY IT, SIRE, SUH...
HUMP
OW DID YOU...?
...BUT AH BELIEVE THAT'S CHECKMATE.
YOU...
A LOWER GODDESS LIKE MAHSELF COULD NEVUH THINK TA HURT YAH, SIRE, SUH.
BUT YOUR PIPE IS A DIFFERENT STORY...
YAH SEE, SIRE, YAH SHOULD BE CAREFUL...
...WHEN DISCUSSING SECRETS AROUND THE CASTLE.
Secrets?
YAH NEVUH KNOW WHO MIGHT BE LISTENING. NOT THAT AH BLAME YAH. CATS ARE LARGELY INVISIBLE.
YAH MUST HAVE THIS PIPE IN THE HUMAN WORLD, OTHERWISE YOU'RE PRETTY MUCH POWERLESS. AREN'T YAH, SIRE?

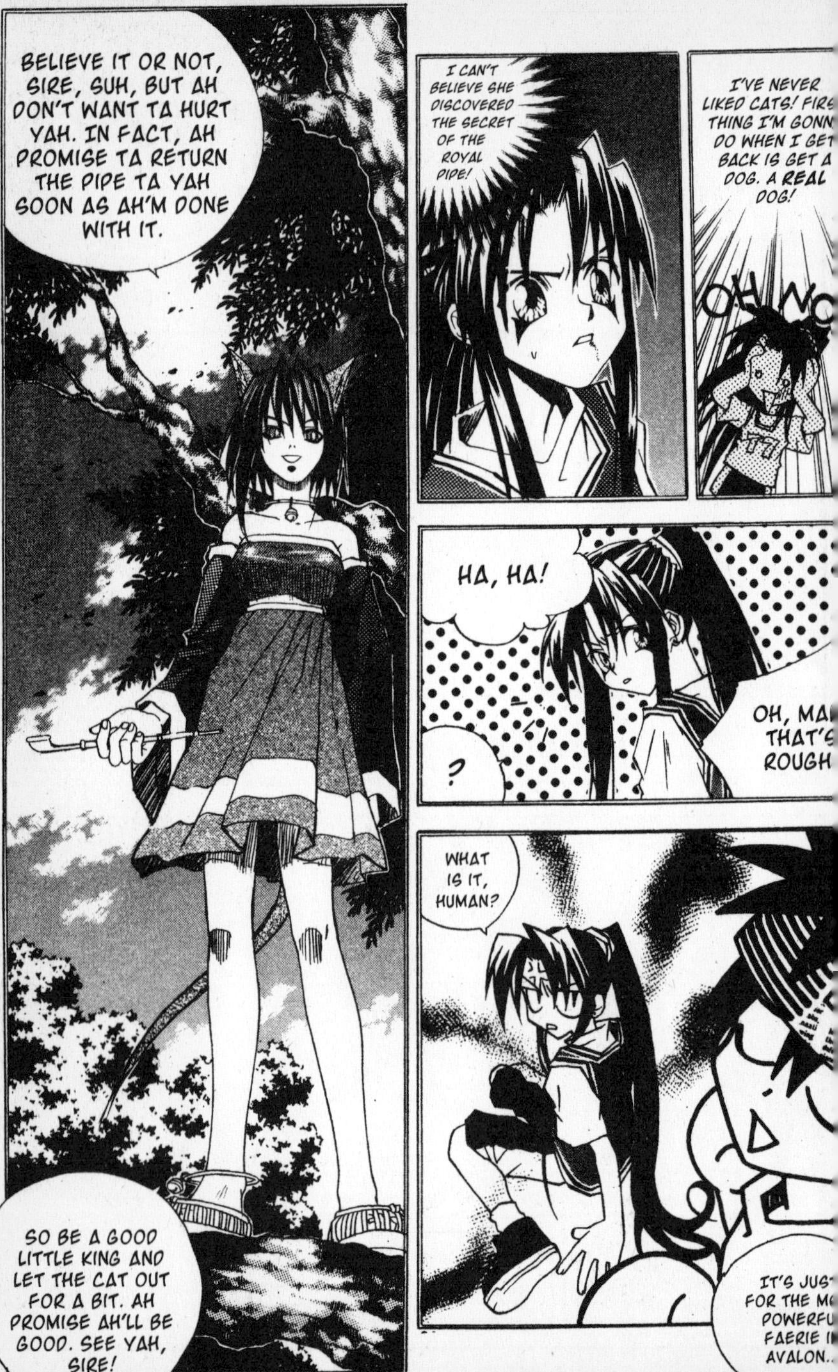
BELIEVE IT OR NOT, SIRE, SUH, BUT AH DON'T WANT TA HURT YAH. IN FACT, AH PROMISE TA RETURN THE PIPE TA YAH SOON AS AH'M DONE WITH IT.
SO BE A GOOD LITTLE KING AND LET THE CAT OUT FOR A BIT. AH PROMISE AH'LL BE GOOD. SEE YAH, SIRE!
I CAN'T BELIEVE SHE DISCOVERED THE SECRET OF THE ROYAL PIPE!
I'VE NEVER LIKED CATS! FIRS THING I'M GONN DO WHEN I GET BACK IS GET A DOG. A REAL DOG!
OH NO
HA, HA!
?
OH, MA THAT'S ROUGH
WHAT IS IT, HUMAN?
IT'S JUST FOR THE M POWERFU FAERIE I AVALON..

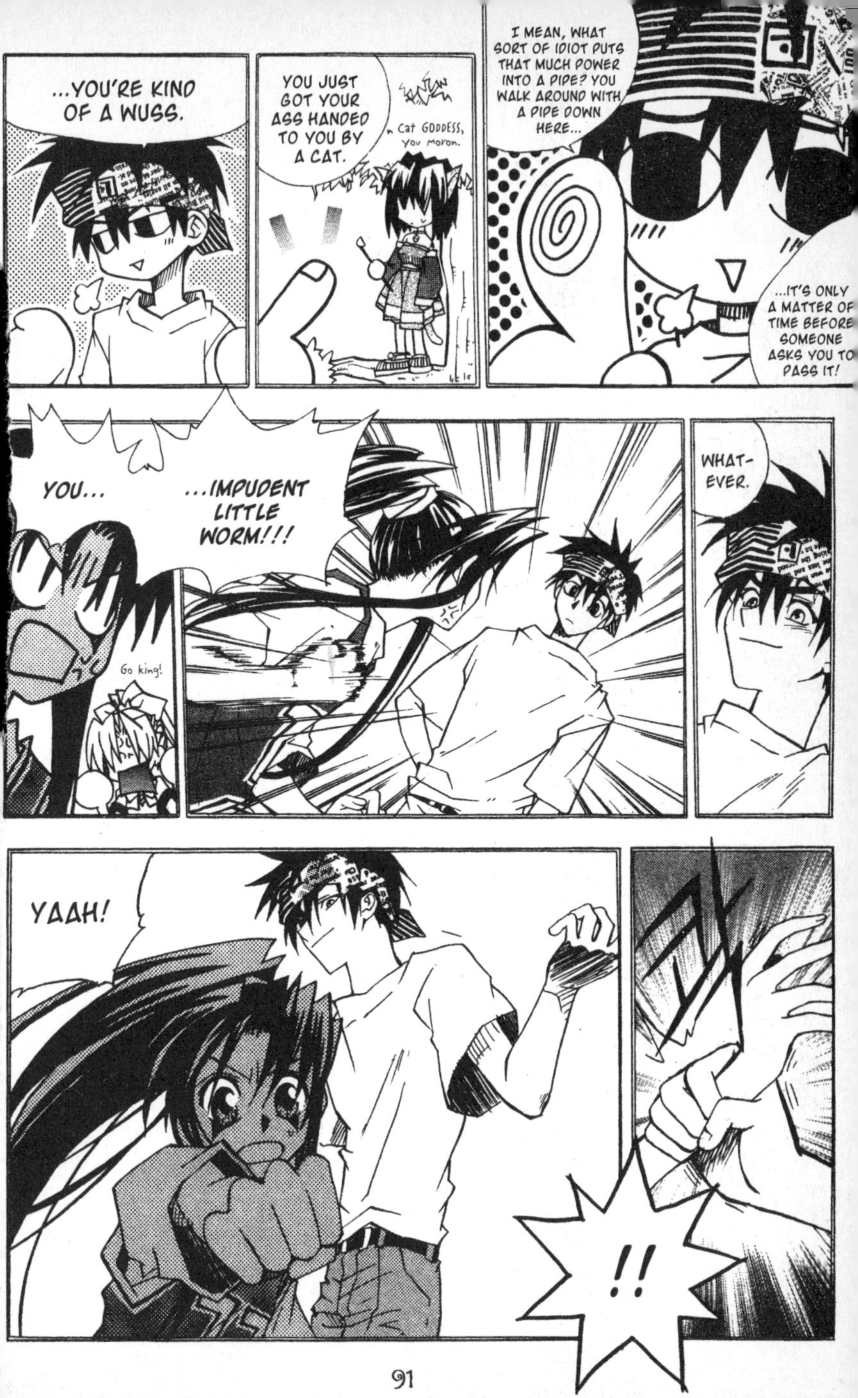
...YOU'RE KIND OF A WUSS.
YOU JUST GOT YOUR ASS HANDED TO YOU BY A CAT.
" Cat GODDESS," You moron.
I MEAN, WHAT SORT OF IDIOT PUTS THAT MUCH POWER INTO A PIPE? YOU WALK AROUND WITH A PIPE DOWN HERE...
...IT'S ONLY A MATTER OF TIME BEFORE SOMEONE ASKS YOU TO PASS IT!
YOU...
...IMPUDENT LITTLE WORM!!!
Go king!
WHAT-EVER.
YAAH!
!!

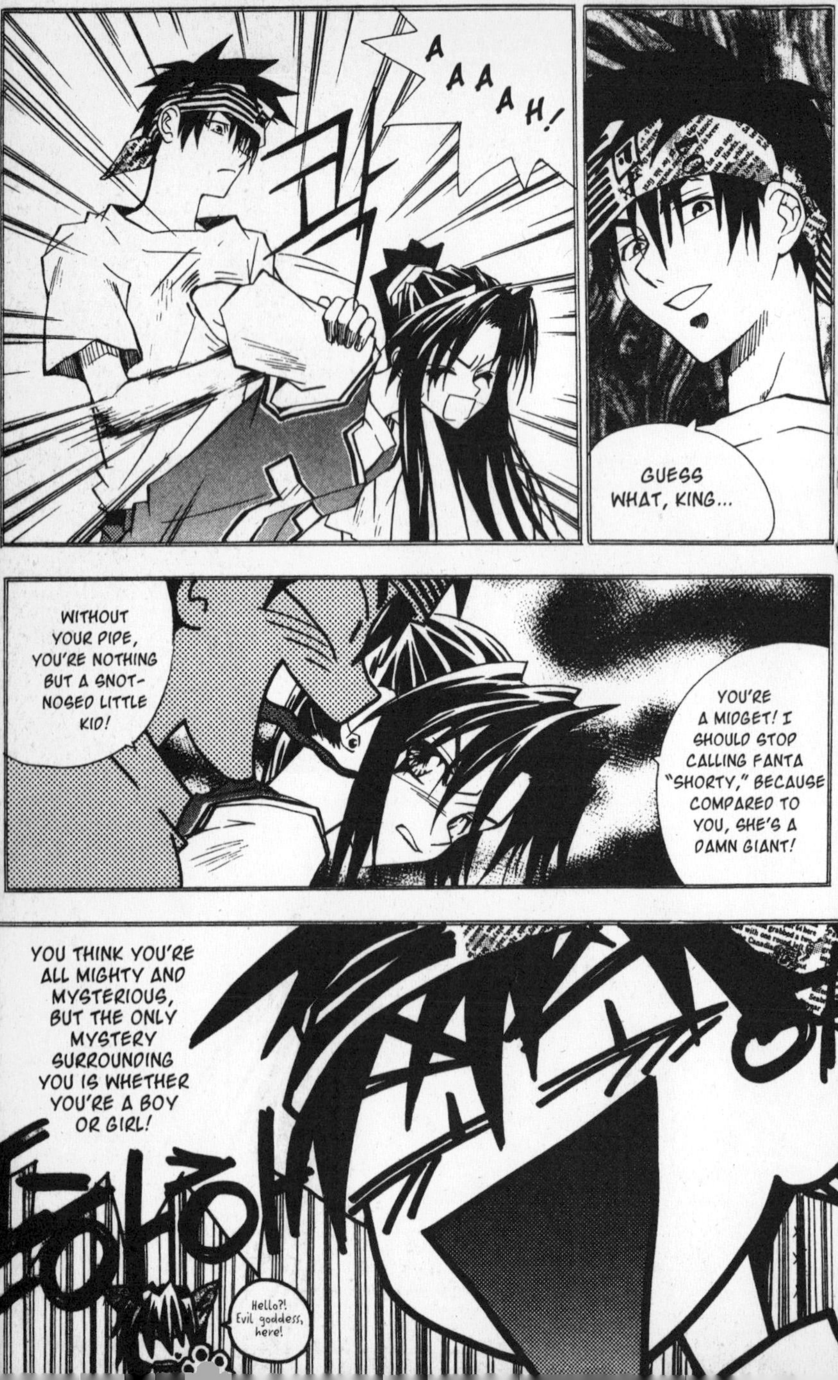
AAAAH!
GUESS WHAT, KING...
WITHOUT YOUR PIPE, YOU'RE NOTHING BUT A SNOT-NOSED LITTLE KID!
YOU'RE A MIDGET! I SHOULD STOP CALLING FANTA "SHORTY," BECAUSE COMPARED TO YOU, SHE'S A DAMN GIANT!
YOU THINK YOU'RE ALL MIGHTY AND MYSTERIOUS, BUT THE ONLY MYSTERY SURROUNDING YOU IS WHETHER YOU'RE A BOY OR GIRL!
Hello?! Evil goddess, here!

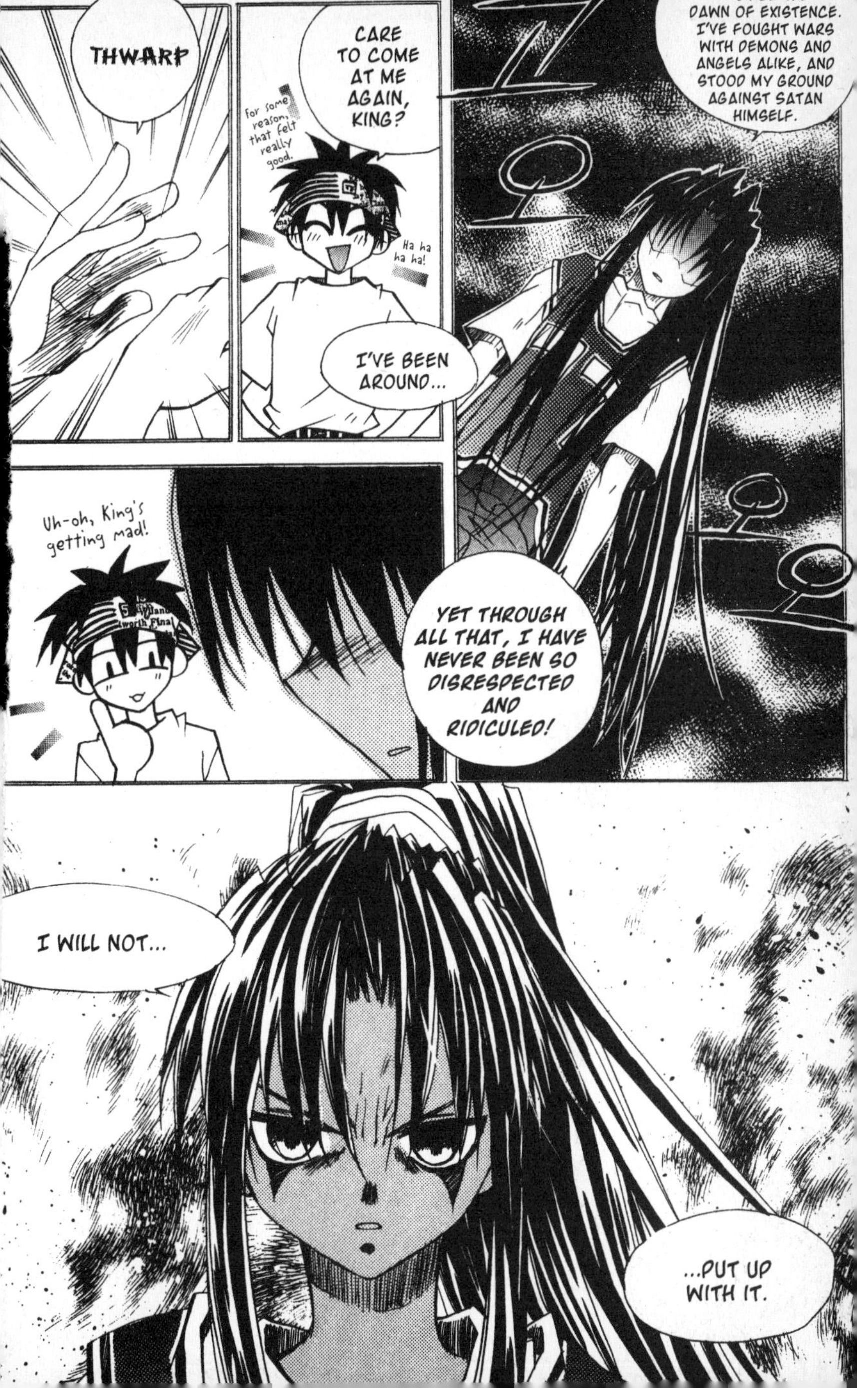
THWARP
CARE TO COME AT ME AGAIN, KING?
For some reason, that felt really good.
Ha ha ha ha!
I'VE BEEN AROUND...
...SINCE THE DAWN OF EXISTENCE. I'VE FOUGHT WARS WITH DEMONS AND ANGELS ALIKE, AND STOOD MY GROUND AGAINST SATAN HIMSELF.
Uh-oh, King's getting mad!
YET THROUGH ALL THAT, I HAVE NEVER BEEN SO DISRESPECTED AND RIDICULED!
I WILL NOT...
...PUT UP WITH IT.

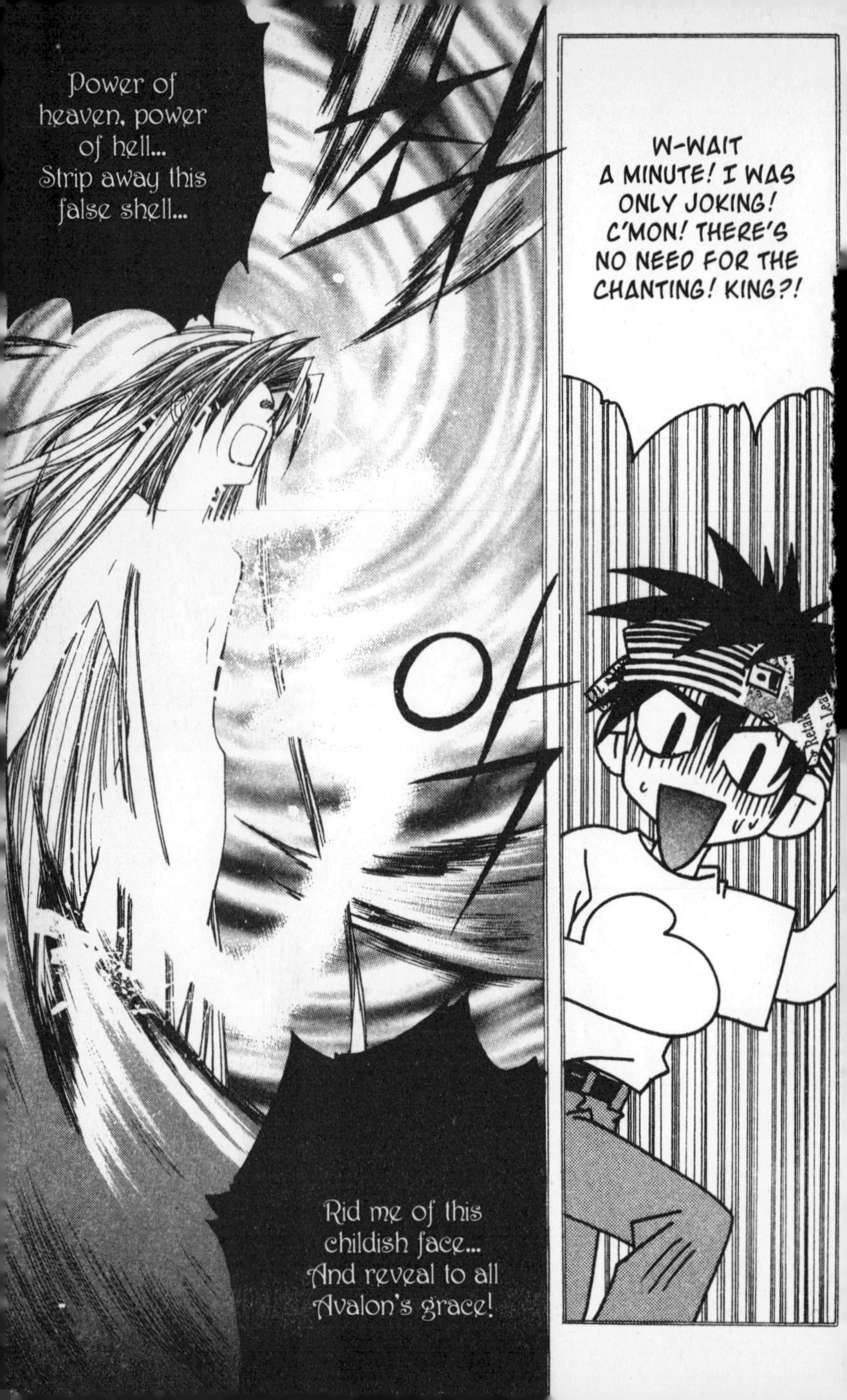

Power of heaven, power of hell... Strip away this false shell...
Rid me of this childish face... And reveal to all Avalon's grace!
W-WAIT A MINUTE! I WAS ONLY JOKING! C'MON! THERE'S NO NEED FOR THE CHANTING! KING?!

AND THERE YOU HAVE IT.

Ryang mouthed off to the king...

...and his highness went a little crazy. Can you blame him? ♡

And where did he get the clothes?

Oh, those! Just a little something I had laying around. Heh, heh...

MEDEA!!!

DAMN!

AH WASN'T PREPARED FOR THIS.

WITH THE KING POWERLESS, TAKIN' CARE OF RYANG WOULD'VE BEEN A SNAP.

COULD HE HAVE UPSET THE KING ON PURPOSE? AH WONDER...

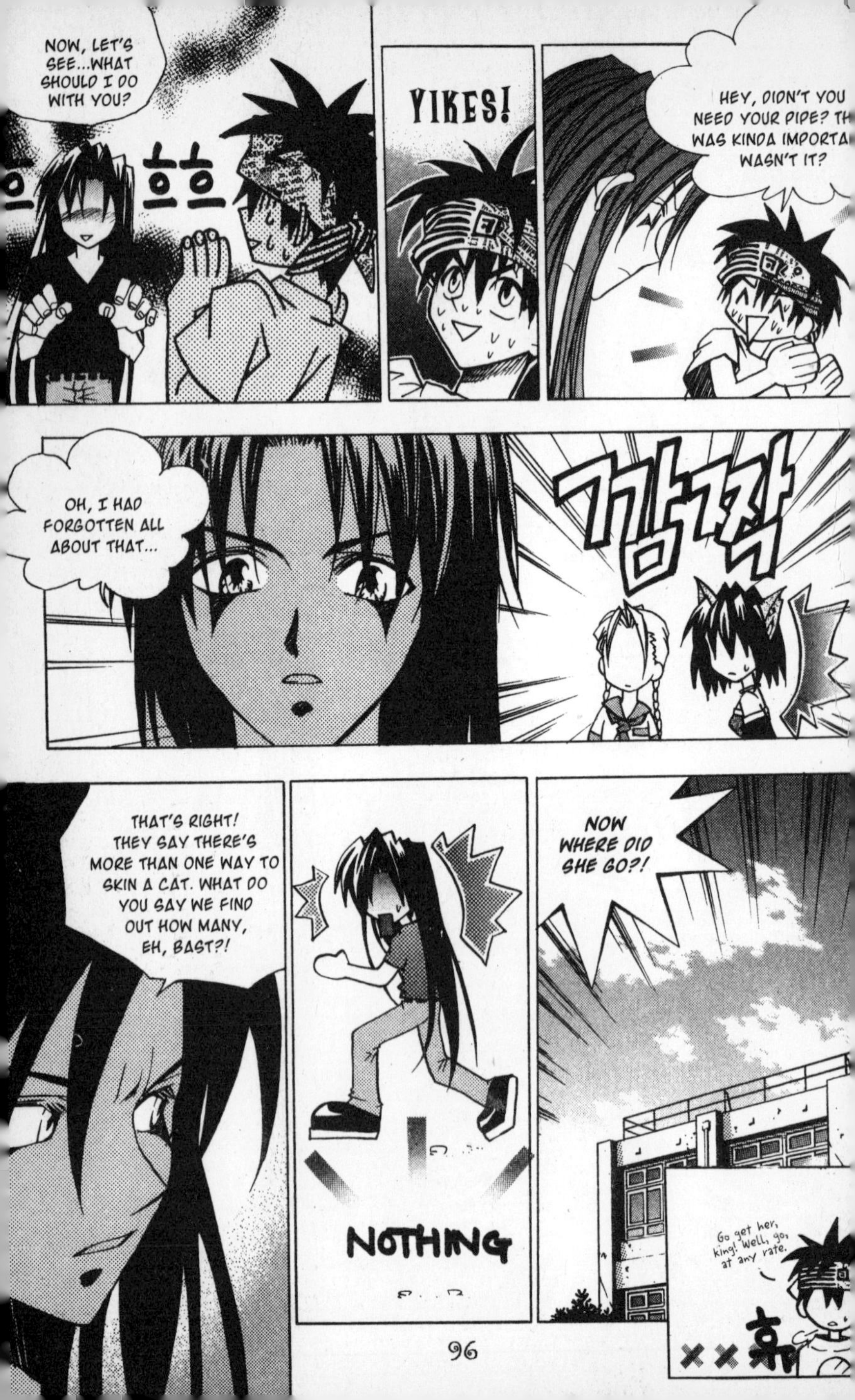
NOW, LET'S SEE...WHAT SHOULD I DO WITH YOU?
흐흐
YIKES!
HEY, DIDN'T YOU NEED YOUR PIPE? TH
WAS KINDA IMPORTA
WASN'T IT?
OH, I HAD FORGOTTEN ALL ABOUT THAT...
깜짝
THAT'S RIGHT! THEY SAY THERE'S MORE THAN ONE WAY TO SKIN A CAT. WHAT DO YOU SAY WE FIND OUT HOW MANY, EH, BAST?!
NOTHING
NOW WHERE DID SHE GO?!
Go get her, king! Well, go, at any rate.
휴

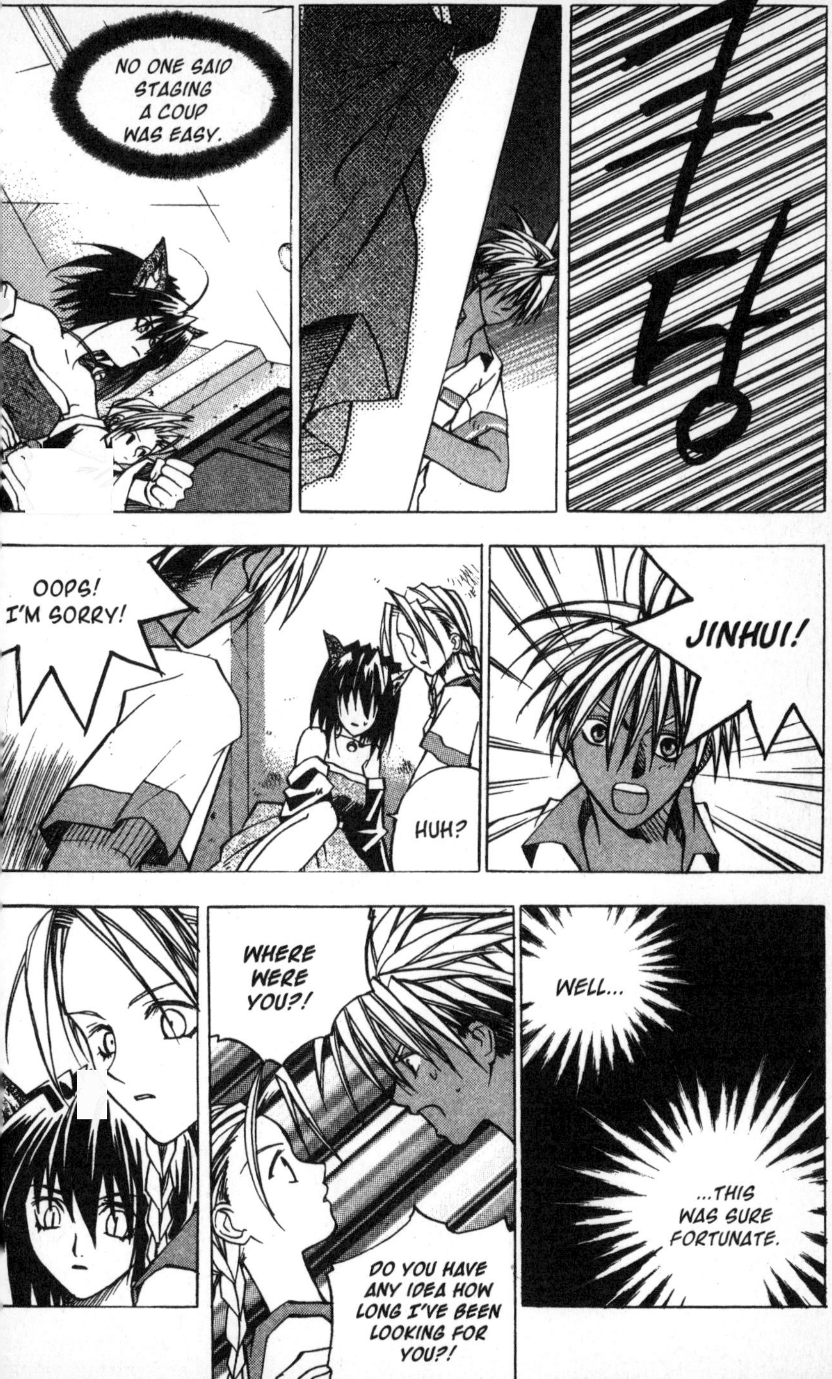
NO ONE SAID STAGING A COUP WAS EASY.
쿠당
OOPS! I'M SORRY!
HUH?
JINHUI!
WHERE WERE YOU?!
DO YOU HAVE ANY IDEA HOW LONG I'VE BEEN LOOKING FOR YOU?!
WELL...
...THIS WAS SURE FORTUNATE.

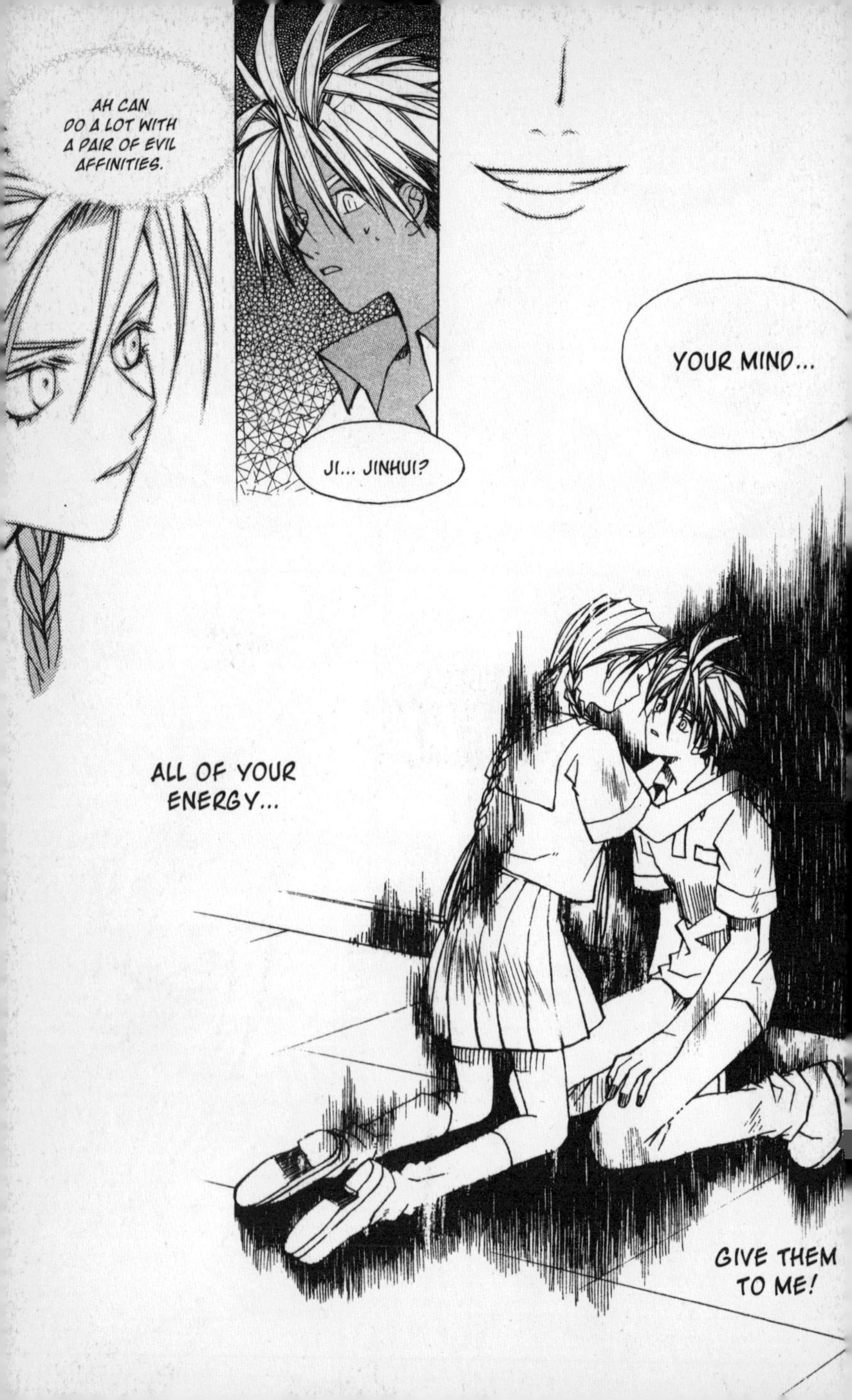
AH CAN DO A LOT WITH A PAIR OF EVIL AFFINITIES.
JI... JINHUI?
YOUR MIND...
ALL OF YOUR ENERGY...
GIVE THEM TO ME!

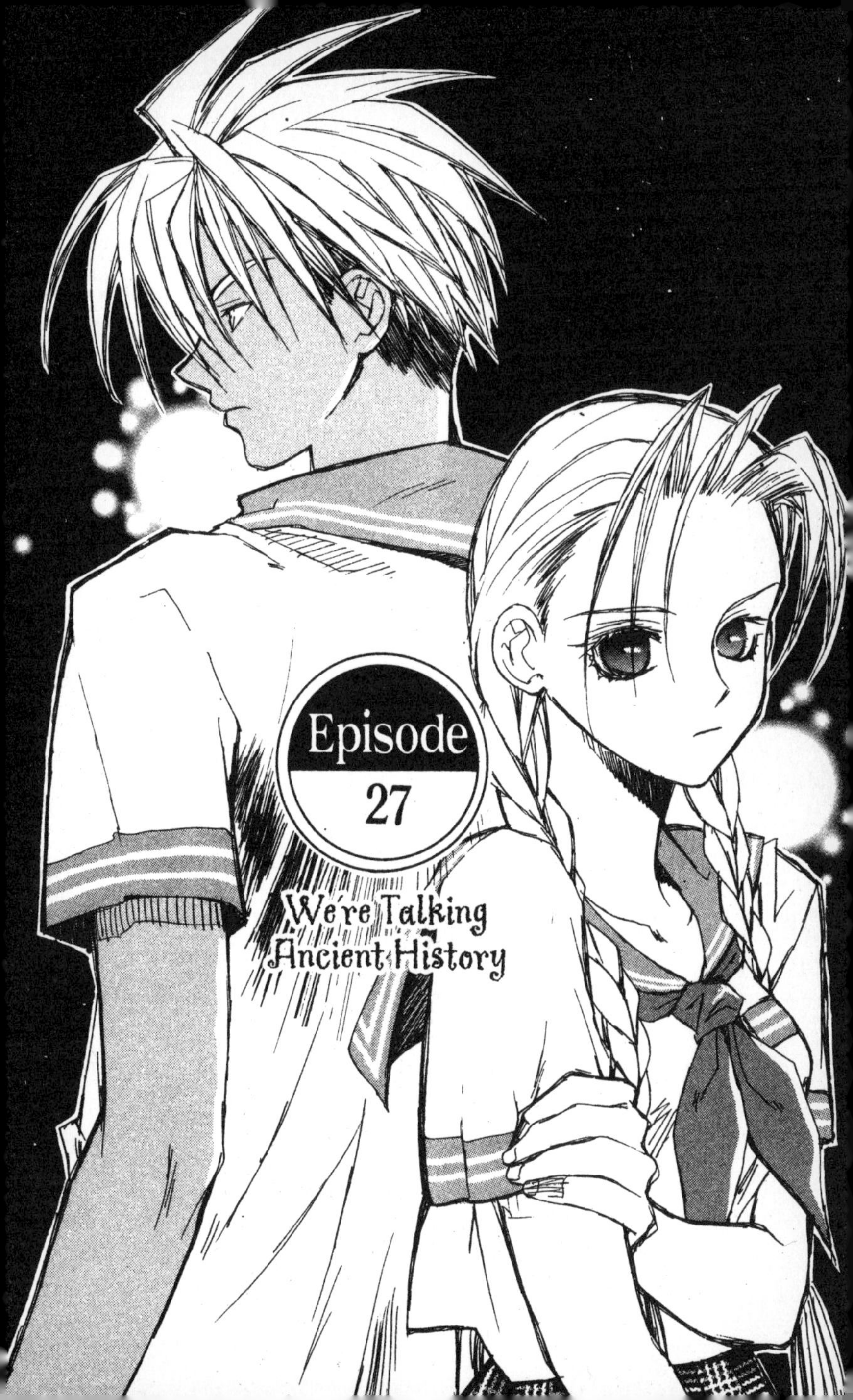
Episode
27
We're Talking
Ancient History

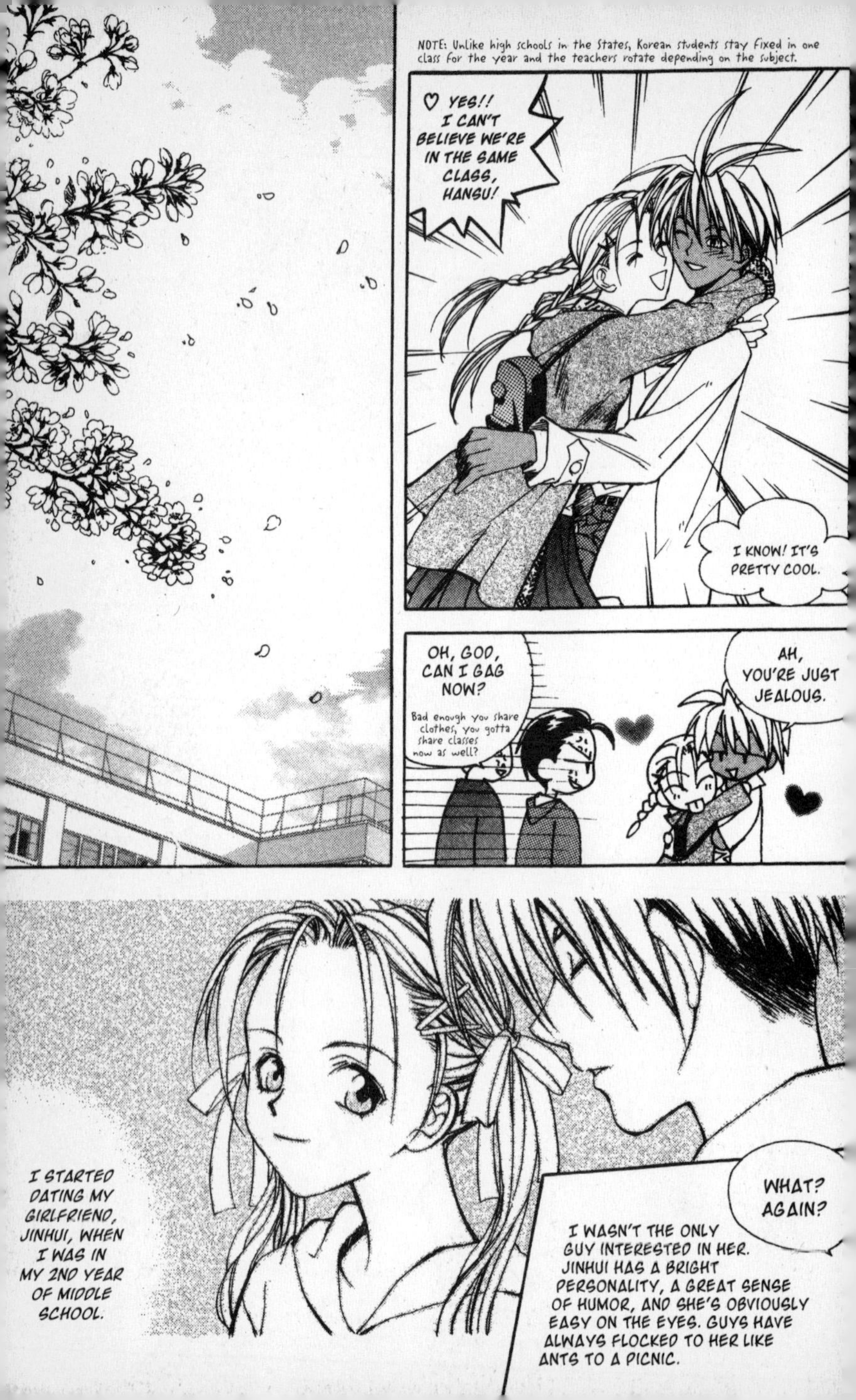
NOTE: Unlike high schools in the States, Korean students stay fixed in one class for the year and the teachers rotate depending on the subject.
♡ YES!! I CAN'T BELIEVE WE'RE IN THE SAME CLASS, HANSU!
I KNOW! IT'S PRETTY COOL.
OH, GOD, CAN I GAG NOW?
Bad enough you share clothes, you gotta share classes now as well?
AH, YOU'RE JUST JEALOUS.
I STARTED DATING MY GIRLFRIEND, JINHUI, WHEN I WAS IN MY 2ND YEAR OF MIDDLE SCHOOL.
WHAT? AGAIN?
I WASN'T THE ONLY GUY INTERESTED IN HER. JINHUI HAS A BRIGHT PERSONALITY, A GREAT SENSE OF HUMOR, AND SHE'S OBVIOUSLY EASY ON THE EYES. GUYS HAVE ALWAYS FLOCKED TO HER LIKE ANTS TO A PICNIC.

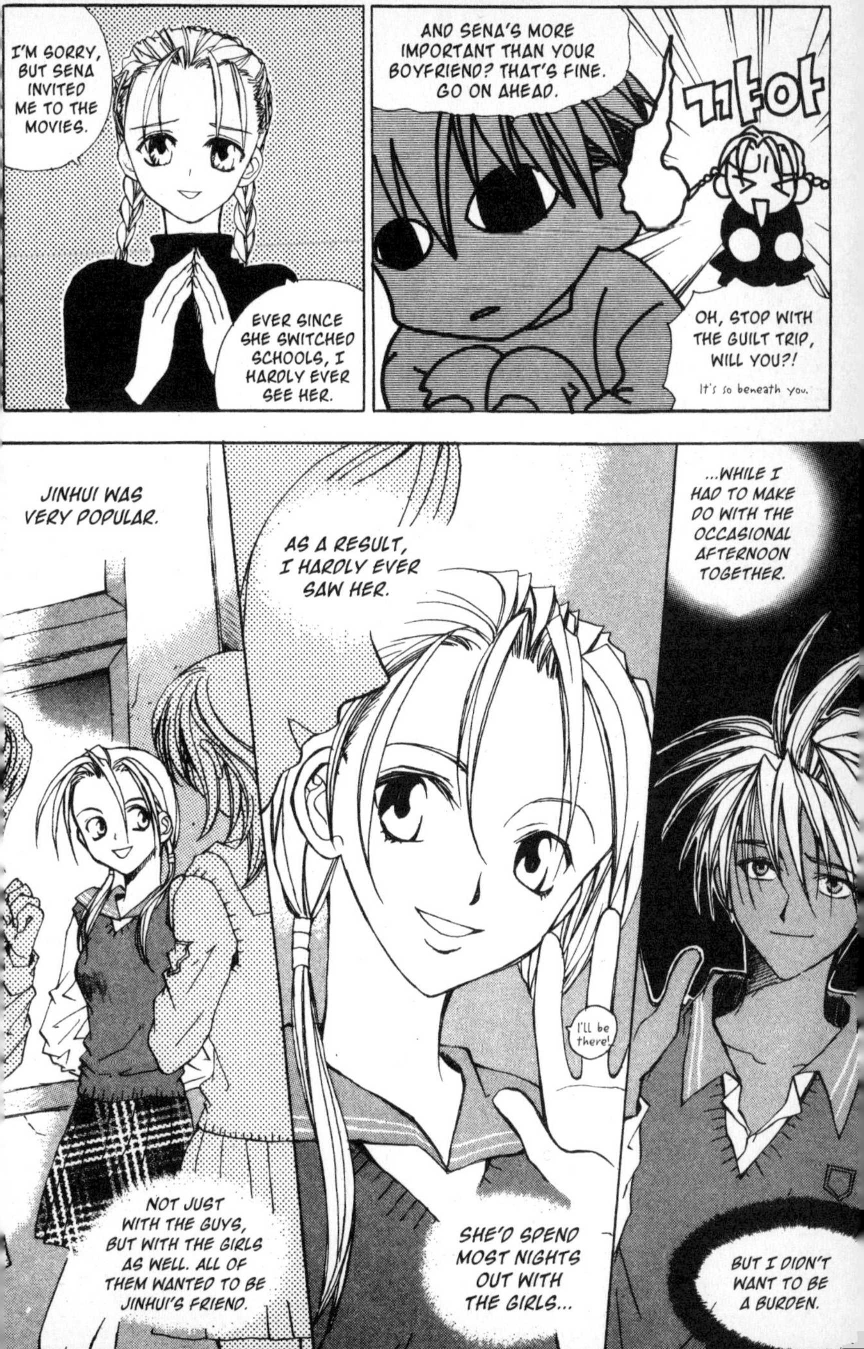
I'M SORRY, BUT SENA INVITED ME TO THE MOVIES.
EVER SINCE SHE SWITCHED SCHOOLS, I HARDLY EVER SEE HER.
AND SENA'S MORE IMPORTANT THAN YOUR BOYFRIEND? THAT'S FINE. GO ON AHEAD.
까아
OH, STOP WITH THE GUILT TRIP, WILL YOU?!
It's so beneath you.
JINHUI WAS VERY POPULAR.
NOT JUST WITH THE GUYS, BUT WITH THE GIRLS AS WELL. ALL OF THEM WANTED TO BE JINHUI'S FRIEND.
AS A RESULT, I HARDLY EVER SAW HER.
I'll be there!
SHE'D SPEND MOST NIGHTS OUT WITH THE GIRLS...
...WHILE I HAD TO MAKE DO WITH THE OCCASIONAL AFTERNOON TOGETHER.
BUT I DIDN'T WANT TO BE A BURDEN.

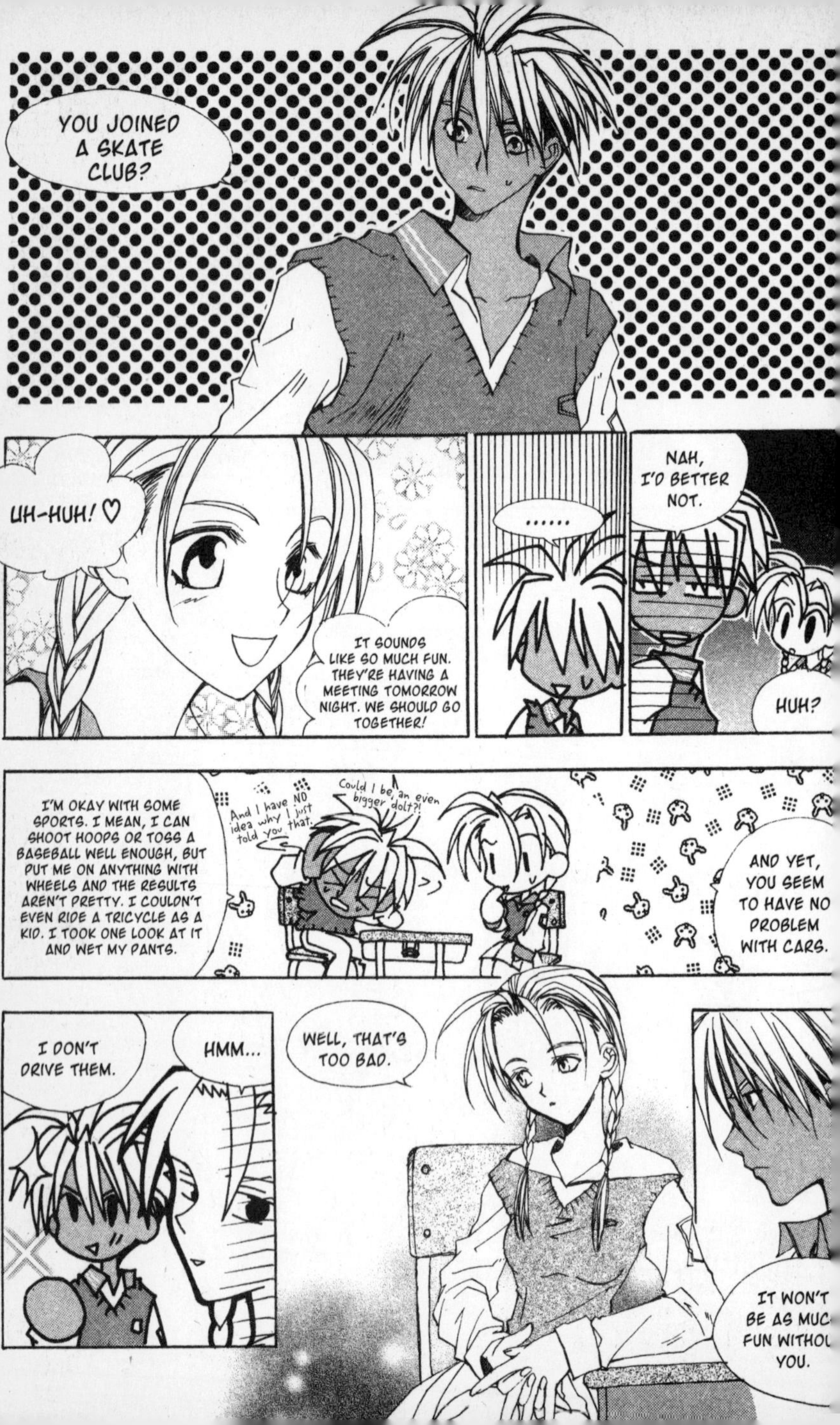
YOU JOINED A SKATE CLUB?
UH-HUH! ♡
IT SOUNDS LIKE SO MUCH FUN. THEY'RE HAVING A MEETING TOMORROW NIGHT. WE SHOULD GO TOGETHER!
......
NAH, I'D BETTER NOT.
HUH?
I'M OKAY WITH SOME SPORTS. I MEAN, I CAN SHOOT HOOPS OR TOSS A BASEBALL WELL ENOUGH, BUT PUT ME ON ANYTHING WITH WHEELS AND THE RESULTS AREN'T PRETTY. I COULDN'T EVEN RIDE A TRICYCLE AS A KID. I TOOK ONE LOOK AT IT AND WET MY PANTS.
And I have NO idea why I just told YOU that.
Could I be an even bigger dolt?!
AND YET, YOU SEEM TO HAVE NO PROBLEM WITH CARS.
I DON'T DRIVE THEM.
HMM...
WELL, THAT'S TOO BAD.
IT WON'T BE AS MUC- FUN WITHOU YOU.

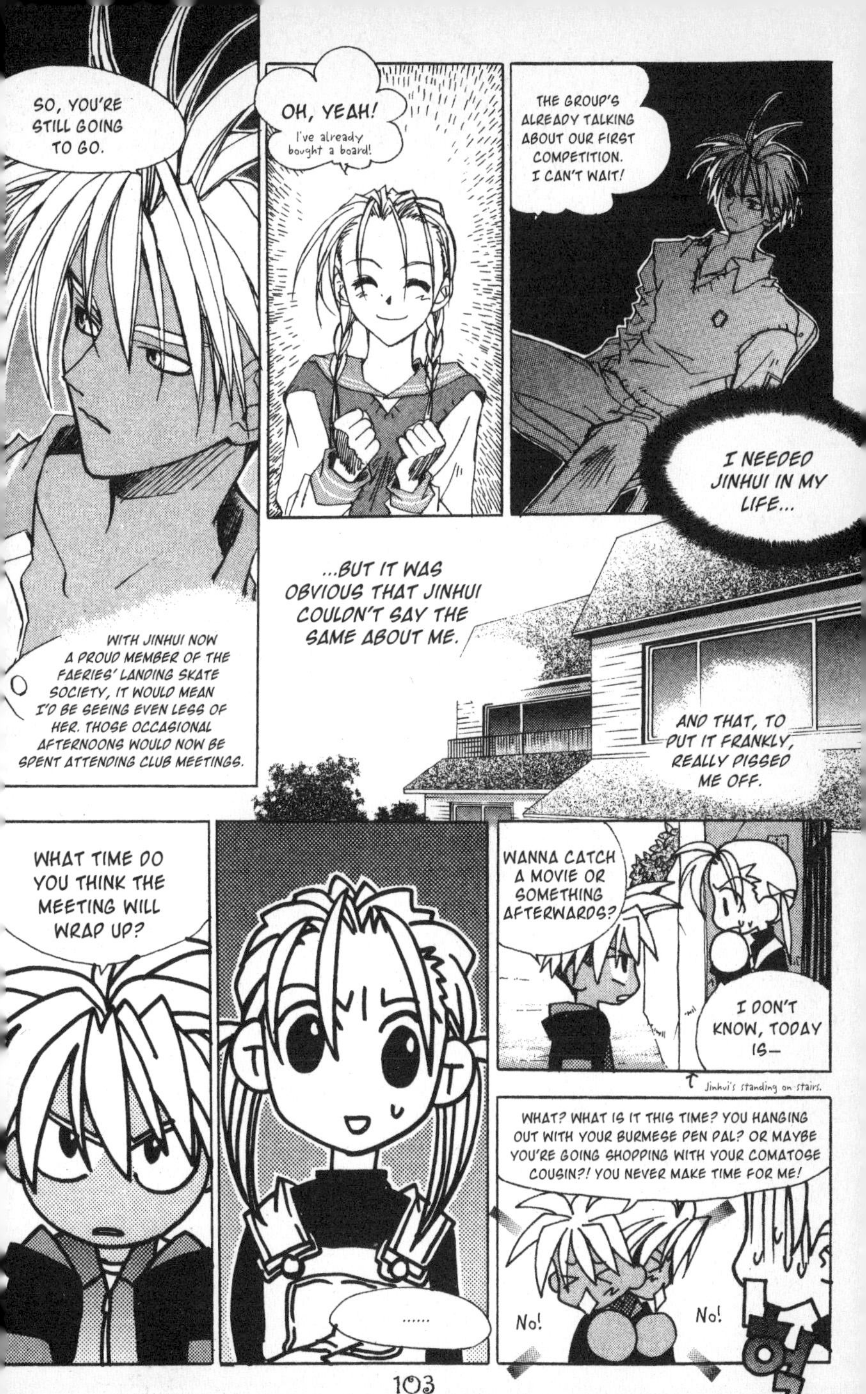
SO, YOU'RE STILL GOING TO GO.
WITH JINHUI NOW A PROUD MEMBER OF THE FAERIES' LANDING SKATE SOCIETY, IT WOULD MEAN I'D BE SEEING EVEN LESS OF HER. THOSE OCCASIONAL AFTERNOONS WOULD NOW BE SPENT ATTENDING CLUB MEETINGS.
OH, YEAH!
I've already bought a board!
THE GROUP'S ALREADY TALKING ABOUT OUR FIRST COMPETITION. I CAN'T WAIT!
I NEEDED JINHUI IN MY LIFE...
...BUT IT WAS OBVIOUS THAT JINHUI COULDN'T SAY THE SAME ABOUT ME.
AND THAT, TO PUT IT FRANKLY, REALLY PISSED ME OFF.
WHAT TIME DO YOU THINK THE MEETING WILL WRAP UP?
......
WANNA CATCH A MOVIE OR SOMETHING AFTERWARDS?
I DON'T KNOW, TODAY IS—
Jinhui's standing on stairs.
WHAT? WHAT IS IT THIS TIME? YOU HANGING OUT WITH YOUR BURMESE PEN PAL? OR MAYBE YOU'RE GOING SHOPPING WITH YOUR COMATOSE COUSIN?! YOU NEVER MAKE TIME FOR ME!
No!
No!

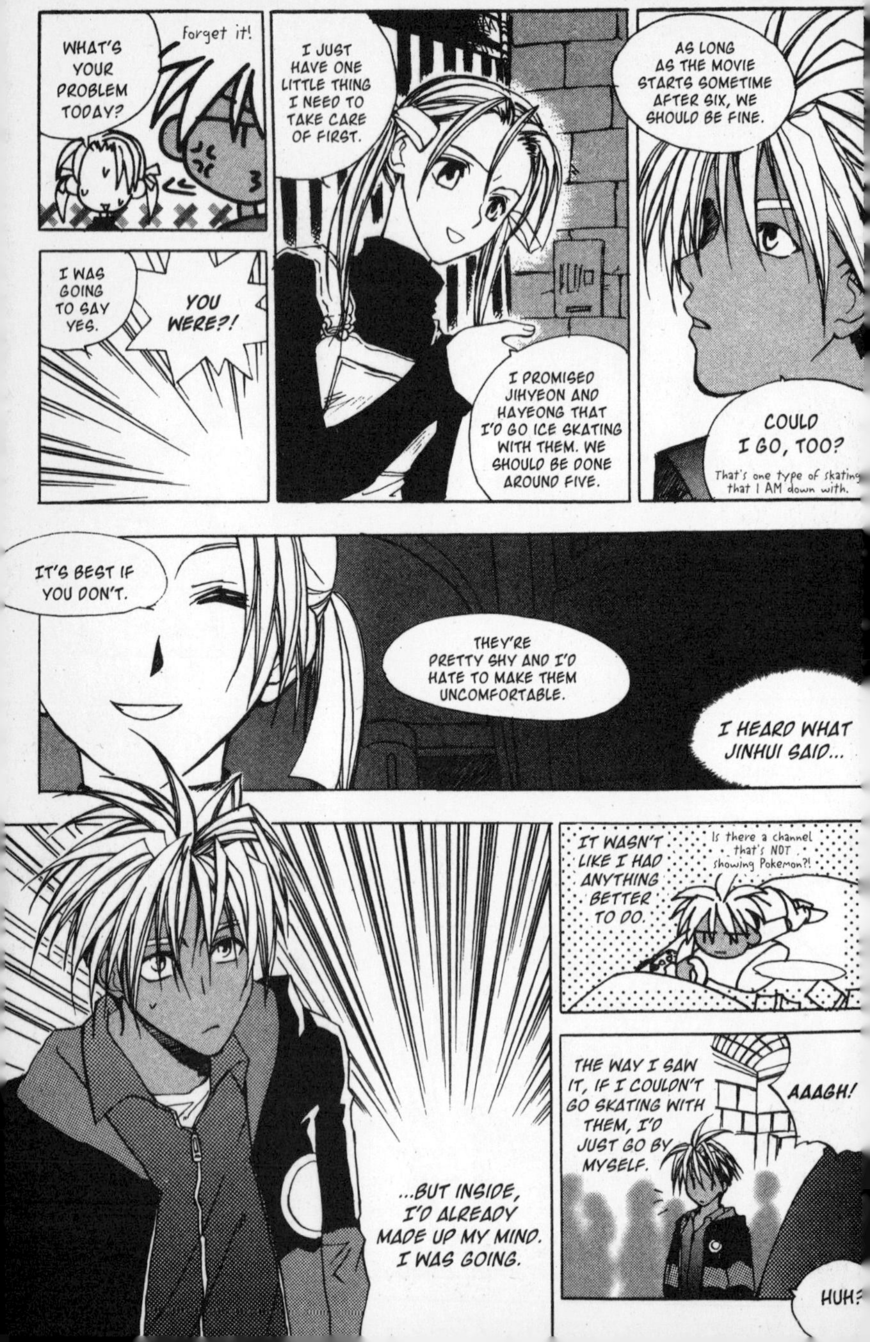
WHAT'S YOUR PROBLEM TODAY?
Forget it!
I WAS GOING TO SAY YES.
YOU WERE?!
I JUST HAVE ONE LITTLE THING I NEED TO TAKE CARE OF FIRST.
I PROMISED JIHYEON AND HAYEONG THAT I'D GO ICE SKATING WITH THEM. WE SHOULD BE DONE AROUND FIVE.
AS LONG AS THE MOVIE STARTS SOMETIME AFTER SIX, WE SHOULD BE FINE.
COULD I GO, TOO?
That's one type of skating that I AM down with.
IT'S BEST IF YOU DON'T.
THEY'RE PRETTY SHY AND I'D HATE TO MAKE THEM UNCOMFORTABLE.
I HEARD WHAT JINHUI SAID...
...BUT INSIDE, I'D ALREADY MADE UP MY MIND. I WAS GOING.
IT WASN'T LIKE I HAD ANYTHING BETTER TO DO.
Is there a channel that's NOT showing Pokemon?!
THE WAY I SAW IT, IF I COULDN'T GO SKATING WITH THEM, I'D JUST GO BY MYSELF.
AAAGH!
HUH?

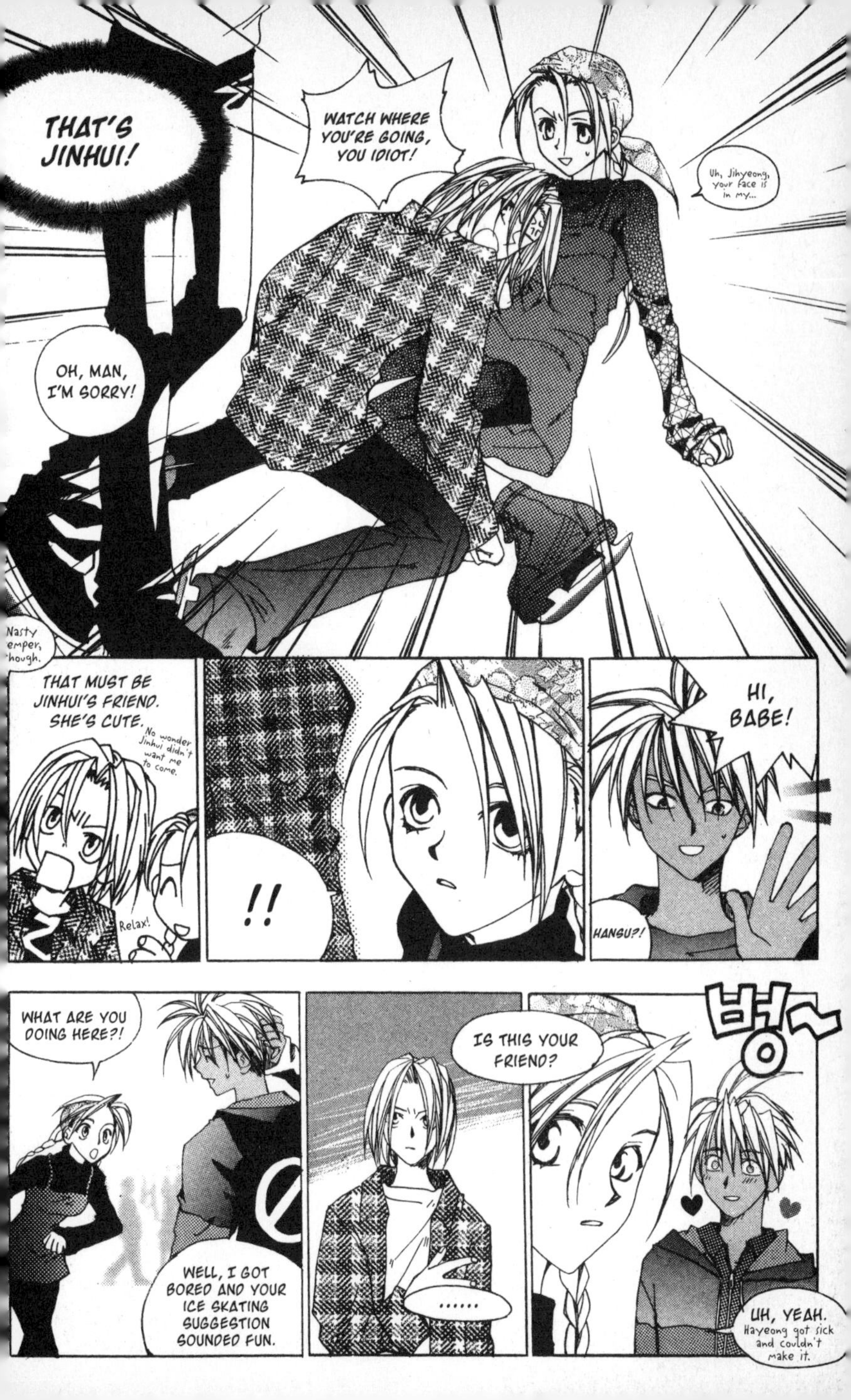

THAT'S JINHUI!
WATCH WHERE YOU'RE GOING, YOU IDIOT!
Uh, Jihyeong, your face is in my...
OH, MAN, I'M SORRY!
Nasty temper, though.
THAT MUST BE JINHUI'S FRIEND. SHE'S CUTE.
No wonder Jinhui didn't want me to come.
Relax!
!!
HI, BABE!
HANSU?!
WHAT ARE YOU DOING HERE?!
WELL, I GOT BORED AND YOUR ICE SKATING SUGGESTION SOUNDED FUN.
......
IS THIS YOUR FRIEND?
벙~
UH, YEAH. Hayeong got sick and couldn't make it.

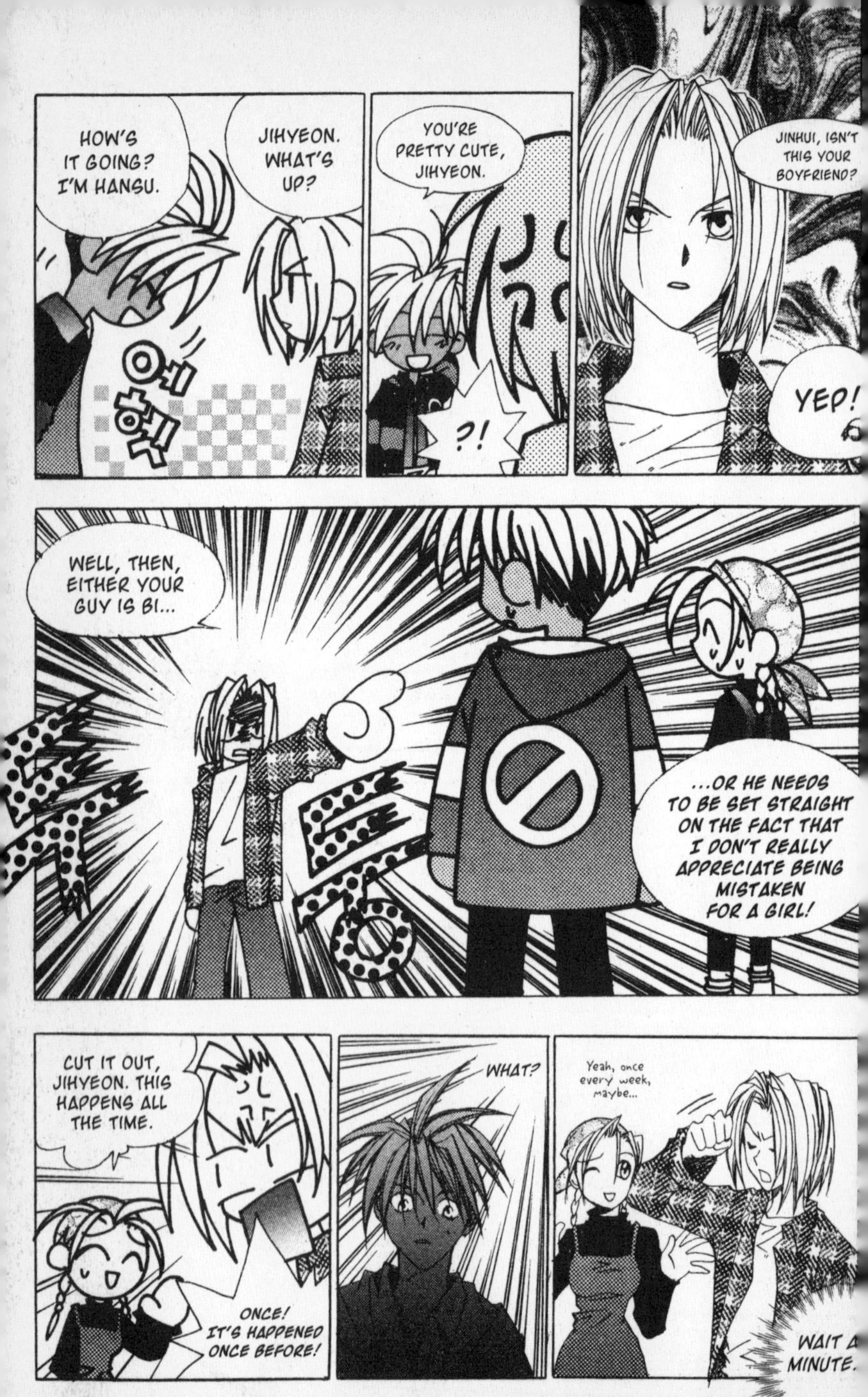
HOW'S IT GOING? I'M HANSU.
JIHYEON. WHAT'S UP?
YOU'RE PRETTY CUTE, JIHYEON.
?!
JINHUI, ISN'T THIS YOUR BOYFRIEND?
YEP!
WELL, THEN, EITHER YOUR GUY IS BI...
...OR HE NEEDS TO BE SET STRAIGHT ON THE FACT THAT I DON'T REALLY APPRECIATE BEING MISTAKEN FOR A GIRL!
CUT IT OUT, JIHYEON. THIS HAPPENS ALL THE TIME.
ONCE! IT'S HAPPENED ONCE BEFORE!
WHAT?
Yeah, once every week, maybe...
WAIT A MINUTE.

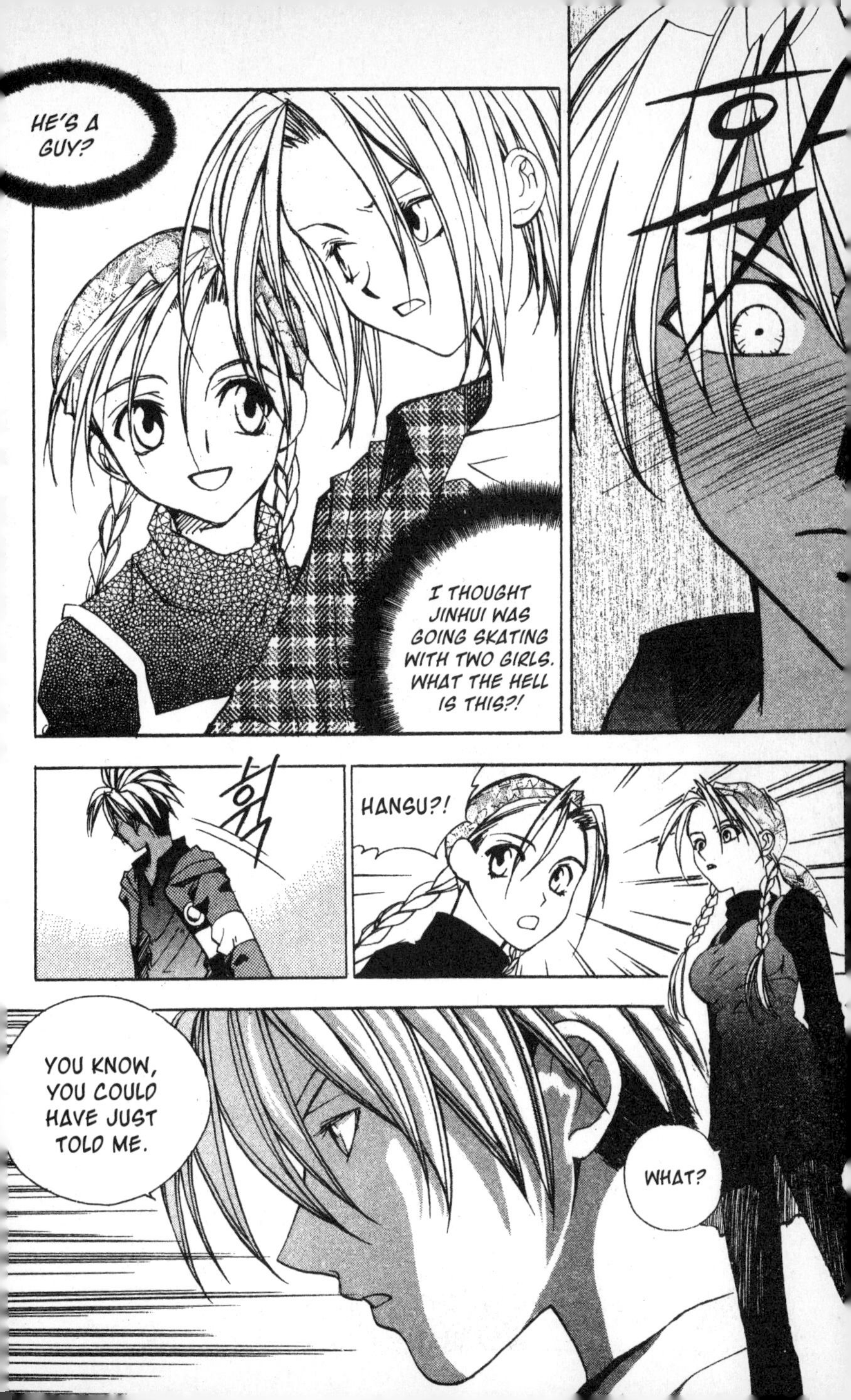
HE'S A GUY?
I THOUGHT JINHUI WAS GOING SKATING WITH TWO GIRLS. WHAT THE HELL IS THIS?!
HANSU?!
YOU KNOW, YOU COULD HAVE JUST TOLD ME.
WHAT?

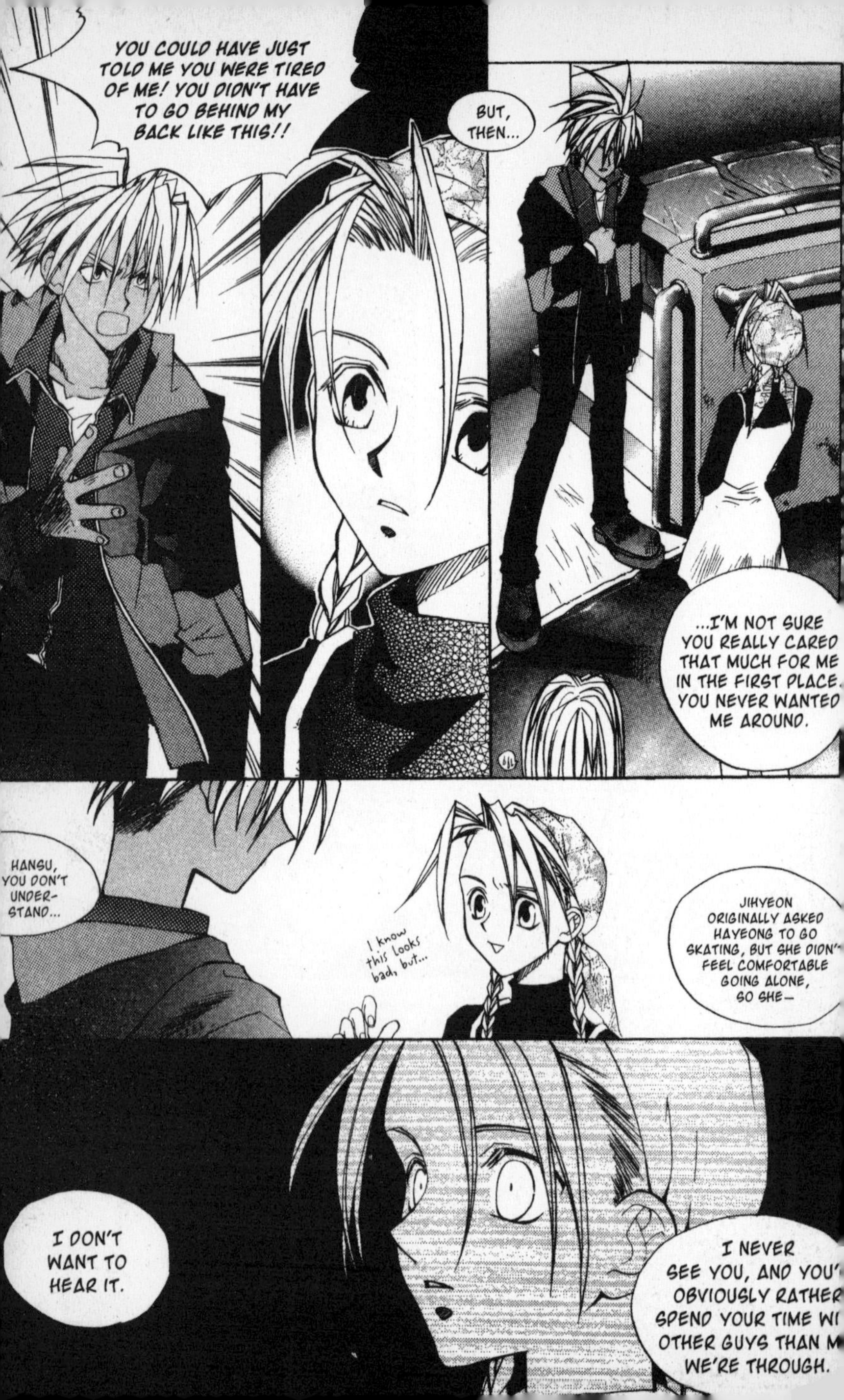
YOU COULD HAVE JUST TOLD ME YOU WERE TIRED OF ME! YOU DIDN'T HAVE TO GO BEHIND MY BACK LIKE THIS!!
BUT, THEN...
...I'M NOT SURE YOU REALLY CARED THAT MUCH FOR ME IN THE FIRST PLACE. YOU NEVER WANTED ME AROUND.
HANSU, YOU DON'T UNDER-STAND...
I know this looks bad, but...
JIHYEON ORIGINALLY ASKED HAYEONG TO GO SKATING, BUT SHE DIDN' FEEL COMFORTABLE GOING ALONE, SO SHE—
I DON'T WANT TO HEAR IT.
I NEVER SEE YOU, AND YOU' OBVIOUSLY RATHER SPEND YOUR TIME WI OTHER GUYS THAN M WE'RE THROUGH.

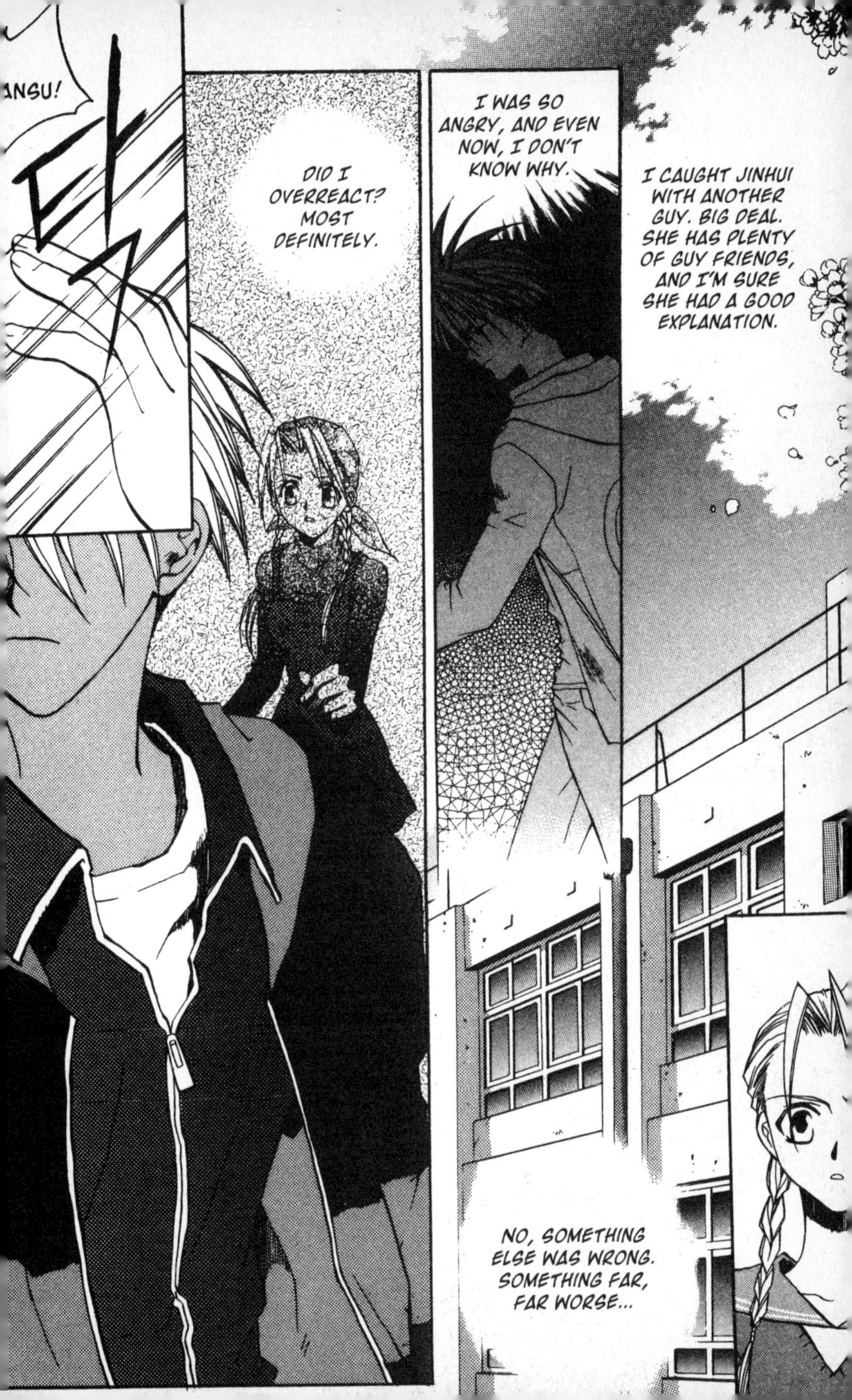

ANSU!
DID I OVERREACT? MOST DEFINITELY.
I WAS SO ANGRY, AND EVEN NOW, I DON'T KNOW WHY.
I CAUGHT JINHUI WITH ANOTHER GUY. BIG DEAL. SHE HAS PLENTY OF GUY FRIENDS, AND I'M SURE SHE HAD A GOOD EXPLANATION.
NO, SOMETHING ELSE WAS WRONG. SOMETHING FAR, FAR WORSE...

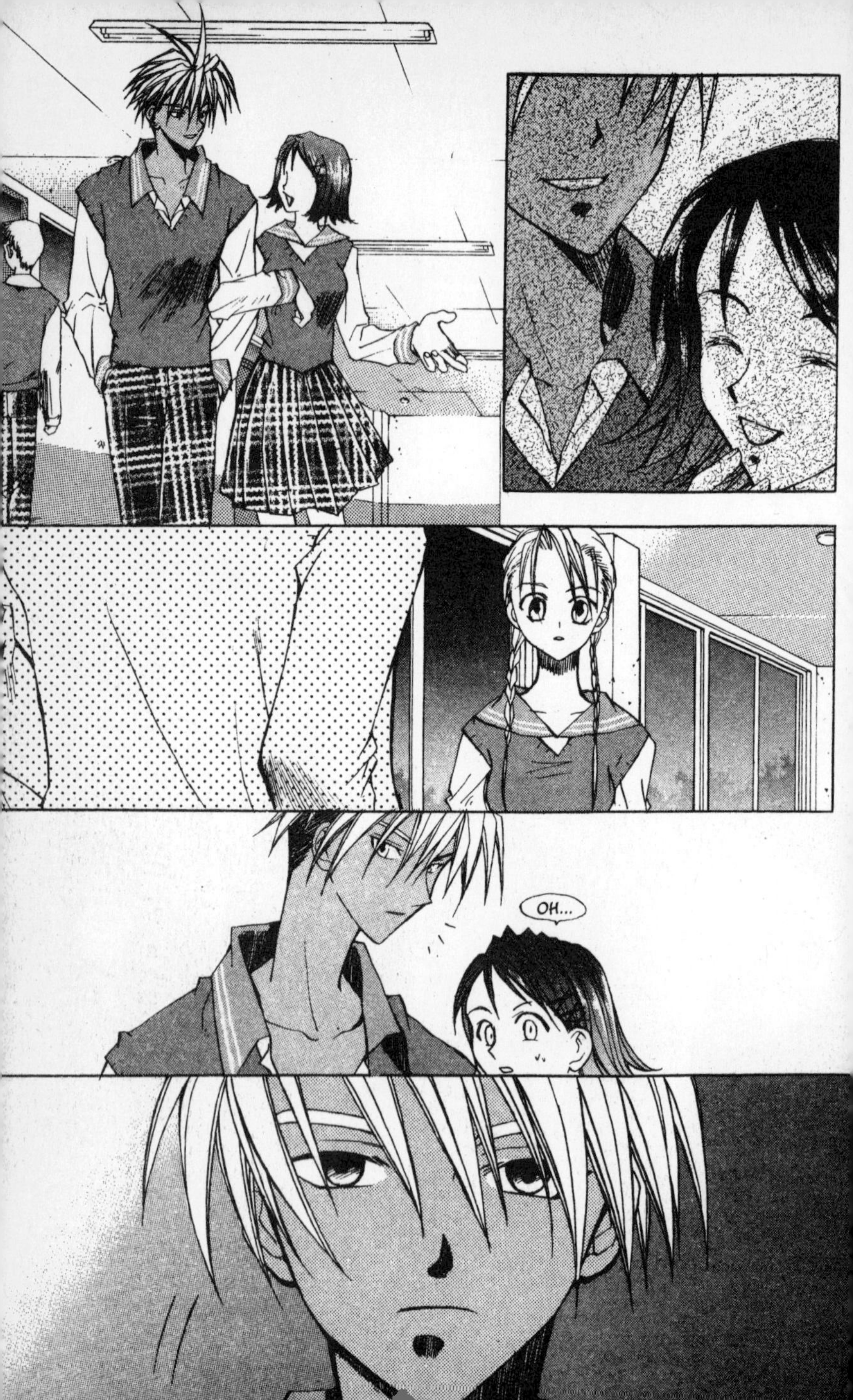
OH...

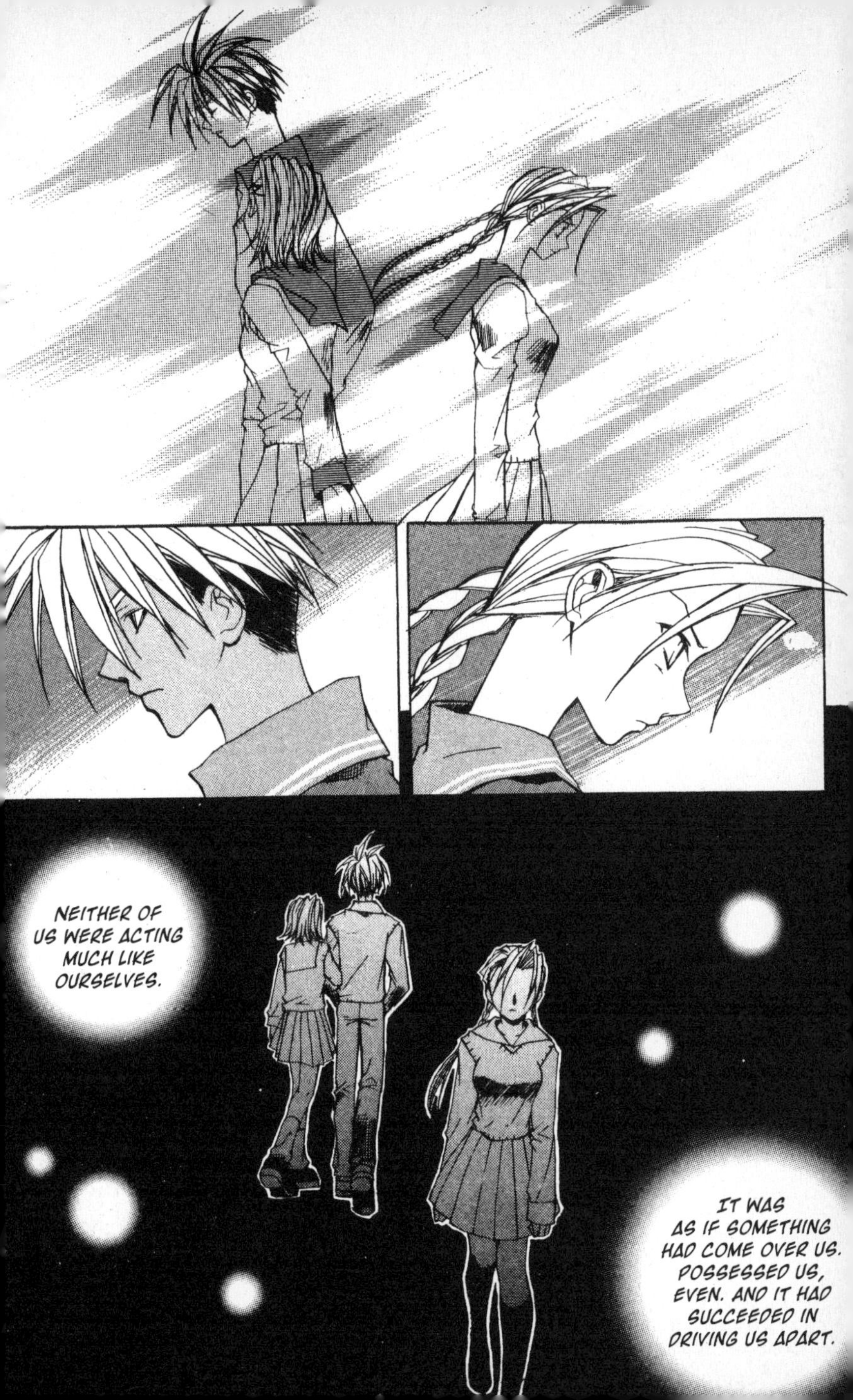

NEITHER OF US WERE ACTING MUCH LIKE OURSELVES.
IT WAS AS IF SOMETHING HAD COME OVER US. POSSESSED US, EVEN. AND IT HAD SUCCEEDED IN DRIVING US APART.

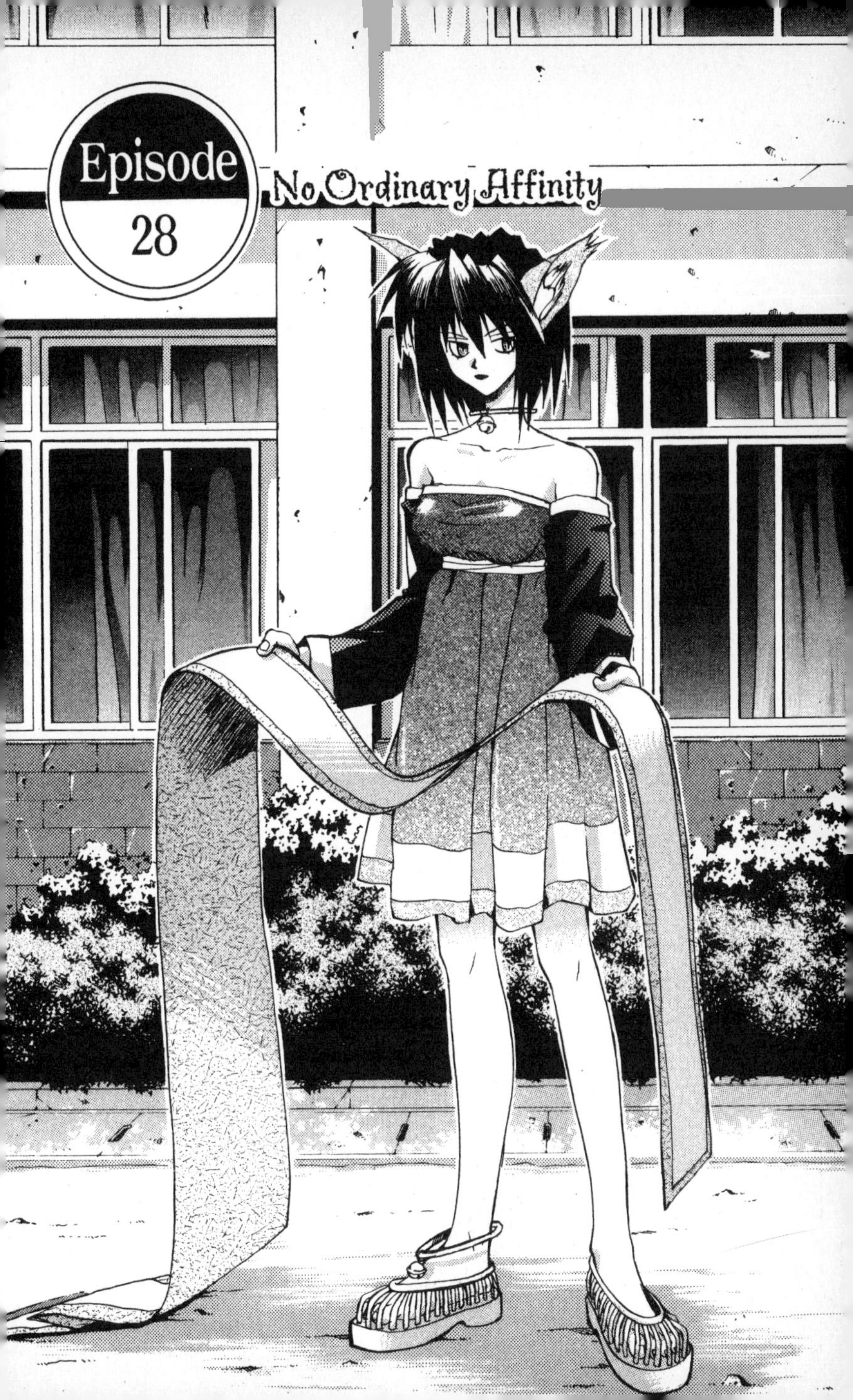
Episode
28
No Ordinary Affinity

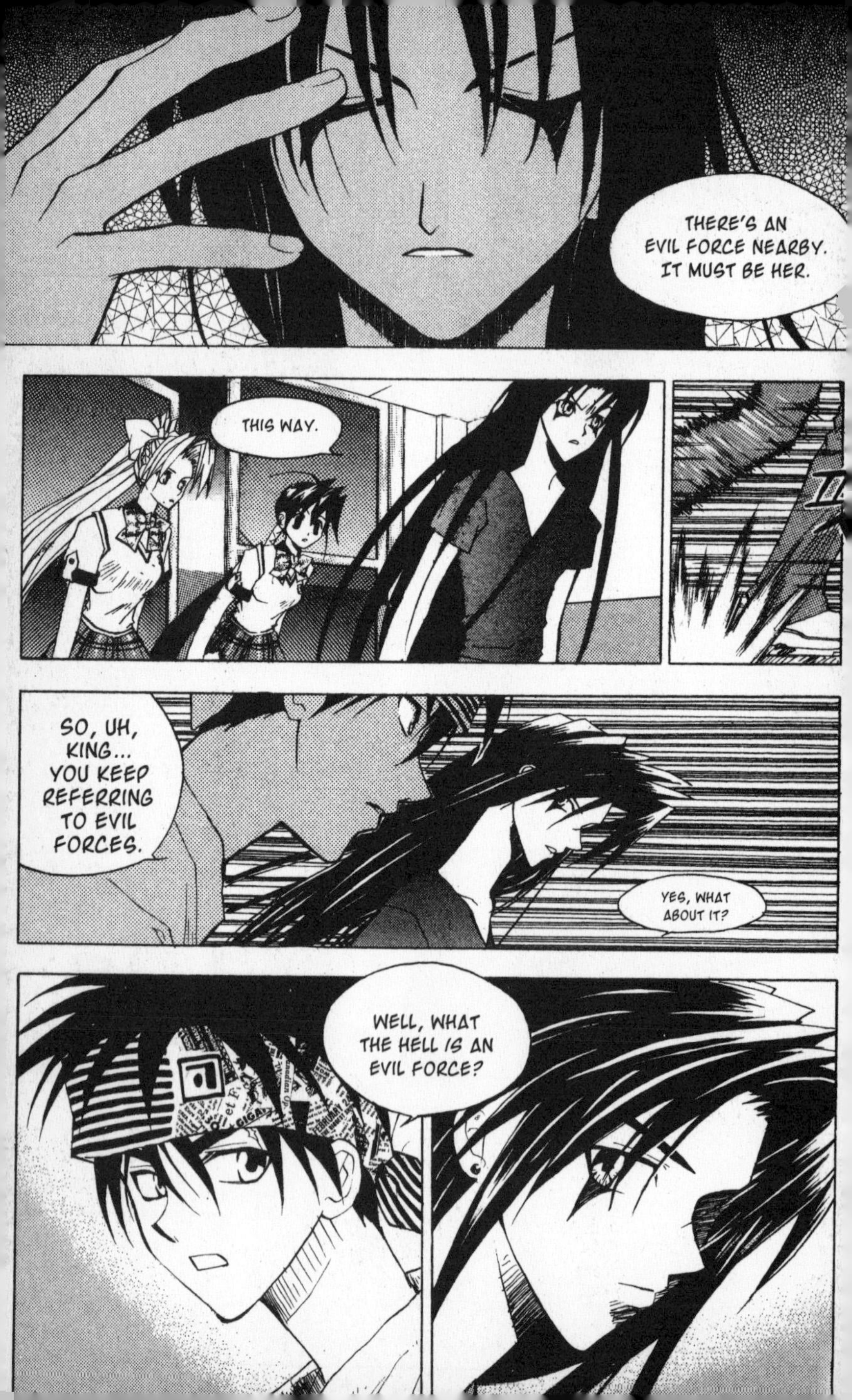
THERE'S AN EVIL FORCE NEARBY. IT MUST BE HER.
THIS WAY.
SO, UH, KING... YOU KEEP REFERRING TO EVIL FORCES.
YES, WHAT ABOUT IT?
WELL, WHAT THE HELL IS AN EVIL FORCE?

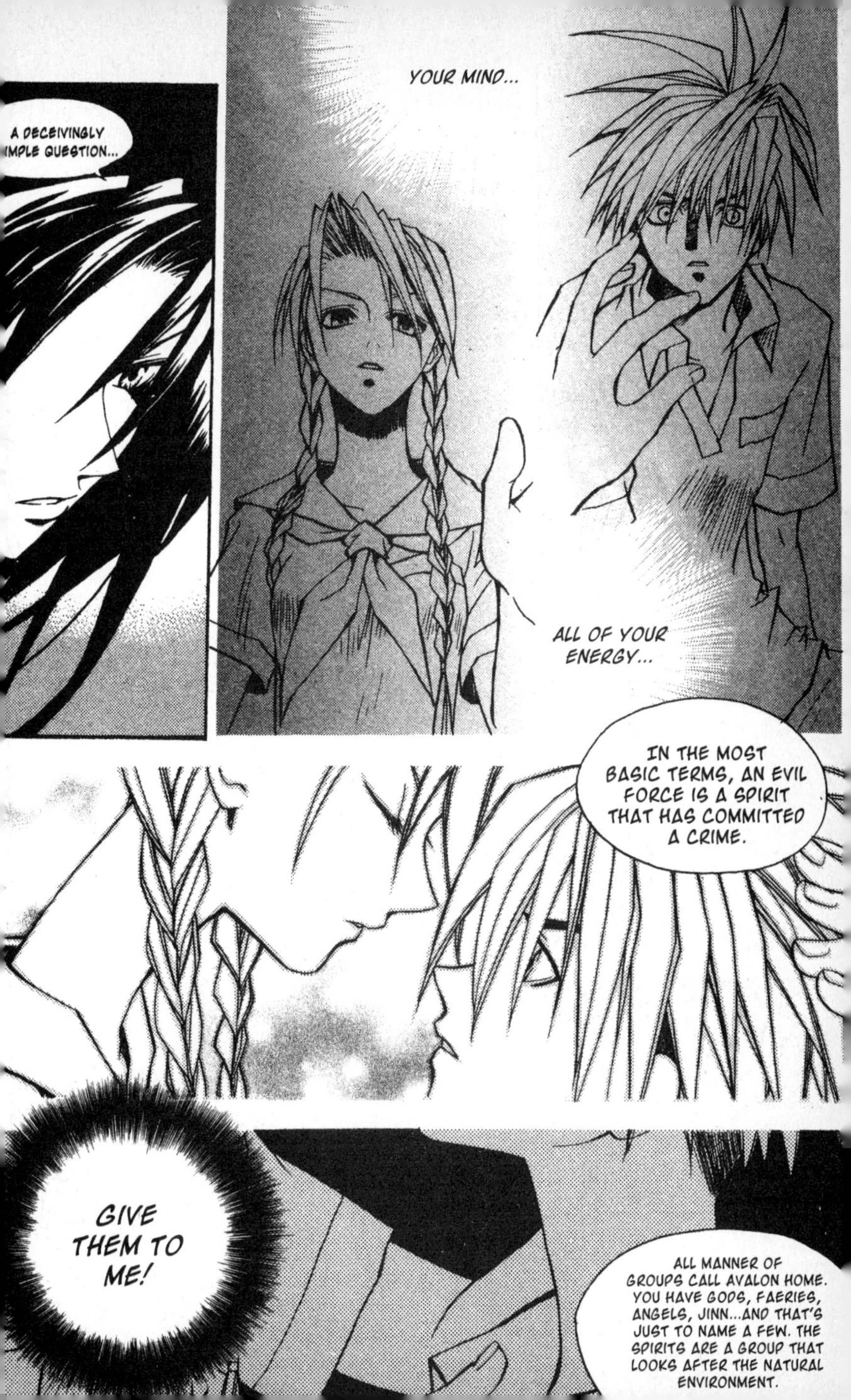
A DECEIVINGLY
IMPLE QUESTION...
YOUR MIND...
ALL OF YOUR ENERGY...
IN THE MOST BASIC TERMS, AN EVIL FORCE IS A SPIRIT THAT HAS COMMITTED A CRIME.
GIVE THEM TO ME!
ALL MANNER OF GROUPS CALL AVALON HOME. YOU HAVE GODS, FAERIES, ANGELS, JINN...AND THAT'S JUST TO NAME A FEW. THE SPIRITS ARE A GROUP THAT LOOKS AFTER THE NATURAL ENVIRONMENT.

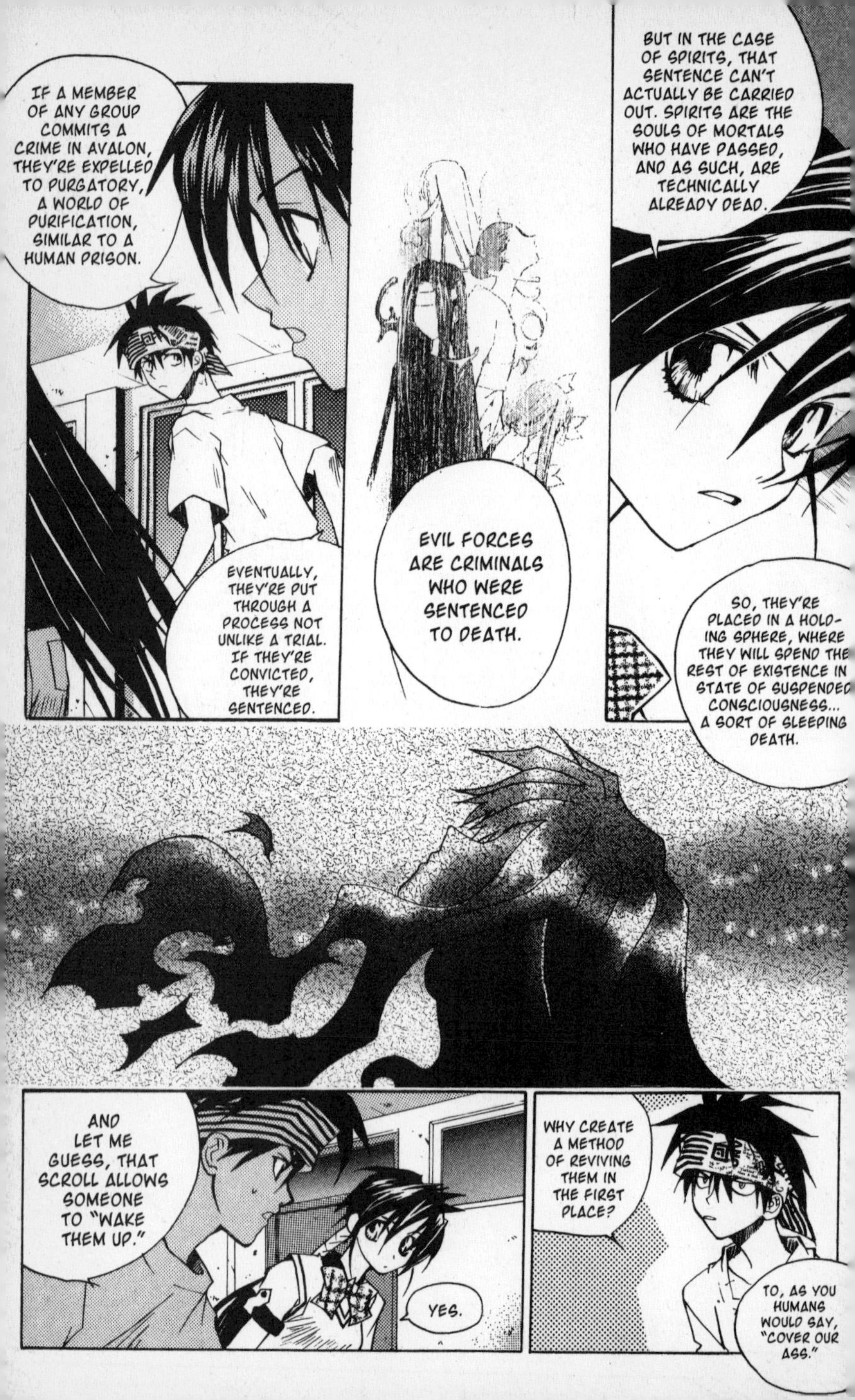
IF A MEMBER OF ANY GROUP COMMITS A CRIME IN AVALON, THEY'RE EXPELLED TO PURGATORY, A WORLD OF PURIFICATION, SIMILAR TO A HUMAN PRISON.
EVENTUALLY, THEY'RE PUT THROUGH A PROCESS NOT UNLIKE A TRIAL. IF THEY'RE CONVICTED, THEY'RE SENTENCED.
EVIL FORCES ARE CRIMINALS WHO WERE SENTENCED TO DEATH.
BUT IN THE CASE OF SPIRITS, THAT SENTENCE CAN'T ACTUALLY BE CARRIED OUT. SPIRITS ARE THE SOULS OF MORTALS WHO HAVE PASSED, AND AS SUCH, ARE TECHNICALLY ALREADY DEAD.
SO, THEY'RE PLACED IN A HOLDING SPHERE, WHERE THEY WILL SPEND THE REST OF EXISTENCE IN STATE OF SUSPENDED CONSCIOUSNESS... A SORT OF SLEEPING DEATH.
AND LET ME GUESS, THAT SCROLL ALLOWS SOMEONE TO "WAKE THEM UP."
YES.
WHY CREATE A METHOD OF REVIVING THEM IN THE FIRST PLACE?
TO, AS YOU HUMANS WOULD SAY, "COVER OUR ASS."

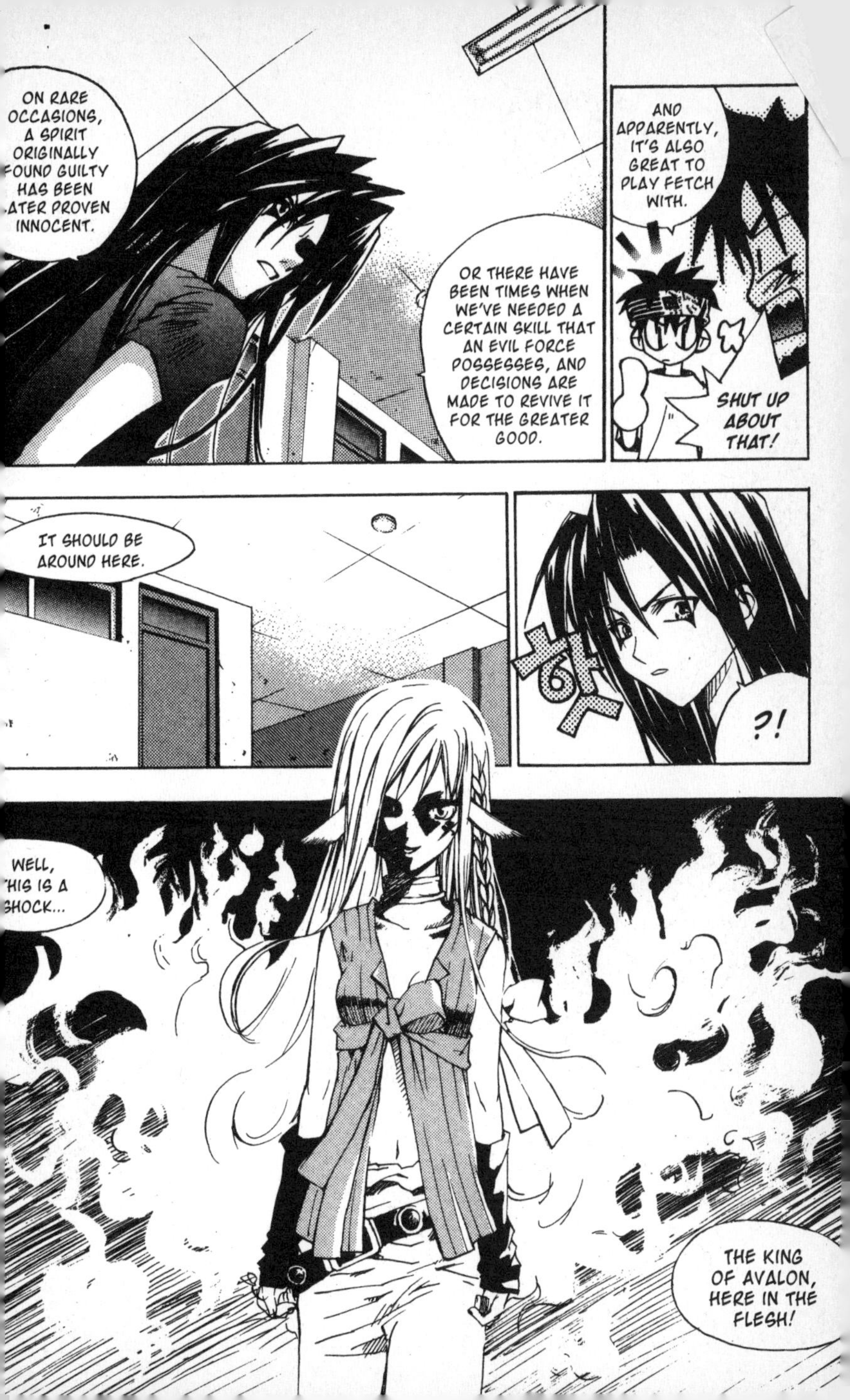
ON RARE OCCASIONS, A SPIRIT ORIGINALLY FOUND GUILTY HAS BEEN ATER PROVEN INNOCENT.
OR THERE HAVE BEEN TIMES WHEN WE'VE NEEDED A CERTAIN SKILL THAT AN EVIL FORCE POSSESSES, AND DECISIONS ARE MADE TO REVIVE IT FOR THE GREATER GOOD.
AND APPARENTLY, IT'S ALSO GREAT TO PLAY FETCH WITH.
SHUT UP ABOUT THAT!
IT SHOULD BE AROUND HERE.
?!
WELL, HIS IS A HOCK...
THE KING OF AVALON, HERE IN THE FLESH!

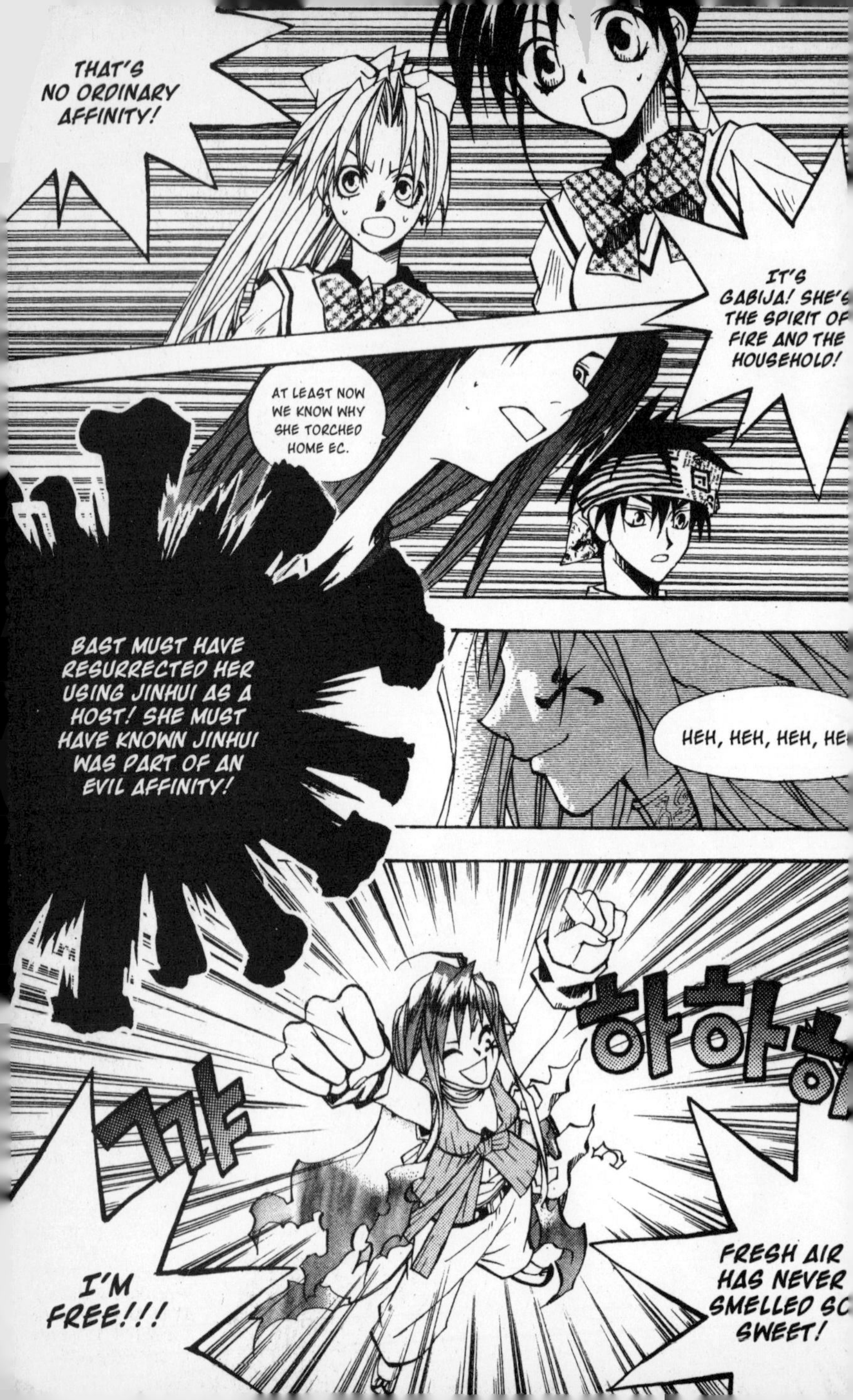
THAT'S NO ORDINARY AFFINITY!
IT'S GABIJA! SHE'S THE SPIRIT OF FIRE AND THE HOUSEHOLD!
AT LEAST NOW WE KNOW WHY SHE TORCHED HOME EC.
BAST MUST HAVE RESURRECTED HER USING JINHUI AS A HOST! SHE MUST HAVE KNOWN JINHUI WAS PART OF AN EVIL AFFINITY!
HEH, HEH, HEH, HE
꺄
하하
I'M FREE!!!
FRESH AIR HAS NEVER SMELLED SC SWEET!

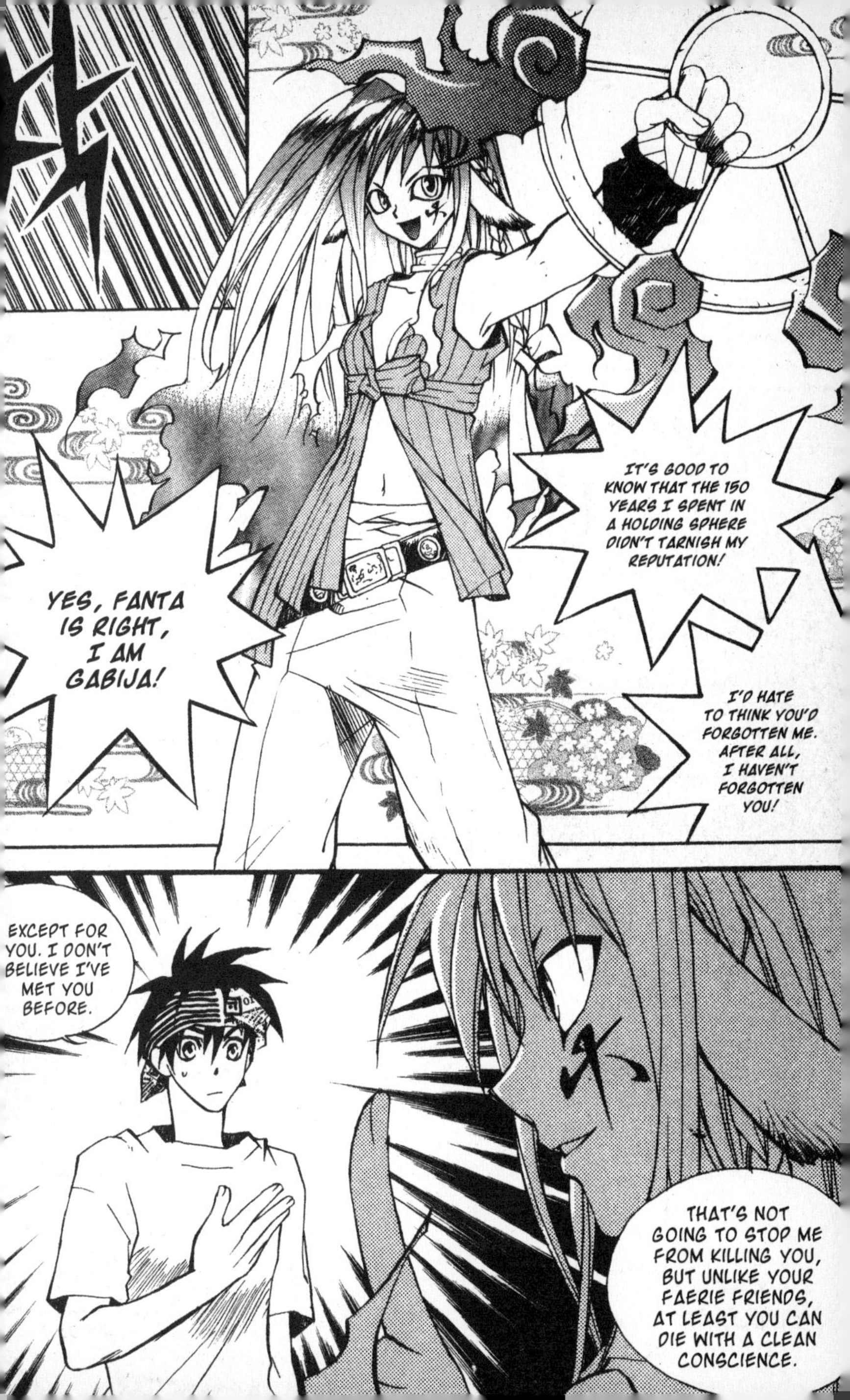
YES, FANTA IS RIGHT, I AM GABIJA!
IT'S GOOD TO KNOW THAT THE 150 YEARS I SPENT IN A HOLDING SPHERE DIDN'T TARNISH MY REPUTATION!
I'D HATE TO THINK YOU'D FORGOTTEN ME. AFTER ALL, I HAVEN'T FORGOTTEN YOU!
EXCEPT FOR YOU. I DON'T BELIEVE I'VE MET YOU BEFORE.
THAT'S NOT GOING TO STOP ME FROM KILLING YOU, BUT UNLIKE YOUR FAERIE FRIENDS, AT LEAST YOU CAN DIE WITH A CLEAN CONSCIENCE.

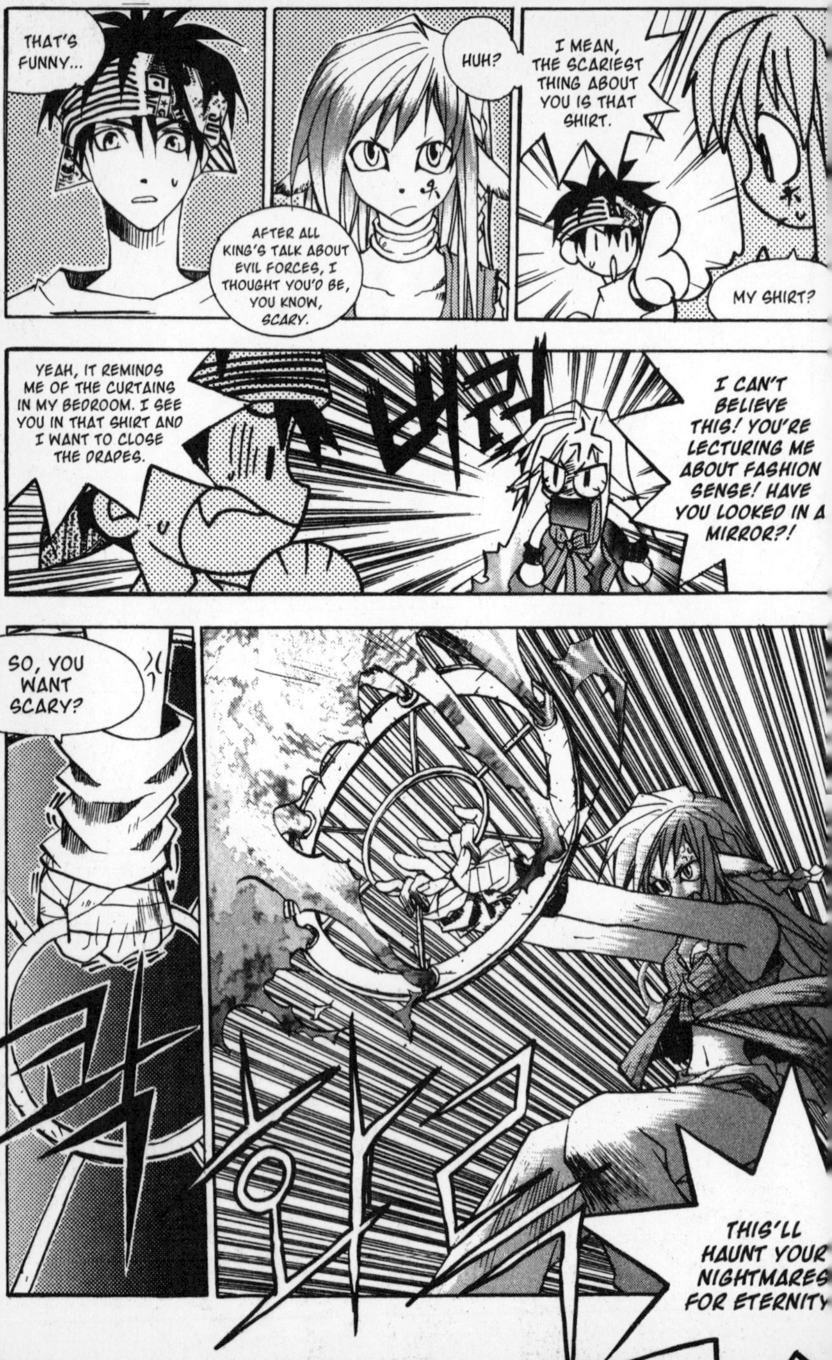
THAT'S FUNNY...
HUH?
AFTER ALL KING'S TALK ABOUT EVIL FORCES, I THOUGHT YOU'D BE, YOU KNOW, SCARY.
I MEAN, THE SCARIEST THING ABOUT YOU IS THAT SHIRT.
MY SHIRT?
YEAH, IT REMINDS ME OF THE CURTAINS IN MY BEDROOM. I SEE YOU IN THAT SHIRT AND I WANT TO CLOSE THE DRAPES.
I CAN'T BELIEVE THIS! YOU'RE LECTURING ME ABOUT FASHION SENSE! HAVE YOU LOOKED IN A MIRROR?!
SO, YOU WANT SCARY?
THIS'LL HAUNT YOUR NIGHTMARES FOR ETERNITY

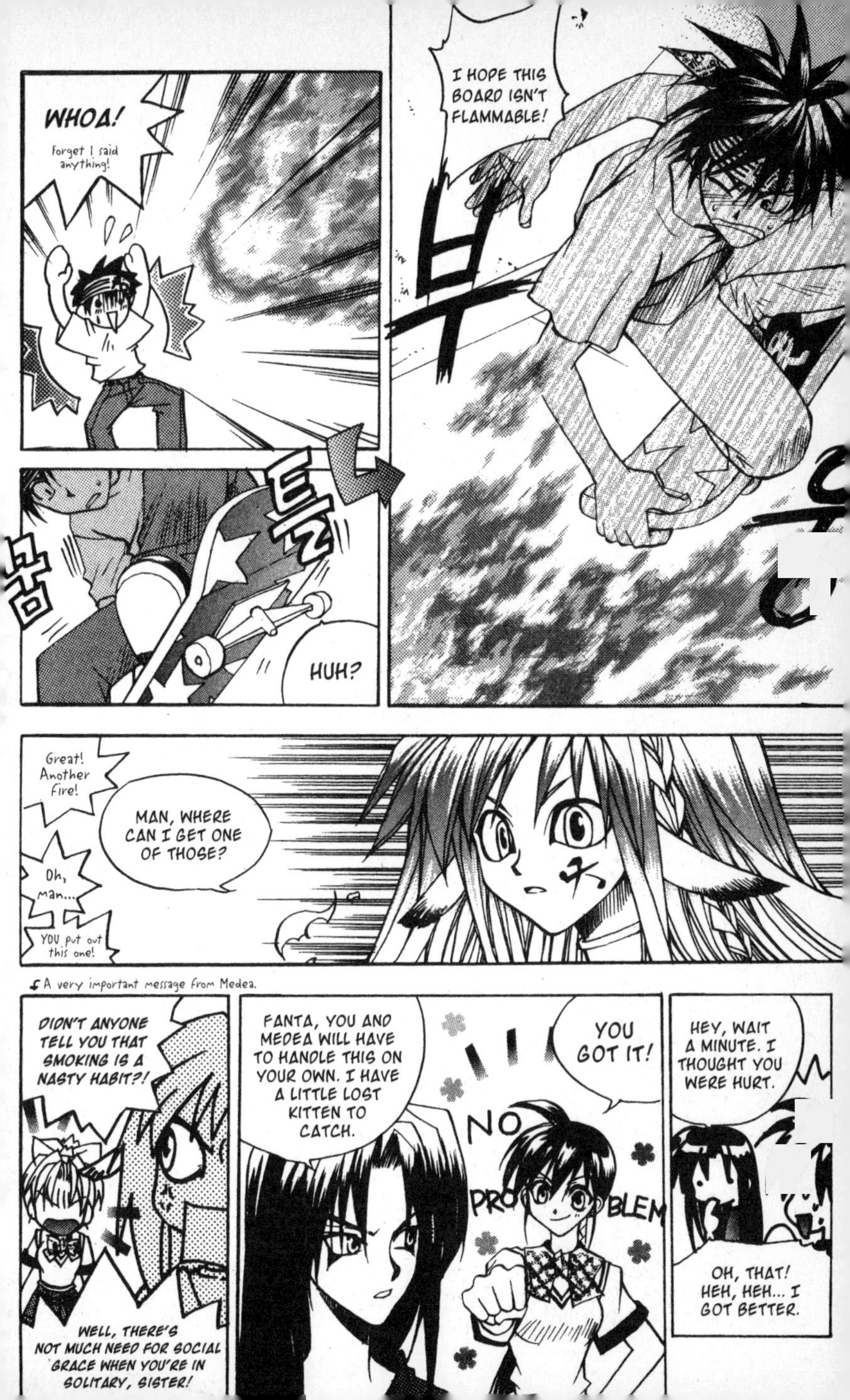
WHOA!
Forget I said anything!
HUH?
I HOPE THIS BOARD ISN'T FLAMMABLE!
Great! Another fire!
MAN, WHERE CAN I GET ONE OF THOSE?
Oh, man...
YOU put out this one!
A very important message from Medea.
DIDN'T ANYONE TELL YOU THAT SMOKING IS A NASTY HABIT?!
WELL, THERE'S NOT MUCH NEED FOR SOCIAL GRACE WHEN YOU'RE IN SOLITARY, SISTER!
FANTA, YOU AND MEDEA WILL HAVE TO HANDLE THIS ON YOUR OWN. I HAVE A LITTLE LOST KITTEN TO CATCH.
YOU GOT IT!
NO PROBLEM
HEY, WAIT A MINUTE. I THOUGHT YOU WERE HURT.
OH, THAT! HEH, HEH... I GOT BETTER.

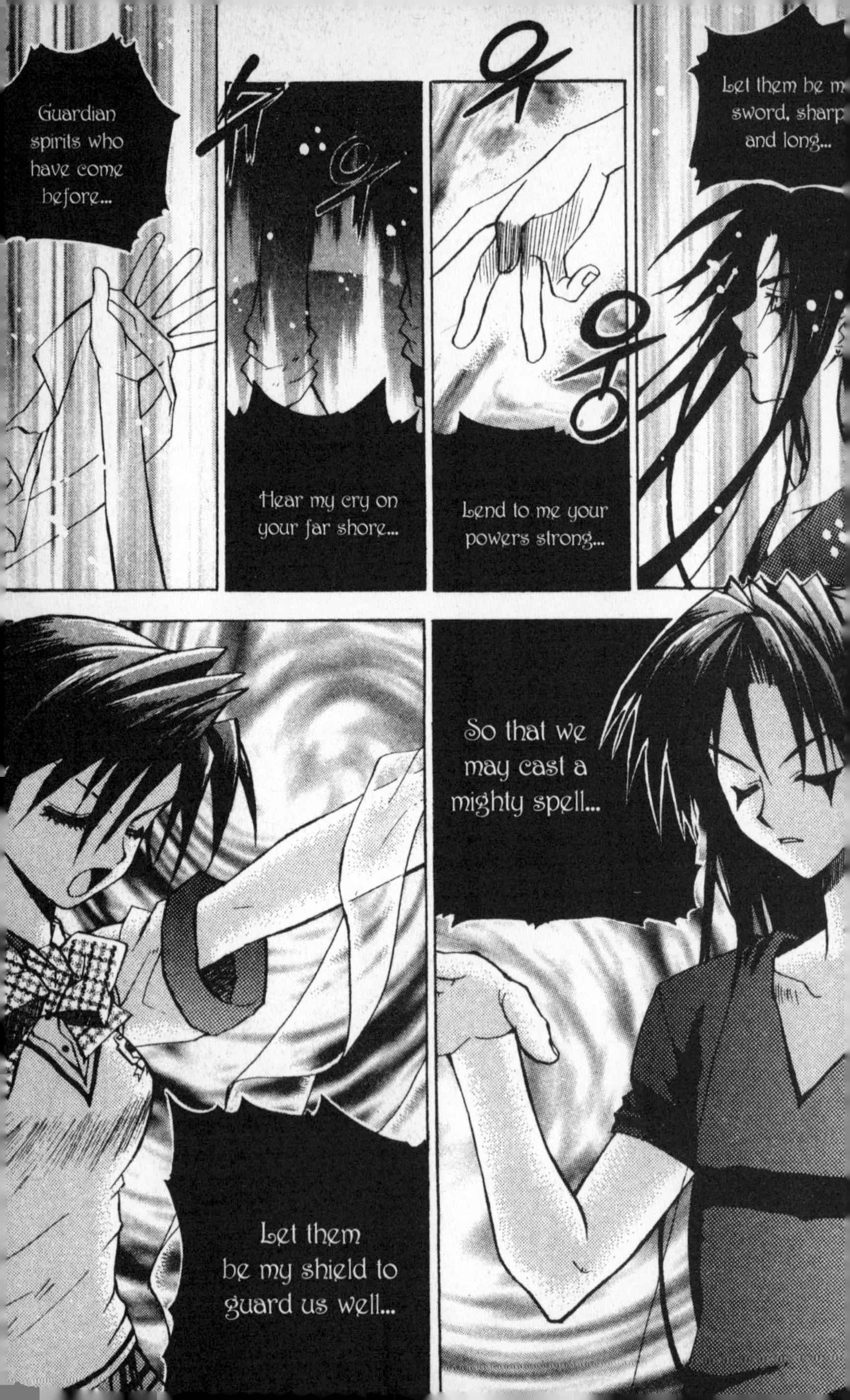

Guardian spirits who have come before...
Hear my cry on your far shore...
Lend to me your powers strong...
Let them be m sword, sharp and long...
Let them be my shield to guard us well...
So that we may cast a mighty spell...

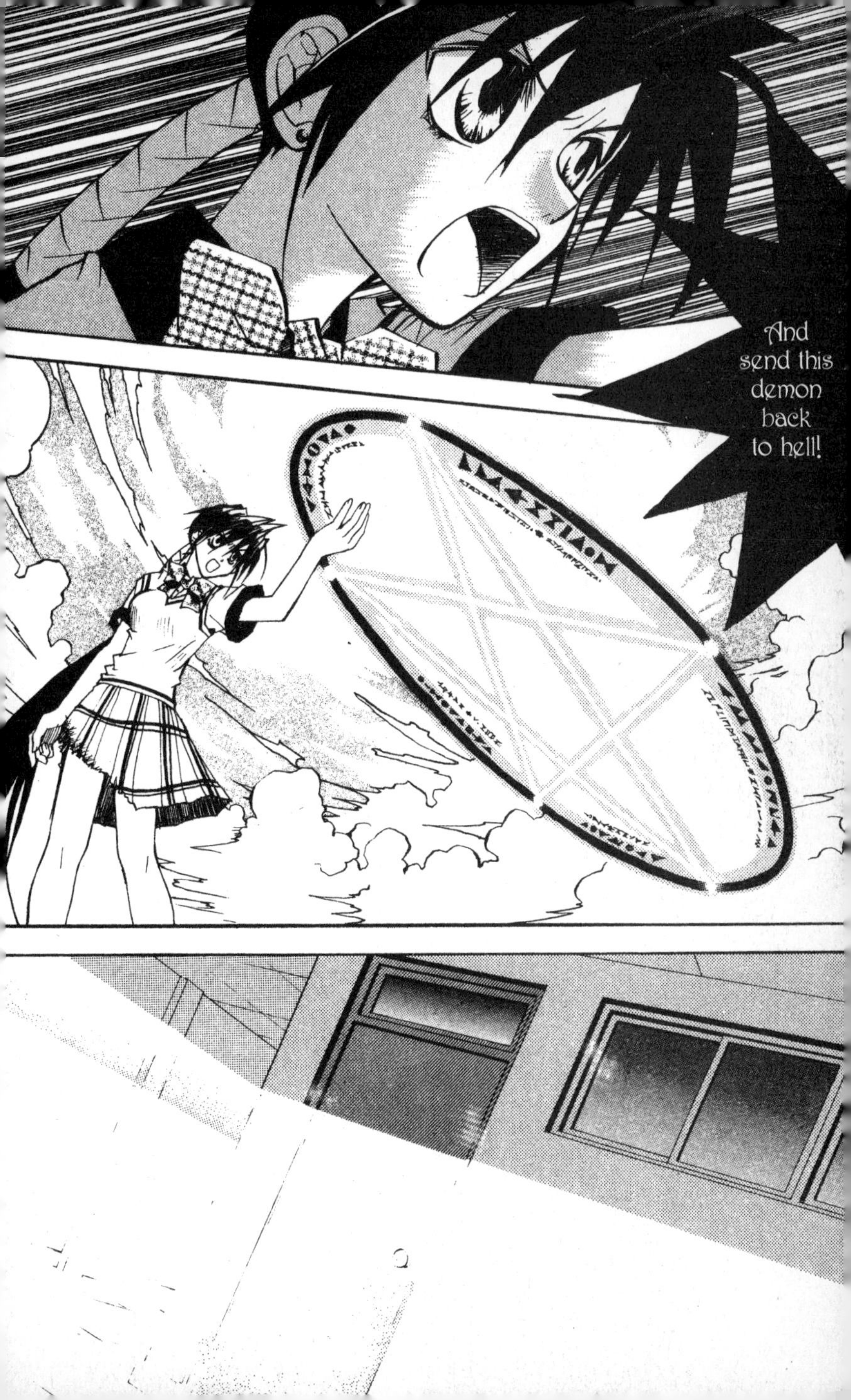
And send this demon back to hell!

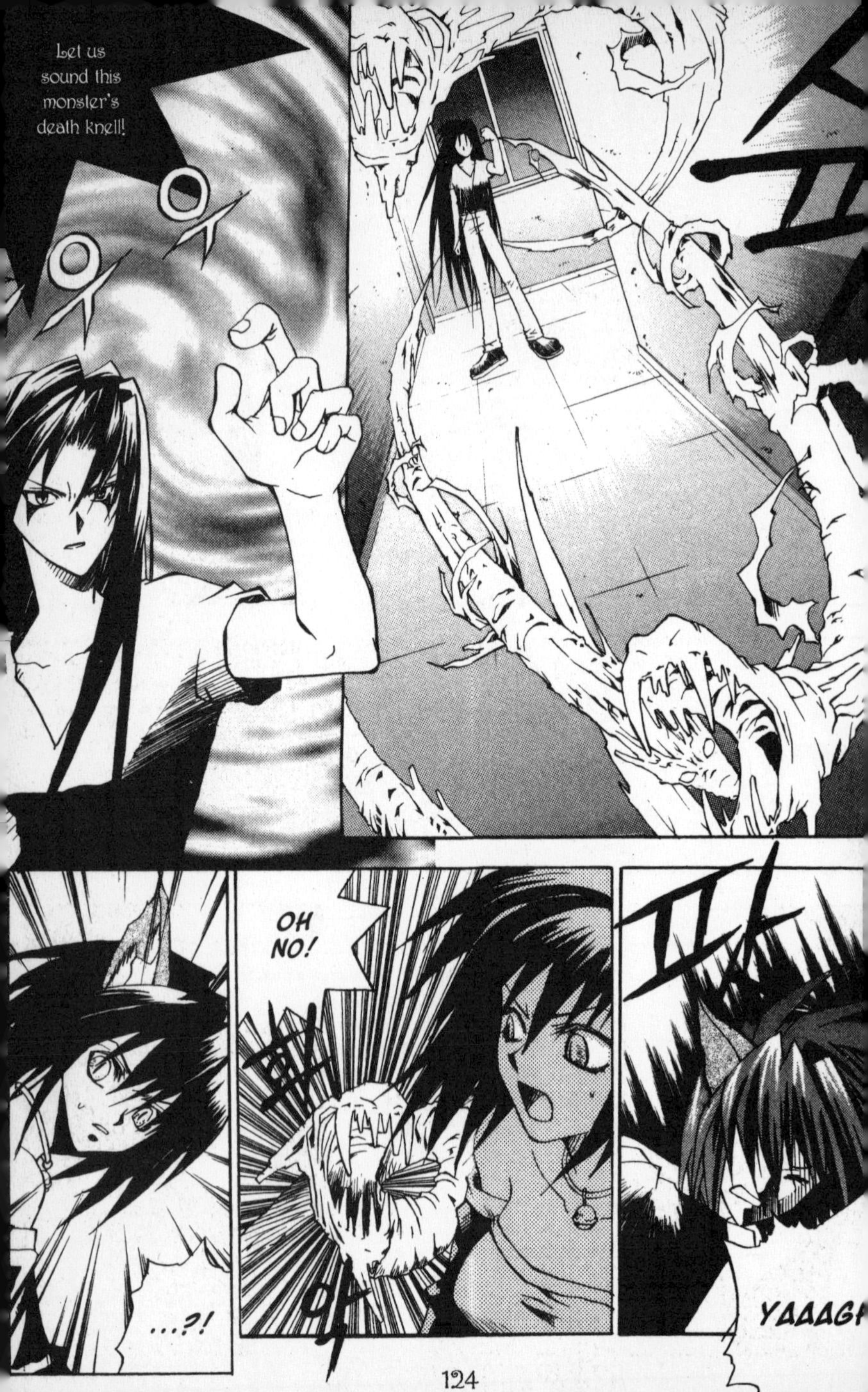
Let us sound this monster's death knell!
...?!
OH NO!
YAAAG!

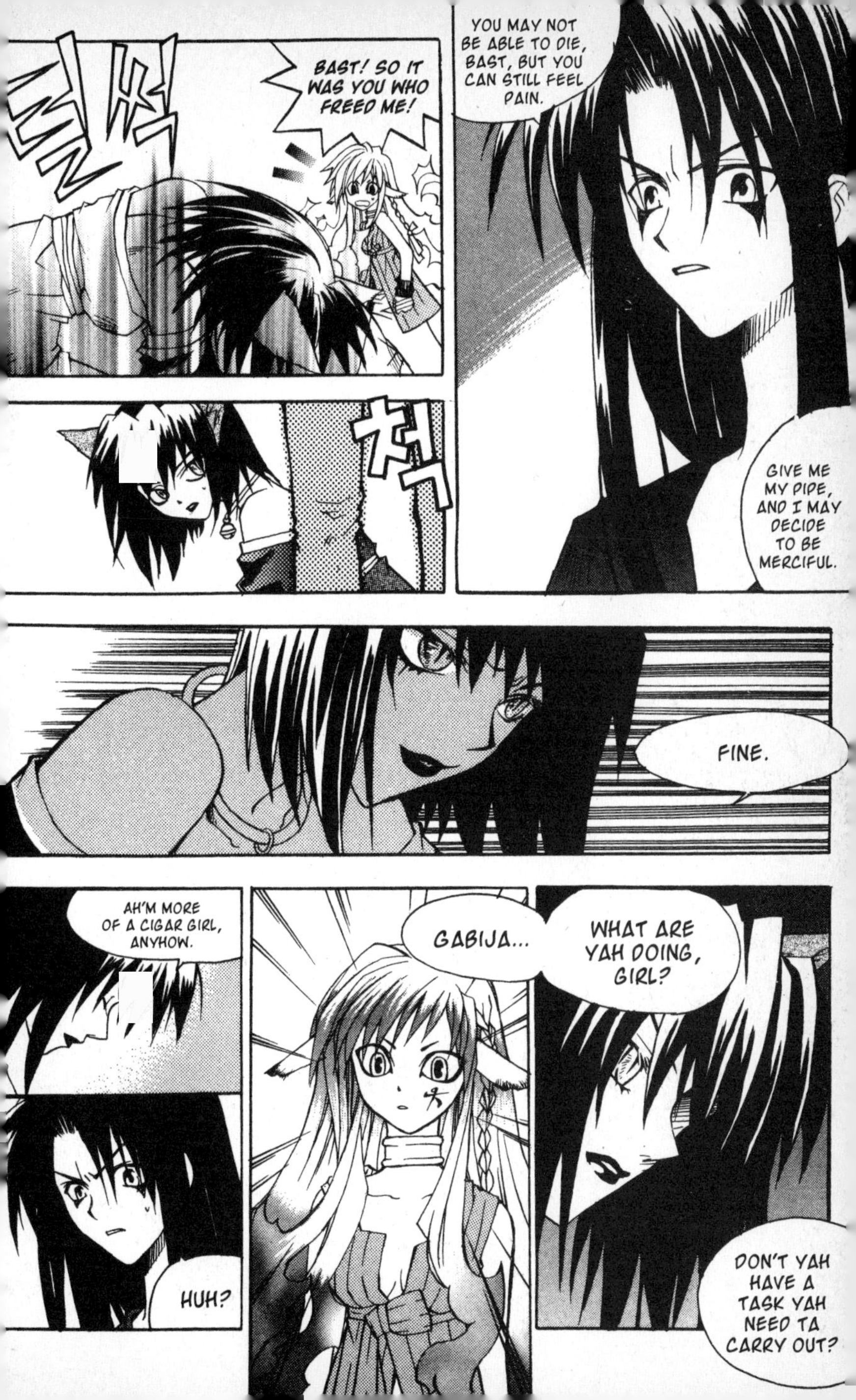
BAST! SO IT WAS YOU WHO FREED ME!
YOU MAY NOT BE ABLE TO DIE, BAST, BUT YOU CAN STILL FEEL PAIN.
GIVE ME MY PIPE, AND I MAY DECIDE TO BE MERCIFUL.
FINE.
AH'M MORE OF A CIGAR GIRL, ANYHOW.
HUH?
GABIJA...
WHAT ARE YAH DOING, GIRL?
DON'T YAH HAVE A TASK YAH NEED TA CARRY OUT?

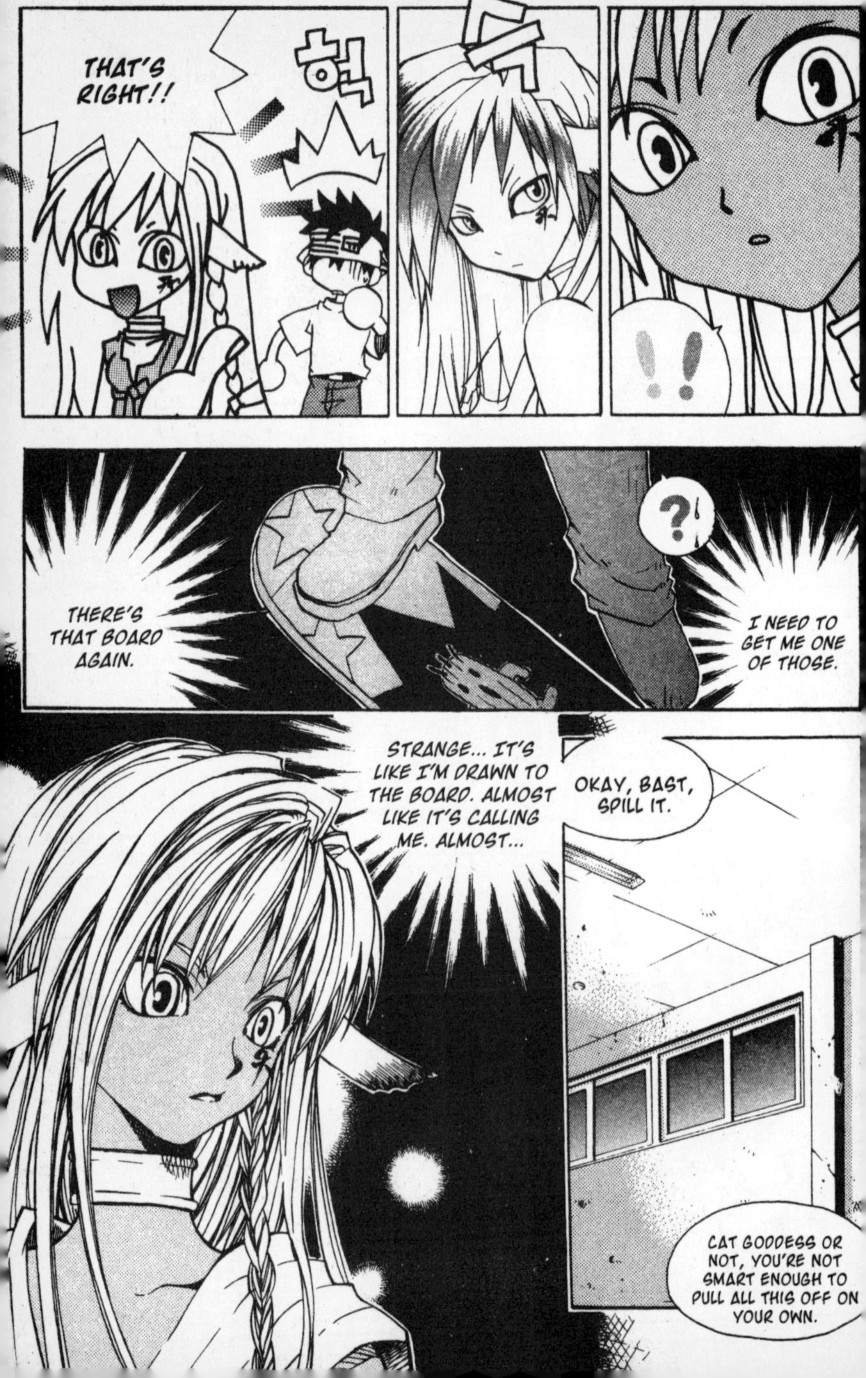
THAT'S RIGHT!!
헉
THERE'S THAT BOARD AGAIN.
I NEED TO GET ME ONE OF THOSE.
STRANGE... IT'S LIKE I'M DRAWN TO THE BOARD. ALMOST LIKE IT'S CALLING ME. ALMOST...
OKAY, BAST, SPILL IT.
CAT GODDESS OR NOT, YOU'RE NOT SMART ENOUGH TO PULL ALL THIS OFF ON YOUR OWN.

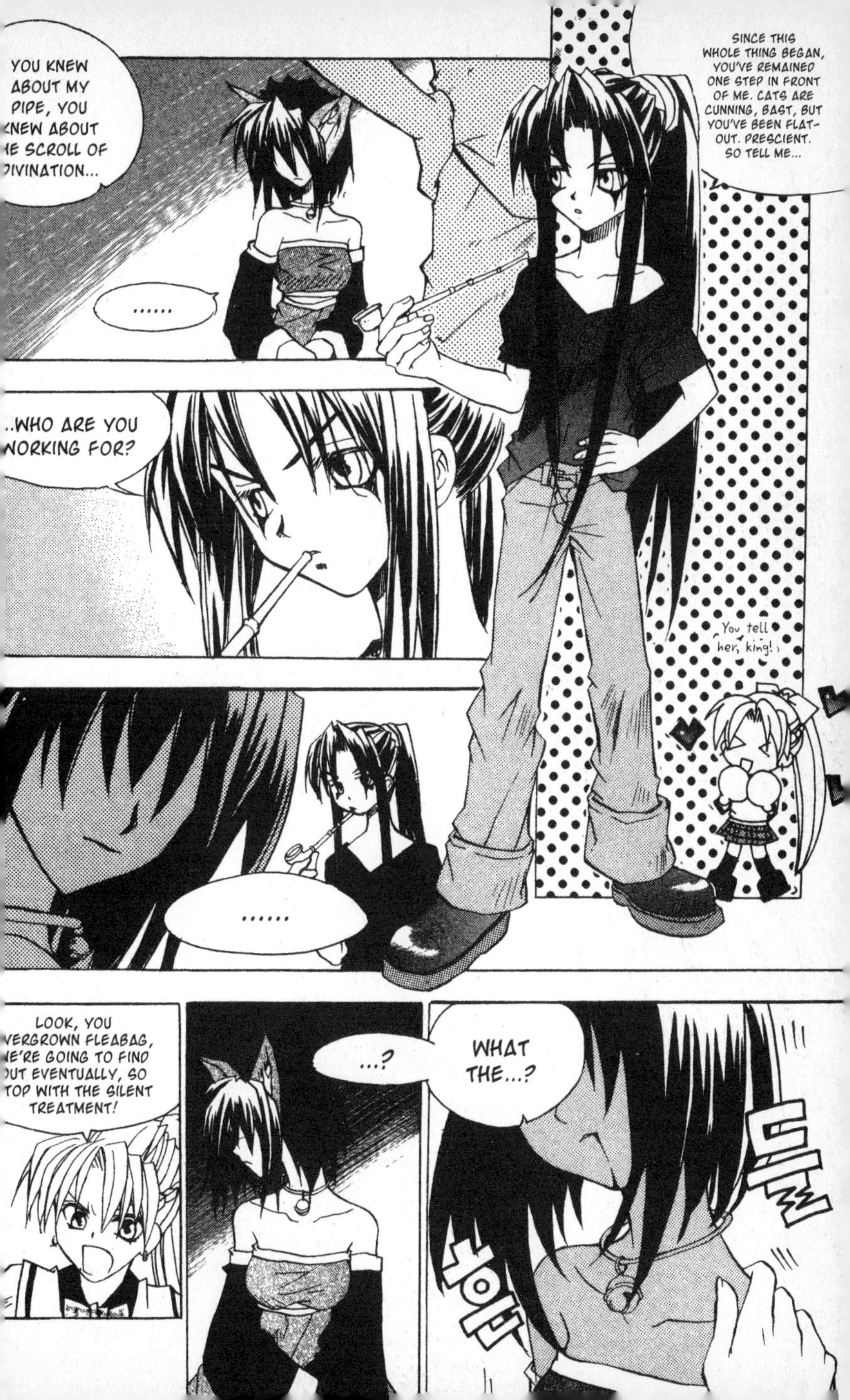

YOU KNEW ABOUT MY PIPE, YOU KNEW ABOUT HE SCROLL OF IVINATION...
......
SINCE THIS WHOLE THING BEGAN, YOU'VE REMAINED ONE STEP IN FRONT OF ME. CATS ARE CUNNING, BAST, BUT YOU'VE BEEN FLAT-OUT. PRESCIENT. SO TELL ME...
..WHO ARE YOU NORKING FOR?
......
You tell her, king!
LOOK, YOU VERGROWN FLEABAG, E'RE GOING TO FIND UT EVENTUALLY, SO TOP WITH THE SILENT TREATMENT!
...?
WHAT THE...?

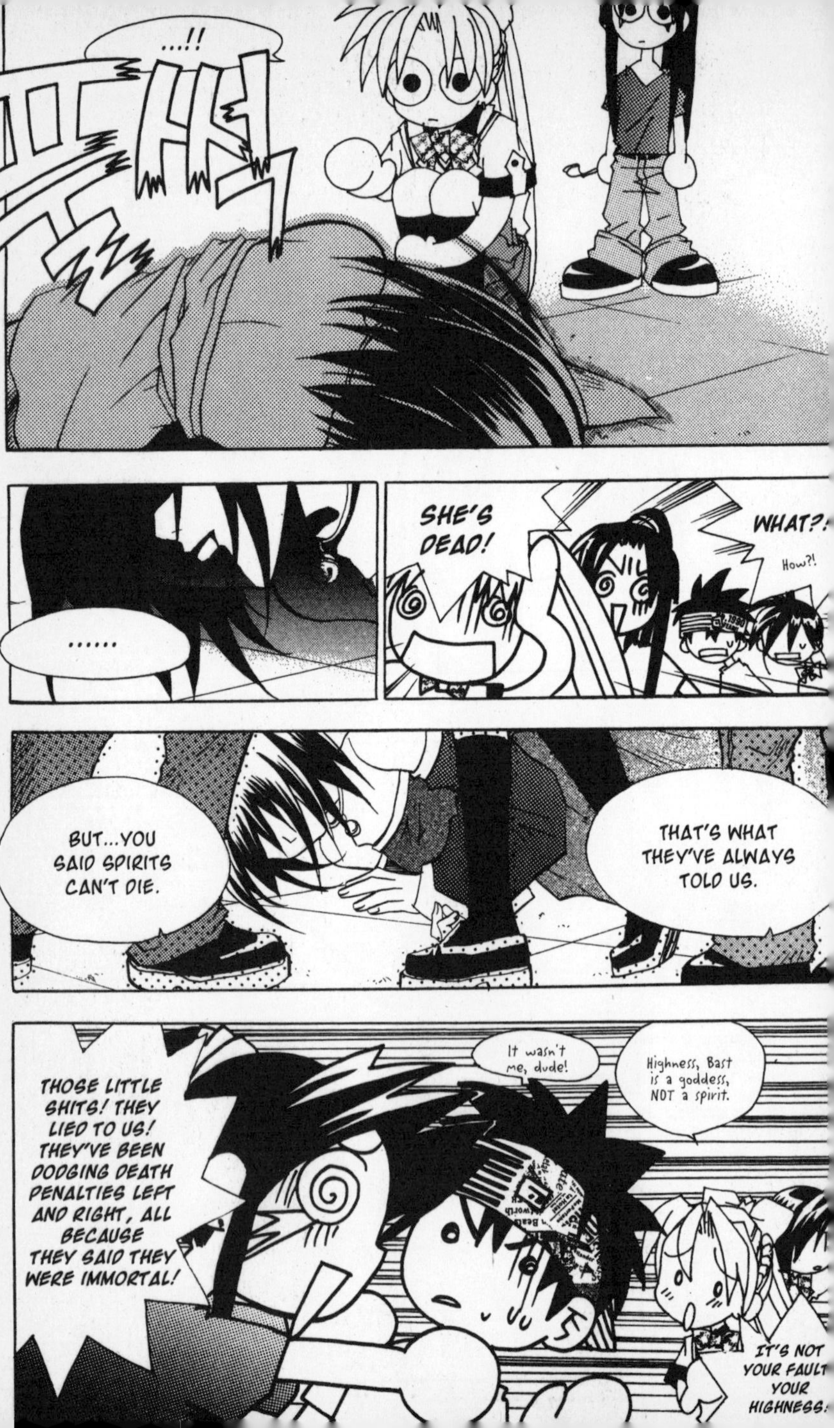
...!!
......
SHE'S DEAD!
WHAT?!
How?!
BUT...YOU SAID SPIRITS CAN'T DIE.
THAT'S WHAT THEY'VE ALWAYS TOLD US.
THOSE LITTLE SHITS! THEY LIED TO US! THEY'VE BEEN DODGING DEATH PENALTIES LEFT AND RIGHT, ALL BECAUSE THEY SAID THEY WERE IMMORTAL!
It wasn't me, dude!
Highness, Bast is a goddess, NOT a spirit.
IT'S NOT YOUR FAULT YOUR HIGHNESS!

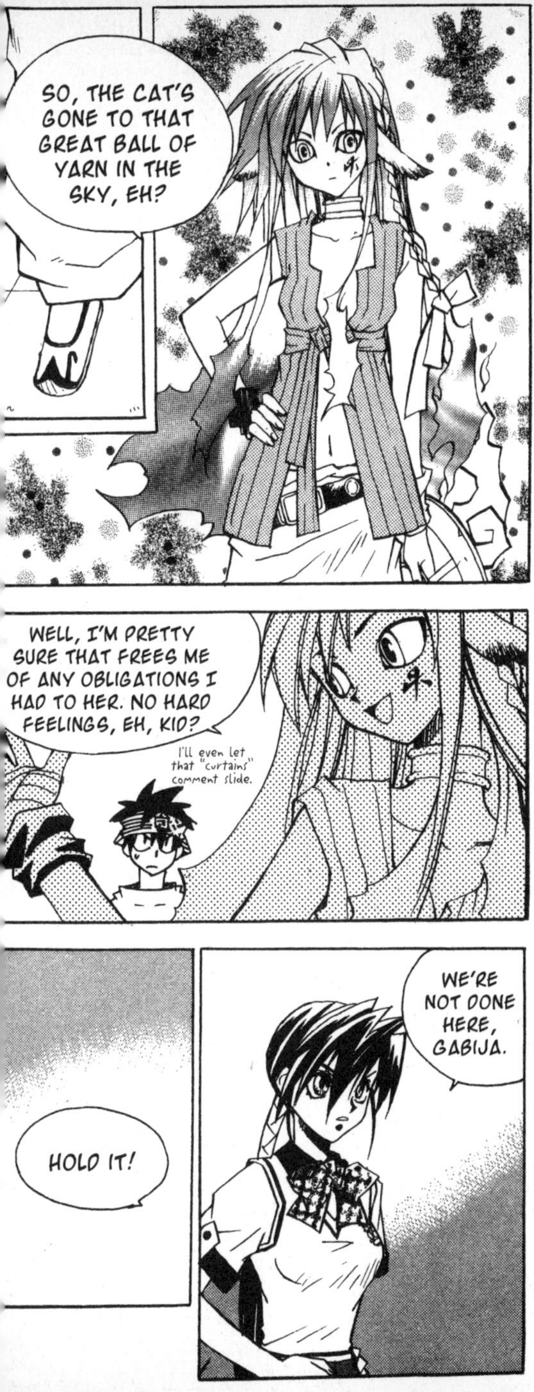
SO, THE CAT'S GONE TO THAT GREAT BALL OF YARN IN THE SKY, EH?
WELL, I'M PRETTY SURE THAT FREES ME OF ANY OBLIGATIONS I HAD TO HER. NO HARD FEELINGS, EH, KID?
I'll even let that "curtains" comment slide.
HOLD IT!
WE'RE NOT DONE HERE, GABIJA.

FREE TALK

Hello! How many episodes has it been? Just like a chronic patient barely getting over the humps of death, I barely make my deadlines for the manuscripts. Ugh... I recently went to Japan for a while. I lot of people asked me if it was fun, but I was so busy that I didn't even get a chance to take one snapshot. It was a lot cooler than our country, so in some ways, it may have been a retreat from the heat. I think I might move. Maybe this will finally be my chance for independence. I can't imagine how dirty and pathetic life would be without my mom. Yesterday was deadline, and one of my cats went missing. I went outside for awhile and she followed me out. I was so distraught. I couldn't so much as pick up a pen. Fortunately, she came back after half a day. I was touched. How could this dumb mommy of cats live without Dambi and Saku? Thanks to the one who gave me the Doraemon pillow at the last sales event. There was so much going on I never got to properly thank you. Also, thank you to whomever it was that gave me the Totoro doll. And to whoever bought me drinks. Thanks to Jeonghun, who got a lot of ice cream from the place where he works part-time. (Oh, I don't have much to write, so now things are getting more personal.) This story will conclude in the next episode. (I'm getting pretty sick of it myself.) I promise to wrap it up with a bang!

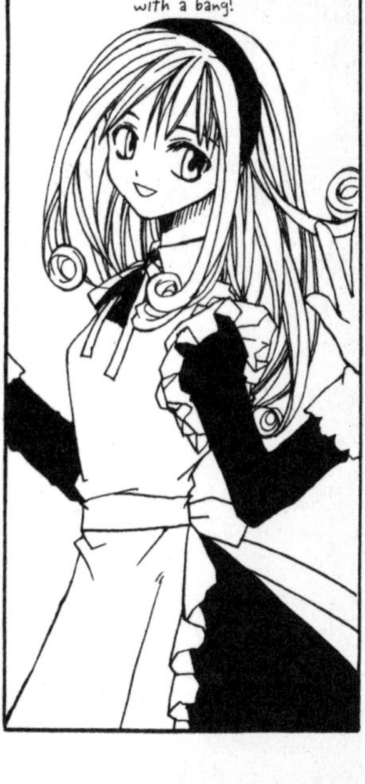

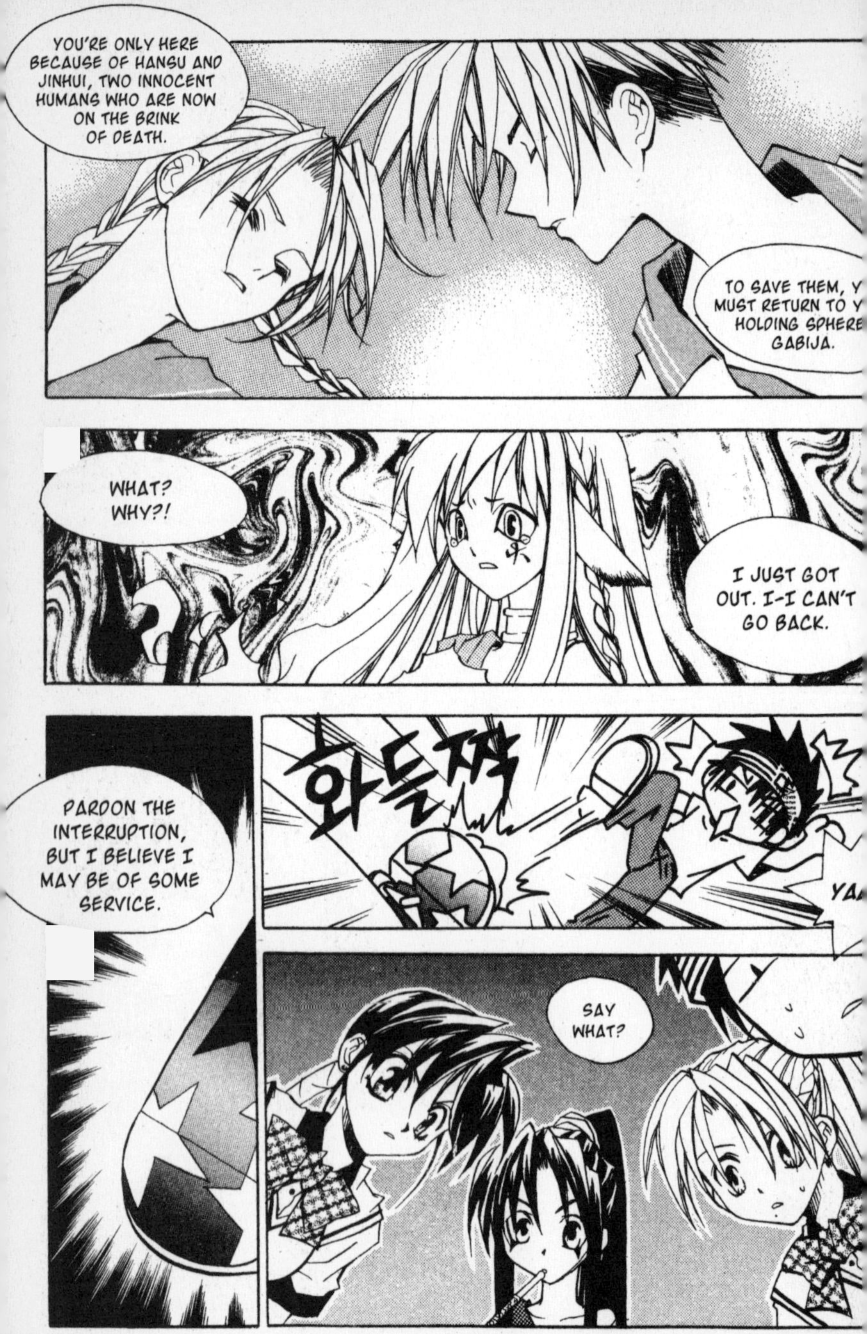
YOU'RE ONLY HERE BECAUSE OF HANSU AND JINHUI, TWO INNOCENT HUMANS WHO ARE NOW ON THE BRINK OF DEATH.
TO SAVE THEM, Y MUST RETURN TO Y HOLDING SPHERE GABIJA.
WHAT? WHY?!
I JUST GOT OUT. I-I CAN'T GO BACK.
PARDON THE INTERRUPTION, BUT I BELIEVE I MAY BE OF SOME SERVICE.
화들짝
YA
SAY WHAT?

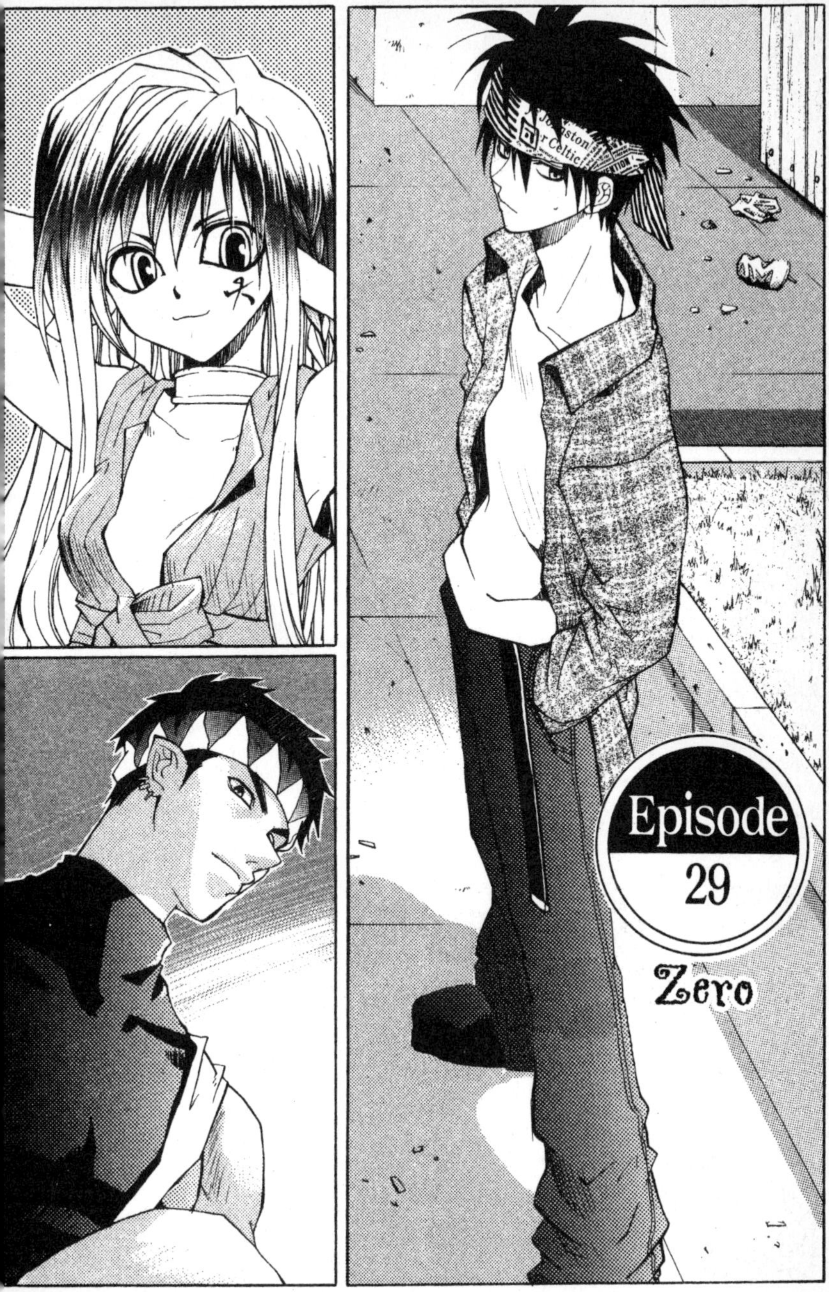
Episode
29
Zero

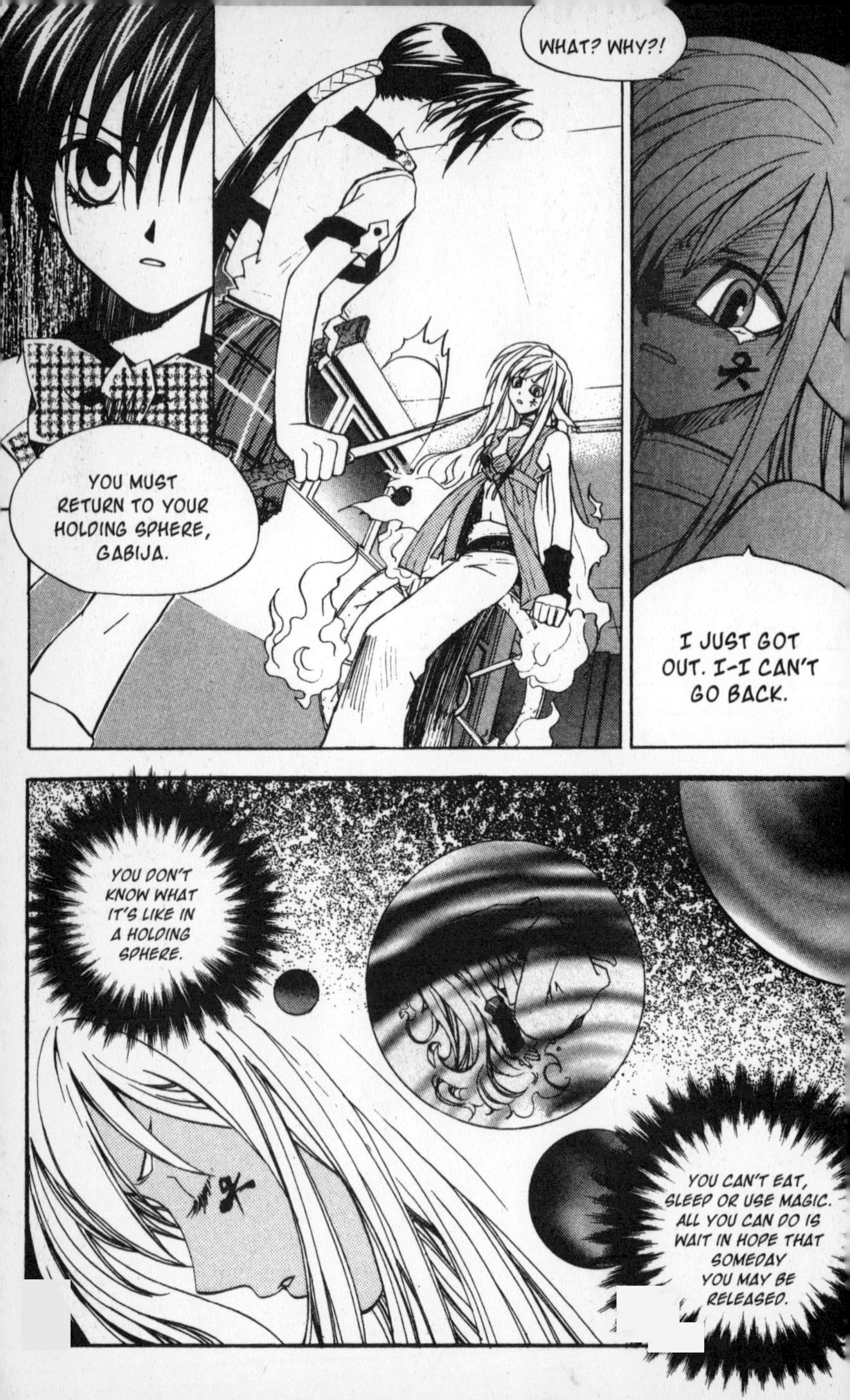
WHAT? WHY?!
YOU MUST RETURN TO YOUR HOLDING SPHERE, GABIJA.
I JUST GOT OUT. I-I CAN'T GO BACK.
YOU DON'T KNOW WHAT IT'S LIKE IN A HOLDING SPHERE.
YOU CAN'T EAT, SLEEP OR USE MAGIC. ALL YOU CAN DO IS WAIT IN HOPE THAT SOMEDAY YOU MAY BE RELEASED.

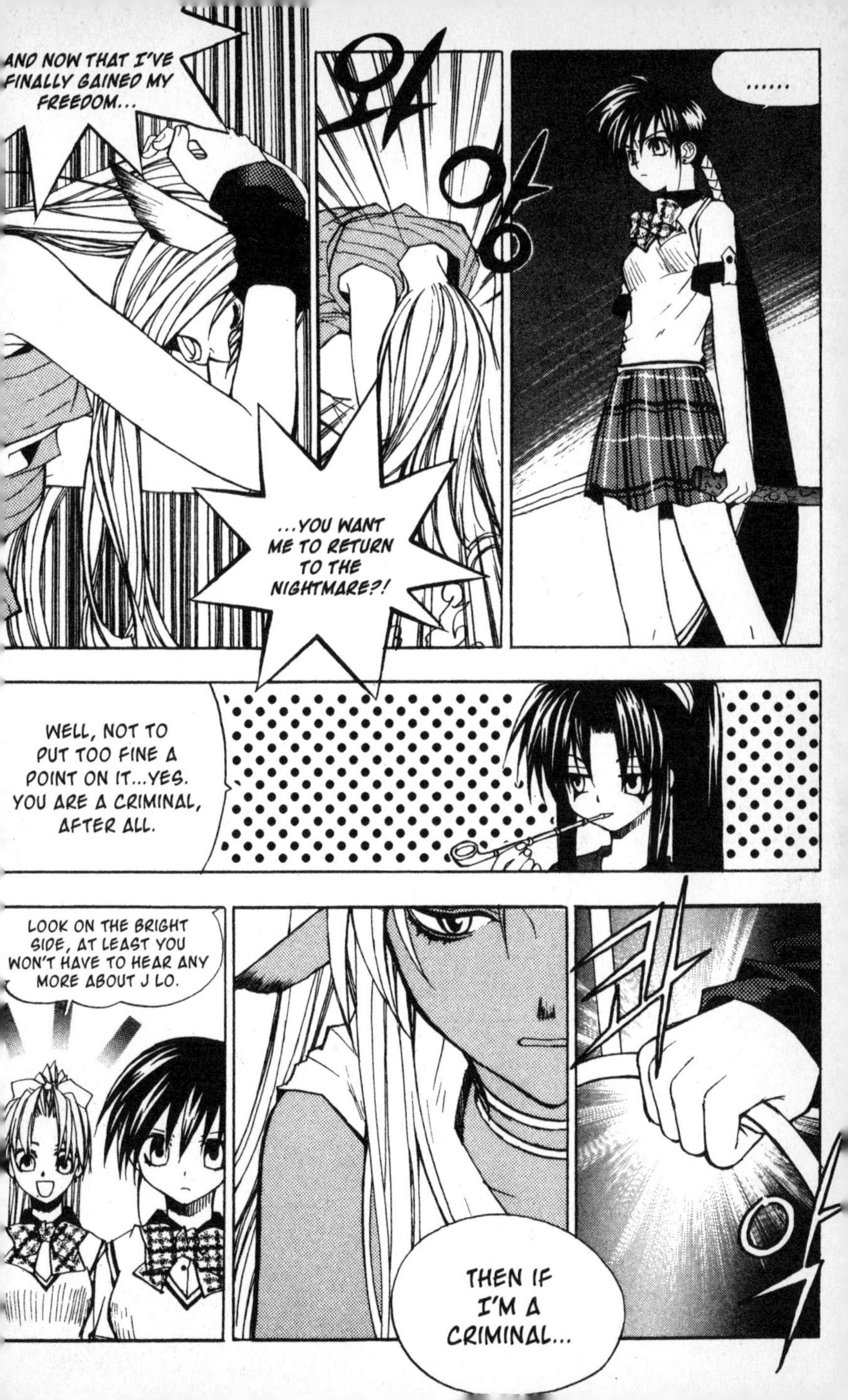
AND NOW THAT I'VE FINALLY GAINED MY FREEDOM...
...YOU WANT ME TO RETURN TO THE NIGHTMARE?!
......
WELL, NOT TO PUT TOO FINE A POINT ON IT...YES. YOU ARE A CRIMINAL, AFTER ALL.
LOOK ON THE BRIGHT SIDE, AT LEAST YOU WON'T HAVE TO HEAR ANY MORE ABOUT J LO.
THEN IF I'M A CRIMINAL...

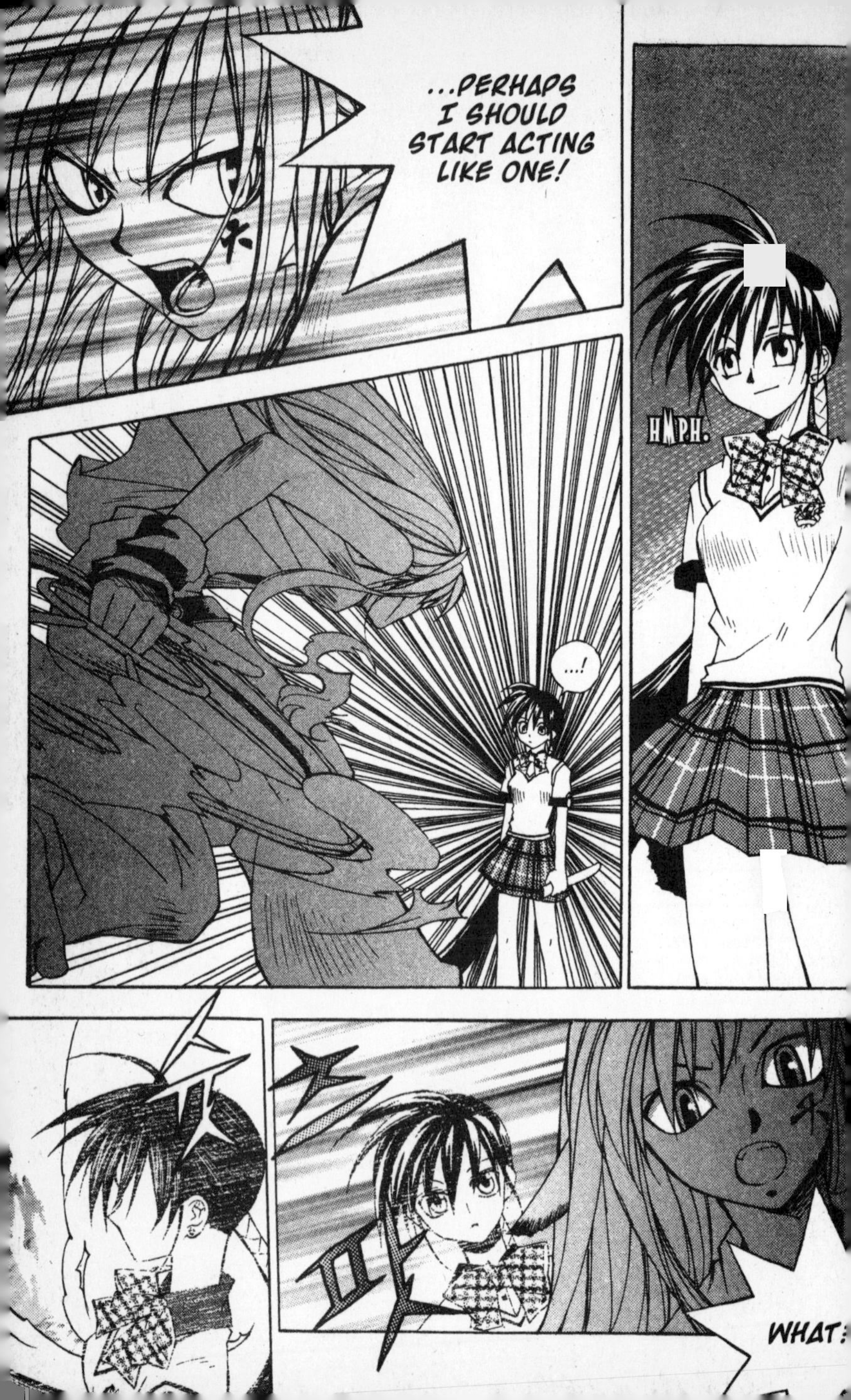
...PERHAPS I SHOULD START ACTING LIKE ONE!
HMPH.
...!
WHAT:

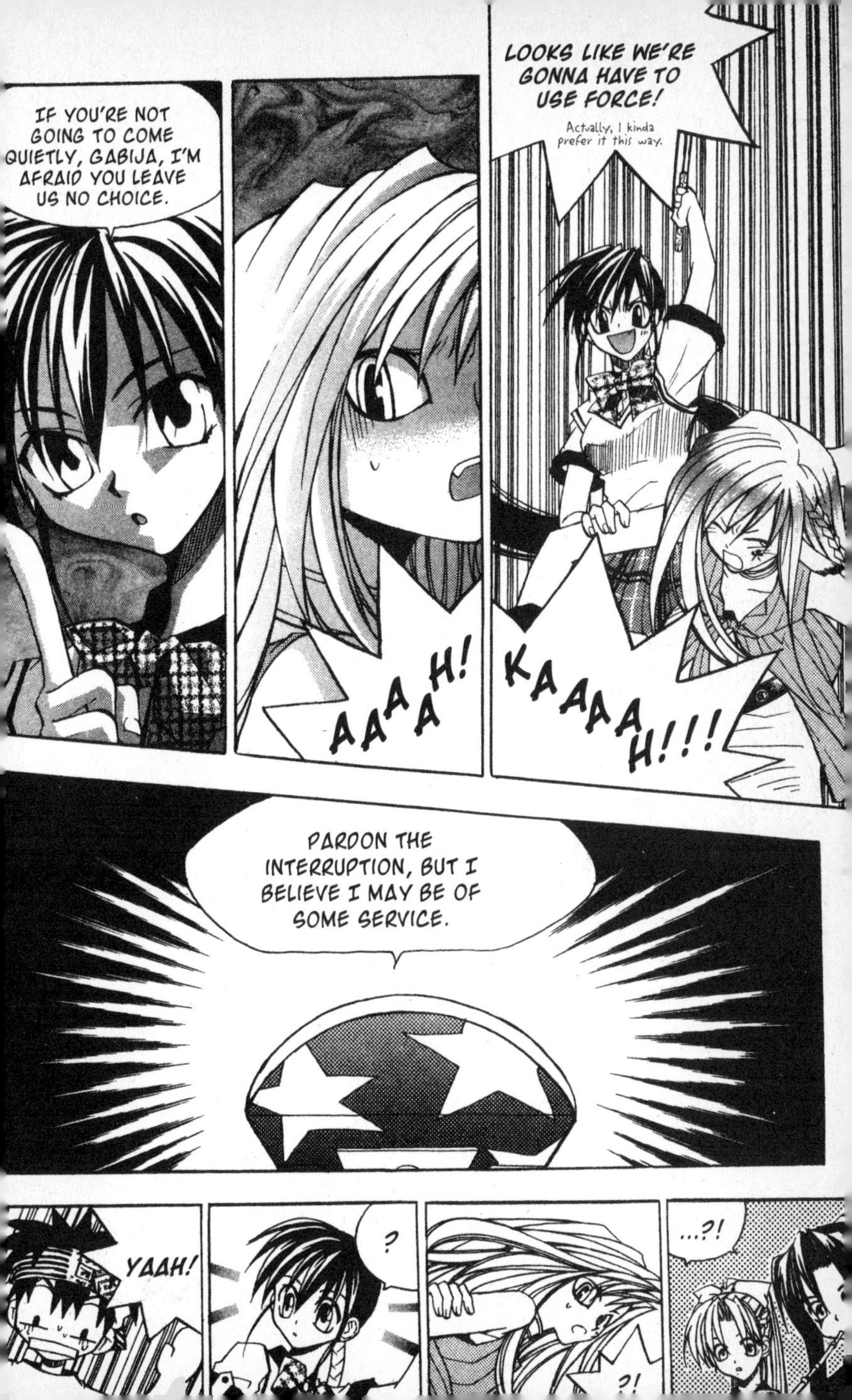
IF YOU'RE NOT GOING TO COME QUIETLY, GABIJA, I'M AFRAID YOU LEAVE US NO CHOICE.
AAAAH!
LOOKS LIKE WE'RE GONNA HAVE TO USE FORCE!
Actually, I kinda prefer it this way.
KAAAAH!!!
PARDON THE INTERRUPTION, BUT I BELIEVE I MAY BE OF SOME SERVICE.
YAAH!
?
?!
...?!

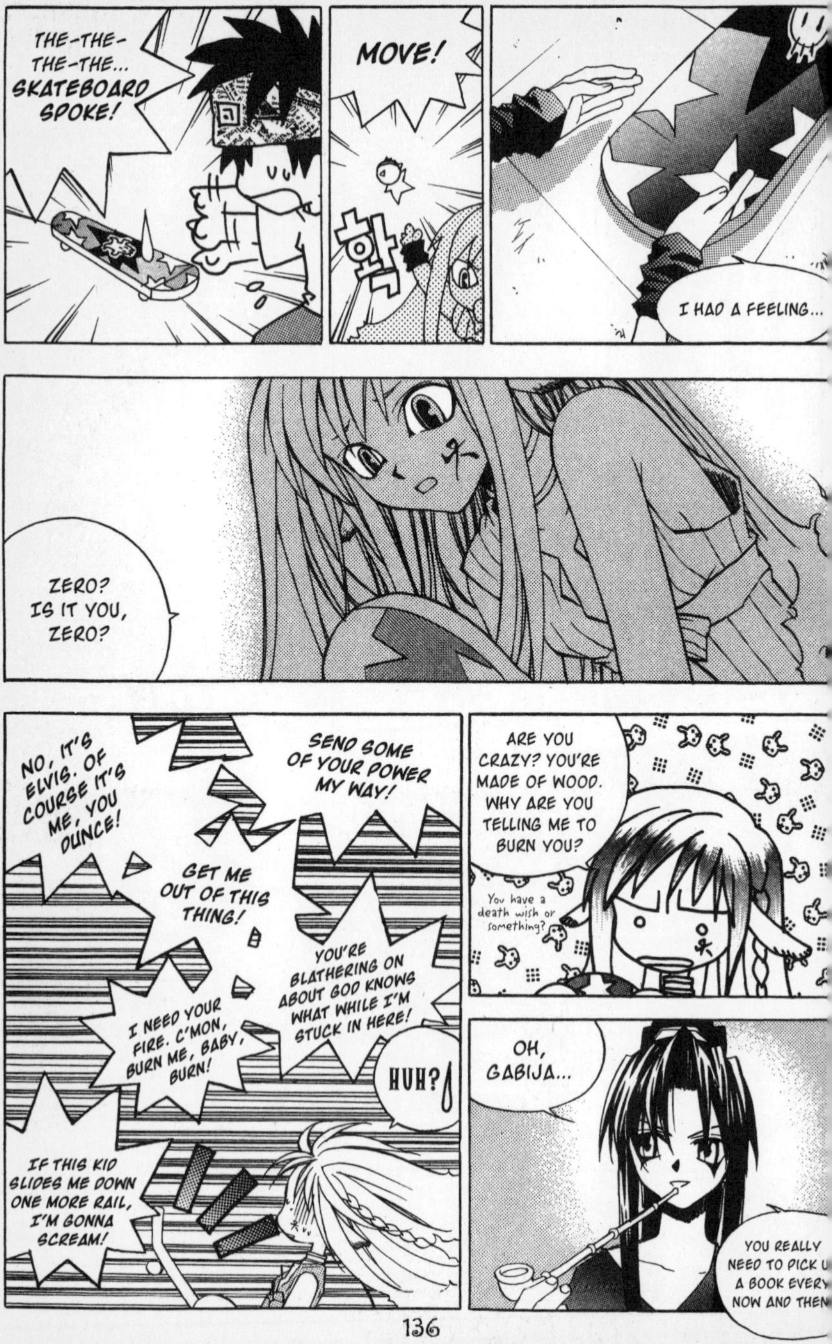
THE-THE-THE-THE... SKATEBOARD SPOKE!
MOVE!
I HAD A FEELING...
ZERO? IS IT YOU, ZERO?
NO, IT'S ELVIS. OF COURSE IT'S ME, YOU DUNCE!
SEND SOME OF YOUR POWER MY WAY!
GET ME OUT OF THIS THING!
YOU'RE BLATHERING ON ABOUT GOD KNOWS WHAT WHILE I'M STUCK IN HERE!
I NEED YOUR FIRE. C'MON, BABY, BURN ME, BABY, BURN!
HUH?
IF THIS KID SLIDES ME DOWN ONE MORE RAIL, I'M GONNA SCREAM!
ARE YOU CRAZY? YOU'RE MADE OF WOOD. WHY ARE YOU TELLING ME TO BURN YOU?
You have a death wish or something?
OH, GABIJA...
YOU REALLY NEED TO PICK U A BOOK EVERY NOW AND THEN

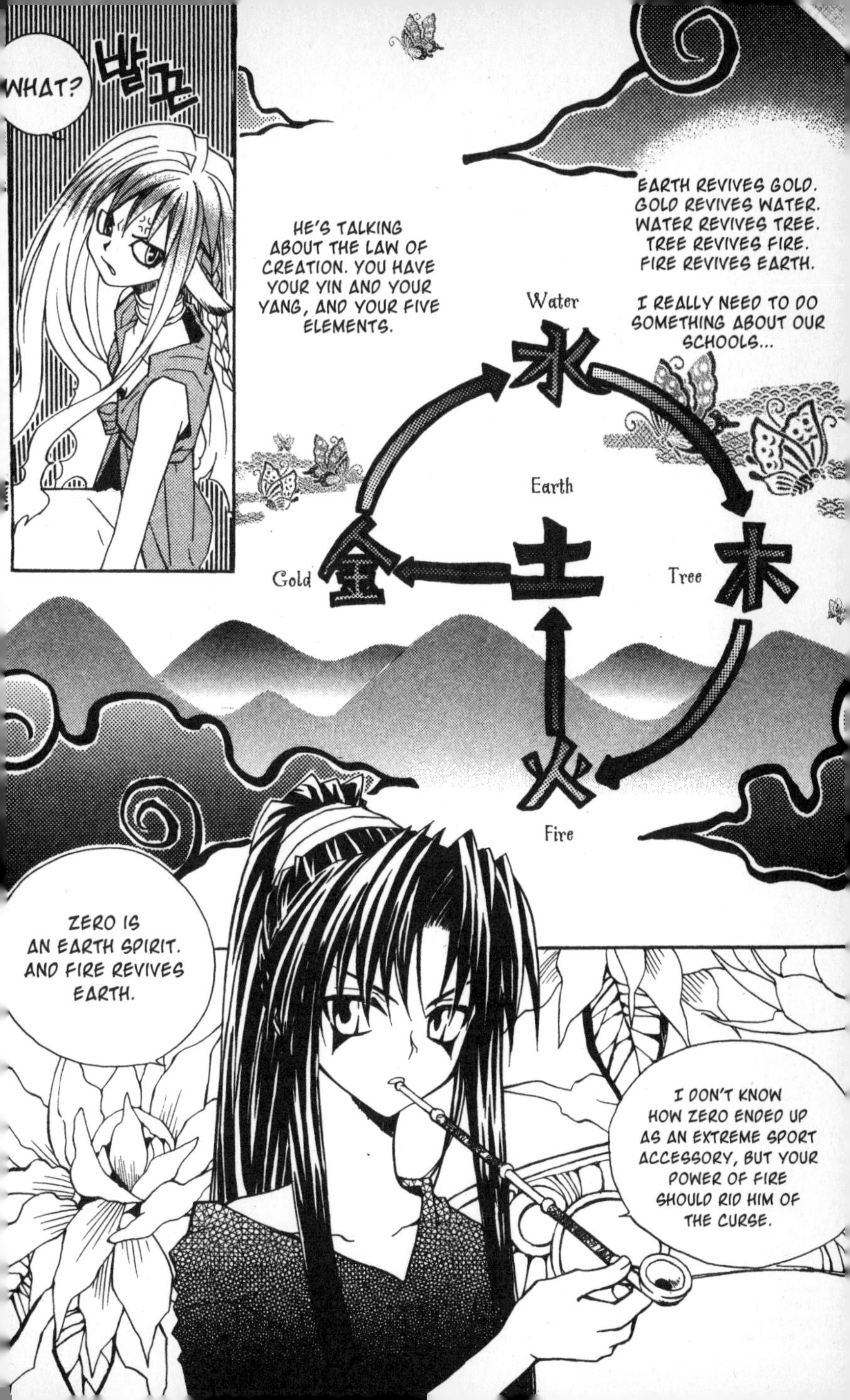
WHAT?
발끈
HE'S TALKING ABOUT THE LAW OF CREATION. YOU HAVE YOUR YIN AND YOUR YANG, AND YOUR FIVE ELEMENTS.
EARTH REVIVES GOLD. GOLD REVIVES WATER. WATER REVIVES TREE. TREE REVIVES FIRE. FIRE REVIVES EARTH.
I REALLY NEED TO DO SOMETHING ABOUT OUR SCHOOLS...
Water
水
Earth
土
Gold
金
Tree
木
火
Fire
ZERO IS AN EARTH SPIRIT. AND FIRE REVIVES EARTH.
I DON'T KNOW HOW ZERO ENDED UP AS AN EXTREME SPORT ACCESSORY, BUT YOUR POWER OF FIRE SHOULD RID HIM OF THE CURSE.

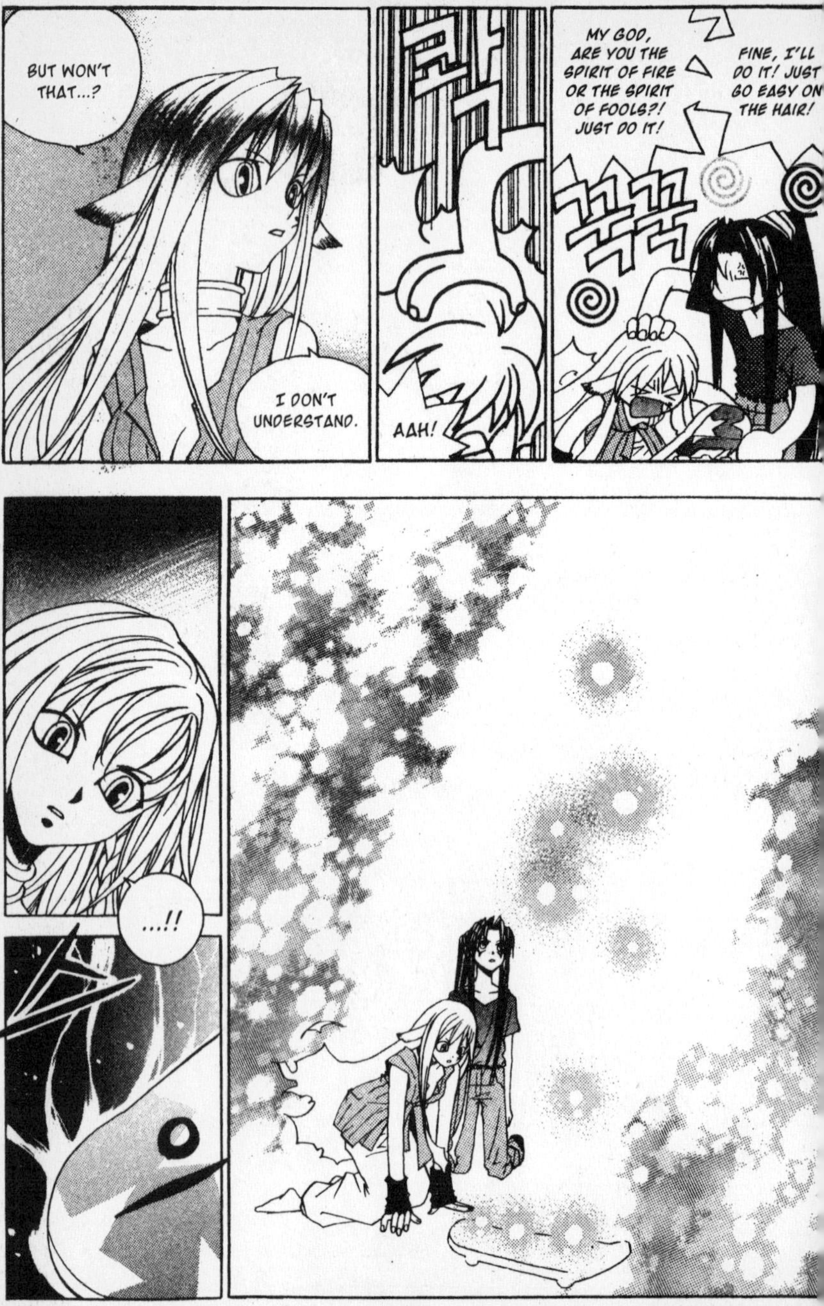
BUT WON'T THAT...?
I DON'T UNDERSTAND.
AAH!
MY GOD, ARE YOU THE SPIRIT OF FIRE OR THE SPIRIT OF FOOLS?! JUST DO IT!
FINE, I'LL DO IT! JUST GO EASY ON THE HAIR!
...!!

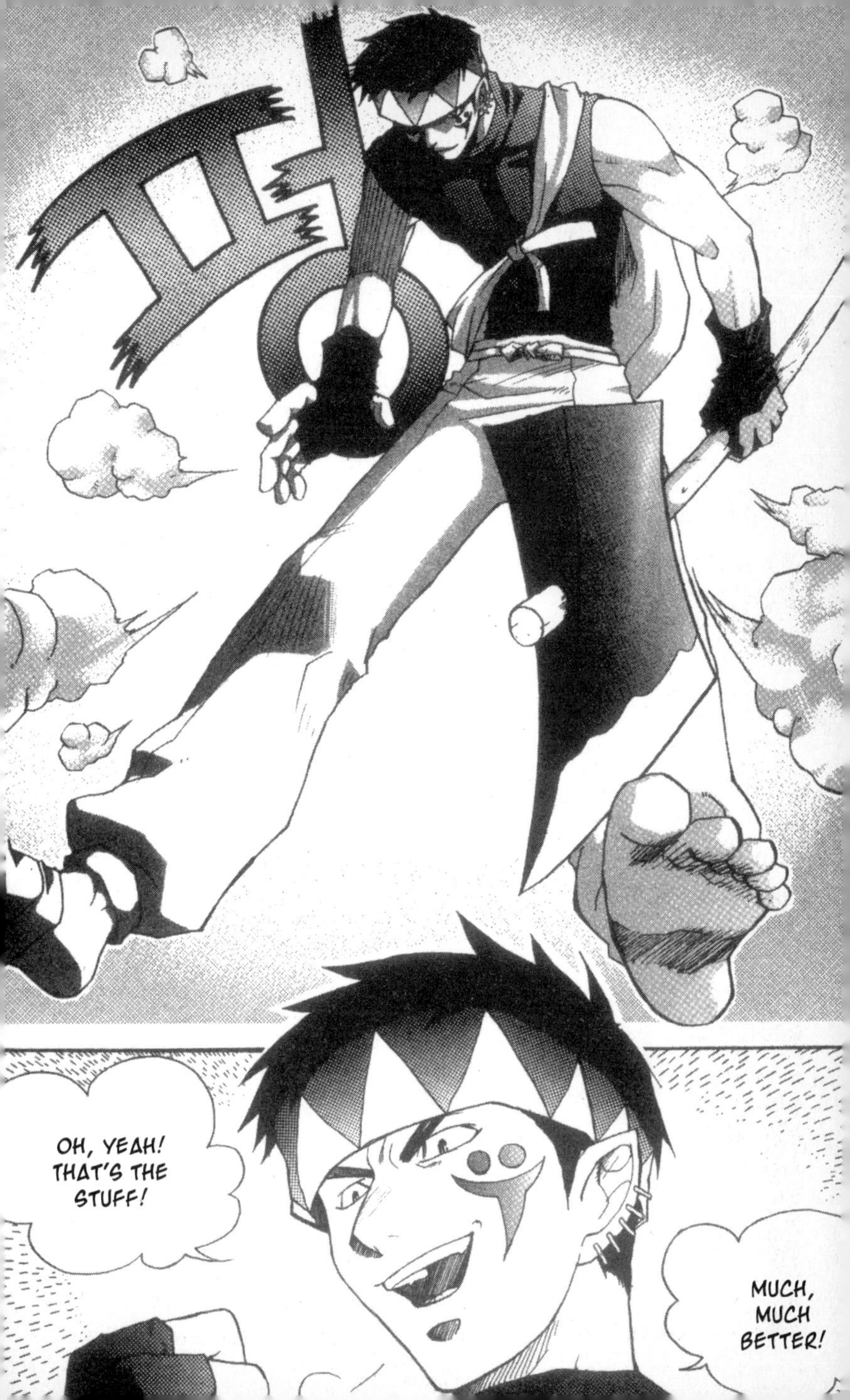
OH, YEAH! THAT'S THE STUFF!
MUCH, MUCH BETTER!

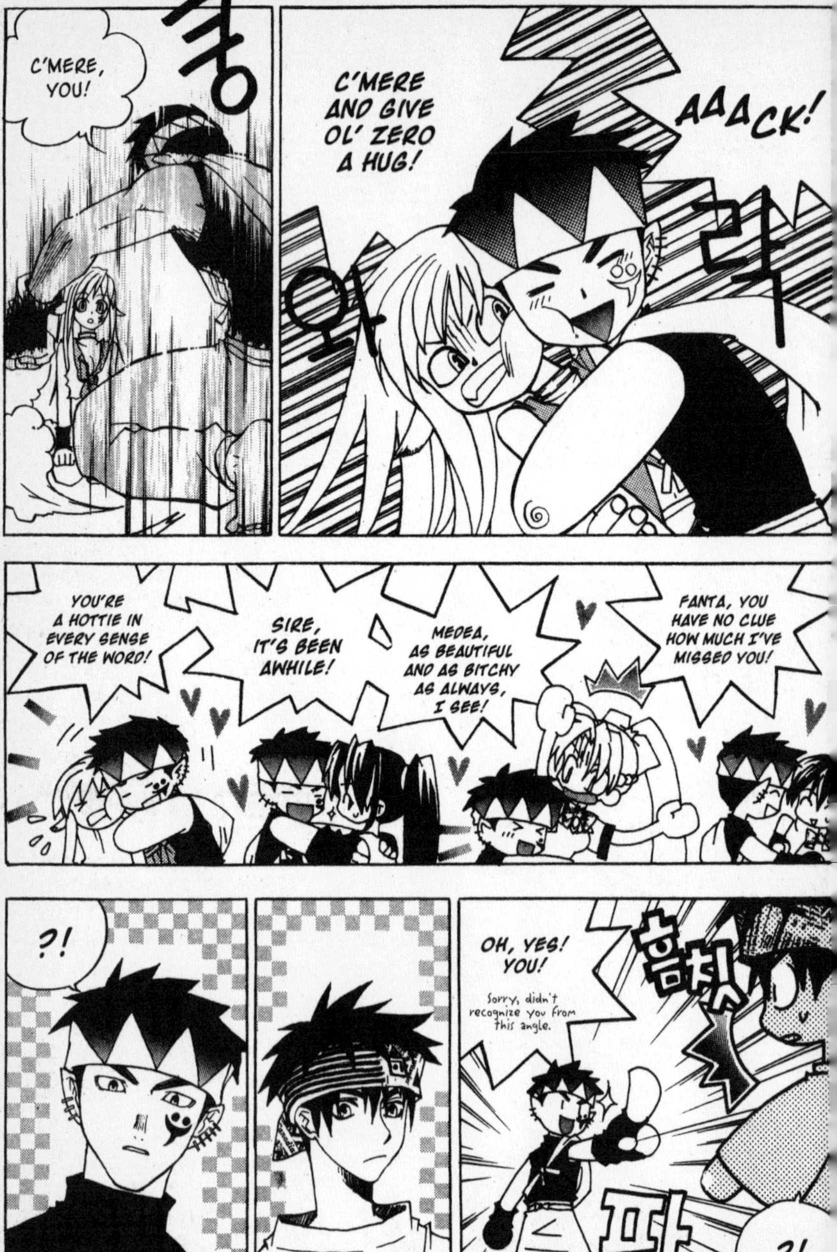
C'MERE, YOU!
C'MERE AND GIVE OL' ZERO A HUG!
AAACK!
YOU'RE A HOTTIE IN EVERY SENSE OF THE WORD!
SIRE, IT'S BEEN AWHILE!
MEDEA, AS BEAUTIFUL AND AS BITCHY AS ALWAYS, I SEE!
FANTA, YOU HAVE NO CLUE HOW MUCH I'VE MISSED YOU!
?!
OH, YES! YOU!
Sorry, didn't recognize you from this angle.
?!

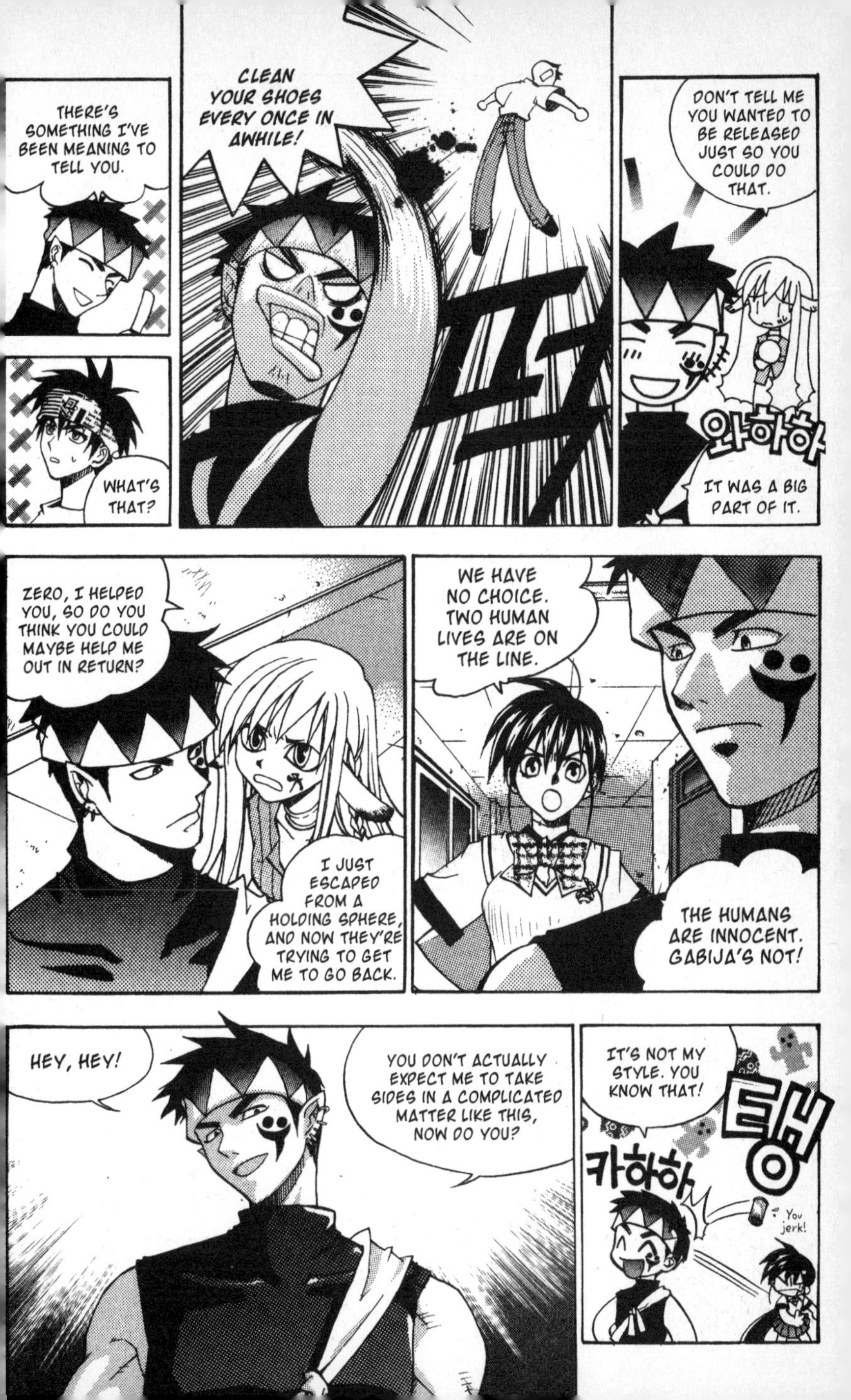
THERE'S SOMETHING I'VE BEEN MEANING TO TELL YOU.
WHAT'S THAT?
CLEAN YOUR SHOES EVERY ONCE IN AWHILE!
퍽
DON'T TELL ME YOU WANTED TO BE RELEASED JUST SO YOU COULD DO THAT.
와하하
IT WAS A BIG PART OF IT.
ZERO, I HELPED YOU, SO DO YOU THINK YOU COULD MAYBE HELP ME OUT IN RETURN?
I JUST ESCAPED FROM A HOLDING SPHERE, AND NOW THEY'RE TRYING TO GET ME TO GO BACK.
WE HAVE NO CHOICE. TWO HUMAN LIVES ARE ON THE LINE.
THE HUMANS ARE INNOCENT. GABIJA'S NOT!
HEY, HEY!
YOU DON'T ACTUALLY EXPECT ME TO TAKE SIDES IN A COMPLICATED MATTER LIKE THIS, NOW DO YOU?
IT'S NOT MY STYLE. YOU KNOW THAT!
카하하
탱
You jerk!

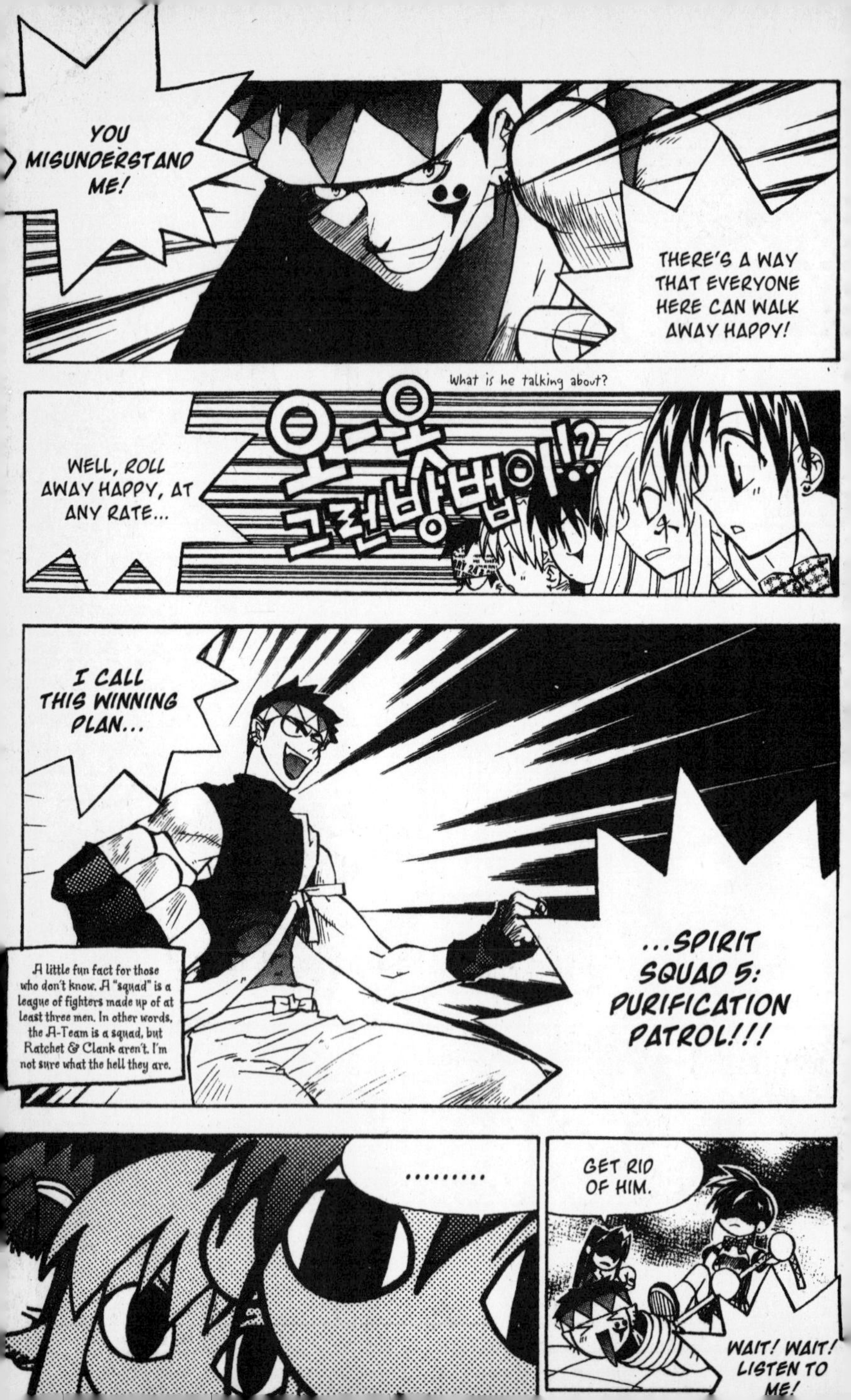
YOU MISUNDERSTAND ME!
THERE'S A WAY THAT EVERYONE HERE CAN WALK AWAY HAPPY!
What is he talking about?
오-옷 그런 방법이!?
WELL, ROLL AWAY HAPPY, AT ANY RATE...
I CALL THIS WINNING PLAN...
A little fun fact for those who don't know. A "squad" is a league of fighters made up of at least three men. In other words, the A-Team is a squad, but Ratchet & Clank aren't. I'm not sure what the hell they are.
...SPIRIT SQUAD 5: PURIFICATION PATROL!!!
....
GET RID OF HIM.
WAIT! WAIT! LISTEN TO ME!

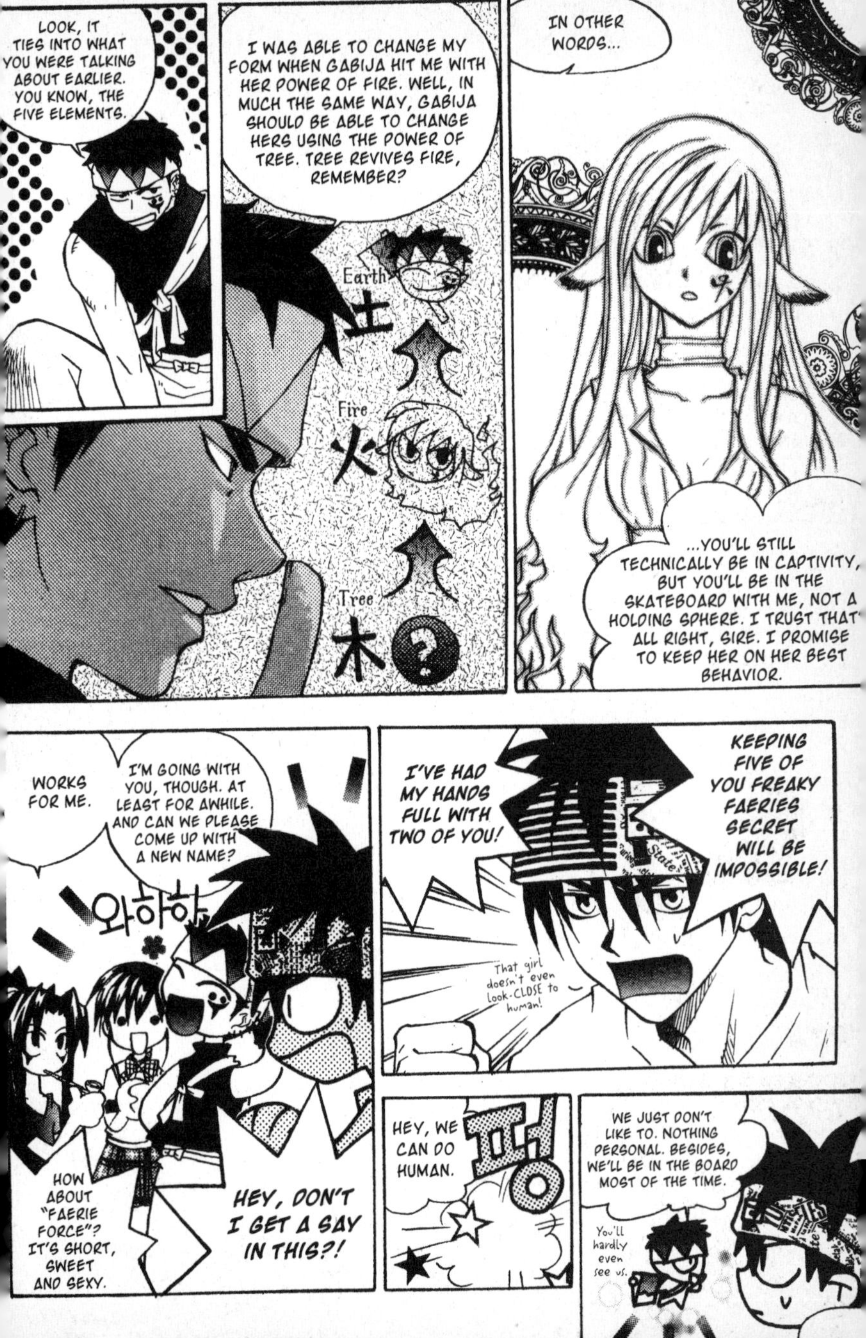
LOOK, IT TIES INTO WHAT YOU WERE TALKING ABOUT EARLIER. YOU KNOW, THE FIVE ELEMENTS.
I WAS ABLE TO CHANGE MY FORM WHEN GABIJA HIT ME WITH HER POWER OF FIRE. WELL, IN MUCH THE SAME WAY, GABIJA SHOULD BE ABLE TO CHANGE HERS USING THE POWER OF TREE. TREE REVIVES FIRE, REMEMBER?
Earth
土
Fire
火
Tree
木
IN OTHER WORDS...
...YOU'LL STILL TECHNICALLY BE IN CAPTIVITY, BUT YOU'LL BE IN THE SKATEBOARD WITH ME, NOT A HOLDING SPHERE. I TRUST THAT ALL RIGHT, SIRE. I PROMISE TO KEEP HER ON HER BEST BEHAVIOR.
WORKS FOR ME.
I'M GOING WITH YOU, THOUGH. AT LEAST FOR AWHILE. AND CAN WE PLEASE COME UP WITH A NEW NAME?
와하하
HOW ABOUT "FAERIE FORCE"? IT'S SHORT, SWEET AND SEXY.
HEY, DON'T I GET A SAY IN THIS?!
I'VE HAD MY HANDS FULL WITH TWO OF YOU!
KEEPING FIVE OF YOU FREAKY FAERIES SECRET WILL BE IMPOSSIBLE!
That girl doesn't even look-CLOSE to human!
HEY, WE CAN DO HUMAN.
WE JUST DON'T LIKE TO. NOTHING PERSONAL. BESIDES, WE'LL BE IN THE BOARD MOST OF THE TIME.
You'll hardly even see us.

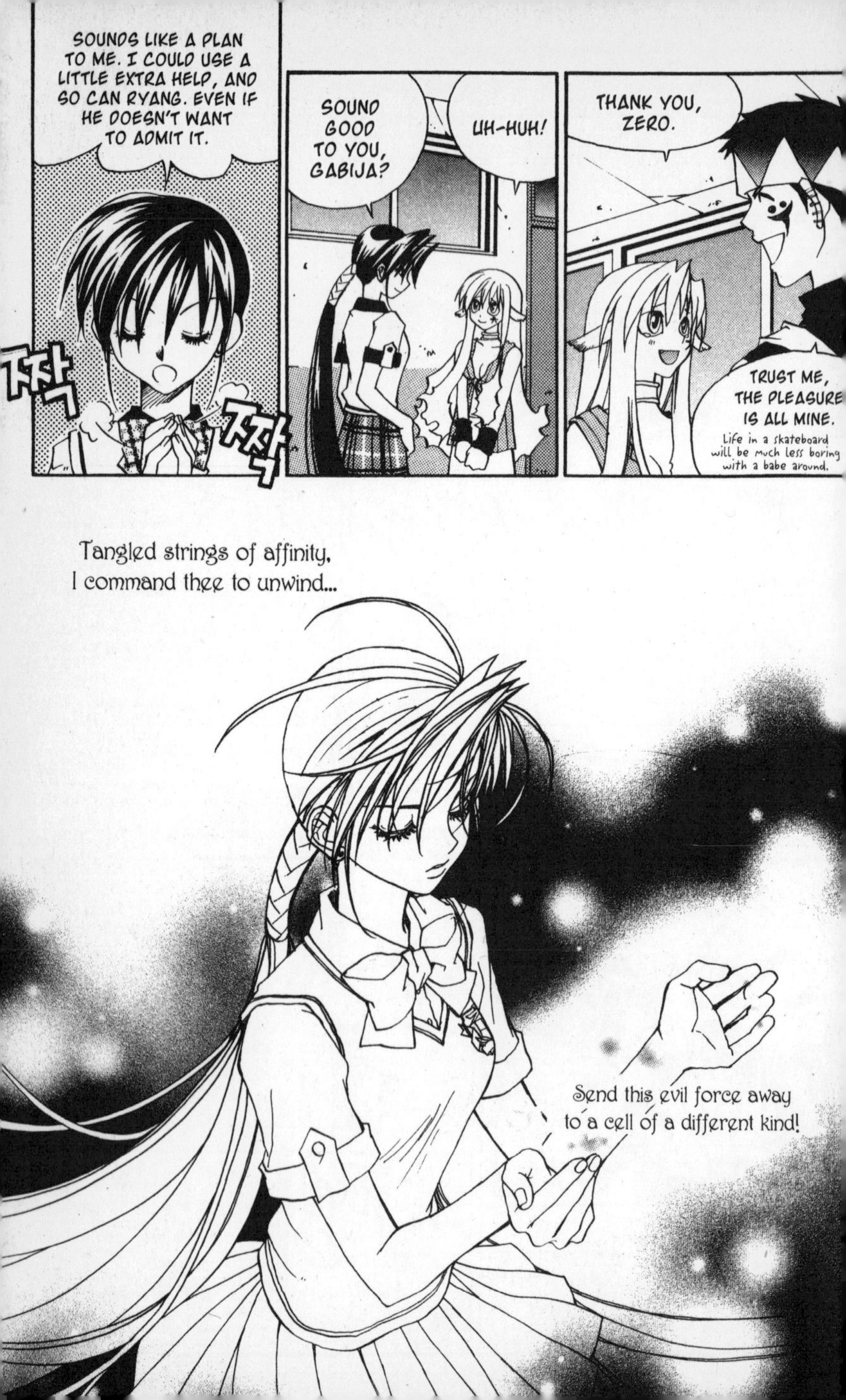
SOUNDS LIKE A PLAN TO ME. I COULD USE A LITTLE EXTRA HELP, AND SO CAN RYANG. EVEN IF HE DOESN'T WANT TO ADMIT IT.
짝
짝
SOUND GOOD TO YOU, GABIJA?
UH-HUH!
THANK YOU, ZERO.
TRUST ME, THE PLEASURE IS ALL MINE.
Life in a skateboard will be much less boring with a babe around.
Tangled strings of affinity, I command thee to unwind...
Send this evil force away to a cell of a different kind!

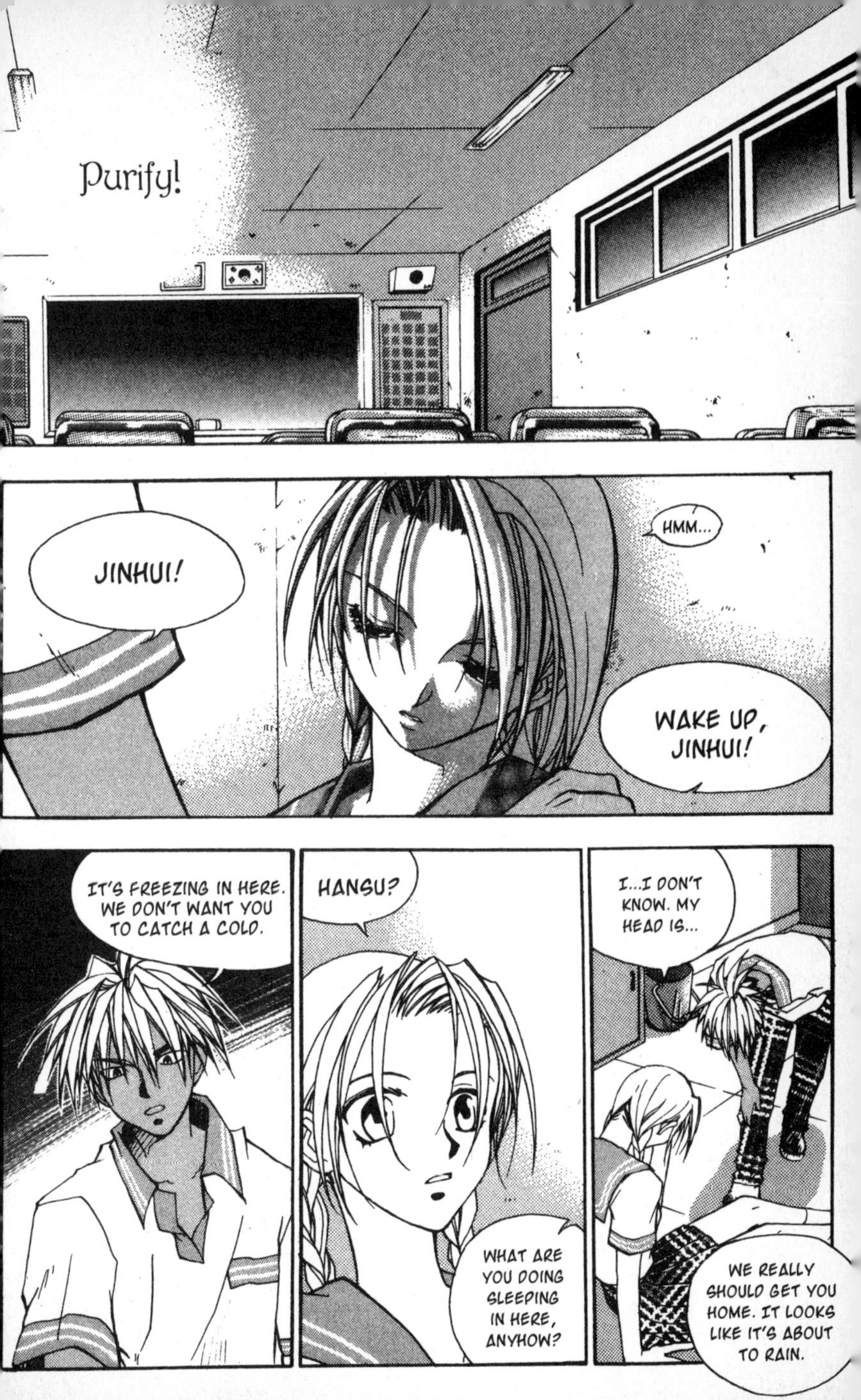
Purify!
JINHUI!
HMM...
WAKE UP, JINHUI!
IT'S FREEZING IN HERE. WE DON'T WANT YOU TO CATCH A COLD.
HANSU?
WHAT ARE YOU DOING SLEEPING IN HERE, ANYHOW?
I...I DON'T KNOW. MY HEAD IS...
WE REALLY SHOULD GET YOU HOME. IT LOOKS LIKE IT'S ABOUT TO RAIN.

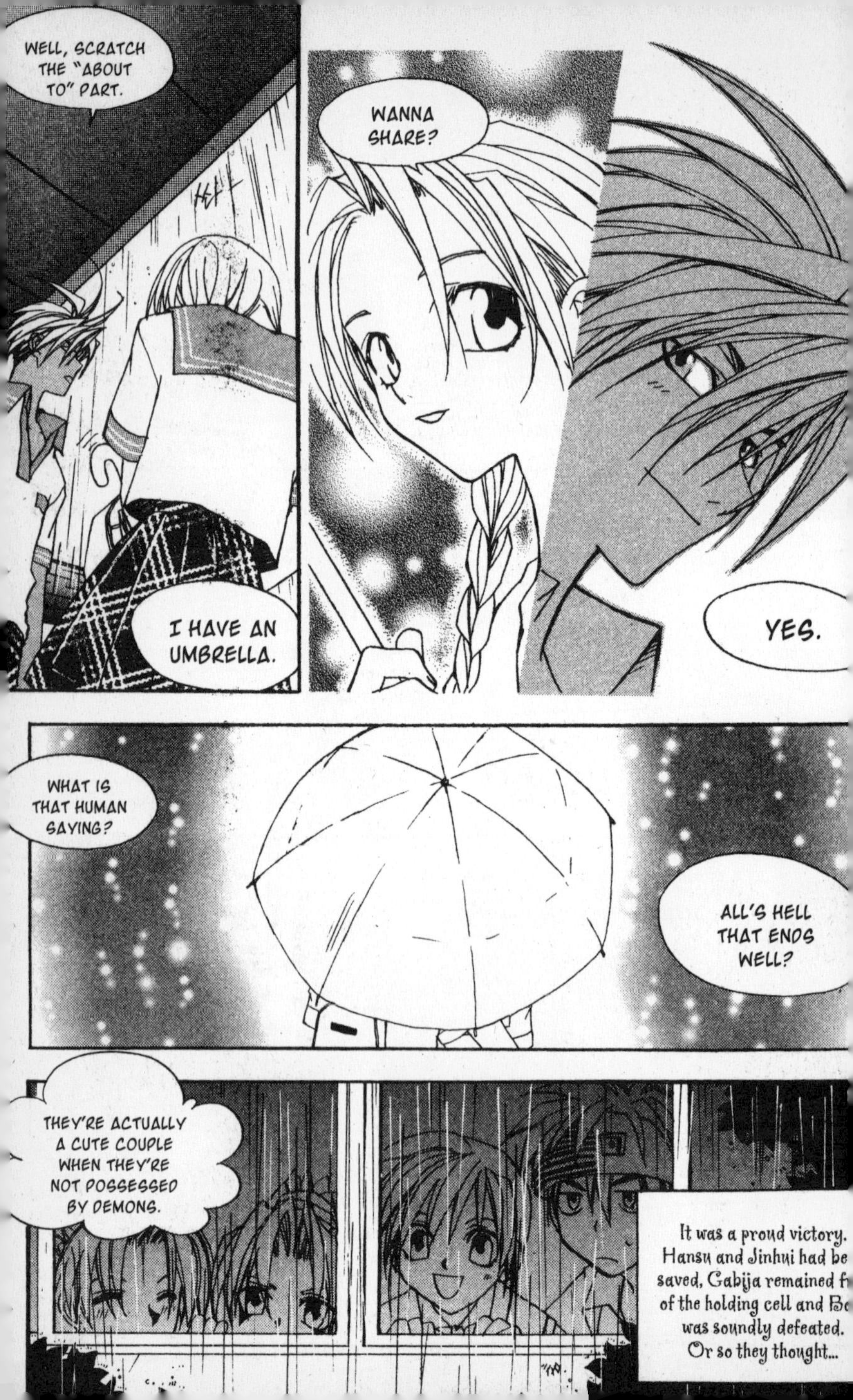
WELL, SCRATCH THE "ABOUT TO" PART.
I HAVE AN UMBRELLA.
WANNA SHARE?
YES.
WHAT IS THAT HUMAN SAYING?
ALL'S HELL THAT ENDS WELL?
THEY'RE ACTUALLY A CUTE COUPLE WHEN THEY'RE NOT POSSESSED BY DEMONS.
It was a proud victory. Hansu and Jinhui had be saved, Gabija remained f of the holding cell and Be was soundly defeated. Or so they thought...

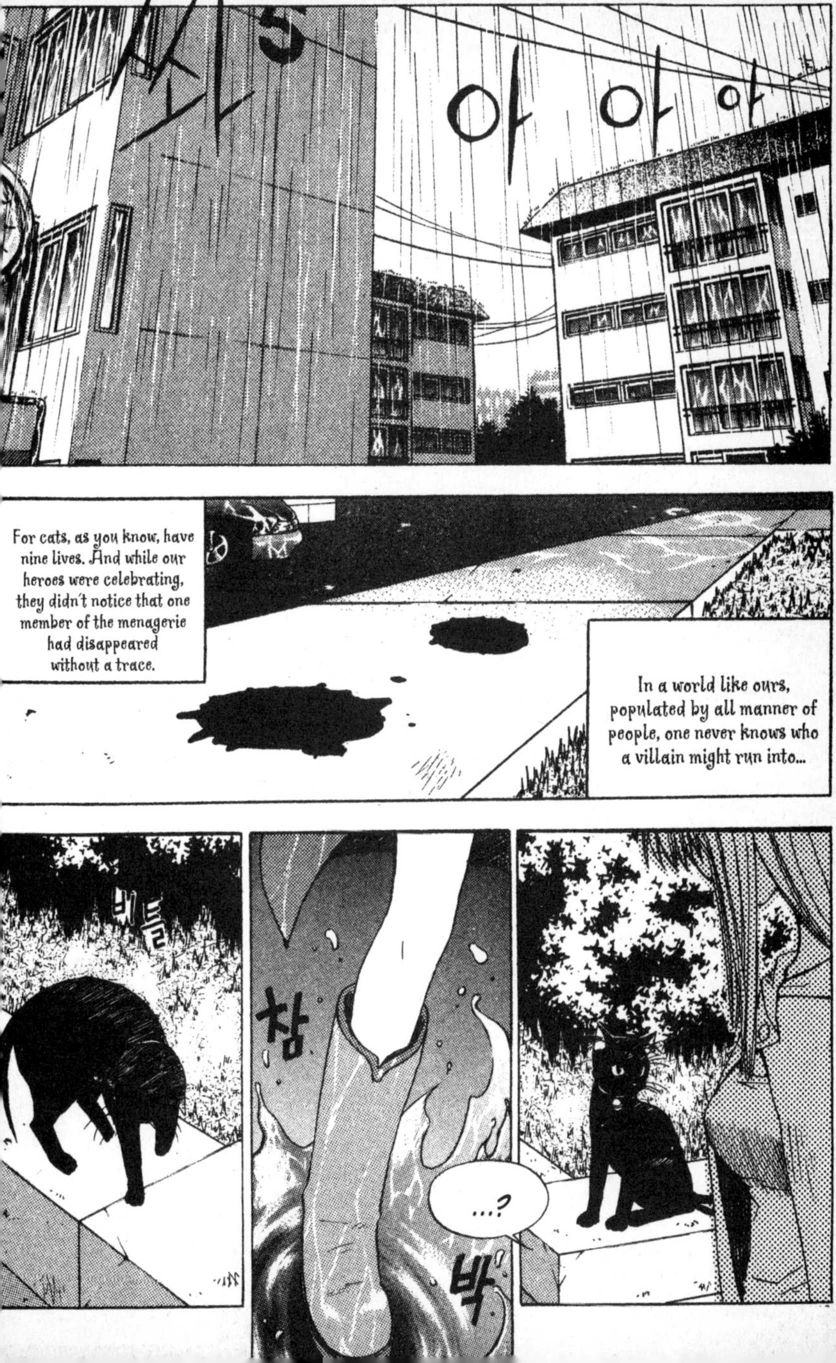
쏴
아 아 아
For cats, as you know, have nine lives. And while our heroes were celebrating, they didn't notice that one member of the menagerie had disappeared without a trace.
In a world like ours, populated by all manner of people, one never knows who a villain might run into...
비틀
참
...?
박

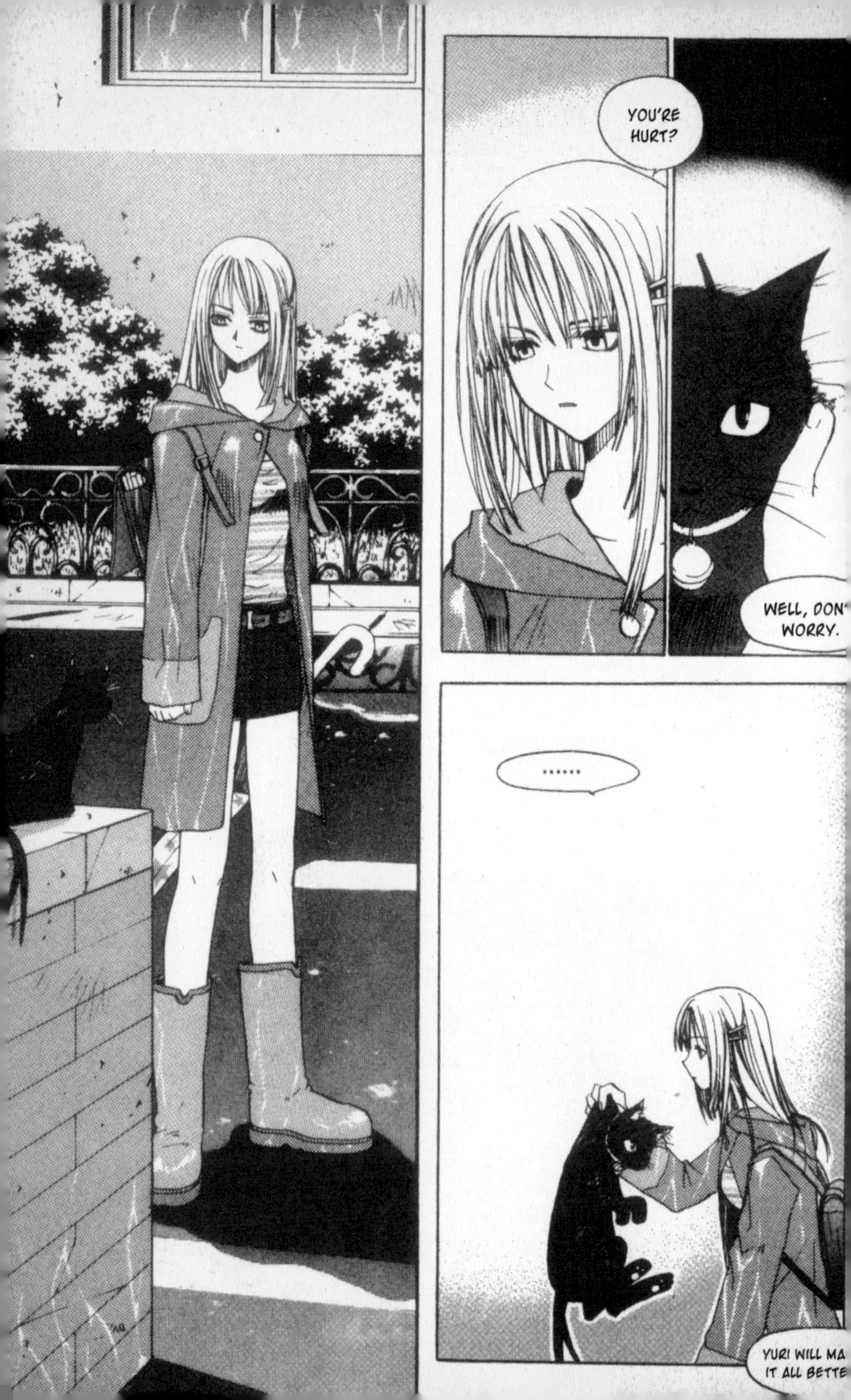
YOU'RE HURT?
WELL, DON'
WORRY.
......
YURI WILL MA
IT ALL BETTE

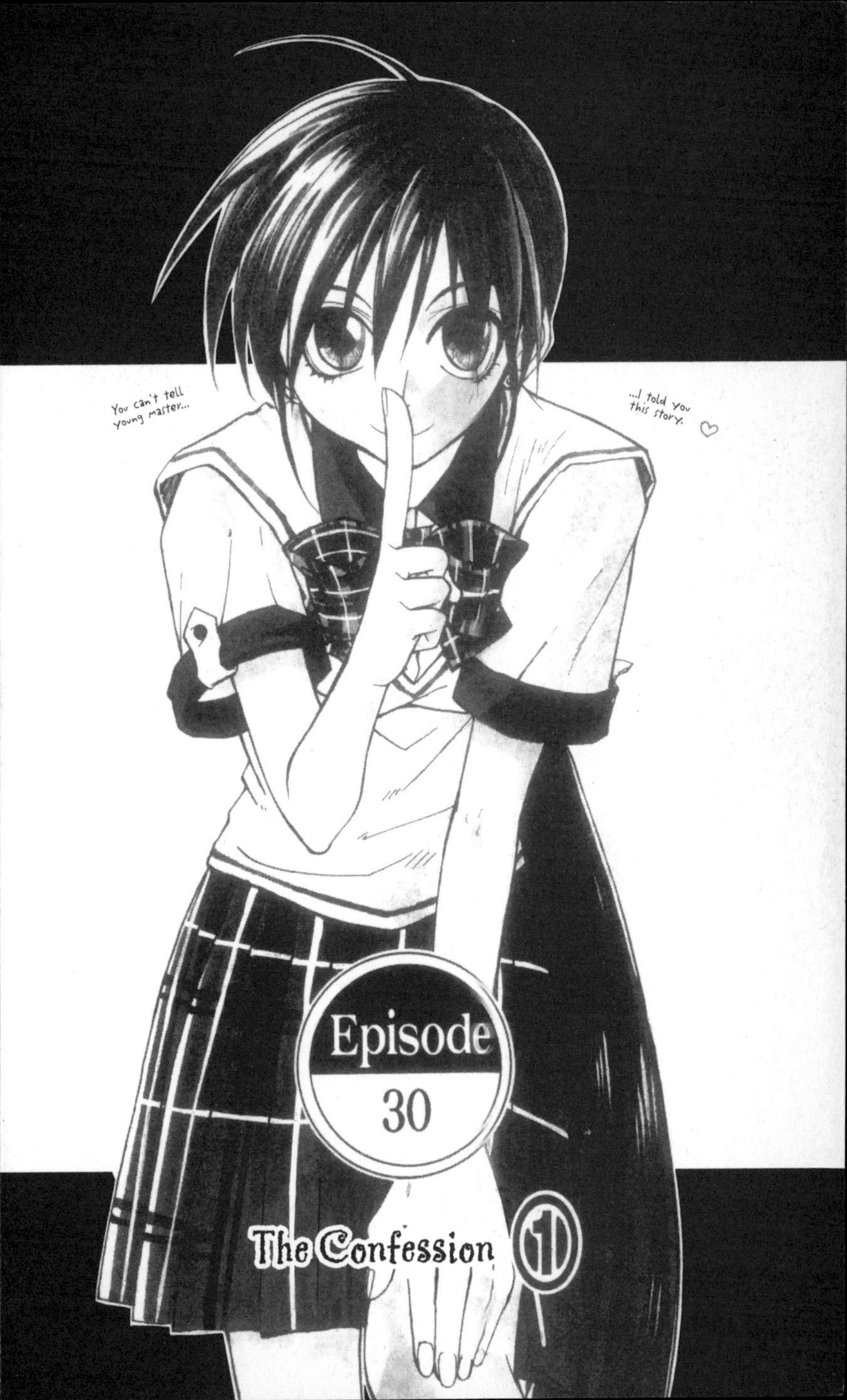
You can't tell young master...
...I told you this story.
Episode
30
The Confession (1)

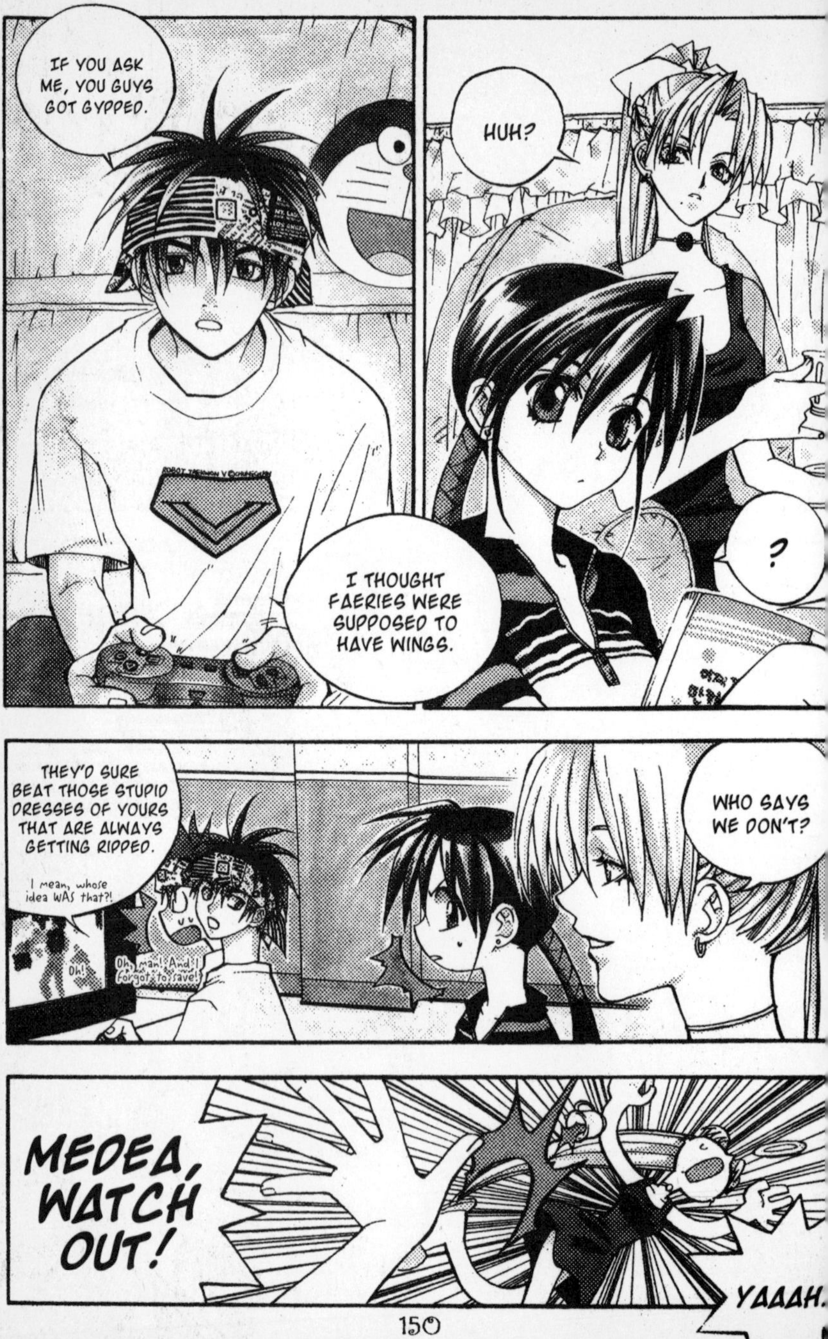

IF YOU ASK ME, YOU GUYS GOT GYPPED.
HUH?
I THOUGHT FAERIES WERE SUPPOSED TO HAVE WINGS.
?
THEY'D SURE BEAT THOSE STUPID DRESSES OF YOURS THAT ARE ALWAYS GETTING RIPPED.
I mean, whose idea WAS that?!
Oh!
Oh, man! And I forgot to save!
WHO SAYS WE DON'T?
MEDEA, WATCH OUT!
YAAAH.

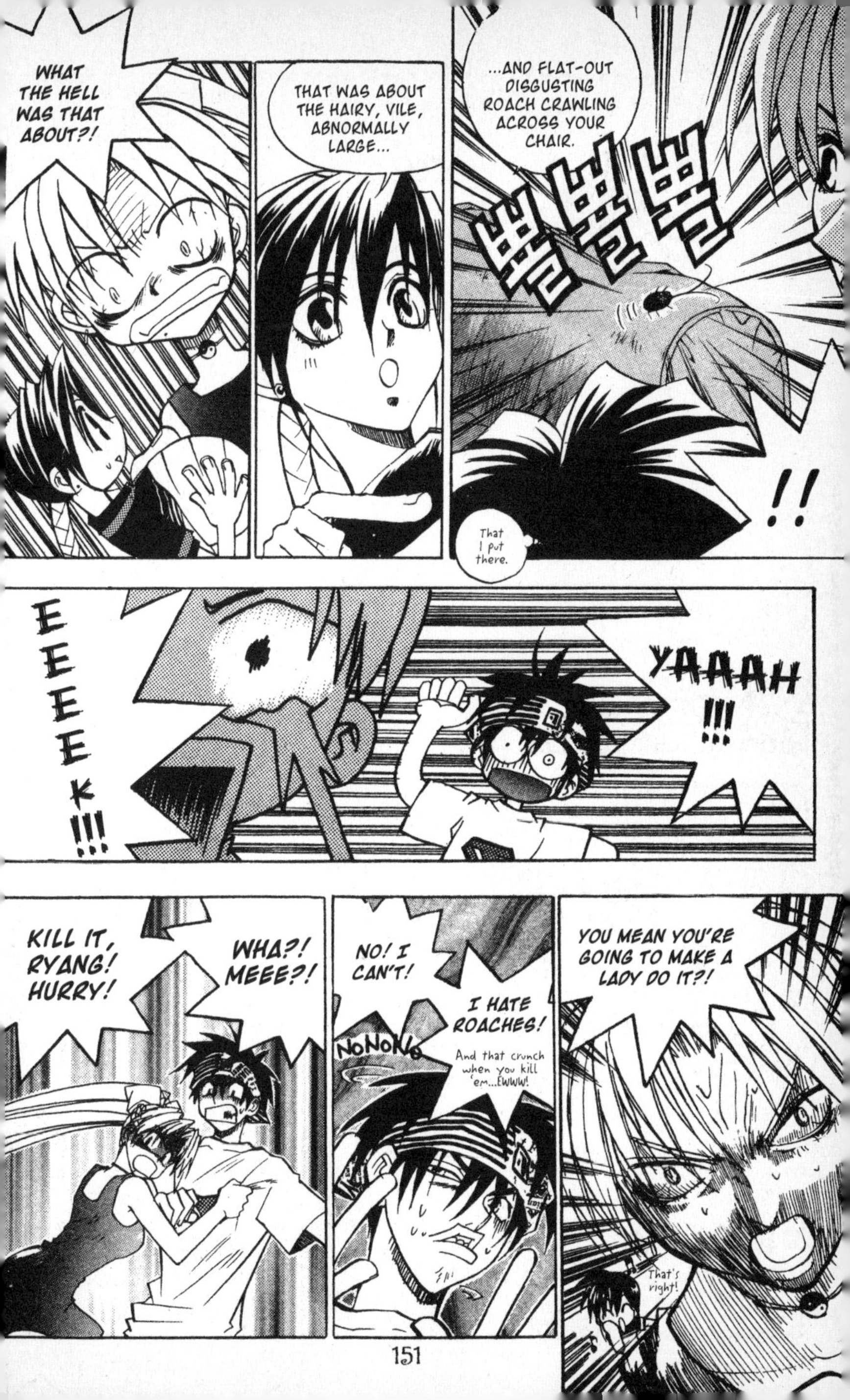
WHAT THE HELL WAS THAT ABOUT?!
THAT WAS ABOUT THE HAIRY, VILE, ABNORMALLY LARGE...
...AND FLAT-OUT DISGUSTING ROACH CRAWLING ACROSS YOUR CHAIR.
뽈뽈뽈
!!
That I put there.
EEEEEK!!!
YAAAH!!!
KILL IT, RYANG! HURRY!
WHA?! MEEE?!
NO! I CAN'T!
NoNoNo
I HATE ROACHES!
And that crunch when you kill 'em...EWWW!
YOU MEAN YOU'RE GOING TO MAKE A LADY DO IT?!
That's right!

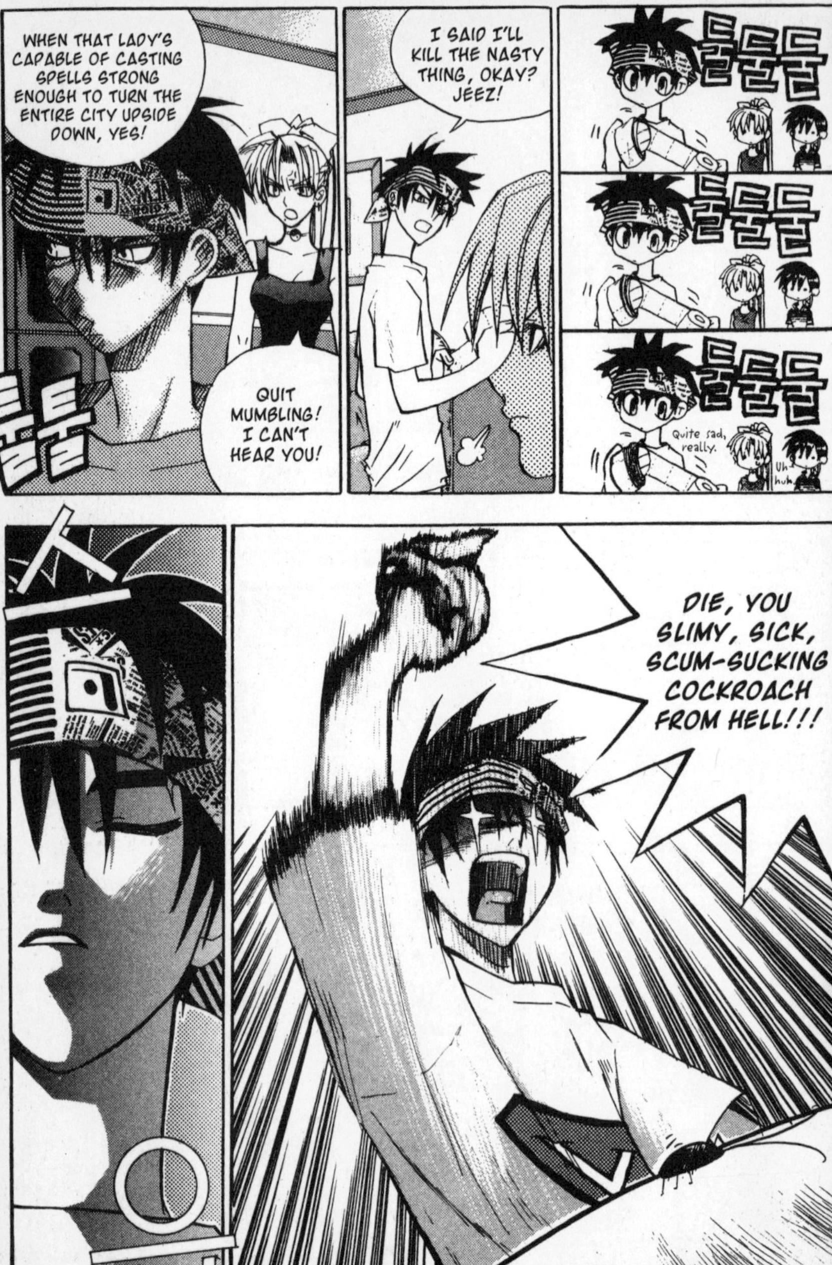
WHEN THAT LADY'S CAPABLE OF CASTING SPELLS STRONG ENOUGH TO TURN THE ENTIRE CITY UPSIDE DOWN, YES!
QUIT MUMBLING! I CAN'T HEAR YOU!
툴툴
I SAID I'LL KILL THE NASTY THING, OKAY? JEEZ!
둘둘둘
둘둘둘
둘둘둘
Quite sad, really.
Uh-huh.
DIE, YOU SLIMY, SICK, SCUM-SUCKING COCKROACH FROM HELL!!!

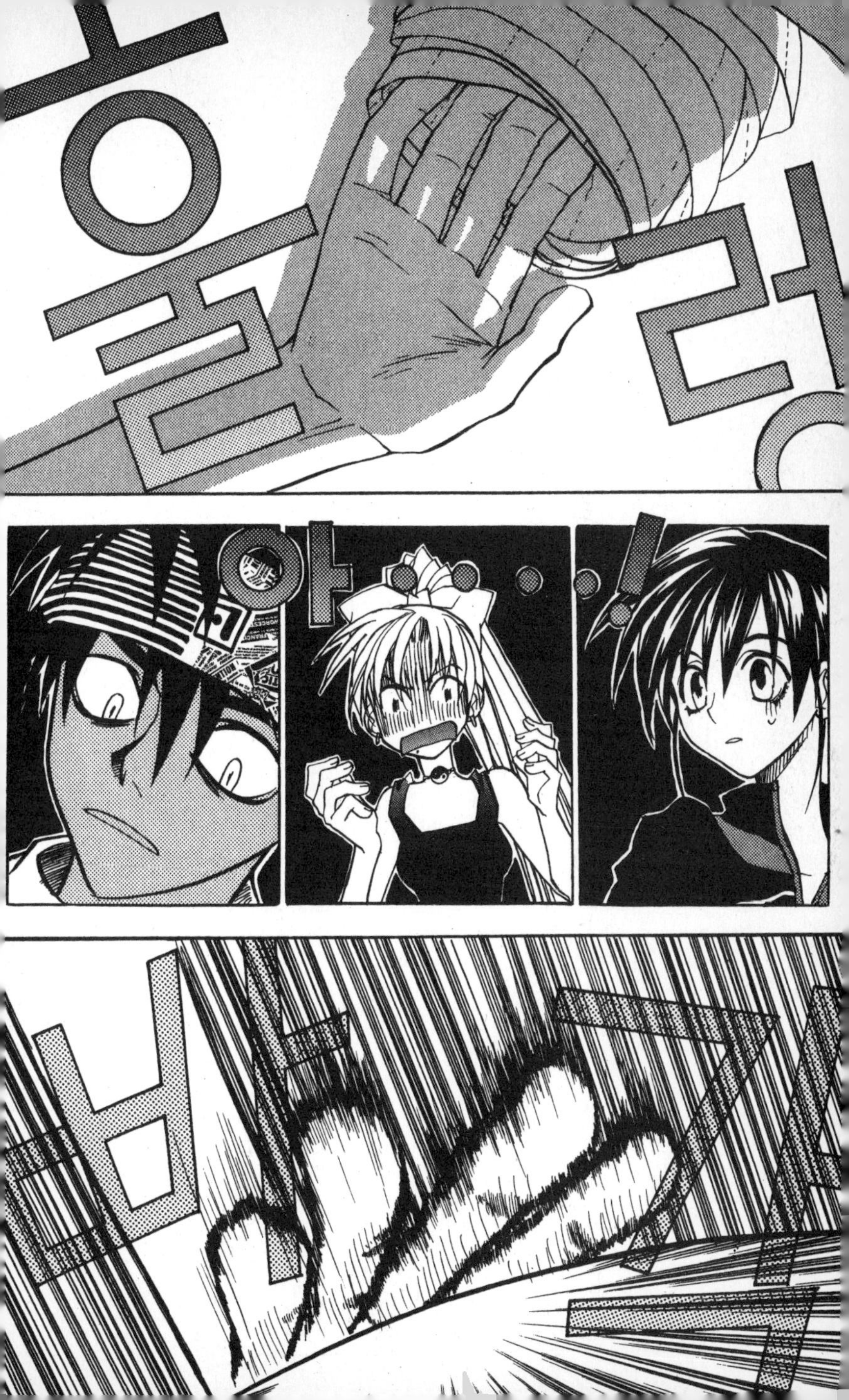
아...!

HEY, REX! DID YOU DO A GOOD JOB WATCHING THE HOUSE?

ARF!

AWW! WHO'S A GOOD BOY? THAT'S RIGHT! WHO'S A GOOD BOY? ♡

ARF! ARF!

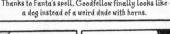

Thanks to Fanta's spell, Goodfellow finally looks like a dog instead of a weird dude with horns.

YOU'RE MY WIDDLE REXY SEXY, AREN'T YOU? AREN'T YOU? THAT'S RIGHT!

GET ME OUT OF HERE!

YOU'RE THE REASON I'VE BEEN COMING HOME SO EARLY!

하하하

WHA

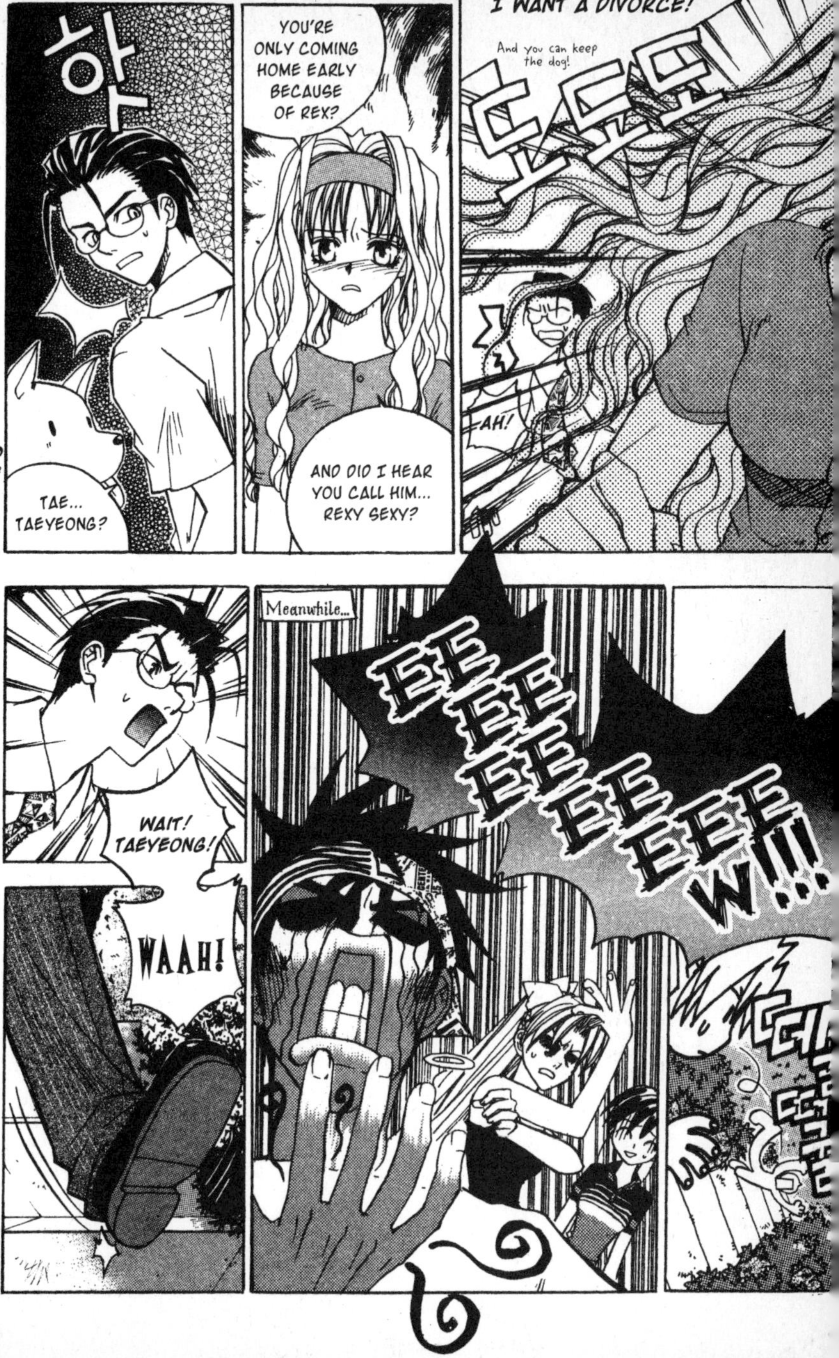
항
TAE... TAEYEONG?
YOU'RE ONLY COMING HOME EARLY BECAUSE OF REX?
AND DID I HEAR YOU CALL HIM... REXY SEXY?
I WANT A DIVORCE!
And you can keep the dog!
AH!
WAIT! TAEYEONG!
WAAH!
Meanwhile...
EEEEEEEEEEEW!!!

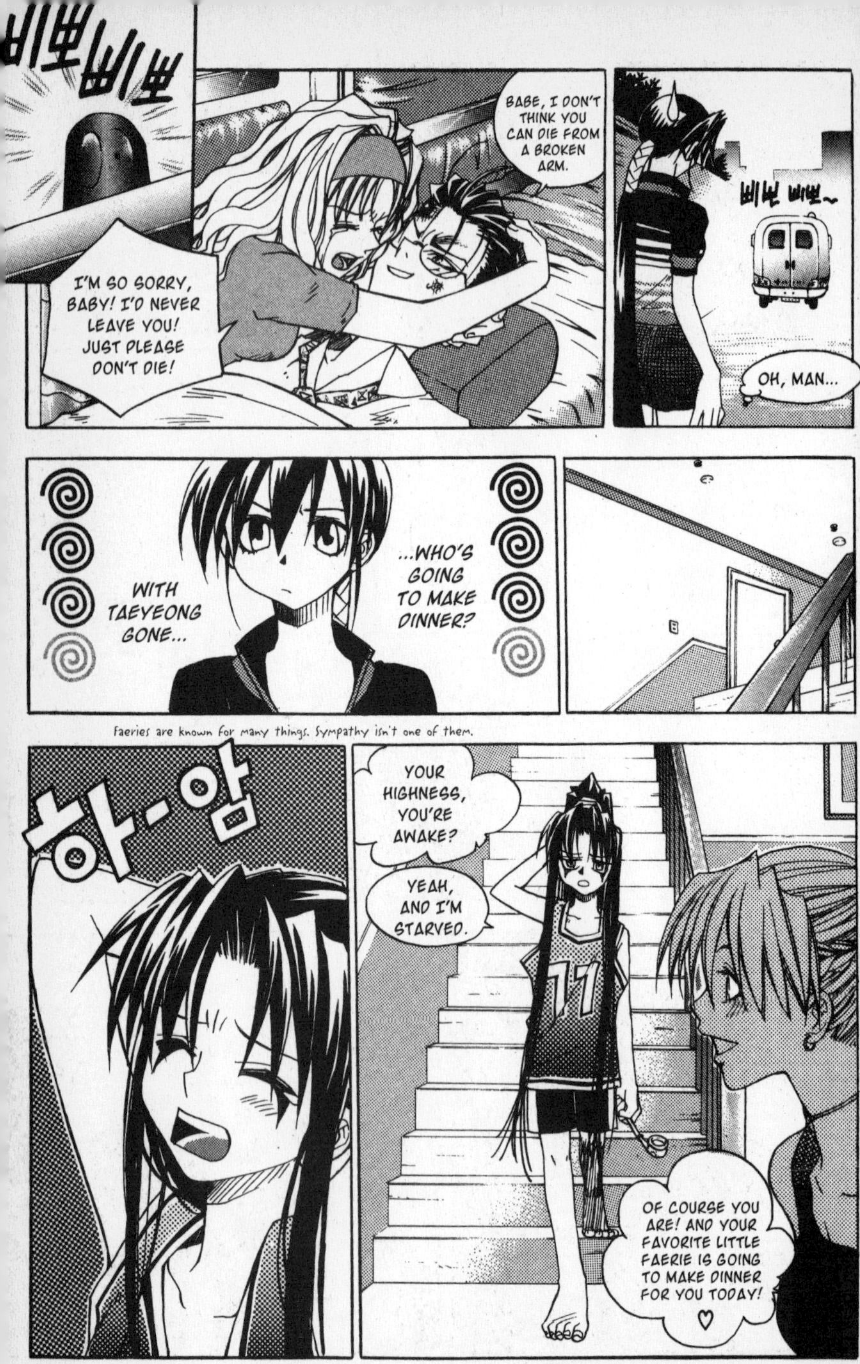
삐뽀 삐뽀
BABE, I DON'T THINK YOU CAN DIE FROM A BROKEN ARM.
I'M SO SORRY, BABY! I'D NEVER LEAVE YOU! JUST PLEASE DON'T DIE!
삐뽀 삐뽀~
OH, MAN...
WITH TAEYEONG GONE...
...WHO'S GOING TO MAKE DINNER?
Faeries are known for many things. Sympathy isn't one of them.
하-암
YOUR HIGHNESS, YOU'RE AWAKE?
YEAH, AND I'M STARVED.
OF COURSE YOU ARE! AND YOUR FAVORITE LITTLE FAERIE IS GOING TO MAKE DINNER FOR YOU TODAY! ♡

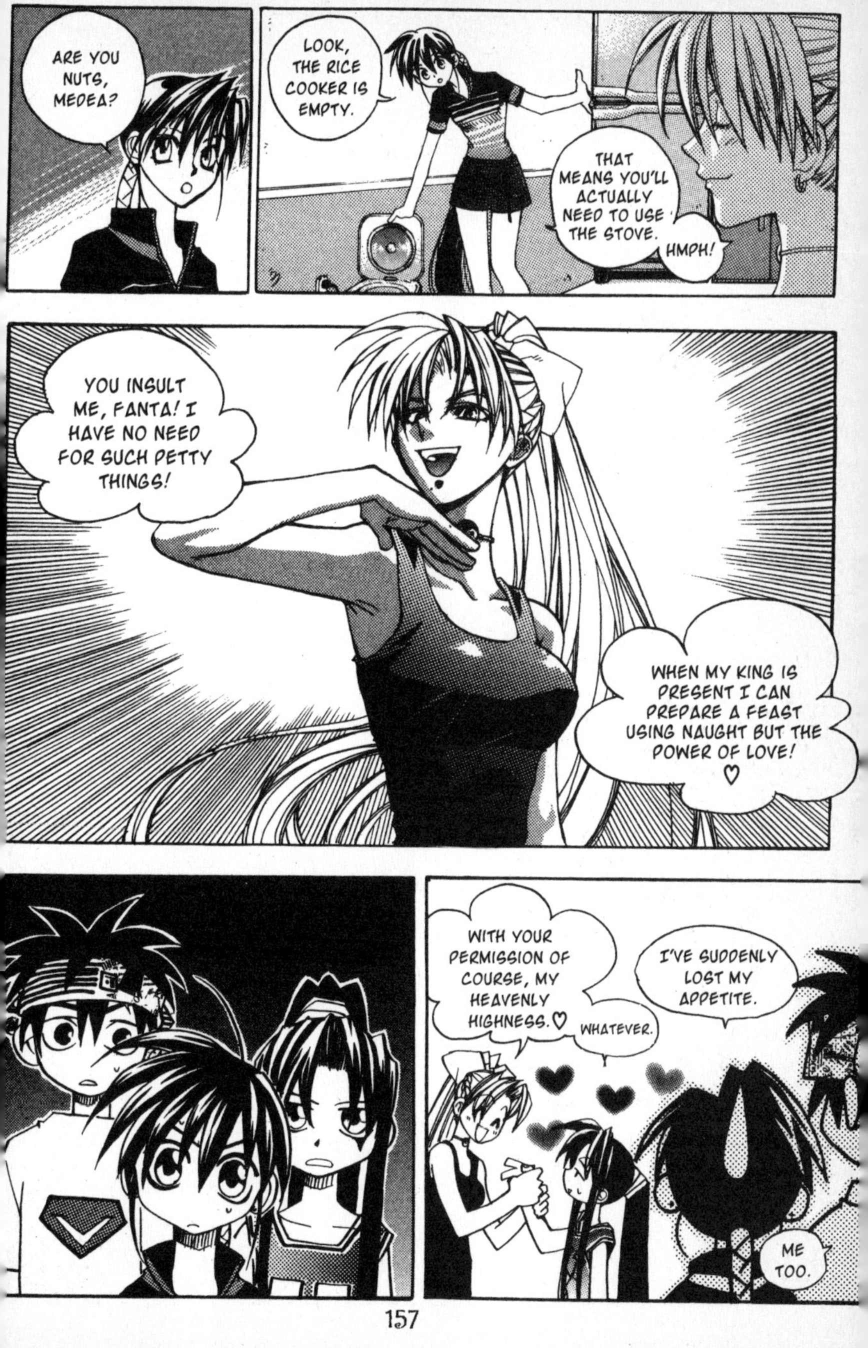
ARE YOU NUTS, MEDEA?
LOOK, THE RICE COOKER IS EMPTY.
THAT MEANS YOU'LL ACTUALLY NEED TO USE THE STOVE.
HMPH!
YOU INSULT ME, FANTA! I HAVE NO NEED FOR SUCH PETTY THINGS!
WHEN MY KING IS PRESENT I CAN PREPARE A FEAST USING NAUGHT BUT THE POWER OF LOVE! ♡
WITH YOUR PERMISSION OF COURSE, MY HEAVENLY HIGHNESS.♡
WHATEVER.
I'VE SUDDENLY LOST MY APPETITE.
ME TOO.

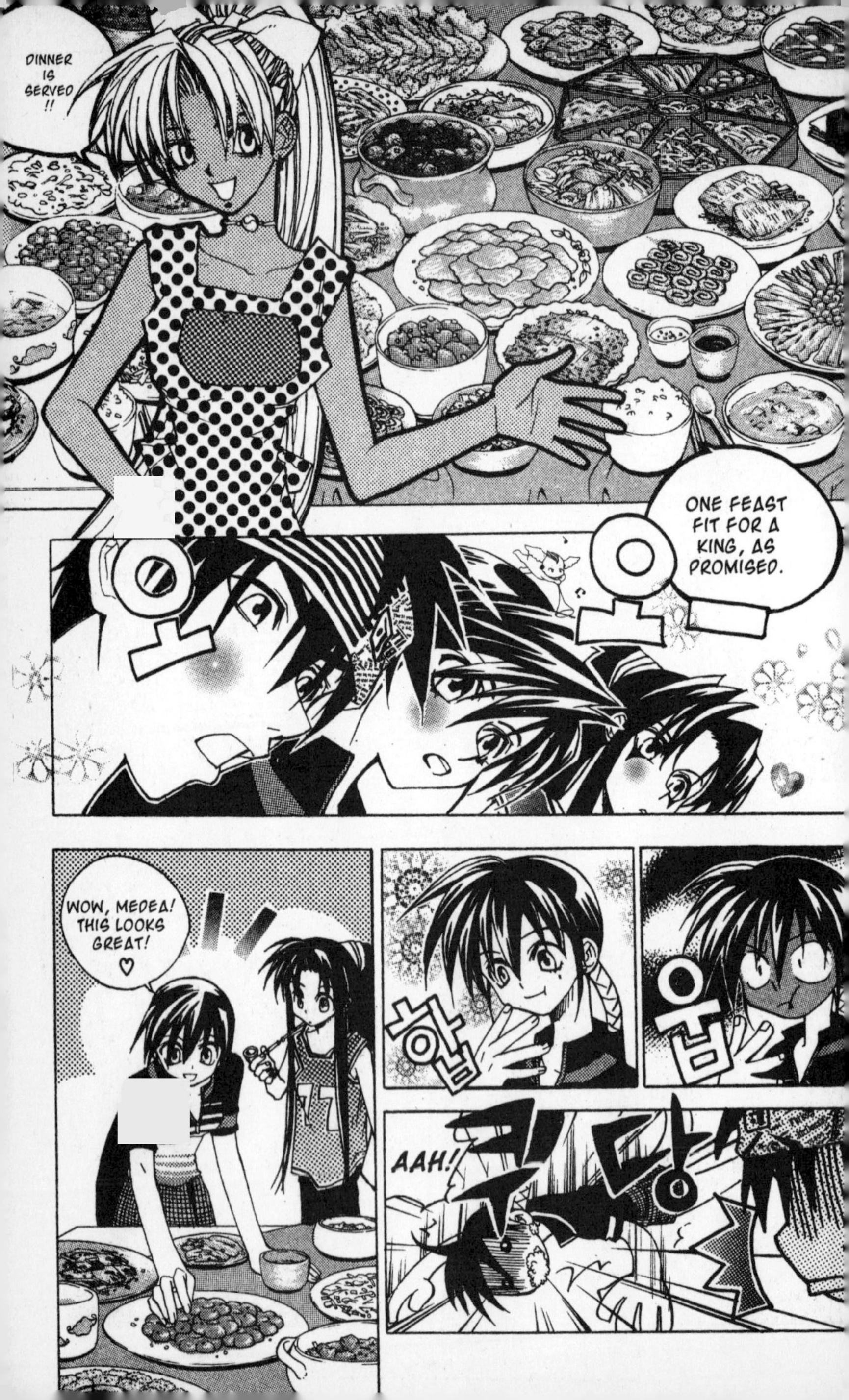
DINNER IS SERVED !!
ONE FEAST FIT FOR A KING, AS PROMISED.
WOW, MEDEA! THIS LOOKS GREAT! ♡
AAH!

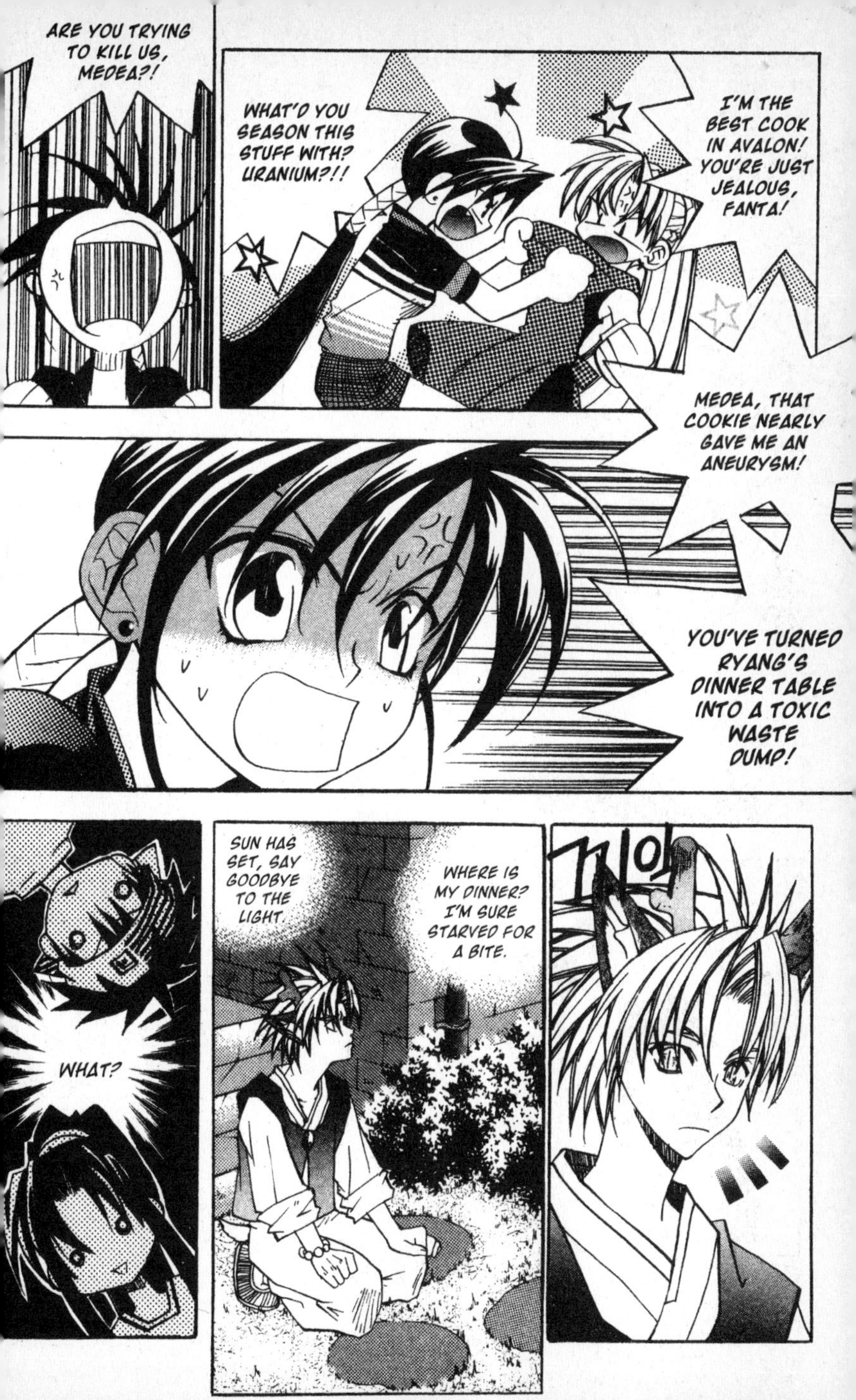
ARE YOU TRYING TO KILL US, MEDEA?!
WHAT'D YOU SEASON THIS STUFF WITH? URANIUM?!!
I'M THE BEST COOK IN AVALON! YOU'RE JUST JEALOUS, FANTA!
MEDEA, THAT COOKIE NEARLY GAVE ME AN ANEURYSM!
YOU'VE TURNED RYANG'S DINNER TABLE INTO A TOXIC WASTE DUMP!
WHAT?
SUN HAS SET, SAY GOODBYE TO THE LIGHT.
WHERE IS MY DINNER? I'M SURE STARVED FOR A BITE.

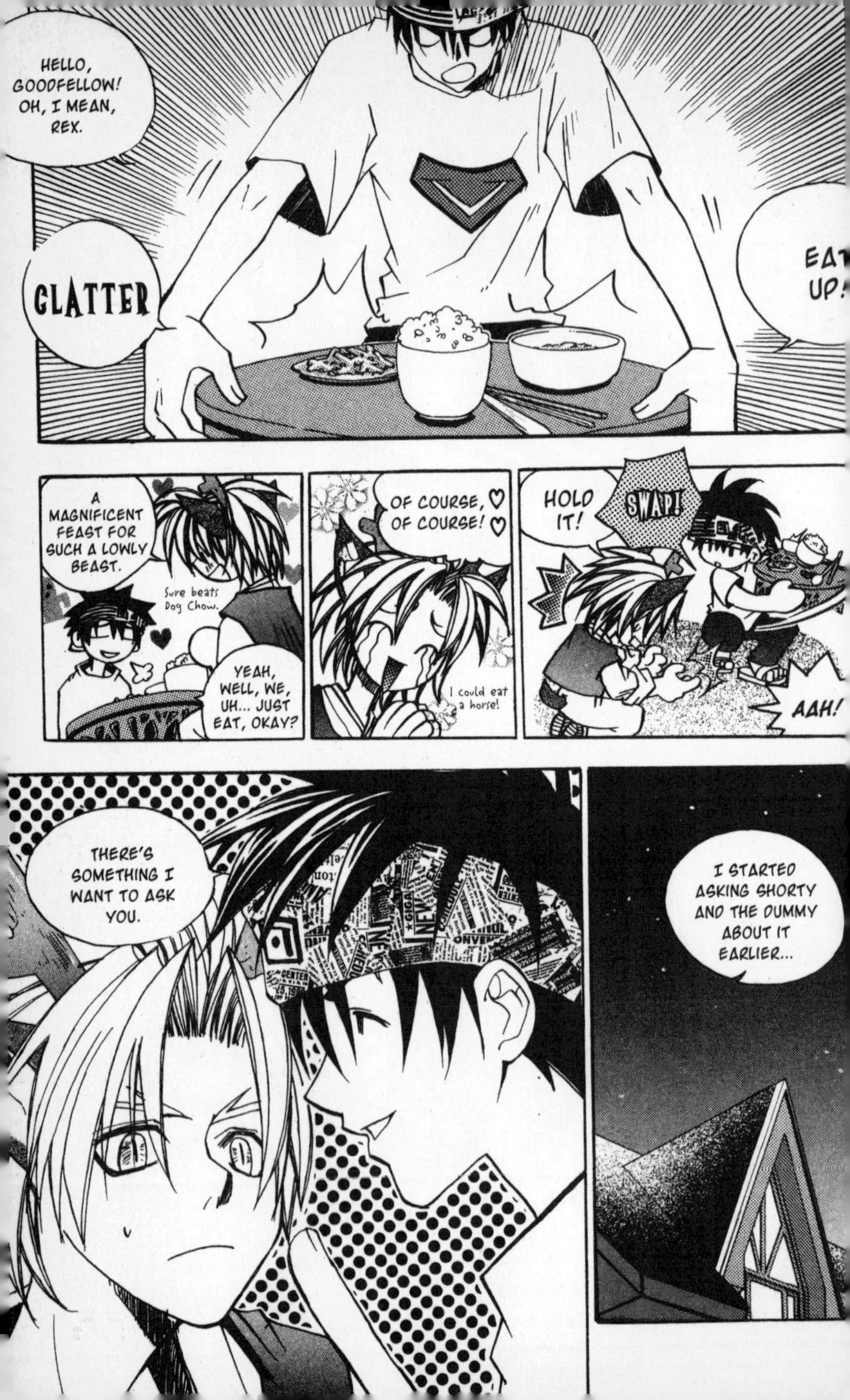
HELLO, GOODFELLOW! OH, I MEAN, REX.
CLATTER
EAT UP!
A MAGNIFICENT FEAST FOR SUCH A LOWLY BEAST.
Sure beats Dog Chow.
YEAH, WELL, WE, UH... JUST EAT, OKAY?
OF COURSE, ♡ OF COURSE! ♡
I could eat a horse!
HOLD IT!
SWAP!
AAH!
THERE'S SOMETHING I WANT TO ASK YOU.
I STARTED ASKING SHORTY AND THE DUMMY ABOUT IT EARLIER...

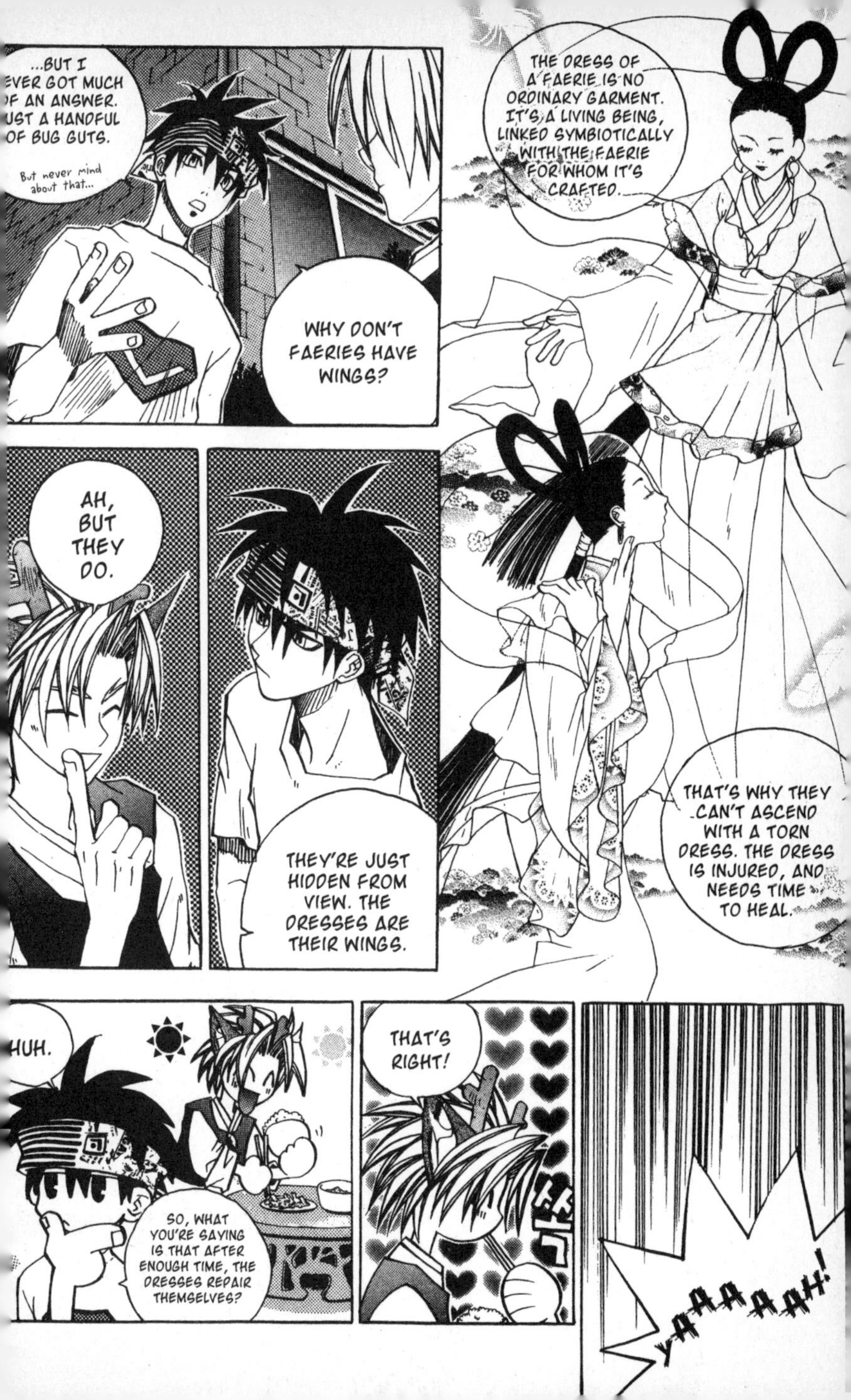
...BUT I
EVER GOT MUCH
F AN ANSWER.
UST A HANDFUL
OF BUG GUTS.
But never mind about that...
WHY DON'T FAERIES HAVE WINGS?
AH, BUT THEY DO.
THEY'RE JUST HIDDEN FROM VIEW. THE DRESSES ARE THEIR WINGS.
THE DRESS OF A FAERIE IS NO ORDINARY GARMENT. IT'S A LIVING BEING, LINKED SYMBIOTICALLY WITH THE FAERIE FOR WHOM IT'S CRAFTED.
THAT'S WHY THEY CAN'T ASCEND WITH A TORN DRESS. THE DRESS IS INJURED, AND NEEDS TIME TO HEAL.
HUH.
SO, WHAT YOU'RE SAYING IS THAT AFTER ENOUGH TIME, THE DRESSES REPAIR THEMSELVES?
THAT'S RIGHT!
YAAAAAH!

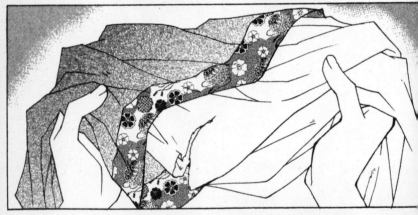

I THINK THE DRESSES ARE STILL IN HUN'S CLOSET.

HUH?

SHORTY?

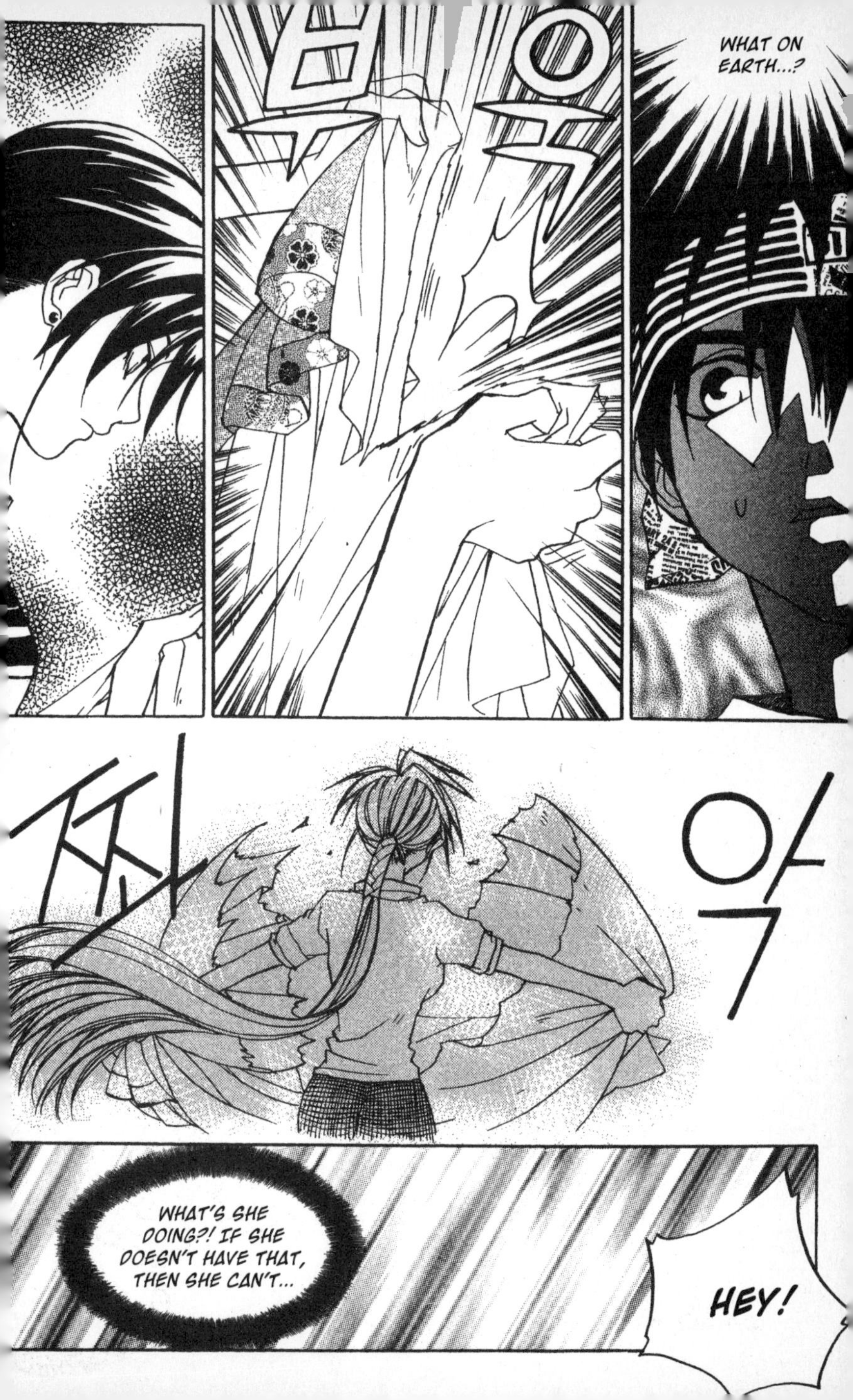
WHAT ON EARTH...?
WHAT'S SHE DOING?! IF SHE DOESN'T HAVE THAT, THEN SHE CAN'T...
HEY!

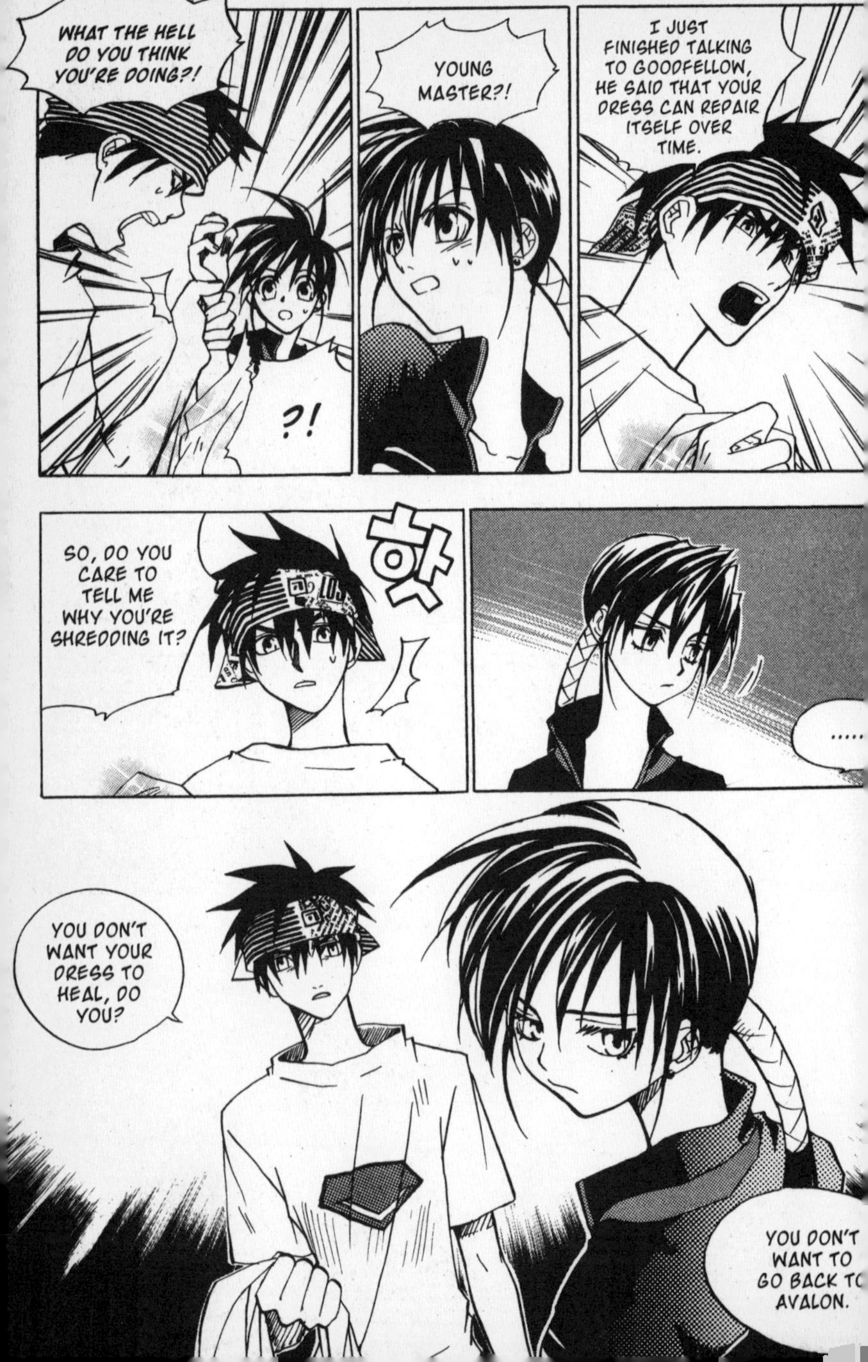
WHAT THE HELL DO YOU THINK YOU'RE DOING?!
?!
YOUNG MASTER?!
I JUST FINISHED TALKING TO GOODFELLOW, HE SAID THAT YOUR DRESS CAN REPAIR ITSELF OVER TIME.
SO, DO YOU CARE TO TELL ME WHY YOU'RE SHREDDING IT?
핫
.....
YOU DON'T WANT YOUR DRESS TO HEAL, DO YOU?
YOU DON'T WANT TO GO BACK TO AVALON.

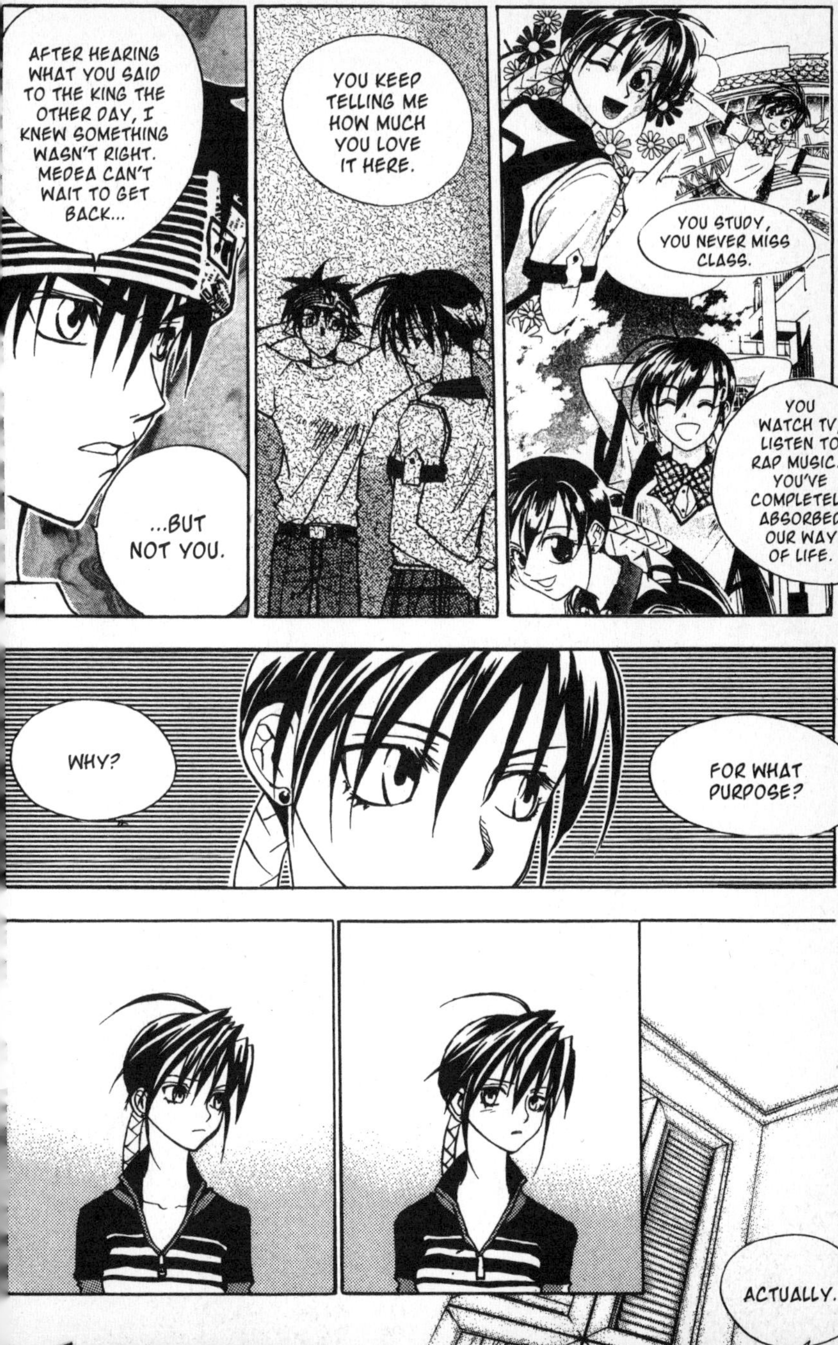
AFTER HEARING WHAT YOU SAID TO THE KING THE OTHER DAY, I KNEW SOMETHING WASN'T RIGHT. MEDEA CAN'T WAIT TO GET BACK...
...BUT NOT YOU.
YOU KEEP TELLING ME HOW MUCH YOU LOVE IT HERE.
YOU STUDY, YOU NEVER MISS CLASS.
YOU WATCH TV, LISTEN TO RAP MUSIC... YOU'VE COMPLETELY ABSORBED OUR WAY OF LIFE.
WHY?
FOR WHAT PURPOSE?
ACTUALLY...

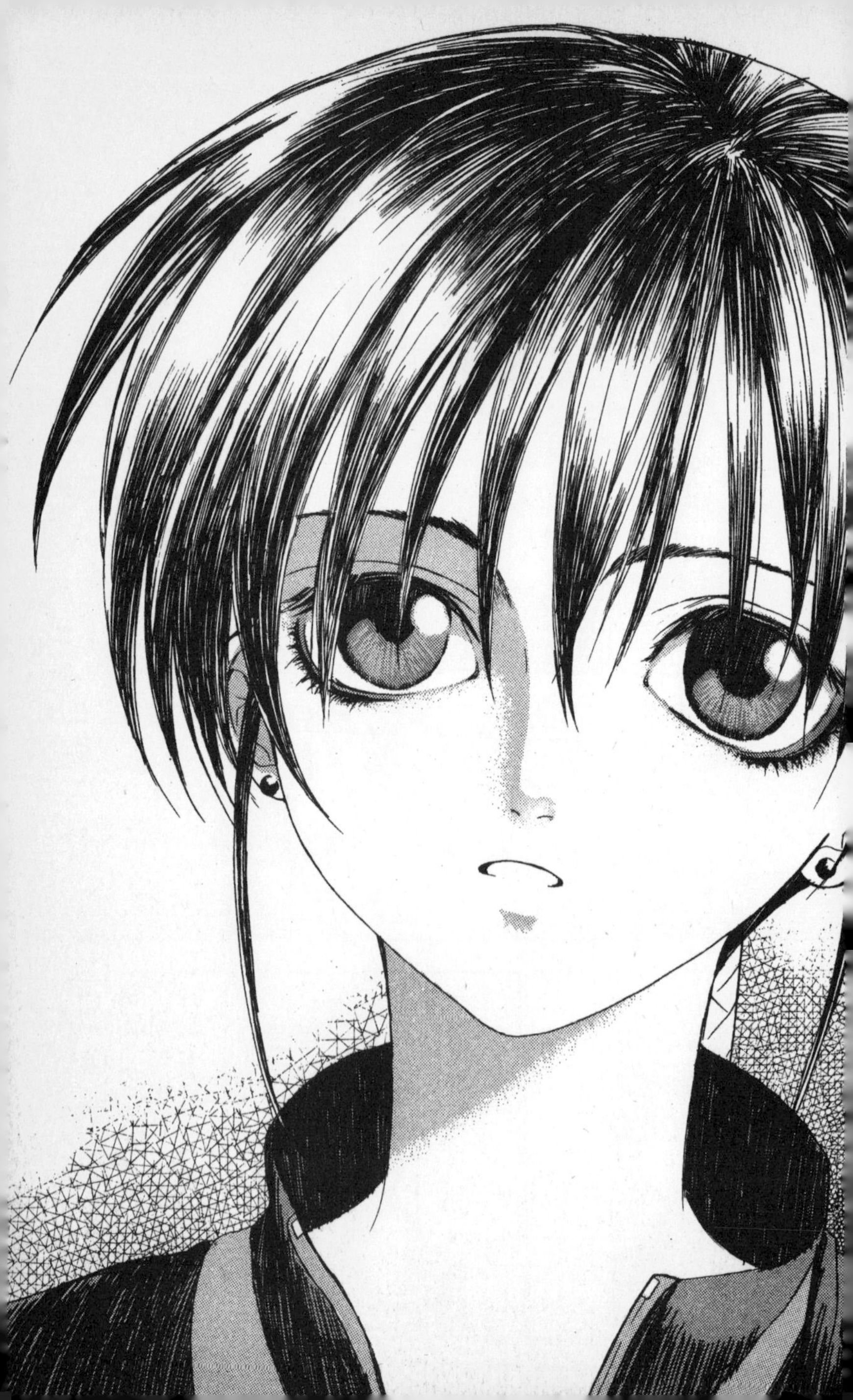

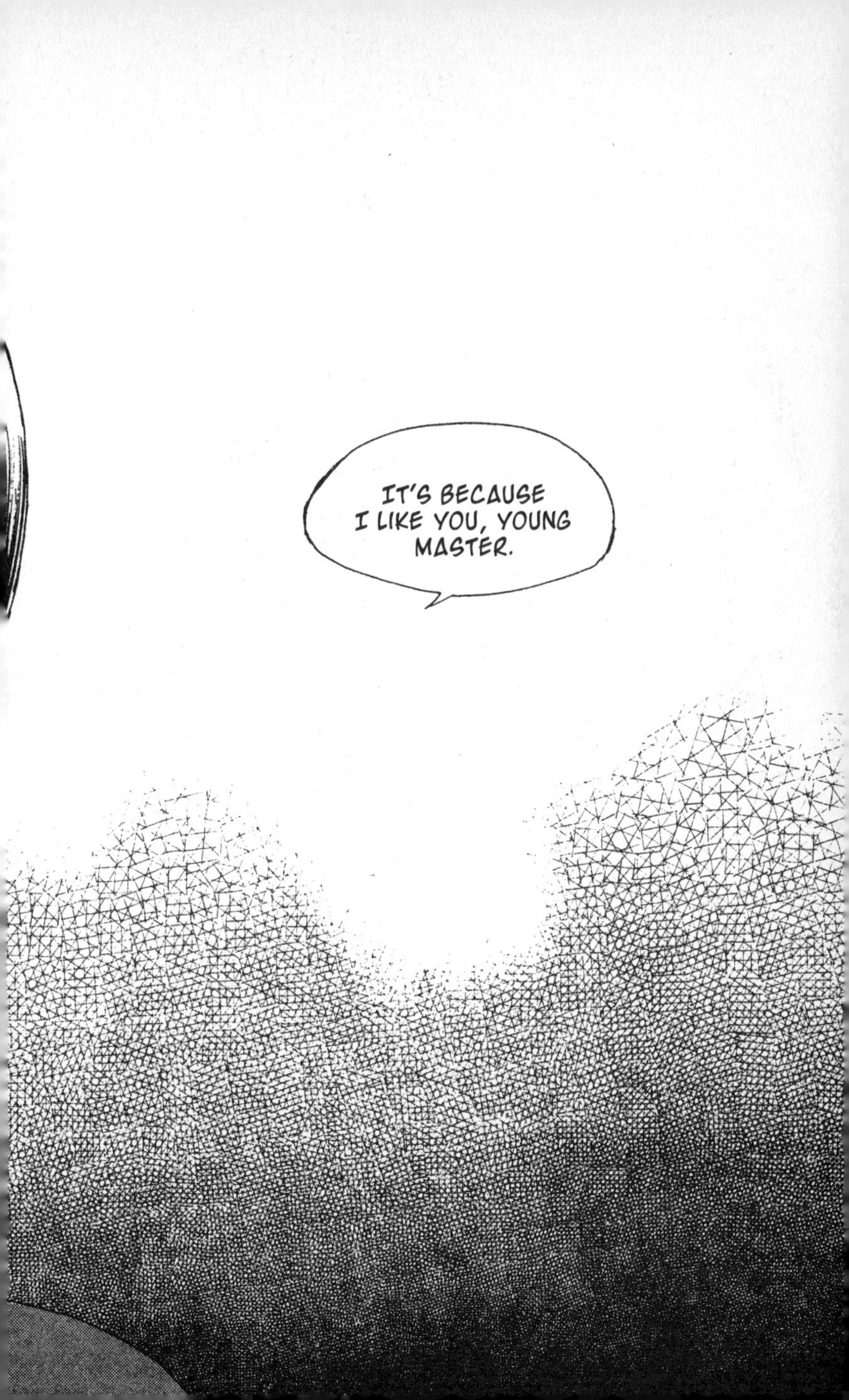
IT'S BECAUSE I LIKE YOU, YOUNG MASTER.

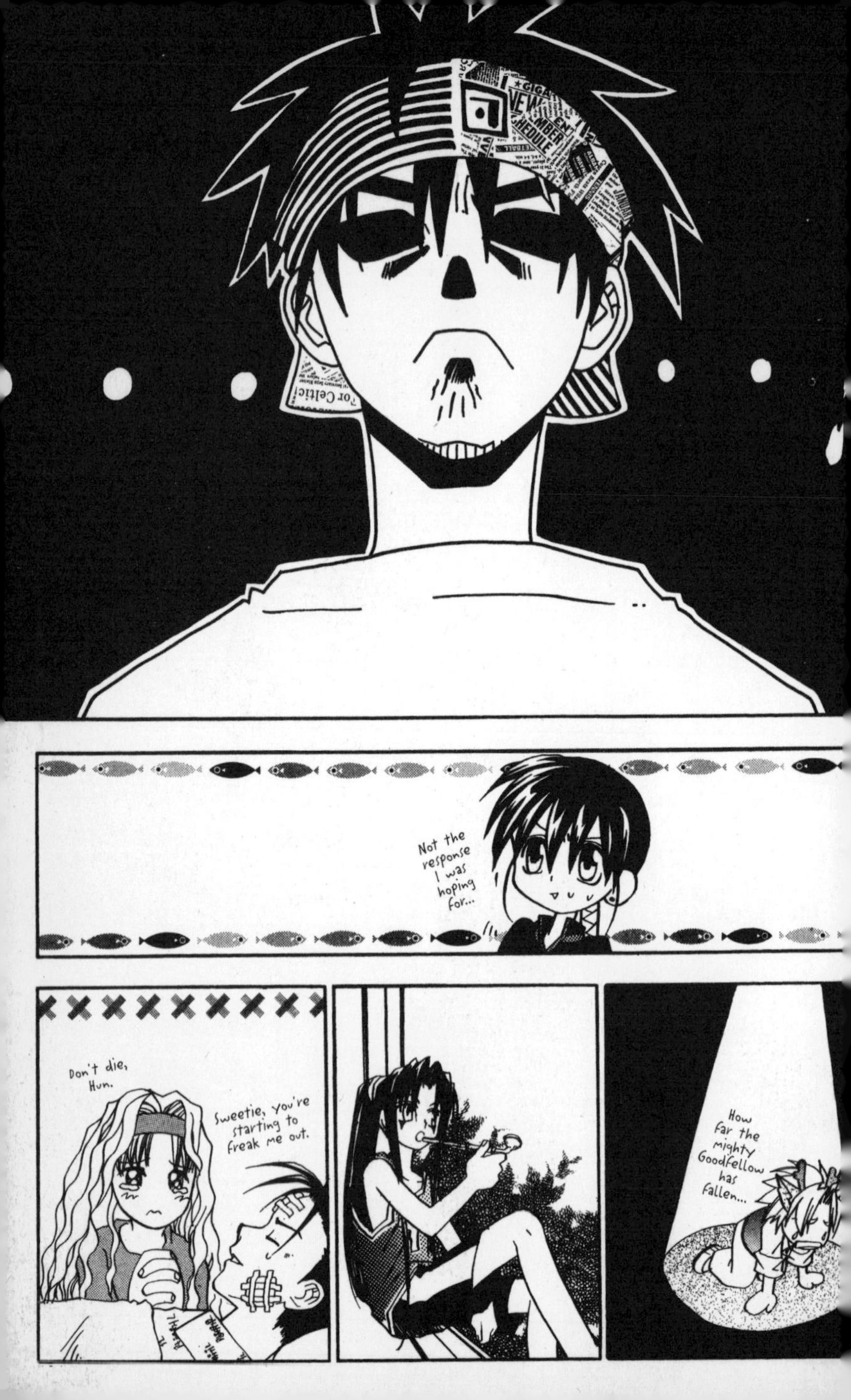
Not the response I was hoping for...
Don't die, Hun.
Sweetie, you're starting to freak me out.
How far the mighty Goodfellow has fallen...

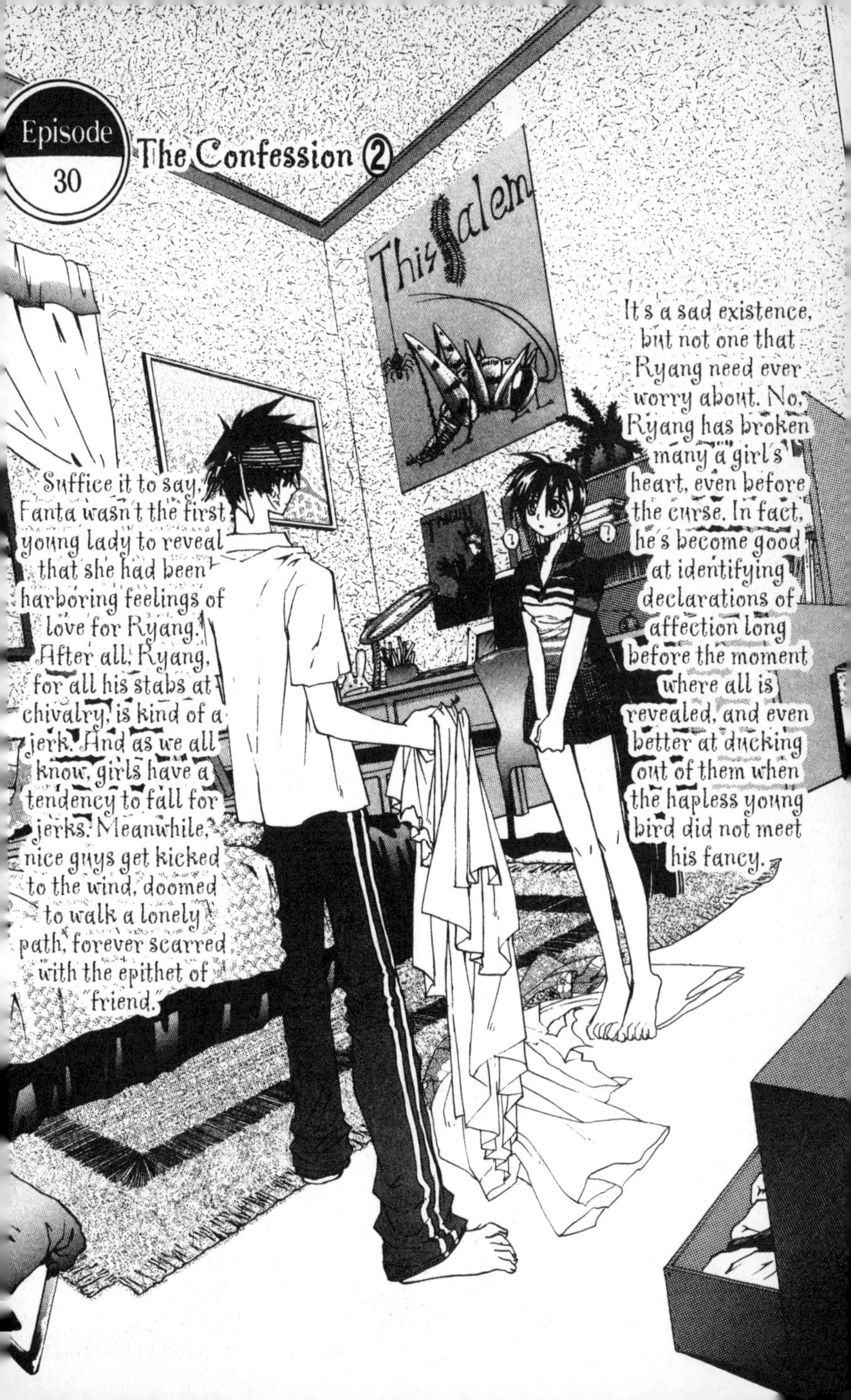
Episode 30
The Confession ②
This Salem
Suffice it to say, Fanta wasn't the first young lady to reveal that she had been harboring feelings of love for Ryang. After all, Ryang, for all his stabs at chivalry, is kind of a jerk. And as we all know, girls have a tendency to fall for jerks. Meanwhile, nice guys get kicked to the wind, doomed to walk a lonely path, forever scarred with the epithet of "friend."
It's a sad existence, but not one that Ryang need ever worry about. No, Ryang has broken many a girl's heart, even before the curse. In fact, he's become good at identifying declarations of affection long before the moment where all is revealed, and even better at ducking out of them when the hapless young bird did not meet his fancy.

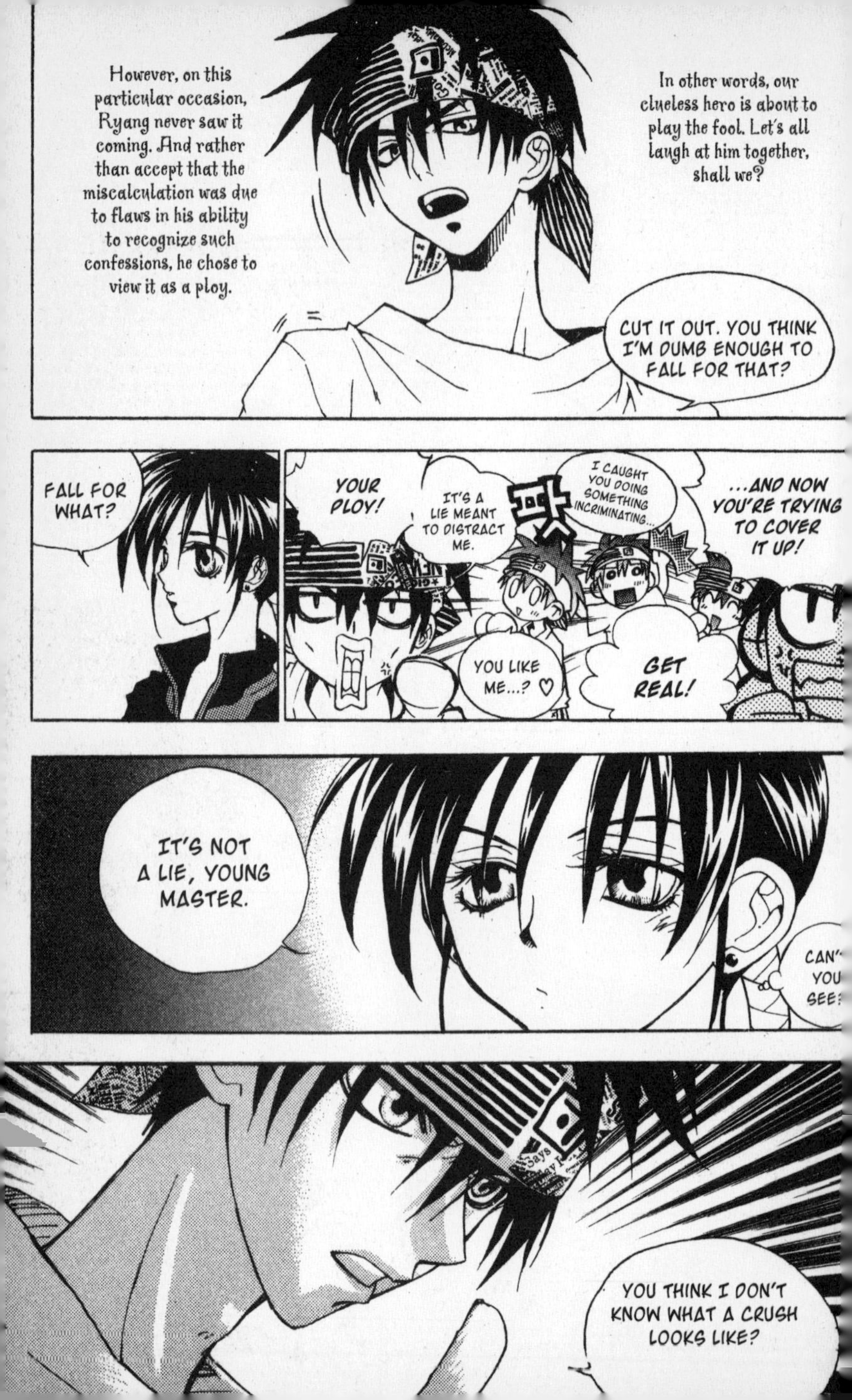
However, on this particular occasion, Ryang never saw it coming. And rather than accept that the miscalculation was due to flaws in his ability to recognize such confessions, he chose to view it as a ploy.
In other words, our clueless hero is about to play the fool. Let's all laugh at him together, shall we?
CUT IT OUT. YOU THINK I'M DUMB ENOUGH TO FALL FOR THAT?
FALL FOR WHAT?
YOUR PLOY!
IT'S A LIE MEANT TO DISTRACT ME.
I CAUGHT YOU DOING SOMETHING INCRIMINATING...
...AND NOW YOU'RE TRYING TO COVER IT UP!
YOU LIKE ME...? ♡
GET REAL!
IT'S NOT A LIE, YOUNG MASTER.
CAN'T YOU SEE?
YOU THINK I DON'T KNOW WHAT A CRUSH LOOKS LIKE?

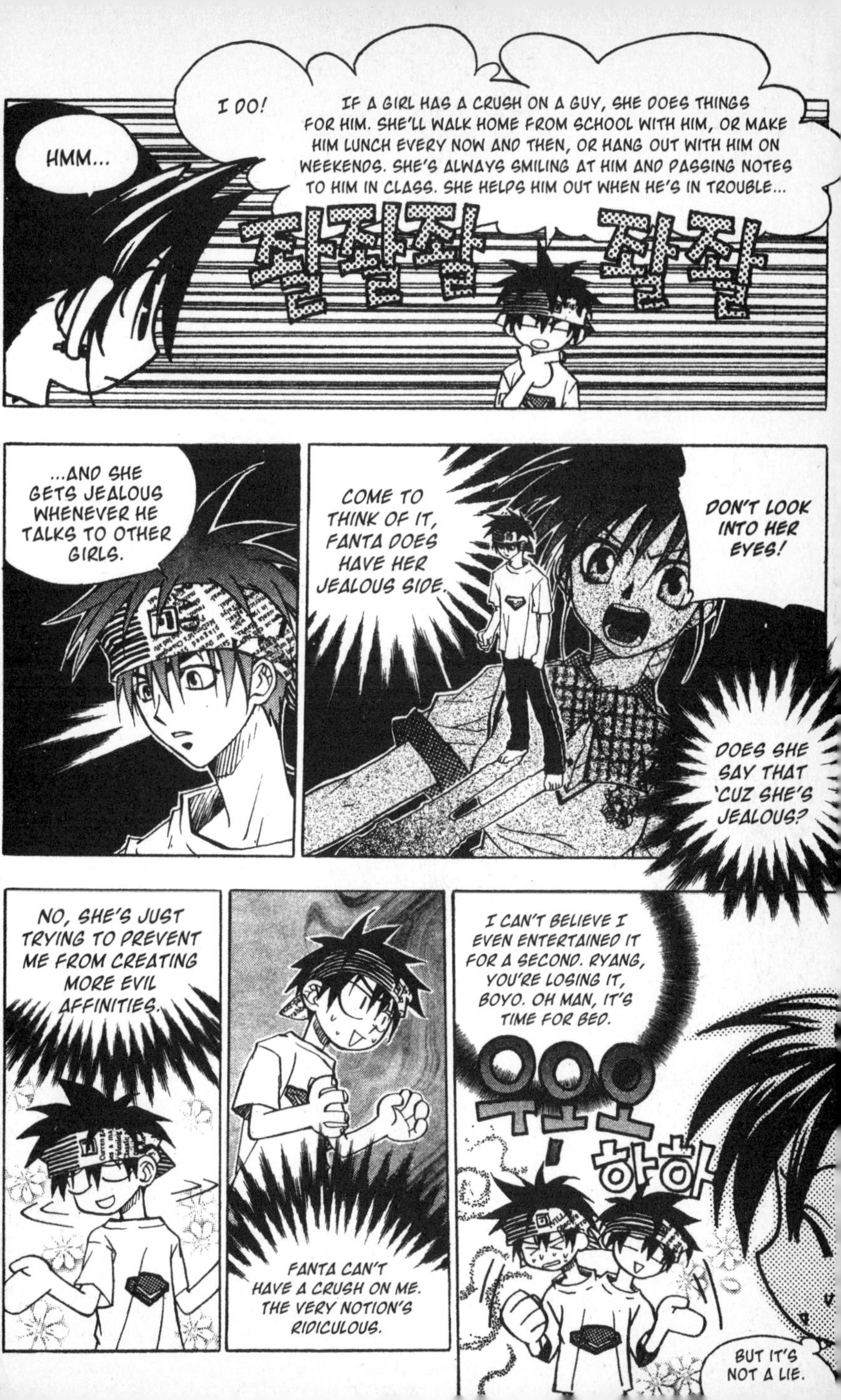

HMM...
I DO!
IF A GIRL HAS A CRUSH ON A GUY, SHE DOES THINGS FOR HIM. SHE'LL WALK HOME FROM SCHOOL WITH HIM, OR MAKE HIM LUNCH EVERY NOW AND THEN, OR HANG OUT WITH HIM ON WEEKENDS. SHE'S ALWAYS SMILING AT HIM AND PASSING NOTES TO HIM IN CLASS. SHE HELPS HIM OUT WHEN HE'S IN TROUBLE...
...AND SHE GETS JEALOUS WHENEVER HE TALKS TO OTHER GIRLS.
COME TO THINK OF IT, FANTA DOES HAVE HER JEALOUS SIDE.
DON'T LOOK INTO HER EYES!
DOES SHE SAY THAT 'CUZ SHE'S JEALOUS?
NO, SHE'S JUST TRYING TO PREVENT ME FROM CREATING MORE EVIL AFFINITIES.
FANTA CAN'T HAVE A CRUSH ON ME. THE VERY NOTION'S RIDICULOUS.
I CAN'T BELIEVE I EVEN ENTERTAINED IT FOR A SECOND. RYANG, YOU'RE LOSING IT, BOYO. OH MAN, IT'S TIME FOR BED.
우오오
하하
BUT IT'S NOT A LIE.

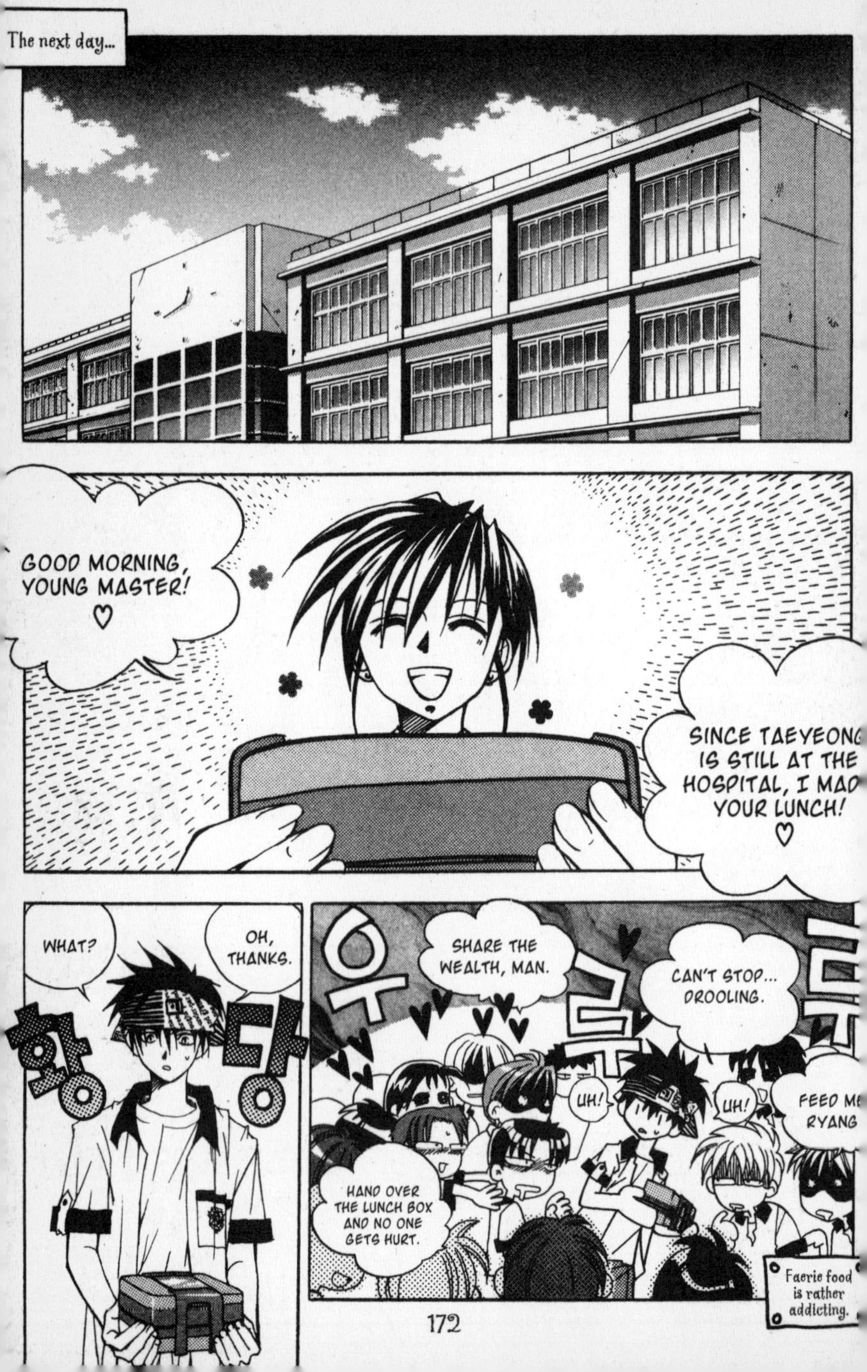
The next day...
GOOD MORNING, YOUNG MASTER! ♡
SINCE TAEYEONG IS STILL AT THE HOSPITAL, I MAD YOUR LUNCH! ♡
WHAT?
OH, THANKS.
SHARE THE WEALTH, MAN.
CAN'T STOP... DROOLING.
UH!
UH!
FEED ME RYANG
HAND OVER THE LUNCH BOX AND NO ONE GETS HURT.
Faerie food is rather addicting.

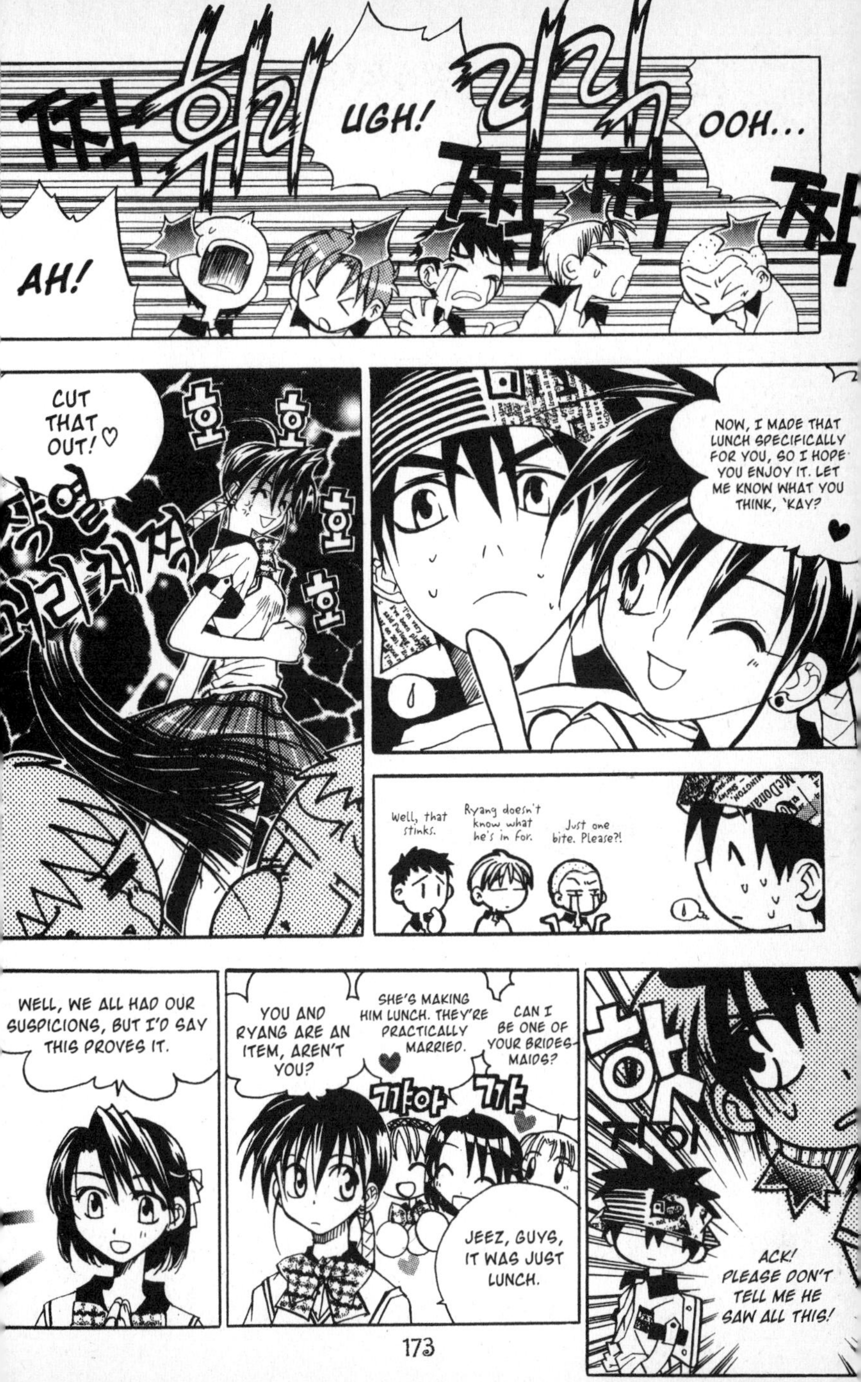
UGH!
OOH...
AH!
CUT THAT OUT! ♡
호 호 호 호
NOW, I MADE THAT LUNCH SPECIFICALLY FOR YOU, SO I HOPE YOU ENJOY IT. LET ME KNOW WHAT YOU THINK, 'KAY?
Well, that stinks.
Ryang doesn't know what he's in for.
Just one bite. Please?!
WELL, WE ALL HAD OUR SUSPICIONS, BUT I'D SAY THIS PROVES IT.
YOU AND RYANG ARE AN ITEM, AREN'T YOU?
SHE'S MAKING HIM LUNCH. THEY'RE PRACTICALLY MARRIED.
CAN I BE ONE OF YOUR BRIDES-MAIDS?
JEEZ, GUYS, IT WAS JUST LUNCH.
ACK! PLEASE DON'T TELL ME HE SAW ALL THIS!

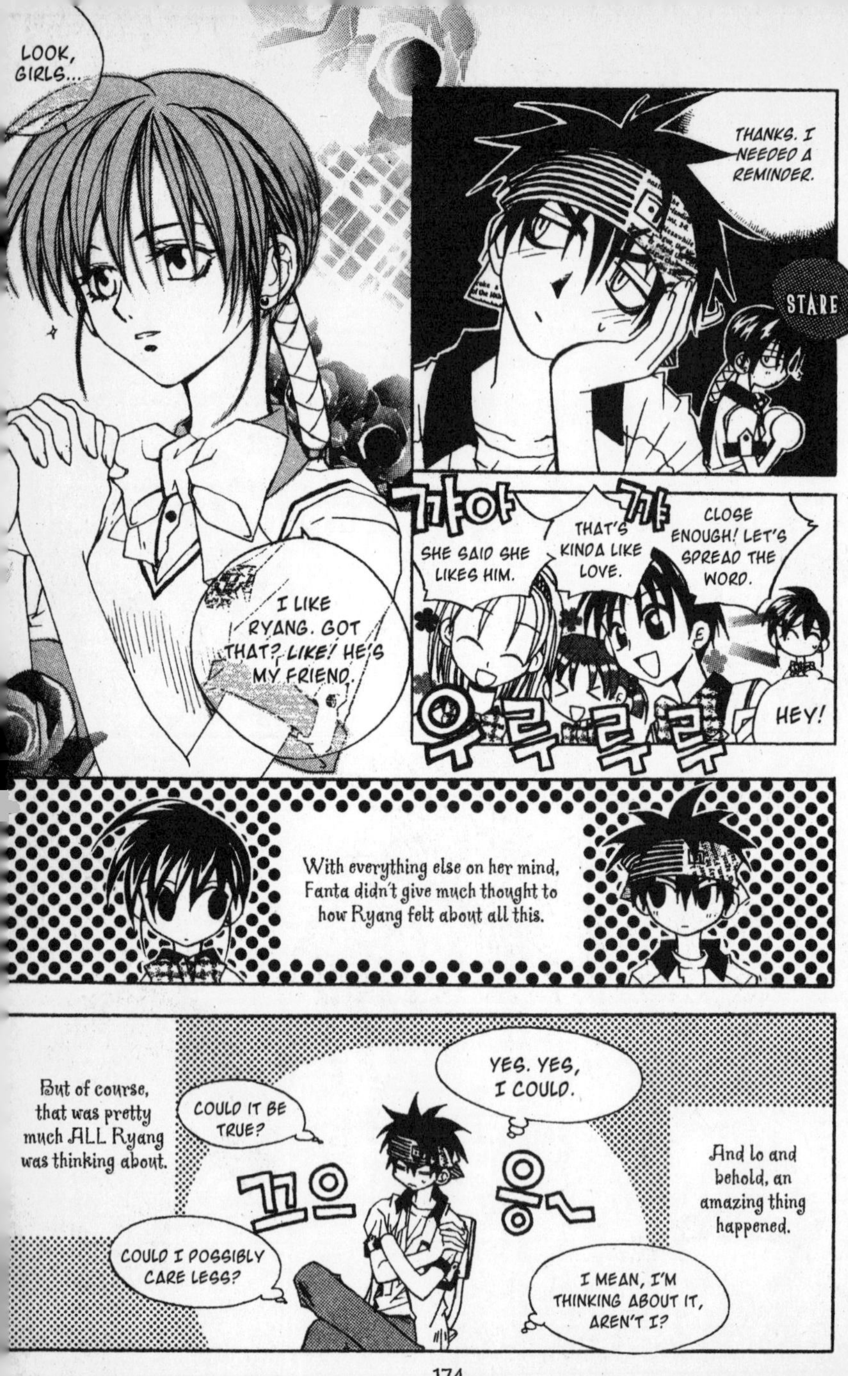

LOOK, GIRLS...
I LIKE RYANG. GOT THAT? LIKE! HE'S MY FRIEND.
THANKS. I NEEDED A REMINDER.
STARE
꺄아 꺄
SHE SAID SHE LIKES HIM.
THAT'S KINDA LIKE LOVE.
CLOSE ENOUGH! LET'S SPREAD THE WORD.
HEY!
With everything else on her mind, Fanta didn't give much thought to how Ryang felt about all this.
But of course, that was pretty much ALL Ryang was thinking about.
COULD IT BE TRUE?
YES. YES, I COULD.
끄으 응~
COULD I POSSIBLY CARE LESS?
I MEAN, I'M THINKING ABOUT IT, AREN'T I?
And lo and behold, an amazing thing happened.

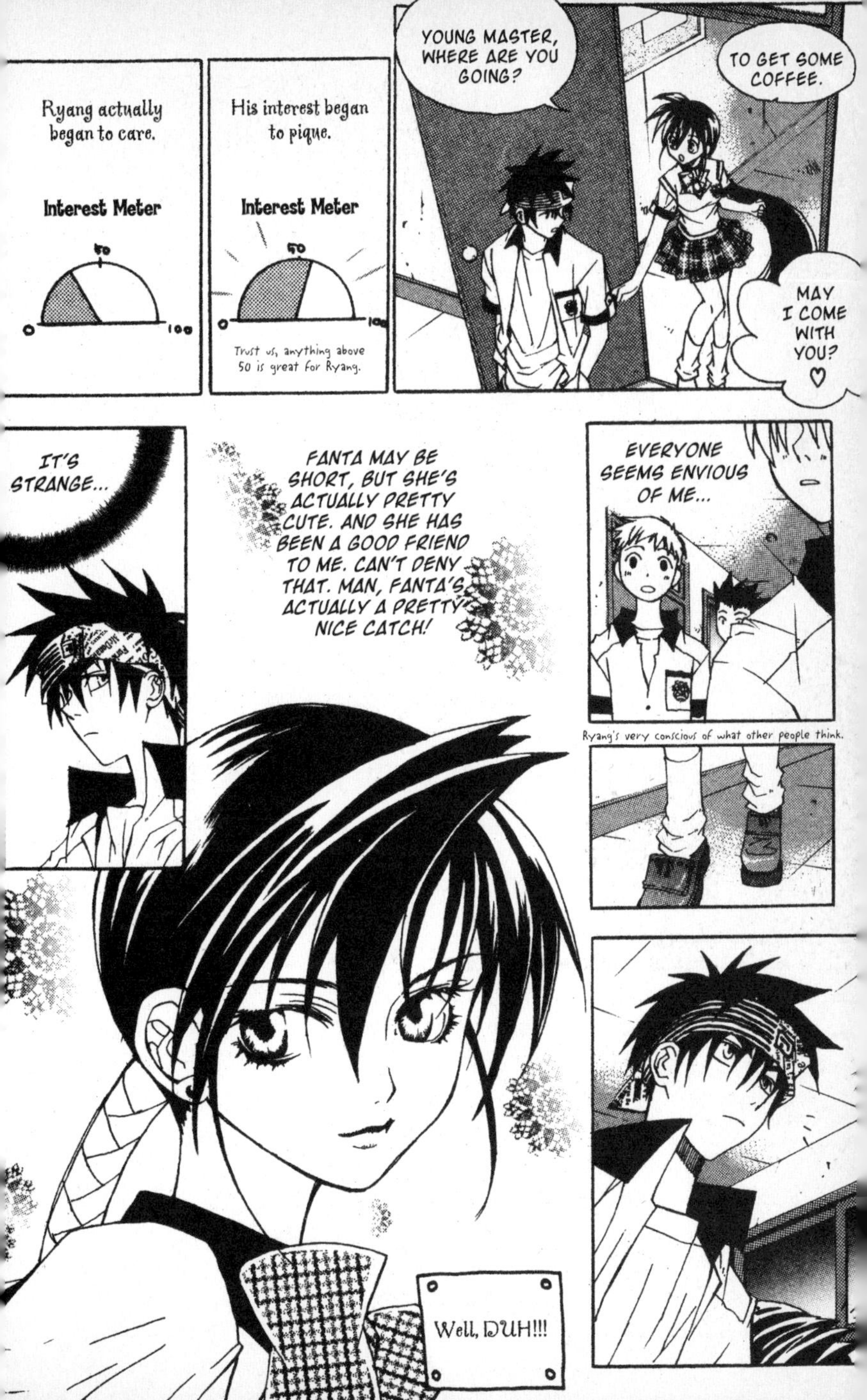
Ryang actually began to care.
Interest Meter
50
0
100
His interest began to pique.
Interest Meter
50
0
100
Trust us, anything above 50 is great for Ryang.
YOUNG MASTER, WHERE ARE YOU GOING?
TO GET SOME COFFEE.
MAY I COME WITH YOU? ♡
IT'S STRANGE...
FANTA MAY BE SHORT, BUT SHE'S ACTUALLY PRETTY CUTE. AND SHE HAS BEEN A GOOD FRIEND TO ME. CAN'T DENY THAT. MAN, FANTA'S ACTUALLY A PRETTY NICE CATCH!
EVERYONE SEEMS ENVIOUS OF ME...
Ryang's very conscious of what other people think.
Well, DUH!!!

!!

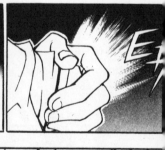

HEY, ISN'T THAT THE GIRL WHO—?

COME ON, FANTA. LET'S GO GET CAFFEINATED.

HUH?

......

!!

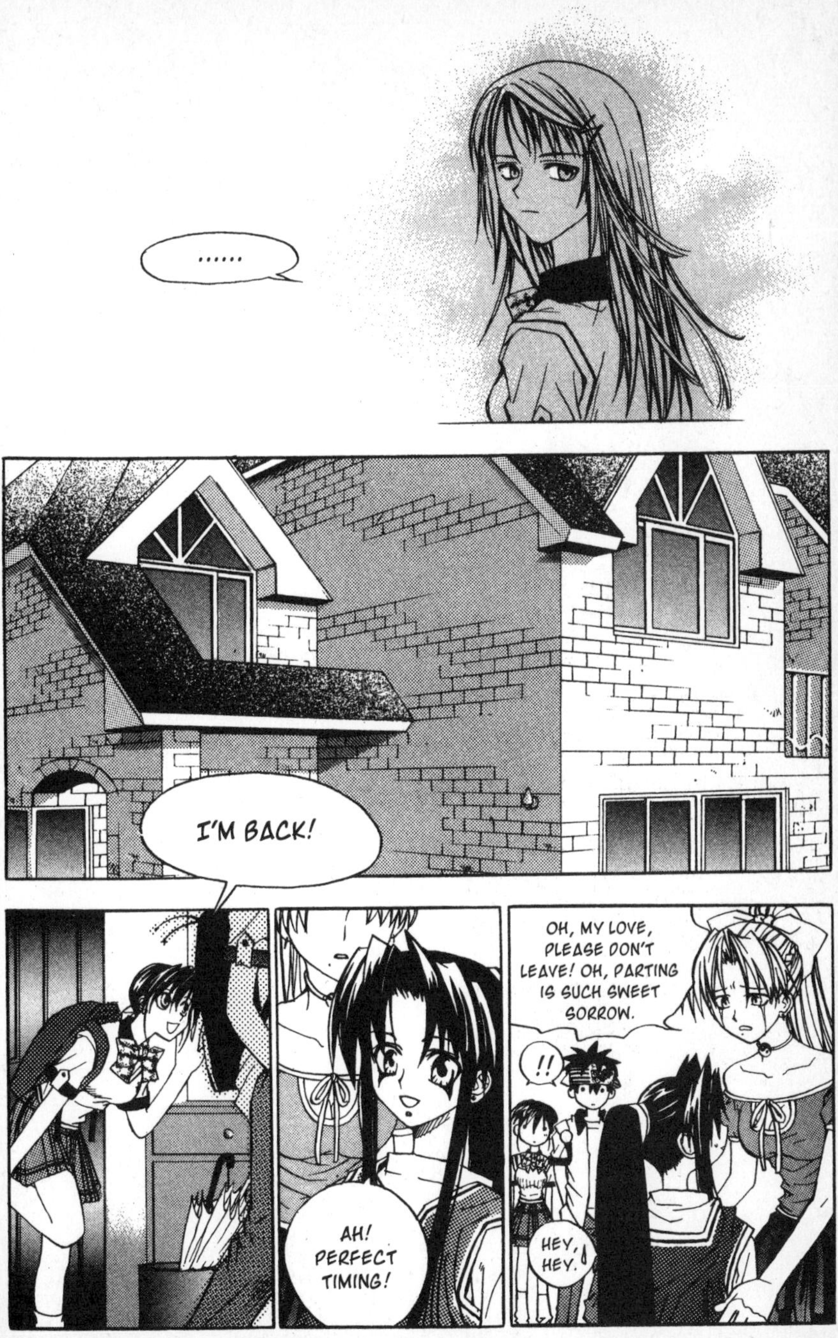
......
I'M BACK!
AH! PERFECT TIMING!
OH, MY LOVE, PLEASE DON'T LEAVE! OH, PARTING IS SUCH SWEET SORROW.
!!
HEY, HEY.

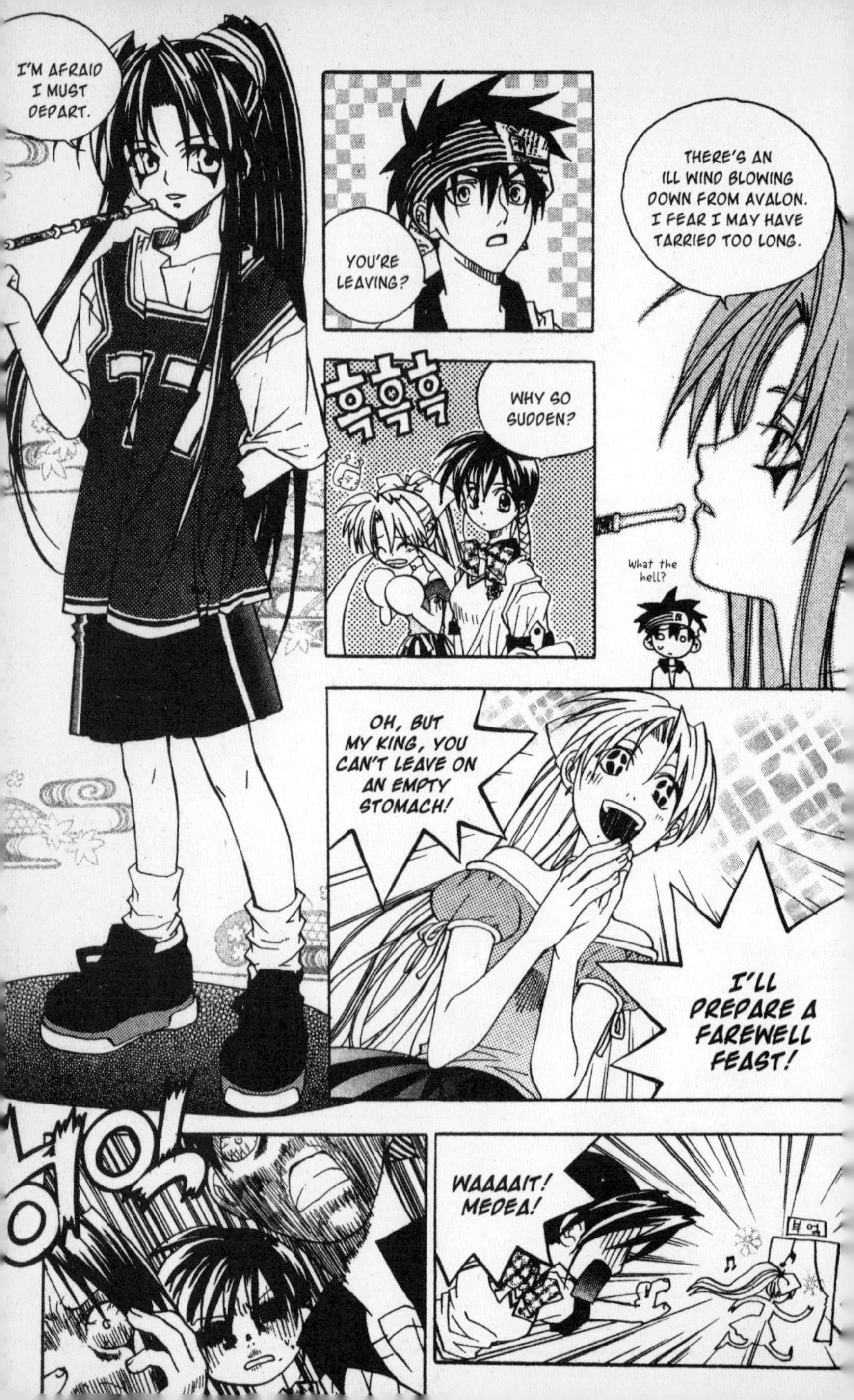
I'M AFRAID I MUST DEPART.
YOU'RE LEAVING?
흑흑흑
WHY SO SUDDEN?
THERE'S AN ILL WIND BLOWING DOWN FROM AVALON. I FEAR I MAY HAVE TARRIED TOO LONG.
What the hell?
OH, BUT MY KING, YOU CAN'T LEAVE ON AN EMPTY STOMACH!
I'LL PREPARE A FAREWELL FEAST!
WAAAAIT! MEDEA!
부엌

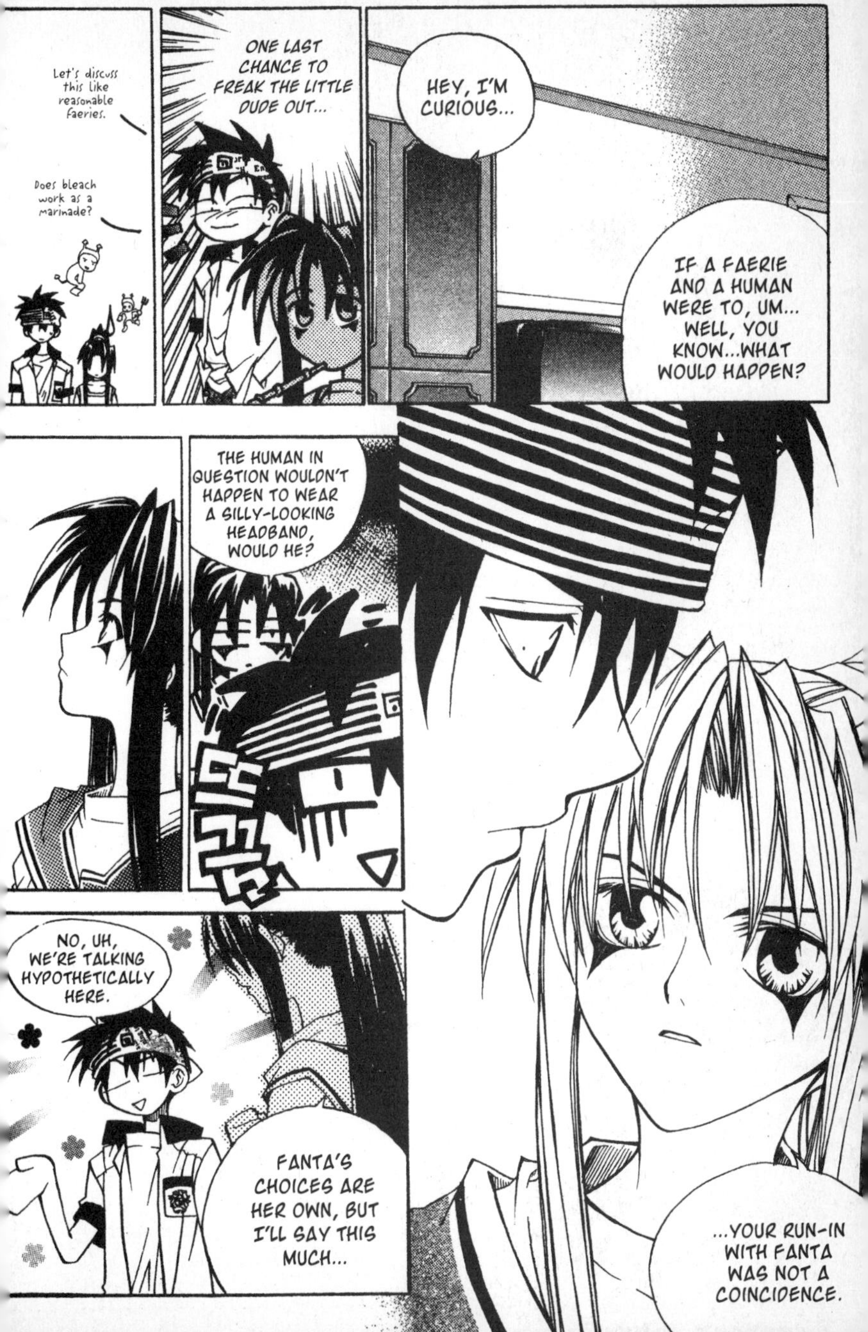
Let's discuss this like reasonable faeries.
Does bleach work as a marinade?
ONE LAST CHANCE TO FREAK THE LITTLE DUDE OUT...
HEY, I'M CURIOUS...
IF A FAERIE AND A HUMAN WERE TO, UM... WELL, YOU KNOW...WHAT WOULD HAPPEN?
THE HUMAN IN QUESTION WOULDN'T HAPPEN TO WEAR A SILLY-LOOKING HEADBAND, WOULD HE?
NO, UH, WE'RE TALKING HYPOTHETICALLY HERE.
FANTA'S CHOICES ARE HER OWN, BUT I'LL SAY THIS MUCH...
...YOUR RUN-IN WITH FANTA WAS NOT A COINCIDENCE.

WHAT?

LET'S GO, GOODFELLOW.

THE KING...

...HAS LEFT THE BUILDING.

I'LL BE SEEING YOU...

AAAAH!

THE KING IS GONE! WHY DIDN'T YOU TELL ME HE WAS ASCENDING?!

Thought I'd do him a favor.

YOU'RE TELLING ME I MISSED HIM?!

OH, FOR CRYIN' OUT LOUD! I'VE BEEN CHASING AFTER THAT BRAT FOR THE ENTIRE BOOK!

WATCH YOUR MOUTH, PAIN.

Though I share your frustration.

Apparently, the king's ill wind was our brothers.

I'm not surprised.

Why are they chasing after him themselves?

A goo question.

See ya faerie fans...

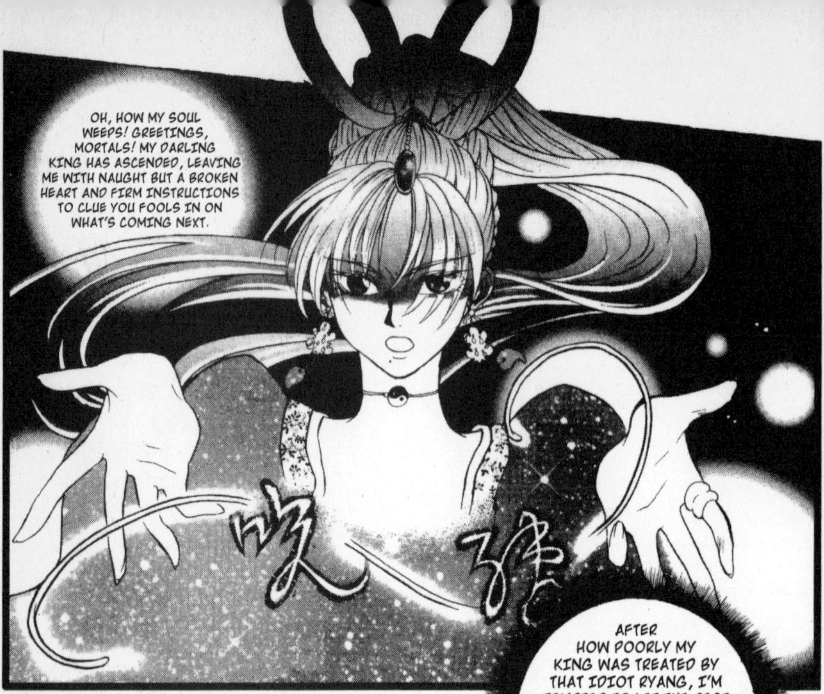
OH, HOW MY SOUL WEEPS! GREETINGS, MORTALS! MY DARLING KING HAS ASCENDED, LEAVING ME WITH NAUGHT BUT A BROKEN HEART AND FIRM INSTRUCTIONS TO CLUE YOU FOOLS IN ON WHAT'S COMING NEXT.
AFTER HOW POORLY MY KING WAS TREATED BY THAT IDIOT RYANG, I'M TEMPTED TO LET THE REST OF YOU FELLOW HUMANS ROT. HOWEVER, AS THIS ORDER CAME FROM MY BELOVED, I MUST FOLLOW IT, AND LOOK GOOD AS I DO, JUST IN CASE HE'S WATCHING.

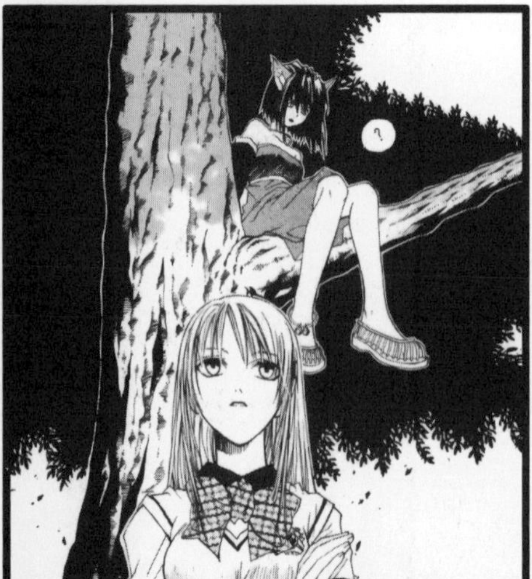
?

ALL YOU FURRIES OUT THERE CAN REJOICE, AS IT APPEARS WE HAVEN'T SEEN THE LAST OF OUR WICKED LITTLE CAT GODDESS. BAST ON HER OWN IS TROUBLE, BUT BAST TEAMED UP WITH THE UTTERLY INSANE YURI...? THE TROUBLE RYANG CAN EXPECT FROM THESE GIRLS FAR OUTWEIGHS THAT OF A SILLY LITTLE AFFINITY.

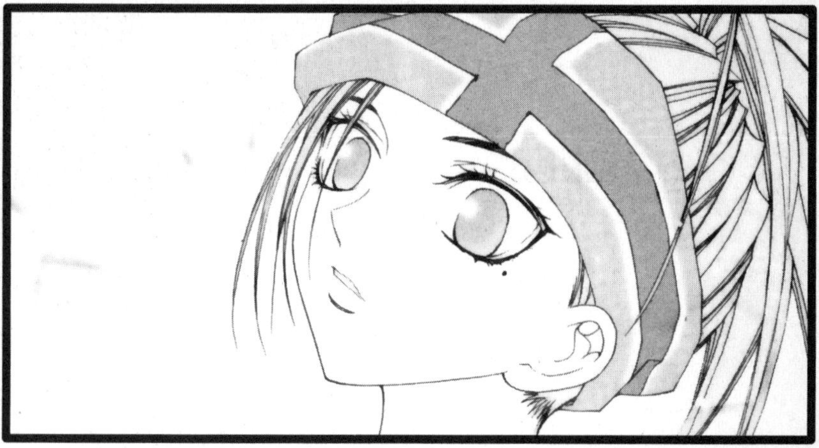

AND SPEAKING OF EVIL AFFINITIES, JINHUI WAS HARDLY THE LAST OF THEM. RYANG DECIDES TO GET PROACTIVE, AND ACTUALLY ***CREATES*** AN EVIL AFFINITY ON PURPOSE! YOU SEE, RYANG THINKS (AND I REALLY WISH HE WOULDN'T DO THAT) THAT AN EVIL AFFINITY IS EASIER TO DEAL WITH IF HE KNOWS WHO THE COUPLE IS. WELL, I'M SURE IT WILL COME AS NO SURPRISE TO HEAR THAT HE THOUGHT WRONG.

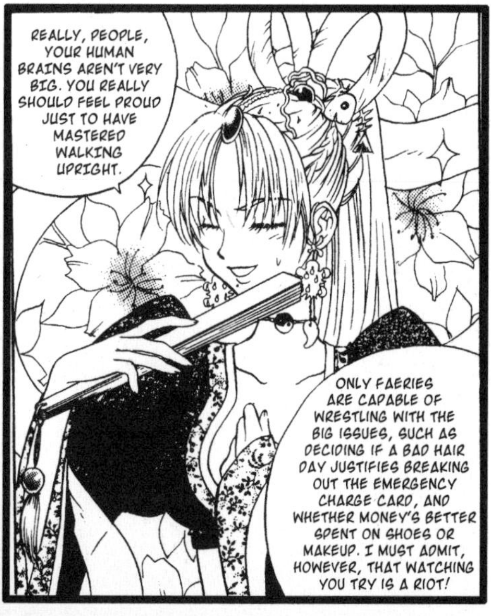
REALLY, PEOPLE, YOUR HUMAN BRAINS AREN'T VERY BIG. YOU REALLY SHOULD FEEL PROUD JUST TO HAVE MASTERED WALKING UPRIGHT.
ONLY FAERIES ARE CAPABLE OF WRESTLING WITH THE BIG ISSUES, SUCH AS DECIDING IF A BAD HAIR DAY JUSTIFIES BREAKING OUT THE EMERGENCY CHARGE CARD, AND WHETHER MONEY'S BETTER SPENT ON SHOES OR MAKEUP. I MUST ADMIT, HOWEVER, THAT WATCHING YOU TRY IS A RIOT!

FAERIES' LANDING

Volume 6

November 2004

ALSO AVAILABLE FROM ◎TOKYOPOP®

MANGA

.HACK//LEGEND OF THE TWILIGHT
@LARGE
ABENOBASHI: MAGICAL SHOPPING ARCADE
A.I. LOVE YOU
AI YORI AOSHI
ANGELIC LAYER
ARM OF KANNON
BABY BIRTH
BATTLE ROYALE
BATTLE VIXENS
BOYS BE...
BRAIN POWERED
BRIGADOON
B'TX
CANDIDATE FOR GODDESS, THE
CARDCAPTOR SAKURA
CARDCAPTOR SAKURA - MASTER OF THE CLOW
CHOBITS
CHRONICLES OF THE CURSED SWORD
CLAMP SCHOOL DETECTIVES
CLOVER
COMIC PARTY
CONFIDENTIAL CONFESSIONS
CORRECTOR YUI
COWBOY BEBOP
COWBOY BEBOP: SHOOTING STAR
CRAZY LOVE STORY
CRESCENT MOON
CROSS
CULDCEPT
CYBORG 009
D•N•ANGEL
DEMON DIARY
DEMON ORORON, THE
DEUS VITAE
DIABOLO
DIGIMON
DIGIMON TAMERS
DIGIMON ZERO TWO
DOLL
DRAGON HUNTER
DRAGON KNIGHTS
DRAGON VOICE
DREAM SAGA
DUKLYON: CLAMP SCHOOL DEFENDERS
EERIE QUEERIE!
ERICA SAKURAZAWA: COLLECTED WORKS
ET CETERA
ETERNITY
EVIL'S RETURN
FAERIES' LANDING
FAKE
FLCL
FLOWER OF THE DEEP SLEEP
FORBIDDEN DANCE
FRUITS BASKET

G GUNDAM
GATEKEEPERS
GETBACKERS
GIRL GOT GAME
GIRLS EDUCATIONAL CHARTER
GRAVITATION
GTO
GUNDAM BLUE DESTINY
GUNDAM SEED ASTRAY
GUNDAM WING
GUNDAM WING: BATTLEFIELD OF PACIFISTS
GUNDAM WING: ENDLESS WALTZ
GUNDAM WING: THE LAST OUTPOST (G-UNIT)
HANDS OFF!
HAPPY MANIA
HARLEM BEAT
HYPER RUNE
I.N.V.U.
IMMORTAL RAIN
INITIAL D
INSTANT TEEN: JUST ADD NUTS
ISLAND
JING: KING OF BANDITS
JING: KING OF BANDITS - TWILIGHT TALES
JULINE
KARE KANO
KILL ME, KISS ME
KINDAICHI CASE FILES, THE
KING OF HELL
KODOCHA: SANA'S STAGE
LAMENT OF THE LAMB
LEGAL DRUG
LEGEND OF CHUN HYANG, THE
LES BIJOUX
LOVE HINA
LUPIN III
LUPIN III: WORLD'S MOST WANTED
MAGIC KNIGHT RAYEARTH I
MAGIC KNIGHT RAYEARTH II
MAHOROMATIC: AUTOMATIC MAIDEN
MAN OF MANY FACES
MARMALADE BOY
MARS
MARS: HORSE WITH NO NAME
MINK
MIRACLE GIRLS
MIYUKI-CHAN IN WONDERLAND
MODEL
MOURYOU KIDEN
MY LOVE
NECK AND NECK
ONE
ONE I LOVE, THE
PARADISE KISS
PARASYTE
PASSION FRUIT
PEACH GIRL
PEACH GIRL: CHANGE OF HEART

TOKYOPOP
From the creator of the #1 best seller Love Hina
A.I. LOVE YOU™
by Ken Akamatsu
A.I. Program Thirty became a real girl...
Can she turn her creator into a real man?
OT
OLDER TEEN AGE 16+
www.TOKYOPOP.com

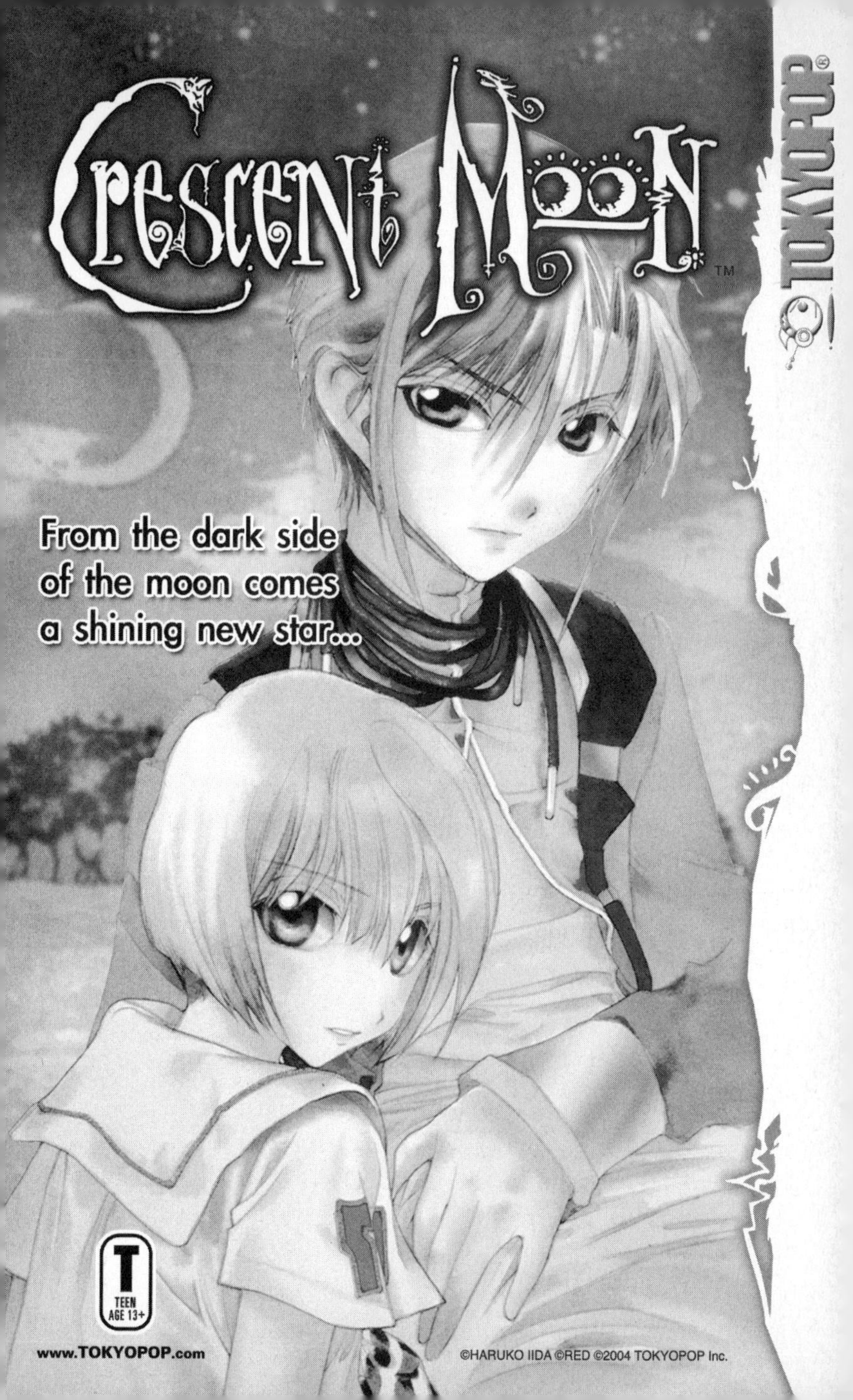
Crescent Moon™
TOKYOPOP®
From the dark side of the moon comes a shining new star...
T TEEN AGE 13+
www.TOKYOPOP.com
©HARUKO IIDA ©RED ©2004 TOKYOPOP Inc.

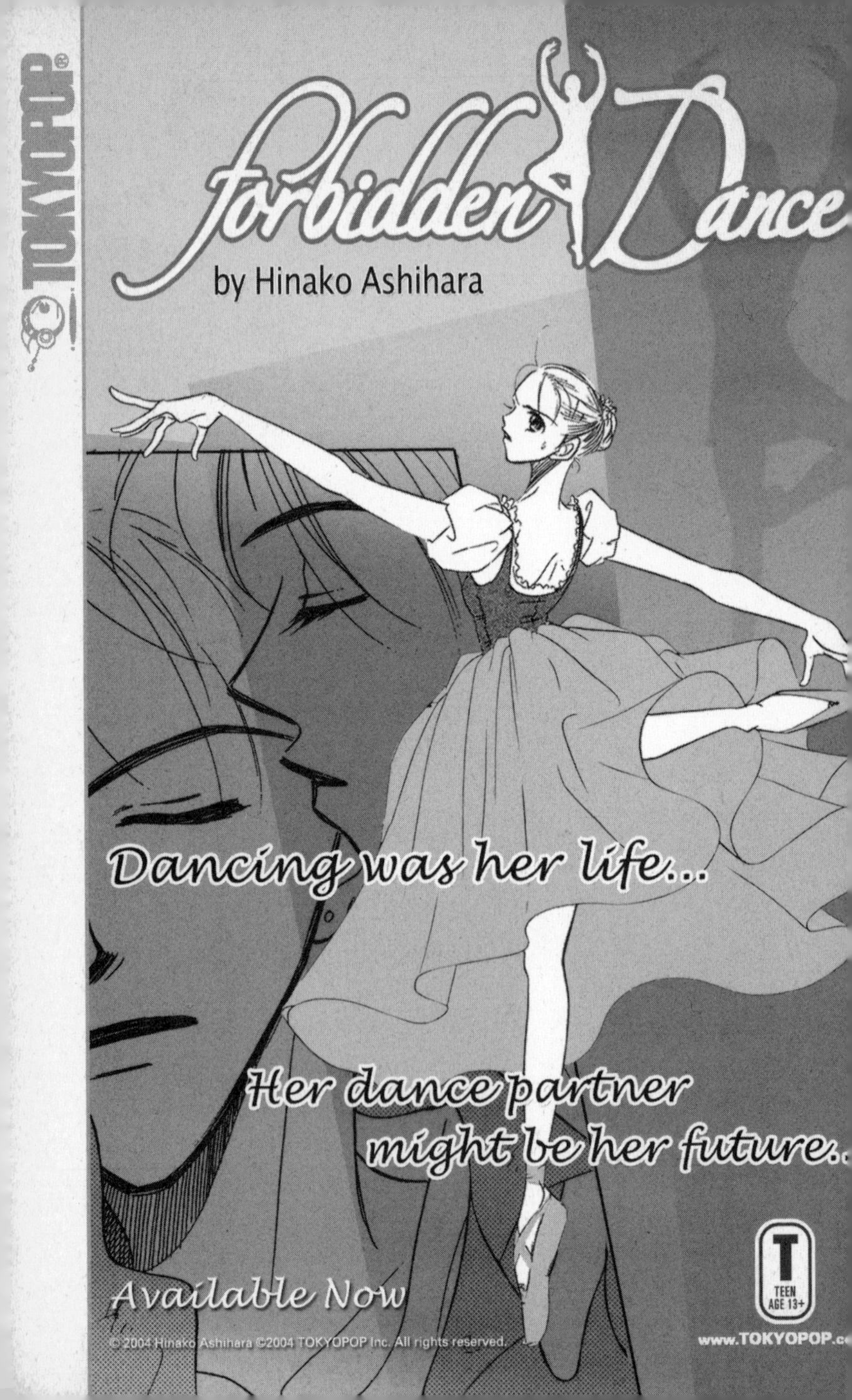
TOKYOPOP®
forbidden Dance
by Hinako Ashihara
Dancing was her life...
Her dance partner
might be her future...
Available Now
T
TEEN
AGE 13+
© 2004 Hinako Ashihara ©2004 TOKYOPOP Inc. All rights reserved.
www.TOKYOPOP.c

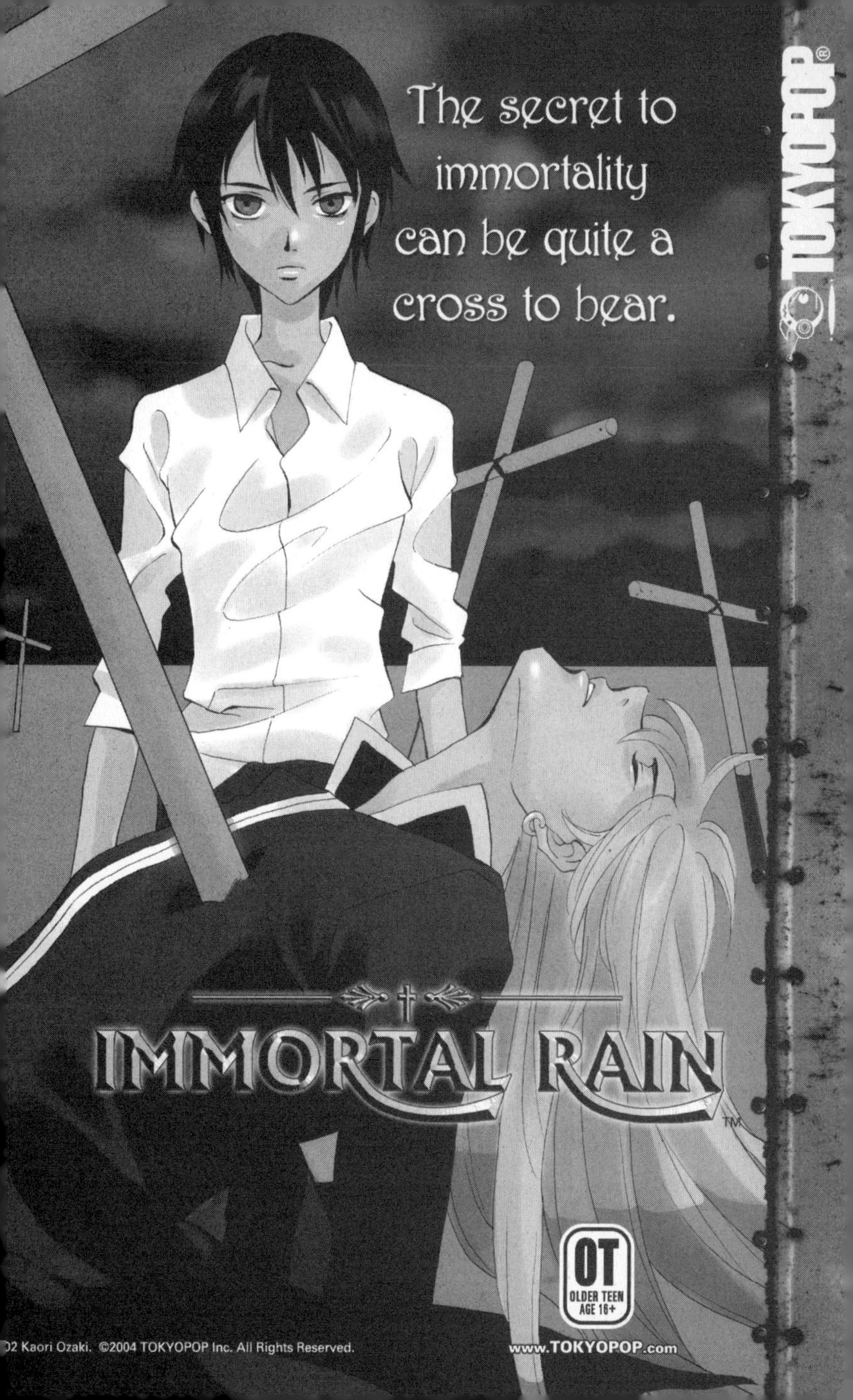
TOKYOPOP®
The secret to immortality can be quite a cross to bear.
IMMORTAL RAIN™
OT OLDER TEEN AGE 16+
02 Kaori Ozaki. ©2004 TOKYOPOP Inc. All Rights Reserved.
www.TOKYOPOP.com

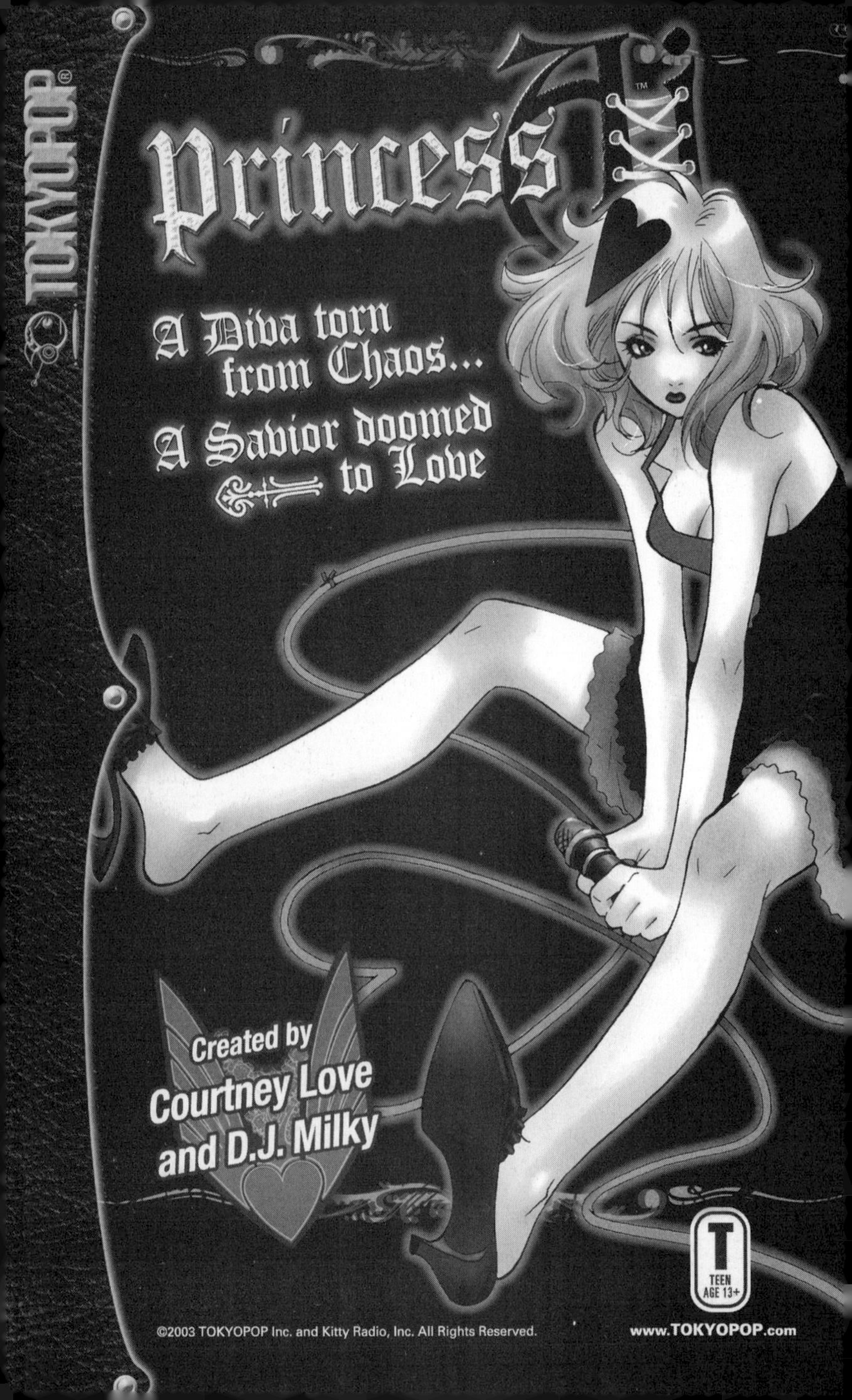
TOKYOPOP
Princess Ai™
A Diva torn from Chaos...
A Savior doomed to Love
Created by
Courtney Love
and D.J. Milky
T
TEEN
AGE 13+
©2003 TOKYOPOP Inc. and Kitty Radio, Inc. All Rights Reserved.
www.TOKYOPOP.com

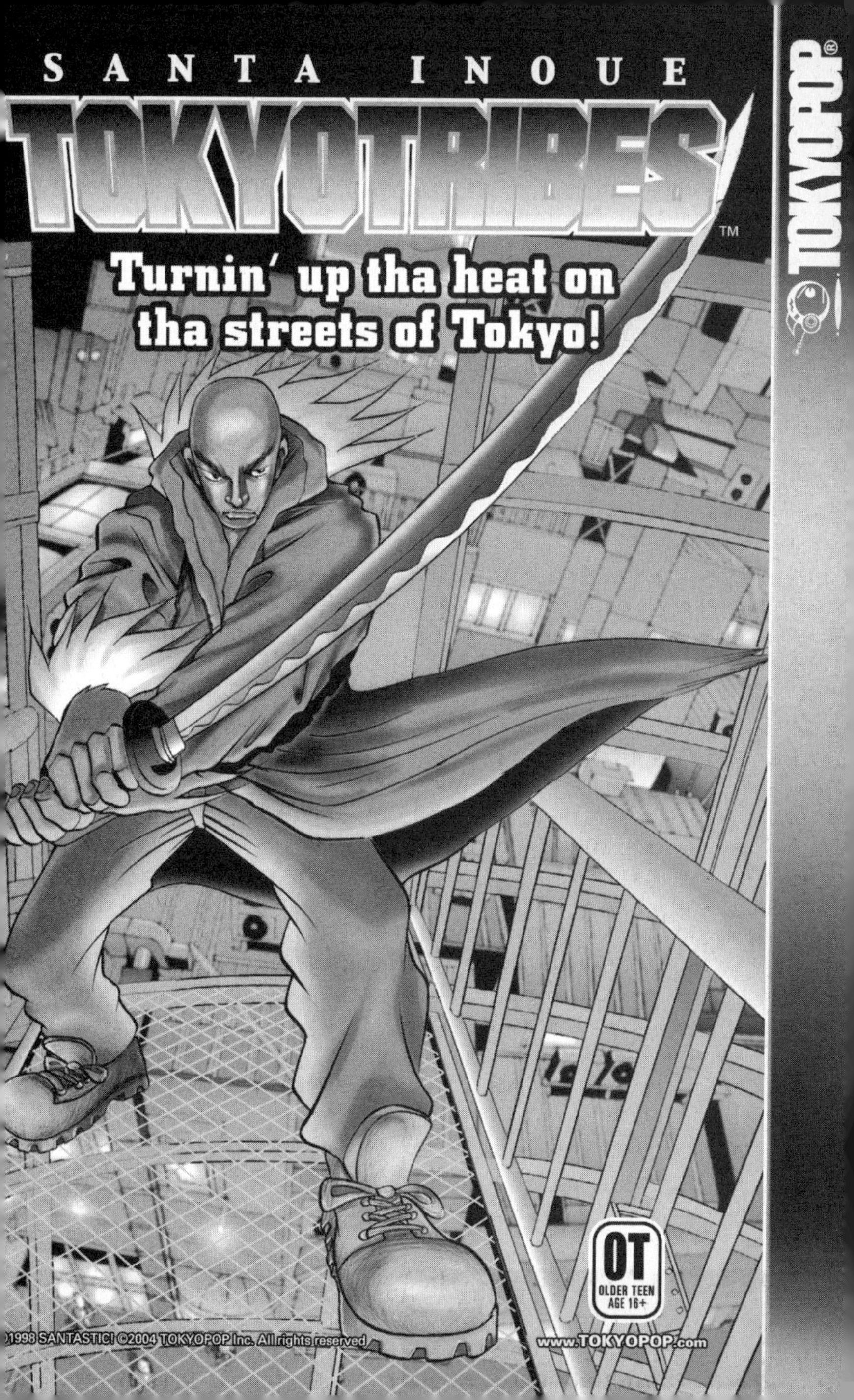
SANTA INOUE
TOKYOTRIBES™
Turnin' up tha heat on tha streets of Tokyo!
OT
OLDER TEEN
AGE 16+
©1998 SANTASTIC! ©2004 TOKYOPOP Inc. All rights reserved
www.TOKYOPOP.com
TOKYOPOP

TOKYOPOP®

BY AHMED HOKE

"[A] MASTERFUL MIX
OF MANGA AND HIP-HOP..."
--THE WASHINGTON POST

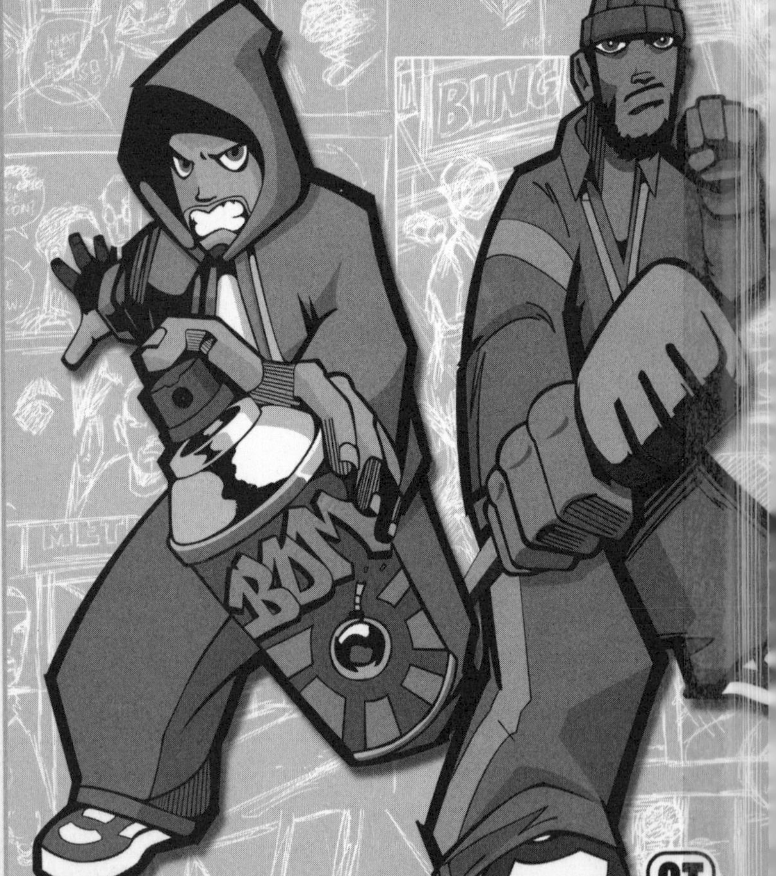

OT
OLDER TEEN
AGE 16+

www.TOKYOPOP.com